世界文学读本

吴 笛 编著

The World Literature Reader

Edited by Wu Di

浙江工商大學出版社
ZHEJIANG GONGSHANG UNIVERSITY PRESS

图书在版编目(CIP)数据

世界文学读本 / 吴笛编著. — 杭州：浙江工商大学出版社，2012.8(2022.8 重印)

ISBN 978-7-81140-550-7

Ⅰ. ①世… Ⅱ. ①吴… Ⅲ. ①英语—汉语—对照读物 ②世界文学—文学史 Ⅳ. ①H319.4:I

中国版本图书馆 CIP 数据核字(2012)第 152212 号

世界文学读本

吴　笛　编著

责任编辑　高林显　沈　娴
责任校对　钟仲南　孙小昭
封面设计　王好驰
责任印制　包建辉
出版发行　浙江工商大学出版社
(杭州市教工路 198 号　邮政编码 310012)
(E-mail:zjgsupress@163.com)
(网址:http://www.zjgsupress.com)
电话:0571-88904980,88831806(传真)
排　　版　杭州朝曦图文设计有限公司
印　　刷　广东虎彩云印刷有限公司绍兴分公司
开　　本　787mm×1092mm　1/16
印　　张　19.25
字　　数　500 千
版 印 次　2012 年 8 月第 1 版　2022 年 8 月第 4 次印刷
书　　号　ISBN 978-7-81140-550-7
定　　价　65.00 元

前　言

10年前，为满足中国语言文学专业本科教学的需要，我们在浙江大学开设了双语课程"世界文学名著选读"，并且编写了适应该课程需要的讲义。此后，又对讲义进行过多次修订。而且，所编讲义也陆续被其他开设了世界文学类双语课程的院校所采用。2007年，该课程获得了"浙江大学双语教学课程建设项目"的立项支持，并在2009年结题验收时，获得优秀项目的称号。现在，在浙江工商大学出版社的大力支持下，在编者对原讲义和教学课件进行认真修订的基础上，本书得以公开出版。

本书的基本框架按照世界文学史的发展脉搏而定。全书共分十章，每章既有对文学发展和作家作品的概述，也选择重要作品供学习者研读，概述内容以及所选作品兼顾世界文学史各个发展时期的重要作家和思潮流派。

就文本选读而言，本书力图选择既在世界文学史上占据重要地位又有艺术鉴赏价值的英文作品，以及西方学者从其他语种翻译成英文的著名作品。所选作品，均为世界文学各个发展时期的具有代表性的经典著作。在编写过程中，注重突出各个时期的创作成就，评介对各个时期以及重点作家的研究现状，以帮助学习者进行深入的研读和鉴赏。由于受到篇幅的限制，对于抒情诗和短篇小说一类的作品，尽可能保持原貌，对于史诗、戏剧、中长篇小说等文本，则为节选，但力图选择原著精彩之处。

为了帮助学习者更好地理解英文文本，绝大多数所选作品的中文译文均附在书的后部，供学习者参考。需要说明的是，所附中文译文大多是得到公认的佳译，为了保持译文的风貌，编者只对少量排印错误或典型错译进行了校订，其中，非英文国家的作品的译文，并非译自英文，而是选自我国各个语种的翻译家从原语种翻译的佳作。这样，在研读过程中，不必拘泥词语的对应。譬如，由于民族语言文化的限定以及译者翻译风格和审美观念的差异，同样译自古希腊语的英文译文和中文译文，有着各自不同的审美特性和艺术特质，更何况同一个文本在译为不同语言的翻译过程中的处理，也是一种文化财富，将这些文本同英文译文进行比较研究，对于探讨文学翻译艺术无疑具有重要的文献价值。

本书主要为世界文学类课程的双语教学而编写，可以作为"外国文学史"以及"外国文学作品选"等世界文学类课程的教材或参考书籍，也可供英文水平较高的文学爱好者研读和鉴赏。希望读者通过对该书的学习，能够对各类英文作品的基本形式要素、修辞手法、艺术技巧等方面有一定的认知，对世界文学史上的重要作家作品有深入的理解，领悟英文作品的内涵和艺术魅力，并熟知一些文学评论类专业术语，为进一步研读、鉴赏和研究英文文学原著以及英文批评论著奠定良好的扎实的基础，并为进一步深造以及借鉴西方文化而探寻理想的发展方向。

吴　笛

2010年夏

Contents

Chapter One Ancient Literature

Ⅰ. Introduction

The ancient literature is the precious cultural heritage of mankind. It could be divided into ancient Greco-Roman literature and ancient Eastern literature.

The time span of ancient Greco-Roman literature extends from the eleventh century BC to the early fifth century AD, a period of some 1,500 years. Ancient Greek literature undergone roughly three periods: the first period is the archaic period. It is from the eleventh century up to the end of the ninth century BC, and the main literary achievements of this period are mythology and epics. The second period is from about the eighth century BC to the fifth century BC, of which the literary achievements are plays and literary theories. The third period is called the Hellenistic Age, lasting from Alexander to the beginning of the Roman Empire. The development of ancient Roman literature can be also divided into three periods: the first period from about the third century BC to the second century BC is famous for comedies. The second period is the Golden Age of Roman literature, lasting from the first century BC to the first century AD, and it is famous for poetry; the great Roman poets Virgil, Horace and Catullus belong to this period. The last period is from the first century AD to the Roman Empire, and it is the declining period of Roman literature, and in this period, the only achievement perhaps is the "new comedy".

Ancient Greece and Rome are generally considered as the two cultural well-springs of the Western world. In poetry, tragedy, and comedy, Greek writers created masterpieces that have inspired, influenced, and challenged generations to the present day. The headstream of all kinds of Western literary forms can be traced in ancient Greece and Rome.

The basic forms of ancient literature include the following three types:

1. Epic. An epic is a long poem which tells the story of a hero, often extending to thousands of lines. The epic remained central and stood at the peak of the generic hierarchy in the history of ancient literature.

The Greek blind poet Homer wrote two connected epics, the *Iliad* and the *Odyssey*, retelling intermingled history and myth of the Mycenaean Age. These two grand epics, standing at the beginning of Greek literature, established most of the literary conventions of the epic poem. The later epic poems are almost composed in the meter which Homer used, a long and swiftly moving line known as the dactylic hexameter in a dignified, self-consciously elevated style.

A kind of epic from Western Asia, written in about 2500 BC, is the Epic of Gilgamesh, a famous epic of ancient Babylon in Mesopotamia on the Euphrates River, and it is considered as the first epic poem of the humankind ever found.

Another important epic is from Rome in 19 BC. It is the great Latin poet Virgil's *Aeneid*. The epic can be divided into two parts based on the disparate subject matter. From Book 1 to Book 6, the author of the epic discusses Aeneas' journey to Italy and from Book 7 to Book 12, the author narrates the war in Italy. These two parts are commonly regarded as reflecting Virgil's ambition to rival Homer by treating both the *Odyssey*'s wandering theme and the *Iliad*'s warfare themes.

2. Lyrical poetry. There are a number of shorter poems written by such lyrical poets as Sappho in Greece and Catullus in Rome. Sappho is regarded as the greatest female poet of antiquity, and her ancient admirers praised her as "the tenth Muse", or even "the female Homer". Catullus is famous for his "Lesbia poems", in which several stages of love relationship are described: initial euphoria, doubts, separation and feelings of loss.

The basic poetical form of the lyric was created in the ancient world, and the traditions of Greek lyric were rooted in oral poetry. Originally, the Greek lyric was a song to be sung to the accompaniment of the lyre.

The lyrical poetry in ancient Greece and Rome and the little collections of lyrical poems known as the Lamentations and the Song of Songs in the Hebrew Bible can be regarded as the early and typical achievements of this literary form.

3. Plays. It is likely that Greek plays emerged from a form which consisted solely of choral songs, possibly song including narrative or praise of Dionysus, a god of wine and of an orgiastic religion celebrating the power and fertility of nature.

Plays are divided into tragedies and comedies. Besides tragedies and comedies, the Greek dramatists regularly wrote satyr-plays, usually as a shorter tailpiece after the tragic trilogy.

Tragedies are generally sad, while comedies are funny with happy endings. Greek tragedies often deal with the mythical events, following the lead of epic. Plato called Homer the pathfinder of tragedy, and subjects connected with the Trojan wars remained particularly prominent.

The oldest tragedies that we still have ever found were written by Aeschylus around 500 BC. We also have tragedies written by Sophocles (around 450 BC) and Euripides (around 425 BC). They are regarded as the three great tragedians in the history of ancient Greek literature. Among the most renowned Greek tragedies are Sophocles' *Oedipus the King* and Aeschylus' *Prometheus Bound*.

The oldest comedies that we still have are by Aristophanes, and were also written around 425 BC. The comedies of Aristophanes are highly political, and frequently constantly allude to the Athens of that time. But, at the same time they are fantastic. In these comedies, reality and imaginative absurdity are closely intertwined.

In ancient Greece and Rome, plays were also written in verse, like lyrical poems or epics, though some comedists made very occasional use of prose passages: "Poetry was older and in some ways more prestigious: the poet had the advantage of elevated and sensuous language, variety of metrical forms, greater freedom in vocabulary and syntax."①

Ⅱ. Greek Mythology

Greek mythology is a group of oral stories in ancient Greece. In terms of theme it can be divided into two parts: the stories about gods, and the heroic tales.

The stories about gods relate to the creation of the universe, the birth of gods and their lives, the nature of the world and the origins of humankind.

The heroic tales are a collection about the heroes and the leaders of the tribe or the founders of the city-states.

The typical characteristics of Greek mythology are as follows:

1. All the chief gods took human forms of beauty and grace and shared the human feelings. Driven by human desires, they frequently gave way to anger and jealousy. They put themselves into ceaseless battles, struggling for power. In the human world they not only experienced competitions and difficulties. but also enjoyed earthly friendship and love.

2. Greek mythology is full of splendid imagination and lively characters, in this way making every story interesting and vivid.

Greek mythology had an enormous influence upon Greek literature "ranging in period and genre from eighth-century BC oral poetry to encyclopedic prose compilations of the early centuries AD"②.

Greek mythology also has an extensive influence on the Western literature. Poets and artists from ancient times to the present day have derived inspiration from Greek mythology and have discovered contemporary significance in these mythological themes.

---

① Richard Rutherford: *Classical Literature: A Concise History*, Blackwell Publishing Ltd. 2005, p. 9.

② Roger D. Woodard ed. *The Cambridge Companion to Greek Mythology*, Cambridge University Press, 2007, p. 1.

The Creation of the World

In the beginning there was only chaos①. Then out of the void appeared Erebus②, the unknowable place where death dwells, and Night. All else was empty, silent, endless darkness. Then somehow Love was born bringing a start of order. From Love came Light and Day. Once there was Light and Day, Gaea③, the earth appeared.

Then Erebus slept with Night, who gave birth to Ether④, the heavenly light, and to Day, the earthly light. Then Night alone produced Doom, Fate, Death, Sleep, Dreams, Nemesis, and others that come to man out of darkness.

Meanwhile Gaea alone gave birth to Uranus⑤, the heavens. Uranus became Gaea's mate covering her on all sides. Together they produced the three Cyclopes⑥, the three Hecatonchires⑦, and twelve Titans⑧.

However, Uranus was a bad father and husband. He hated the Hecatonchires. He imprisoned them by pushing them into the hidden places of the earth, Gaea's womb. This angered Gaea and she plotted against Uranus. She made a flint sickle and tried to get her children to attack Uranus. All were too afraid except the youngest Titan, Cronus⑨.

Gaea and Cronus set up an ambush of Uranus as he lay with Gaea at night. Cronus grabbed his father and castrated him, with the stone sickle, throwing the severed genitals into the ocean. The fate of Uranus is not clear. He either died, withdrawing from the earth, or exiled himself to Italy. As he departed he promised that Cronus and the Titans would be punished. From his spilt blood came the Giants, the Ash Tree Nymphs, and the Erinyes. From the sea foam where his genital organ fell came Aphrodite.

---

① chaos [ˈkeɪɔs] *n.* the disordered state of unformed matter and infinite space supposed in some cosmogonic views to have existed before the ordered universe (混沌)。

② Erebus [ˈerɪbəs] *n.* the dark region of the underworld through which the dead must pass before they reach Hades (厄瑞玻斯,阳间与阴间当中的黑暗区域)。

③ Gaea [ˈdʒiːə] *n.* the goddess of the earth, who bore and married Uranus and became the mother of the Titans and the Cyclopes (盖亚)。

④ Ether [ˈiːθə] *n.* the regions of space beyond the earth's atmosphere (苍天;以太)。

⑤ Uranus [ˈjuːərənəs] *n.* the earliest supreme god, a personification of the sky, who was the son and consort of Gaea and the father of the Cyclopes and the Titans (乌拉诺斯天神); the seventh planet from the sun (天王星)。

⑥ Cyclopes [ˈsaɪklɔpəz]: Cyclops 的复数形式。Cyclops [saɪklɔps] *n.* one-eyed giants, include Arges, Brontes, and Sterops (独眼巨人)。

⑦ Hecatonchires [ˌhekətɔnˈkaɪriːz] *n.* 赫卡同刻伊瑞斯,百手三巨人。

⑧ Titan [ˈtaɪt(ə)n] *n.* 提坦巨神。

⑨ Cronus [ˈkrəunəs] *n.* a Titan who ruled the universe until dethroned by his son Zeus (克罗诺斯,提坦巨神之一)。

Cronus became the next ruler. He imprisoned the Cyclopes and the Hecatonchires in Tartarus[①]. He married his sister Rhea. Under his rule the Titans had many offspring. He ruled for many ages. However, Gaea and Uranus both had prophesied that he would be overthrown by a son. To avoid this Cronus swallowed each of his children as they were born. Rhea was angry at the treatment of the children and plotted against Cronus. When it came time to give birth to her sixth child, Rhea hid herself, then she left the child to be raised by Nymphs. To conceal her act she wrapped a stone in swaddling cloths and passed it off as the baby to Cronus, who swallowed it.

This child was Zeus[②]. He grew into a handsome youth on Crete[③]. He consulted Metis on how to defeat Cronus. She prepared a drink for Cronus designing to make him vomit[④] up the other children. Rhea convinced Cronus to accept his son and Zeus was allowed to return to Mount Olympus as Cronus's cupbearer. This gave Zeus the opportunity to slip Cronus the specially prepared drink. This worked as planned and the other five children were vomited up. Being gods they were unharmed. They were thankful to Zeus and made him their leader.

Cronus was yet to be defeated. He and the Titans, except Prometheus, Epimetheus, and Oceanus, fought to retain their power. Atlas became their leader in battle and it looked for some time as though they would win and put the young gods down. However, Zeus was cunning. He went down to Tartarus and freed the Cyclopes and the Hecatonchires. Prometheus joined Zeus as well. He returned to battle with his new allies. The Cyclopes provided Zeus with lighting bolts for weapons. The Hecatonchires he set in ambush armed with boulders. With the time right, Zeus retreated, drawing the Titans into the Hecatonchires' ambush. The Hecatonchires rained down hundreds of boulders with such a fury the Titans thought the mountains were falling on them. They broke and ran, giving Zeus victory.

Zeus exiled the Titans who had fought against him into Tartarus. Except for Atlas, who was singled out for the special punishment of holding the world on his shoulders.

However, even after this victory Zeus was not safe. Gaea was angry that her children had been imprisoned, and gave birth to a last offspring, Typhoeus[⑤]. Typhoeus was so fearsome that most of the gods fled. However, Zeus faced the monster and flung his lighting bolts that was able to kill it. Typhoeus was buried under Mount Etna in Sicily.

Much later a final challenge to Zeus' rule was made by the Giants. They went so far

---

① Tartarus [ˈtɑːtərəs] *n.* the abysmal regions below Hades where the Titans were confined; an infernal region (地狱底下暗无天日之深渊)。

② Zeus [zjuːs] *n.* the principal god of the Greek pantheon and ruler of the heavens (宙斯)。

③ Crete [kriːt] *n.* 克利特岛。

④ vomit [ˈvɔmɪt] *v.* to eject (contents of the stomach) through the mouth (呕吐)。

⑤ Typhoeus [taɪˈfəʊjuːs] *n.* 百头巨怪。

as to attempt to invade Mount Olympus, piling mountain upon mountain in an effort to reach the top. But, the gods had grown strong and with the help of Heracles[①] the Giants were subdued or killed.

Io

Zeus fell in love with Io[②] and seduced her. To try to keep Hera from noticing, he covered the world with a thick blanket of clouds. This backfired, arousing Hera's suspicions. She came down from Mount Olympus and began dispersing the clouds. Zeus did some quick thinking and changed Io's form from being a lovely maiden. So as the clouds dispersed Hera found Zeus standing next to a white heifer[③]. He then swore that he had never seen the cow before, and it had just sprang right out of the earth. Seeing right through this, Hera complimented the cow and asked to have it as a present. As turning such a reasonable request down would have given the whole thing away, Zeus presented her with the cow.

She sent the cow away and arranged Argus[④] to watch over it. Since Argus had a hundred eyes and could have some of them sleep while others were awake he made a fine watchman. Desperate, Zeus sent Hermes[⑤] to fetch Io. Disguised as a shepherd, Hermes had to employ all his skill as a musician and story teller to gain Argus' confidence and lull him to sleep. Once Argus fell asleep, Hermes killed him. As a memorial, Hera took his eyes and set them into the tail of her favorite bird, the peacock.

While Io was now free, Hera sent the mother of all gad-flies to sting the still bovine Io. This pushed her near madness, trying to escape she wandered the world. During her wanders she came across Prometheus[⑥] while chained. He gave her hope. He predicted that she would have to wander for many years. But, she would eventually be changed back into human form and would bear a child. He predicted that a descendant of this child would be a great hero and set him free.

His predictions came true. During her wanderings many geographical features were named after her including the Ionian Sea, and the Bosporus[⑦] (which means ford of the

---

① Heracles [ˈherəkliːz] *n.* the son of Zeus and Alcmene, a hero of extraordinary strength (赫拉克勒斯)。

② Io [ˈaɪəʊ] *n.* a maiden who was loved by Zeus and transformed by Hera into a cow (伊娥)。

③ heifer [ˈhefə] *n.* a young cow, especially one that has not yet given birth to a calf (小母牛)。

④ Argus [ˈɑːgəs] *n.* a giant with a hundred eyes (阿耳戈斯,百眼巨人)。

⑤ Hermes [ˈhɜːmiːz] *n.* the god of commerce, invention, cunning, and theft, who also served as messenger (赫耳墨斯)。

⑥ Prometheus [prəˈmɪθjuːs] *n.* a Titan who stole fire from Olympus and gave it to humankind, for which Zeus chained him to a rock and sent an eagle to eat his liver, which grew back daily (普罗米修斯)。

⑦ Bosporus [ˈbɔspərəs] *n.* a narrow strait separating European and Asian Turkey and joining the Black Sea with the Sea of Marmara (博斯普鲁斯海峡)。

cow). She eventually reached the Nile where Zeus did restore her to human form. She bore Apis[①] and eleven generations later her descendant Heracles would set Prometheus free.

Ⅲ. Homer

Homer was a legendary ancient Greek blind poet, the author of the great epic poems, the *Iliad* and the *Odyssey*.

The ancient Greeks generally believed that Homer was a historical individual, but modern scholars are skeptical. Some depict Homer as a wandering minstrel who collected and composed the epic poems from oral works. Some modern scholars even tend to be affected by the so-called "Homeric question", an expression which refers to the disputes over the authorship and composition of the two epics. It is generally accepted that *Iliad* and *Odyssey* draw on and probably form part of a long tradition of oral poetry, an inherited body of material repeatedly re-worked and re-performed over many generations, so that the precise date of "composition" is theoretically difficult and practically impossible to define.

The great epic the *Iliad* deals with the war against the city of Troy, while the *Odyssey* deals with the return of Odysseus after the Trojan War to his home island of Ithaca. Rather than recounting the Trojan War from start to finish, Homer narrates a short episode in the *Iliad*. It describes the events of last 51 days of the ten-year siege of Troy. It begins with Achilles' anger and ends with Hector's funeral.

Iliad[②]

(Excerpt)

Athena[③] went after Hector in the form and with the voice of Deiphobus[④]. She came close up to him and said, "Dear brother, I see you are hard pressed by Achilles who is chasing you at full speed round the city of Priam[⑤], let us await his onset and stand on our defence."

And Hector answered, "Deiphobus, you have always been dearest to me of all my

---

① Apis [ˈeɪpɪs] *n.* the son of Zeus and Io and a king of Egypt (埃皮斯,神牛)。

② 译文参见本书第 225 至 226 页。

③ Athena [əˈθiːnə] *n.* the goddess of wisdom and the arts (雅典娜)。

④ Deiphobus a son of Priam and Hecuba and the prince of Troy, became leader of the Trojan army following the death of Hector (得伊福玻斯)。

⑤ Priam [ˈpraɪəm] *n.* the father of Paris, Hector, and Cassandra and king of Troy, who was killed when his city fell to the Greeks (普里阿摩斯)。

brothers, children of Hecuba[①] and Priam, but henceforth I shall rate you yet more highly, inasmuch as you have ventured outside the wall for my sake when all the others remain inside."

Then Athena said, "Dear brother, my father and mother went down on their knees and implored me, as did all my comrades, to remain inside. So great a fear has fallen upon them all; but I was in an agony of grief when I beheld you; now, therefore, let us two make a stand and fight, and let there be no keeping our spears in reserve, that we may learn whether Achilles[②] shall kill us and bear off our spoils to the ships, or whether he shall fall before you."

Thus did Athena inveigle[③] him by her cunning, and when the two were now close to one another, great Hector was the first to speak. "I will-no longer fly you, son of Peleus[④]," said he, "as I have been doing hitherto, three times have I fled round the mighty city of Priam, without daring to withstand you, but now, let me either slay or be slain, for I am in the mind to face you. Let us, then, give pledges to one another by our gods, who are the fittest witnesses and guardians of all covenants[⑤]; let it be agreed between us that if Zeus vouchsafes me the longer stay and I take your life, I am not to treat your dead body in any unseemly fashion, but when I have stripped you of your armour, I am to give up your body to the Achaeans[⑥], and do you likewise."

Achilles glared at him and answered, "Fool, prate[⑦] not to me about covenants. There can be no covenants between men and lions, wolves and lambs can never be of one mind, but hate each other out and out an through. Therefore there can be no understanding between you and me, nor may there be any covenants between us, till one or other shall fall and glut grim Mars[⑧] with his life's blood. Put forth all your strength; you have need now to prove yourself indeed a bold soldier and man of war. You have no more chance, and Pallas Athena will forthwith vanquish you by my spear: you shall now pay me in full for the grief you have caused me on account of my comrades whom you have killed in battle."

He poised his spear as he spoke and hurled it. Hector saw it coming and avoided it; he watched it and crouched down so that it flew over his head and stuck in the ground beyond; Athena then snatched it up and gave it back to Achilles without Hector's seeing

① Hecuba [ˈhekjʊbə] *n.* the wife of Priam and mother of Hector, Paris, and Cassandra in Homer's Iliad (赫卡柏,普里阿摩斯的妻子,赫克托耳、帕里斯和卡桑德拉的母亲)。

② Achilles [əˈkɪliːz] *n.* the hero of Homer's Iliad, the son of Peleus and Thetis (阿喀琉斯)。

③ inveigle [ɪnˈviːgl] *vt.* to obtain by cajolery (诱骗)。

④ Peleus [ˈpeliəs] *n.* a son of Aeacus and the father of Achilles (珀琉斯,阿喀琉斯之父)。

⑤ covenant [ˈkʌvɪnənt] *n.* a binding agreement; a compact (盟约;契约)。

⑥ Achaean [əˈkiːən] *n.* 阿开亚人;希腊人。

⑦ prate [preɪt] *v./n.* to utter idly or to little purpose; idle chatter (空谈)。

⑧ Mars [mɑːz] *n.* 战神。

her; Hector thereon said to the son of Peleus, "You have missed your aim, Achilles, peer of the gods, and Zeus has not yet revealed to you the hour of my doom, though you made sure that he had done so. You were a false-tongued liar when you deemed that I should forget my valour and quail before you. You shall not drive spear into the back of a runaway — drive it, should heaven so grant you power, drive it into me as I make straight towards you; and now for your own part avoid my spear if you can — would that you might receive the whole of it into your body; if you were once dead the Trojans would find the war an easier matter, for it is you who have harmed them most."

He poised his spear as he spoke and hurled it. His aim was true for he hit the middle of Achilles' shield, but the spear rebounded[①] from it, and did not pierce it. Hector was angry when he saw that the weapon had sped from his hand in vain, and stood there in dismay for he had no second spear. With a loud cry he called Deiphobus and asked him for one, but there was no man; then he saw the truth and said to himself, "Alas! the gods have lured me on to my destruction. I deemed that the hero Deiphobus was by my side, but he is within the wall, and Athena has inveigled me; death is now indeed exceedingly[②] near at hand and there is no way out of it — for so Zeus and his son Apollo, the far-darter have willed it, though heretofore they have been ever ready to protect me. My doom has come upon me; let me not then die ingloriously and without a struggle, but let me first do some great thing that shall be told among men hereafter."

As he spoke he drew the keen blade that hung so great and strong by his side, and gathering himself together be sprang on Achilles like a soaring eagle which swoops[③] down from the clouds on to some lamb or timid hare — even so did Hector brandish his sword and spring upon Achilles. Achilles mad with rage darted towards him, with his wondrous shield before his breast, and his gleaming helmet[④], made with four layers of metal, nodding fiercely forward. The thick tresses of gold which Hephaestus[⑤] had crested the helmet floated round it, and as the evening star that shines brighter than all others through the stillness of night, even such was the gleam of the spear which Achilles poised in his right hand, fraught with the death of noble Hector.

He eyed his fair flesh over and over to see where he could best wound it, but all was protected by the goodly armour of which Hector had spoiled Patroclus[⑥] after he had slain him, save only the throat where the collar-bones divide the neck from the shoulders, and this is a most deadly place: here then did Achilles strike him as he was coming on towards

---

① rebound [rɪˈbaund] *v.* to spring or bounce back after hitting or colliding with something (回弹)。

② exceedingly [ɪkˈsiːdɪŋli] *adv.* extremely (非常地;极度地)。

③ swoop [swuːp] *v./n.* to move in a sudden sweep; the act or an instance of swooping (猛扑)。

④ helmet [ˈhelmɪt] *n.* a head covering of hard material (头盔;钢盔)。

⑤ Hephaestus [hɪˈfiːstəs] *n.* the god of fire and metalworking (赫菲斯托斯;火和锻冶之神)。

⑥ Patroclus [pəˈtrəkləs] *n.* a Greek warrior, attendant, and friend to Achilles, who was killed by Hector in the Trojan War (普特洛克勒斯)。

him, and the point of his spear went right through the fleshy part of the neck, but it did not sever his windpipe[①] so that he could still speak. Hector fell headlong, and Achilles vaunted over him saying, "Hector, you deemed that you should come off scatheless when you were spoiling Patroclus, and recked not of myself who was not with him. Fool that you were: for I, his comrade, mightier far than he, was still left behind him at the ships, and now I have laid you low. The Achaeans shall give him all due funeral rites, while dogs and vultures[②] shall work their will upon yourself."

Ⅳ. Sappho

Sappho (610 BC～580 BC) was a great Greek poetess, whose poetry was so renowned that Greek philosopher Plato referred to her two centuries after her death as the "tenth muse". Sappho was born on the island of Lesbos, a cultural center at that time. Although the details of her life are deficient, it appears that she was born to an aristocratic family and was a contemporary of Greek lyric poet Alcaeus. According to tradition, Alcaeus was Sappho's lover. According to another legend, Sappho's death was consistent with her passionate personality. It is because of her unrequited love for a beautiful young boatman named Phaon that she jumped from the steep cliffs on the island of Leucas into the sea. Perhaps it is only an invention, but many people believe it is a true event.

Sappho wrote nine books of odes and a number of wedding songs, elegies, and hymns, but most of her poetry was destroyed centuries later by church authorities, and only a few fragments still exist. The fragmentary remains of Sappho's poems indicate that she taught her art to a group of young women, to whom she was devotedly attached and whose bridal odes she composed when they left her to be married.

Sappho's poems are marked by beauty of diction, simplicity of form, and intensity of emotion. She invented the verse form known as Sapphic, a four-line stanza in which the first three lines are each 11 syllables long and the fourth is 5 syllables long. This form influenced many later Greek poets.

Blest as the Immortal Gods Is He[③]

Blest as the immortal gods is he,
The youth who fondly sits by thee[④],
And hears and sees thee all the while

---

① windpipe [ˈwɪndpaɪp] *n.* 气管。

② vulture [ˈvʌltʃə(r)] *n.* 秃鹰；贪婪的人。

③ 译文参见本书第226页。

④ thee: you (古英语 thee 是 thou 的宾格)。

Softly speak and sweetly smile.

'Twas[①] this deprived my soul of rest,
And raised such tumults in my breast;
For while I gazed, in transport tost,
My breath was gone, my voice was lost:
My bosom glowed; the subtle flame

Ran quick through all my vital frame[②];
O'er[③] my dim eyes a darkness hung;
My ears with hollow murmurs rung.

In dewy damps my limbs were chilled;
My blood with gentle horror thrilled;
My feeble pulse forgot to play;
I fainted, sank, and died away.

Tr. by Ambrose Philips

On the Throne of Many Hues, Immortal Aphrodite[④]

On the throne of many hues, Immortal Aphrodite[⑤],
Child of Zeus, weaving wiles — I beg you
Not to subdue my spirit, Queen,
With pain or sorrow

But come — if ever before
Having heard my voice from far away
You listened, and leaving your father's
Golden home you came

In your chariot yoked with swift, lovely
Sparrows bringing you over the dark earth
Thick-feathered wings swirling down
From the sky through mid-air

---

① 'Twas: It was.

② frame: the structure of a human or animal body; physique (身体结构;体格)。

③ o'er: over.

④ 译文参见本书第 226 至 227 页。

⑤ Aphrodite [ˌæfrəˈdaɪti] *n.* the goddess of love and beauty (阿芙洛蒂忒)。

Arriving quickly — you, Blessed One,
With a smile on your unaging face
Asking again what have I suffered
And why am I calling again

And in my wild heart what did I most wish
To happen to me: "Again whom must I persuade
Back into the harness of your love?
Sappho, who wrongs you?

For if she flees, soon she'll pursue,
She doesn't accept gifts, but she'll give,
If not now loving, soon she'll love
Even against her will."

Come to me now again, release me from
This pain, everything my spirit longs
To have fulfilled, fulfill, and you
Be my ally.

Tr. by Diane Rayor

Ⅴ. Anacreon

Anacreon (570 BC～488 BC), the Greek lyric poet, was born in Teos, an Ionian city on the coast of Asia Minor. He was known for his satires and short poems. His favorite themes were wine and passionate desire. His poetry, graceful and elegant, celebrates the joys of wine and love. He was one of the most popular poets of his time. He invented a poetic form of verse called Anacreonic.

Anacreon's actual works are claimed to have filled at least five volumes, but only a few fragments of his poems have been preserved. His poems are marked by urbanity, simplicity, delicate and vivid expressions and airy quality.

The eighteenth century saw great interest in English imitations of Anacreon. One result was a popular song, "Anacreon in Heaven", which later supplied the tune for the American national anthem.

Drinking Song[①]

Drink from my cup, dear! Live my life — be still
Young with my youth! Have one heart, word and will,
One love for both; let one wreath shade our eyes;
Be mad when I am — wise when I am wise.

Tr. by E. Arnold

Roving God, Whose Playfellows[②]

Roving god, whose playfellows[③]
Over the mountains' airy brows
In happy chase are led;
Where Love, who breaks the heart of pride,
Or Nymphs[④] amuse thee, violet-eyed,
Or Aphrodite keeps thy side,
The goddess rosy Red —
Lord Dionysus[⑤], I kneel to thee;
Stoop to me of thy charity
And this my prayer receive:
Dear Lord, thy best persuasion[⑥] use,
Bid Cleobulus[⑦] not refuse
The gift of love I give.

Tr. by T. F. Higham

Ⅵ. Sophocles

Sophocles (496 BC～406 BC), an Athenian writer, is believed to have written 118 plays, but only seven of them remain. The most famous of Sophocles' tragedies are those

---

① 译文参见本书第 227 页。

② 译文参见本书第 227 页。

③ playfellow [ˈpleɪfeləʊ] *n.* play mate (游戏伙伴)。

④ Nymph [nɪmf] *n.* 林泽仙女。In Greek and Roman mythology, any of numerous minor deities represented as beautiful maidens inhabiting and sometimes personifying features of nature such as trees, waters, and mountains were called Nymph.

⑤ Dionysus [ˌdaɪəˈnaɪsəs] *n.* 酒神狄俄尼索斯。

⑥ persuasion [pəˈsweɪʒən] *n.* the act of persuading; the ability to persuade (说服;说服力)。

⑦ Cleobulus: 克勒布罗斯 (阿那克里翁当年所钟情的少年)。

concerning Oedipus and Antigone: these are often known as the Theban plays, consisting of three plays: *Antigone*, *King Oedipus*, and *Oedipus at Colonus*. All three plays concern the fate of Thebes during and after the reign of King Oedipus. *King Oedipus* (also translated as *Oedipus the King*, *Oedipus Tyrannus* or *Oedipus Rex*) is his most important play and it is regarded as the representative of all the Greek tragedies.

Greek tragedy is often based on the Greek mythology. The story of Oedipus belongs to Theban cycle of legends. It is considered the most tragic story ever told.

In this play, it is the evil fate that made Oedipus guilty. Laius, King of Thebes, was informed that any child born to his wife, Jocasta, would kill him. So, when the queen had a baby-boy, Laius sent the trusted slave to leave the baby on a mountainside for wolves to eat. But Oedipus did not die as his father wished, and he became the prince of Corinth. When he became a young man, Oedipus only knew that he was the son of the King and Queen of Corinth, so, when he learned from the priestess that would kill his father and marry his mother he decided to leave immediately from Corinth and go to Thebes. It is in the Thebes, he accidentally killed an old man, the very king! Then, he met the Sphinx, sitting on her rock at a crossroad. Sphinx ate anyone who could not give the right answer to her riddle, but Oedipus answered correctly; and the Sphinx threw herself down from a cliff. Having saved the city of Thebes from this monster, Oedipus found a hero's welcome. The Thebans gratefully proclaimed Oedipus king and he married the widowed Queen Jocasta.

In *King Oedipus* by Sophocles, Oedipus, the protagonist, was a pure-hearted king. He had ruled Thebes happily for many years. All was well, till the plague suddenly struck Thebes. Oedipus cared of his people, anxious to find out the cause of the plague and he got the answer: Gods were angry because the death of the old king remained unavenged. Oedipus pronounced a curse on the murderer, and promised to banish him as soon as he was found. From the prophet Tiresias and others he soon found the truth. So, Jocasta hung herself; Oedipus grabbed the pin from her dress and poked out his eyes and went to exile.

Here is the selection from the play translated by the great poet William Butler Yeats.

King Oedipus①

(Excerpt)

[*Jocasta*② *enters from the palace.*]

Jocasta. It has come into my head, citizens of Thebes, to visit every altar of the Gods, a wreath in my hand and a dish of incense. For all manner of alarms trouble the soul of

---

① 译文参见本书第227至229页。

② Jocasta [dʒəʊ'kæstə] *n.* a queen of Thebes who unknowingly married her own son, Oedipus (伊俄卡斯忒)。

Oedipus[①], who instead of weighing new oracles[②] by old, like a man of sense, is at the mercy of every mouth that speaks terror. Seeing that my words are nothing to him, I cry to you, Lysian Apollo, whose altar is the first I meet: I come, a suppliant, bearing symbols of prayer; O make us clean, for now we are all afraid, seeing him afraid, even as they who see the helmsman afraid.

[*Enter Messenger.*]

Messenger. May I learn from you, strangers, where is the home of King Oedipus? Or better still, tell me where he himself is, if you know.

Chorus. This is his house, and he himself, stranger, is within it, and this lady is the mother of his children.

Messenger. Then I call a blessing upon her, seeing what man she has married.

Jocasta. May God reward those words with a like blessing, stranger! But what have you come to seek or to tell?

Messenger. Good news for your house, lady, and for your husband.

Jocasta. What news? From whence have you come?

Messenger. From Corinth, and you will rejoice at the message I am about to give you; yet, maybe, it will grieve you.

Jocasta. What is it? How can it have this double power?

Messenger. The people of Corinth, they say, will take him for king.

Jocasta. How then? Is old Polybus no longer on the throne?

Messenger. No. He is in his tomb.

Jocasta. What do you say? Is Polybus dead, old man?

Messenger. May I drop dead if it is not the truth.

Jocasta. Away! Hurry to your master with this news. O oracle of the Gods, where are you now? This is the man whom Oedipus feared and shunned lest he should murder him, and now this man has died a natural death, and not by the hand of Oedipus.

[*Enter Oedipus.*]

Oedipus. Jocasta, dearest wife, why have you called me from the house?

Jocasta. Listen to this man, and judge to what the oracles of the Gods have come.

Oedipus. And he — who may he be? And what news has he?

Jocasta. He has come from Corinth to tell you that your father, Polybus, is dead.

Oedipus. How, stranger? Let me have it from your own mouth.

Messenger. If I am to tell the story, the first thing is that he is dead and gone.

Oedipus. By some sickness or by treachery?

Messenger. A little thing can bring the aged to their rest.

---

① Oedipus [ˈiːdɪpəs] *n.* a son of Laius and Jocasta, who was abandoned at birth and unwittingly killed his father and then married his mother (俄狄浦斯)。

② oracle [ˈɔrəkl] *n.* a command or revelation from God (神谕)。

Oedipus. Ah! He died, it seems, from sickness?

Messenger. Yes; and of old age.

Oedipus. Alas! Alas! Why, indeed, my wife, should one look to that Pythian seer, or to the birds that scream above our heads? For they would have it that I was doomed to kill my father. And now he is dead — hid already beneath the earth. And here am I — who had no part in it, unless indeed he died from longing for me. If that were so, I may have caused his death; but Polybus has carried the oracles with him into Hades — the oracles as men have understood them and they are worth nothing.

Jocasta. Did I not tell you so, long since?

Oedipus. You did, but fear misled me.

Jocasta. Put this trouble from you.

Oedipus. But surely I must needs fear my mother's bed?

Jocasta. Nay, what should mortal fear, for whom the decrees of fortune are supreme, and who hash clear foresight of nothing? 'Tis best to live at random, as one may. But fear not thou touching wedlock[①] with thy mother. Many men ere now have so fared in dreams also: but he to whom these things are as nought bears his life most easily.[②]

Oedipus. Those bold words would sound better, were not my mother living. But as it is — I have some grounds for fear; yet you have said well.

Jocasta. Yet your father's death is a sign that all is well.

Oedipus. I know that: but I fear because of her who lives.

Messenger. Who is this woman who makes you afraid?

Oedipus. Merope, old man, the wife of Polybus.

Messenger. What is there in her to make you afraid?

Oedipus. A dreadful oracle sent from Heaven, stranger.

Messenger. Is it a secret, or can you speak it out?

Oedipus. Loxias said that I was doomed to marry my own mother, and to shed my father's blood. For that reason I fled from my house in Corinth; and I did right, though there is great comfort in familiar faces.

Messenger. Was it indeed for that reason that you went into exile?

Oedipus. I did not wish, old man, to shed my father's blood.

Messenger. King, have I not freed you from that fear?

Oedipus. You shall be fittingly rewarded.

Messenger. Indeed, to tell the truth, it was for that I came; to bring you home and be the better for it —

Oedipus. No! I will never go to my parents' home.

Messenger. Oh, my son, it is plain enough, you do not know what you do.

---

① wedlock [ˈwedlɔk] *n.* the state of being married; matrimony (婚姻;结婚状态)。

② These five lines from the translation by Sir Richard Claverhouse Jebb.

Oedipus. How, old man? For God's love, tell me.

Messenger. If for these reasons you shrink from going home.

Oedipus. I am afraid lest Phoebus has spoken true.

Messenger. You are afraid of being made guilty through Merope?

Oedipus. That is my constant fear.

Messenger. A vain fear.

Oedipus. How so, if I was born of that father and mother?

Messenger. Because they were nothing to you in blood.

Oedipus. What do you say? Was Polybus not my father?

Messenger. No more nor less than myself.

Oedipus. How can my father be no more to me than you who are nothing to me?

Messenger. He did not beget you any more than I.

Oedipus. No? Then why did he call me his son?

Messenger. He took you as a gift from these hands of mine.

Oedipus. How could he love so dearly what came from another's hands?

Messenger. He had been childless.

Oedipus. If I am not your son, where did you get me?

Messenger. In a wooded valley of Cithaeron.

Oedipus. What brought you wandering there?

Messenger. I was in charge of mountain sheep.

Oedipus. A shepherd — a wandering, hired man.

Messenger. A hired man who came just in time.

Oedipus. Just in time — had it come to that?

Messenger. Have not the cords left their marks upon your ankles?

Oedipus. Yes, that is an old trouble.

Messenger. I took your feet out of the spancel①.

Oedipus. I have had those marks from the cradle.

Messenger. They have given you the name you bear. ②

Oedipus. Tell me, for God's sake, was that deed my mother's or my father's?

Messenger. I do not know he who gave you to me knows more of that than I.

Oedipus. What? You had me from another? You did not chance on me yourself?

Messenger. No. Another shepherd gave you to me.

Oedipus. Who was he? Can you tell me who he was?

Messenger. I think that he was said to be of Laius' household.

Oedipus. The king who ruled this country long ago?

Messenger. The same — the man was herdsman in his service.

---

① spancel [ˈspænsl] *n.* a noose for tethering animals(拴畜绳)。

② Oedipus means "swollen-feet".

Oedipus. Is he alive, that I might speak with him?

Messenger. You people of this country should know that.

Oedipus. Is there any one here present who knows the herd he speaks of? Any one who has seen him in the town pastures? The hour has come when all must be made clear.

Chorus. I think he is the very herd you sent for but now; Jocasta can tell you better than I.

Jocasta. Why ask about that man? Why think about him? Why waste a thought on what this man has said? What he has said is of no account.

Oedipus. What, with a clue like that in my hands and fail to find out my birth?

Jocasta. For God's sake, if you set any value upon your life, give up this search — my misery is enough.

Oedipus. Though I be proved the son of a slave, yes, even of three generations of slaves, you cannot be made base-born.

Jocasta. Yet, hear me, I implore you. Give up this search.

Oedipus. I will not hear of anything but searching the whole thing out.

Jocasta. I am only thinking of your good — I have advised you for the best.

Oedipus. Your advice makes me impatient.

Jocasta. May you never come to know who you are, unhappy man!

Oedipus. Go, some one, bring the herdsman here — and let that woman glory in her noble blood.

Jocasta. Alas, alas, miserable man! Miserable! That is all that I can call you now or for ever. [*She goes out.*]

Chorus. Why has the lady gone, Oedipus, in such a transport of despair? Out of this silence will burst a storm of sorrows.

Oedipus. Let come what will. However lowly my origin is I will discover it. That woman, with all a woman's pride, grows red with shame at my base birth. I think myself the child of Good Luck, and that the years are my foster-brothers. Sometimes they have set me up, and sometimes thrown me down, but he that has Good Luck for mother can suffer no dishonour. That is my origin, nothing can change it, so why should I renounce this search into my birth?

Tr. by William Butler Yeats

Ⅷ. Catullus

The Roman poet Catullus (87 BC～54 BC) is often considered the greatest writer of Latin lyric verse. It is thought that Catullus was born in or near Verona and went to Rome about 62 BC, where he achieved prominence in a group of young poets who wrote Latin verse inspired by the Greek poets of the Hellenistic Age.

Among the most famous of Catullus's works are the so-called "Lesbia poems", which variously express the deep passion, devotion, hatred and scorn for a mysterious lady, identified as Lesbia (apparently after the Greek poet Sappho who lived on Lesbos). And scholars identified the poet's Lesbia with a real woman named Clodia. This beautiful but unscrupulous married woman had been unfaithful to the young poet when the two were lovers. Although the focus is on Lesbia, many of the poems express self-doubt, self-criticism, and self-pity. Whatever the exact facts of the affair may be, critics generally agree that the Lesbia poems rank among the most intense and effective expressions of passion in Roman literature. In these poems, the conflicting emotions dwell within him at the same time. The poem "Let Us Live, My Lesbia" is one of the representatives of the Lesbia poems, and it is famous for its Carpe Diem theme.

Catullus's creation of Lesbia is the first of many important creations in which male poets summon through their poetry the image of a woman whom they love, and express the deep conflicting emotions dwelling within them at the same time.

Catullus's influence is seen not only on the love poetry of later Latin poets such as Ovid and Horace, but also on the marriage odes of English poets of the Renaissance and of the 17th century such as Robert Herrick, Ben Jonson, and Edmund Spenser.

Tears for Lesbia's Sparrow①

Sparrow, my sweet girl's delight,
Whom she plays with, holds to her breast,
Whom, greedy, she gives her little finger to,
Often provoking you to a sharp bite,
Whenever my shining desire wishes
To play with something she loves,
I suppose, while strong passion abates,
It might be a small relief from her pain:
Might I toy with you as she does
And ease the cares of a sad mind!

Let Us Live, My Lesbia②

Let us live, my Lesbia, and let us love,
And let us judge all the rumors of the old men
To be worth just one penny!
The suns are able to fall and rise:

① 译文参见本书第 229 页。
② 译文参见本书第 230 页。

When that brief light has fallen for us,
We must sleep a never ending night.
Give me a thousand kisses, then another hundred,
Then another thousand, then a second hundred,
Then yet another thousand more, then another hundred.
Then, when we have made many thousands,
We will mix them all up so that we don't know,
And so that no one can be jealous of us when he finds out
How many kisses we have shared.

Tr. by Rudy Negenborn

Ⅷ. Hebrew Bible

The Hebrew Bible is a collection of the sacred writings of the Christian religion. It is written partly in prose and partly in verse and exploits various literary types, including narrative stories and lyrical poems. The Bible is the most popular and the most influential work of all literatures.

The Hebrew Bible not only deals with God's creations and ancient Jewish legends, but also contains collections of philosophical and lyrical poems. The collection of philosophical poems entitled as Proverbs embodies the thoughts of ancient people and the lyrical collection known as the Song of Solomon has long puzzled the readers because its themes seem to have nothing to do with the religious concerns of the rest of the Bible. Some people even think that it is among the best of the erotic love poetry of the world. The book appears to be a collection of poetry on the theme of human love, largely in the form of a dialogue between a man and a woman. The poems typically presuppose two primary figures: a male lover and a female lover. Some scholars consider that there are three figures and there is a plot in it. In this plot, Solomon married the Shulamite Woman and added her to his harem. She was the most beautiful woman that Solomon ever saw. She was the closest to a Right Woman that he ever found. But she had a Shepherd Lover, who was her Right Man, who, though only a shepherd boy, in her eyes surpassed the glory of Solomon. And thus the collection becomes more complicated than it appears. Like much poetry, its complex meanings make it both evocative and enigmatic.

The Song of Songs has played a fascinating role in Western culture. It has been a test case and a workshop for allegorical method. It has been a mainstay of asceticism and an impetus for mysticism.

There are many English versions of the Bible, among them, King James Version (KJV), American Standard Version (ASV) and New International Version (NIV) are famous and popular translations, and what we select here are from NIV.

Genesis[①]

(Excerpt)

In the beginning God created the heavens and the earth. Now the earth was formless and empty, darkness was over the surface of the deep, and the Spirit of God was hovering over the waters. And God said, "Let there be light," and there was light. God saw that the light was good, and he separated the light from the darkness. God called the light "day", and the darkness he called "night". And there was evening, and there was morning — the first day.

And God said, "Let there be an expanse between the waters to separate water from water." So God made the expanse and separated the water under the expanse from the water above it. And it was so. God called the expanse "sky". And there was evening, and there was morning — the second day.

And God said, "Let the water under the sky be gathered to one place, and let dry ground appear." And it was so. God called the dry ground "land", and the gathered waters he called "seas". And God saw that it was good. Then God said, "Let the land produce vegetation: seed-bearing plants and trees on the land that bear fruit with seed in it, according to their various kinds." And it was so. The land produced vegetation: plants bearing seed according to their kinds and trees bearing fruit with seed in it according to their kinds. And God saw that it was good. And there was evening, and there was morning — the third day.

And God said, "Let there be lights in the expanse of the sky to separate the day from the night, and let them serve as signs to mark seasons and days and years, and let them be lights in the expanse of the sky to give light on the earth." And it was so. God made two great lights — the greater light to govern the day and the lesser light to govern the night. He also made the stars. God set them in the expanse of the sky to give light on the earth, to govern the day and the night, and to separate light from darkness. And God saw that it was good. And there was evening, and there was morning — the fourth day.

And God said, "Let the water teem[②] with living creatures, and let birds fly above the earth across the expanse of the sky." So God created the great creatures of the sea and every living and moving thing with which the water teems, according to their kinds, and every winged bird according to its kind. And God saw that it was good. God blessed them and said, "Be fruitful and increase in number and fill the water in the seas, and let the birds increase on the earth." And there was evening, and there was morning — the fifth day.

---

① 引自《圣经·创世纪》第一章和第二章。译文参见本书第 230 页。

② teem [tiːm] *v.* 大量出现。teem with：充满。

And God said, "Let the land produce living creatures according to their kinds: livestock[1], creatures that move along the ground, and wild animals, each according to its kind." And it was so. God made the wild animals according to their kinds, the livestock according to their kinds, and all the creatures that move along the ground according to their kinds. And God saw that it was good.

Then God said, "Let us make man in our image, in our likeness, and let them rule over the fish of the sea and the birds of the air, over the livestock, over all the earth, and over all the creatures that move along the ground." So God created man in his own image. In the image of God he created him; male and female he created them. God blessed them and said to them, "Be fruitful and increase in number; fill the earth and subdue[2] it. Rule over the fish of the sea and the birds of the air and over every living creature that moves on the ground." Then God said, "I give you every seed-bearing plant on the face of the whole earth and every tree that has fruit with seed in it. They will be yours for food. And to all the beasts of the earth and all the birds of the air and all the creatures that move on the ground — everything that has the breath of life in it — I give every green plant for food." And it was so. God saw all that he had made, and it was very good. And there was evening, and there was morning — the sixth day.

Thus the heavens and the earth were completed in all their vast array. By the seventh day God had finished the work he had been doing; so on the seventh day he rested from all his work. And God blessed the seventh day and made it holy, because on it he rested from all the work of creating that he had done. This is the account of the heavens and the earth when they were created.

When the Lord God made the earth and the heavens — and no shrub of the field had yet appeared on the earth and no plant of the field had yet sprung up, for the Lord God had not sent rain on the earth and there was no man to work the ground, but streams came up from the earth and watered the whole surface of the ground — the Lord God formed the man from the dust of the ground and breathed into his nostrils[3] the breath of life, and the man became a living being.

Proverbs[4]

(Excerpt)

When I was a boy in my father's house, still tender, and an only child of my mother, he taught me and said, "Lay hold of my words with all your heart; keep my commands and you will live.

---

① livestock [ˈlaɪvstɔk] *n.* domestic animals (家畜;牲畜)。

② subdue [sʌbˈdjuː] *vt.* to conquer and subjugate (征服)。

③ nostrIl [ˈnɔstrɪl] *n.* either of the external openings of the nose; a naris (鼻孔)。

④ 引自《圣经·箴言》第四章,译文参见本书第 230 至 231 页。

Get wisdom, get understanding; do not forget my words or swerve[1] from them.

Do not forsake[2] wisdom, and she will protect you; love her, and she will watch over you.

Wisdom is supreme; therefore get wisdom. Though it cost all you have (Or whatever else you get), get understanding.

Esteem her, and she will exalt[3] you; embrace her, and she will honour you.

She will set a garland of grace on your head and present you with a crown of splendour.

Listen, my son, accept what I say, and the years of your life will be many.

I guide you in the way of wisdom and lead you along straight paths.

When you walk, your steps will not be hampered; when you run, you will not stumble.

Hold on to instruction, do not let it go; guard it well, for it is your life.

Do not set foot on the path of the wicked or walk in the way of evil men.

Avoid it, do not travel on it; turn from it and go on your way."

Song of Songs[4]

(Excerpt)

Lover
How beautiful you are, my darling!
Oh, how beautiful!
Your eyes behind your veil are doves.
Your hair is like a flock of goats
descending from Mount Gilead[5].
Your teeth are like a flock of sheep just shorn,
coming up from the washing.
Each has its twin;
not one of them is alone.
Your lips are like a scarlet ribbon;
your mouth is lovely.
Your temples behind your veil
are like the halves of a pomegranate.
Your neck is like the tower of David,

---

① swerve [swɜːv] *v.* 突然转向。swerve from：背离。

② forsake [fəˈseɪk] *vt.* to give up; renounce (放弃；抛弃)。

③ exalt [ɪgˈzɔːlt] *vt.* to raise in rank, character, or status; elevate (提升；提高；赞美)。

④ 引自《圣经·雅歌》第四章，译文参见本书第 231 页。

⑤ Mount Gilead：基列山。

built with elegance;
on it hang a thousand shields,
all of them shields of warriors.
Your two breasts are like two fawns,
like twin fawns of a gazelle[①]
that browse among the lilies.
Until the day breaks
and the shadows flee,
I will go to the mountain of myrrh
and to the hill of incense.
All beautiful you are, my darling;
there is no flaw in you.

Come with me from Lebanon, my bride,
come with me from Lebanon.
Descend from the crest of Amana,
from the top of Senir, the summit of Hermon,
from the lions' dens
and the mountain haunts of the leopards.
You have stolen my heart, my sister, my bride;
you have stolen my heart
with one glance of your eyes,
with one jewel of your necklace.
How delightful is your love, my sister, my bride!
How much more pleasing is your love than wine,
and the fragrance of your perfume than any spice!
Your lips drop sweetness as the honeycomb, my bride;
milk and honey are under your tongue.
The fragrance of your garments is like that of Lebanon.

You are a garden locked up, my sister, my bride;
you are a spring enclosed, a sealed fountain.
Your plants are an orchard of pomegranates
with choice[②] fruits,

① gazelle [gəˈzel] *n.* 瞪羚。
② choice [tʃɔɪs] *adj.* of very fine quality (上等的)。

with henna[①] and nard[②],
nard and saffron[③],
calamus[④] and cinnamon[⑤],
with every kind of incense tree,
with myrrh and aloes[⑥]
and all the finest spices.
You are a garden fountain,
a well of flowing water
streaming down from Lebanon.
Beloved
Awake, north wind,
and come, south wind!
Blow on my garden,
that its fragrance may spread abroad.
Let my lover come into his garden
and taste its choice fruits.

---

① henna [ˈhenə] *n.* 指甲花;指甲花染料。
② nard [nɑːd] *n.* 甘松;甘松香。
③ saffron [ˈsæfrən] *n.* 番红花。
④ calamus [ˈkæləməs] *n.* 省藤属植物;菖蒲。
⑤ cinnamon [ˈsɪnəmən] *n.* 肉桂;肉桂色。
⑥ aloe [ˈæləʊ] *n.* 芦荟;芦荟油。

Chapter Two Medieval Literature

Ⅰ. Introduction

The period in the history of Europe between the ancient time and the Renaissance that lasted from about 350 to about 1450 is called the Middle Ages. At the beginning of the Middle Ages, the western half of the Roman Empire began to fragment into smaller, weaker kingdoms. By the end of the Middle Ages, many modern European states had taken shape. During this time, the precursors of many modern institutions, such as universities and bodies of representative government, were created.

Actually, no single event ended the ancient world and began the Middle Ages. In fact, no one who lived in what is now called the Middle Ages ever thought of themselves as living in it. In the Middle Ages, perhaps people thought they were living in modern times, just as the modern people think today.

The term "Middle Ages" was invented by people during the Renaissance, a period of cultural and literary change in the 14th, 15th, and 16th centuries. The term was not meant as a compliment. During the Renaissance, people thought that their own age and the time of ancient Greece and Rome were advanced and civilized. They called the period between themselves and the ancient world "medium aevum". The adjective "medieval" comes from the Latin words for this term, *medium* (middle) and *aevum* (age).

Historians adopted this term even though it was originally meant to belittle the period. Since the Middle Ages covers such a large span of time, historians divided it into three parts: the Early Middle Ages, lasting from about 350 to about 1050; the High Middle Ages, lasting from about 1050 to about 1300; and the Late Middle Ages, lasting from about 1300 to about 1450. Historians used to believe that most of the cultural, economic, and political achievements of the Middle Ages occurred in the second period.

In the Middle Ages, the literary achievements include the following four types: religious literature, knightly literature, heroic epic and ballads, and urban literature. The greatest achievement of religious literature was made by the greatest writer of this period, Dante. The knightly literature consists of two parts: knight's lyrical poems and knight's romance. A heroic epic is an extended narrative poem, celebrating the feats of a legendary or traditional hero. The representatives of them are the Anglo-Saxon *Beowulf*, the French

Song of Roland, the Spanish *Song of the Cid*, the Germanic *Niebelungenlied*, and the Old Russian *Song of Igor's Campaign*. From the later 13th century, we see the rise of urban literature, which came forth because of the urbanization.

The knightly literature perhaps is the most important and typical literary form in the medieval period. The best-known knight's lyrical poems are the Provençal poems, popular in France. And knight's romance uses narrative verse or prose to sing knightly adventures or other heroic deeds. The hero is usually the knight, who sets out on a journey to accomplish some missions, meet the evil giant, and encounter with the beautiful beloved. So, the knight romance often expresses the knight's love for a particular lady who inspires him to do great deeds, in order to be worthy of her love or to win her favour.

Romance drew from three rich sources of character and adventure: the legends of Charlemagne, the legends of ancient Greece and Rome, and the British legends of King Arthur and the Knights of the Round Table. *Tristram and Isolde* perhaps is the best-known Arthurian legend, and it is a tragic romance.

Ⅱ. Dante Alighieri

Dante Alighieri (1265～1321), the great Italian poet and one of the supreme figures in the history of world literature, is admired for the depth of his spiritual vision and for the range of his intellectual accomplishment.

Dante was born into a family of the lower nobility in Florence between late May and early June 1265. He lost his mother in his childhood, and his father died when Dante was 18 years old. The most significant event of his youth, according to his own account, was his meeting in 1274 with Beatrice, the woman whom he loved, and whom he exalted in *The New Life* and later in his greatest work the *Divine Comedy*.

The New Life is Dante's first important literary work. It was written not long after the death of Beatrice. It is composed of sonnets and canzoni woven together with a prose commentary. The work narrates the course of Dante's love for Beatrice, his premonition of her death in a dream, her actual death, and his ultimate resolve to write a work that would be a worthy monument to her memory. *The New Life* clearly exhibits the influence of the love poetry of the Provençal troubadours and represents the finest work of the school "sweet new style" of contemporary Florentine poetry. It transcends the Provençal tradition in that it not only describes the poet's love in terms of a lofty idealism but suggests a spiritual significance in the object of his adoration. *The New Life*, in its sustained intensity of feeling, is one of the greatest verse sequences in European literature.

The epic poem the *Divine Comedy* is Dante's greatest work. It includes three sections: *Hell*, in which the great classical poet Virgil leads Dante on a trip through hell; *Purgatory*, in which Virgil leads Dante up the mountain of purification; and *Paradise*, in which Dante travels through heaven. The *Divine Comedy* is the greatest Christian work with profound vision of the Medieval Christian world and at the same time it expresses the humanist ideas which foreshadowed the spirit of the Renaissance.

My Lady Carries Love Within Her Eyes[①]

My lady carries Love within her eyes,
Whereby whate'er she looks at gentle grows.
Towards her, where she passes, each man draws,
And, greeted by her, tremblingly replies.

His forehead bent, he pales and nearly dies,
So deeply his defects he sees and knows.
Envy and pride dare not stay to her close:
Then help me, ladies, praise her to the skies.
Every most humbling thought and every bliss
Rise in the heart of one who hears her speak,
So that who sees her first is firstly blest.

And if her faintest smile be manifest,
To tell it, word is vain, and mind is weak
So new and dear a miracle it is.

So Winsome and So Worthy Seems to Me[②]

So winsome[③] and so worthy seems to me
My lady, when she greets a passer-by,
That every tongue can only babble[④] shy
And eager glances lose temerity.

Sweetly and dressed in all humility,
Away she walks from all she's praised by,
And truly seems a thing come from the sky
To show on earth what miracles can be.

---

① 译文参见本书第 231 至 232 页。
② 译文参见本书第 232 页。
③ winsome ['wɪnsəm] *adj.* charming (迷人的)。
④ babble ['bæbl] *v.* to utter a meaningless confusion of words or sounds (含混地说)。

So much she pleases every gazing eye,
She gives a sweetness through it to the heart,
Which he who does not feel it fails to guess.

A spirit full of love and tenderness
Seems from her features ever to depart,
That, reaching for the soul, says softly "Sigh."

Ⅲ. Provençal Poems

Provençal poems are the lyrical poems that originated in Southern France in the twelfth and thirteenth centuries. They were composed by the troubadours and sung by minstrels. The most important theme of Provençal poetry is the passionate love. It reaches rare heights of virtuosity and variety in its celebration of courtly, or chivalric, love. And "dawn song" or "aubade" is the most loved form for this subject. It is often a dialogue between the lovers separating at dawn.

Pierre Rogiers's "Who Has Not Looked upon Her Brow" and Bertran d'Alamano's "Dawn Song" are the often-quoted ones of the Provençal poems. The five stanzas of "Dawn Song" with couplet rhyme express the deep pain of two lovers' parting at dawn after they have spent their sweet night. The speaker of the poem is the cavalier. Although his love to the lady is illegal, it is a positive attack towards the feudalistic marriage and medieval asceticism.

Who Has Not Looked upon Her Brow

Pierre Rogiers

Who has not looked upon her brow
Has never dreamed of perfect bliss,
But once to see her is to know
What beauty, what perfection, is.

Her charms are of the growth of heaven,
She decks the night with hues of day:
Blest are the eyes to which'tis given
On her to gaze the soul away!

Tr. by Costello

Dawn Song[①]

Bertran d'Alamano

A knight beside his sweet desire
Between his kisses makes inquire:
Sweet, what is to do my dear?
Dark must end as day draws near.
I hear the watchman's "Up away;"
On the heels of[②] dawn runs day.

Sweet, if day and dawn for ever
Ended were that lovers sever[③],
Best of blessings where true knight
Lies beside his best delight.
I hear the watchman's "Up away;"
On the heels of dawn runs day.

Sweet, be sure there is no smarting
Pain can match with lover's parting;
I myself can count its pains
By how little night remains.
I hear the watchman's "Up away;"
On the heels of dawn runs day.

Sweet, I go but leave thee knowing
I am thine wherever going;
Keep me ever in thy mind
For my heart remains behind.
I hear the watchman's "Up away;"
On the heels of dawn runs day.

Sweet, without you death would find me,
Love put all my life behind me.
I'll be back as soon as fled,

---

① 译文参见本书第 232 页。

② on the heels of: 紧随……之后。

③ sever [ˈsevə] *vt.* to cut through something, separating it into two parts; to divide (切断;使……分离)。

For without you I am dead.
I hear the watchman's "Up away;"
On the heels of dawn runs day.

Tr. by Willard Trask

Ⅳ. English Ballads

A ballad is a form of verse, often a narrative and set to music. English ballads originated in the later medieval period and were used extensively until the 19th century. The basic form of English ballads is the four-line stanza, known as a quatrain. This kind of ballad stanza consists of alternating four-and three-stress lines, and usually the second and the fourth line rhyme.

The ballad "Get Up and Bar the Door" is about a battle of wills between a couple. The husband tries to maintain his power but the wife refuses because she does not want to be treated like a doormat. The ballad makes the point that being stubborn has no benefits, by being stubborn they lost pudding and subjected their possessions to be stolen.

In the poem "The Twa Corbies", there is a conversation between two ravens. They discuss in some gruesome detail the meal they will make out of the new-slain knight, plucking out his eye and using his hair for their nests. Some themes are believed to be portrayed in this poem: the fragility of life, the idea that life goes on after death, and a pessimistic viewpoint on life and love.

Get Up and Bar the Door①

It fell about the Martinmas② time,
And a gay time it was then,
When our goodwife③ got puddings to make.
And she's boild them in the pan.

The wind sae cauld④ blew south and north,
And blew into the floor;
Quoth our goodman⑤ to our goodwife,

---

① 译文参见本书第 232 至 233 页。

② Martinmas [ˈmɑːtɪnməs] *n.* a Christian feast observed in commemoration of the death and burial of Saint Martin of Tours (圣马丁节,11 月 11 日)。

③ goodwife [ˈgʊdwaɪf] *n.* the mistress of the house, the wife (女主人)。

④ sae cauld: so cold.

⑤ goodman [ˈgʊdmæn] *n.* the master of the house, the husband (男主人)。

"Gae out[1] and bar the door."

"My hand is in my hussyfskap[2],
Goodman, as ye may see;
An[3] it shoud nae be barrd this hundred year,
It's no be barrd for me[4]."

They made a paction[5] tween them twa[6],
They made it firm and sure,
That the first word whaeer[7] shoud speak,
Shoud rise and bar the door.

Then by there came two gentlemen,
At twelve o'clock at night,
And they could neither see house nor hall,
Nor coal nor candle-light.

"Now whether is this a rich man's house,
Or whether is it a poor?"
But neer[8] a word wad[9] ane o them[10] speak,
For barring of the door.

And first they ate the white puddings,
And then they ate the black;
Tho muckle[11] thought the goodwife to herself,
Yet neer a word she spake.

Then said the one unto the other,

---

① gae out: go out.
② hussyfskap: house-keeping.
③ an: if.
④ It's no be barrd for me: It's not going to be barred by me.
⑤ paction: pack.
⑥ twa: two.
⑦ whaeer: whoever.
⑧ neer: never
⑨ wad: would.
⑩ ane o them: one of them.
⑪ muckle: much.

"Here, man, tak ye my knife;
Do ye tak aff[①] the auld[②] man's beard,
And I'll kiss the goodwife."

"But there's nae water in the house,
And what shall we do then?"
"What ails ye at the pudding-broo[③],
That boils into the pan?"

O up then started our goodman,
An angry man was he:
"Will ye kiss my wife before my een[④],
And scad[⑤] me wi pudding-bree[⑥]?"

Then up and started our goodwife,
Gied[⑦] three skips on the floor:
"Goodman, you've spoken the foremost word[⑧],
Get up and bar the door."

The Twa Corbies[⑨]

As I was walking all alane[⑩],
I heard twa corbies making a mane[⑪]:
The tane unto the t'other[⑫] did say,
"Whaur[⑬] shall we gang and dine the day?"

---

① tak aff: take off.
② auld: old.
③ pudding-broo: broth of pudding.
④ before my een: before my eyes (当着我的面)。
⑤ scad: scald (烫伤)。
⑥ wi pudding-bree: with pudding-broth.
⑦ gied: gave.
⑧ you've spoken the foremost word: you've been the first to speak.
⑨ twa corbies: two ravens. 译文参见本书第 233 页。
⑩ alane: alone.
⑪ mane: moan.
⑫ The tane unto the t'other: the one unto the other.
⑬ whaur: where.

"O doun beside yon auld fail[1] dyke[2],
I wot there lies a new-slain knight;
And naebody kens[3] that he lies there
But his hawk, his hound, and his lady fair.

"His hound is to the hunting gane,
His hawk to fetch the wild-fowl hame,
His lady's ta'en another mate,
Sae we may mak' our dinner sweet.

O we'll sit on his white hause[4] bane,
And I'll pyke[5] out his bonny blue een;
Wi' ae lock o' his gowden hair
We'll theek[6] our nest when it blaws bare.

"Mony a one[7] for him makes mane,
But nane shall ken whaur he is gane.
Over his banes when they are bare,
The wind shall blaw for evermair."

Ⅴ. Omar Khayyam

Omar Khayyam (1048～1131), a Persian poet, is known to English-speaking readers chiefly through the translation of *The Rubaiyat* by Edward J. Fitzgerald.

Omar Khayyam is believed to have composed more than one thousand Rubaiyat (quatrains). Some are known to be authentic and are attributed to him, while others seem to be combinations or condensations of his poetry, and whose origins are more dubious.

The Rubaiyat of Omar Khayyam is among the few masterpieces that have been translated into most languages, including English, French, German, Italian, Russian, Chinese and Arabic.

The most famous translation of *The Rubaiyat* of Omar Khayyam from Farsi into

---

① fail: turf.
② dyke [daɪk] *n.* 沟渠;堤坝。
③ naebody kens: nobody knows.
④ hause: neck.
⑤ pyke: pick.
⑥ theek: thatch.
⑦ mony a one: many men.

English was undertaken in 1859 by the English writer Edward J. Fitzgerald. In quite a many of his translations, he combined a few of the Rubaiyat to compose one, and sometimes it is difficult to trace and correspond the original to the translated version. However, he tried his utmost to adhere to the spirit of the original poetry, and because of his translations, *The Rubaiyat* is widely spread around the world.

The Rubaiyat①

12

A book of Verses underneath the Bough,
A Jug of Wine, a Loaf of Bread — and thou②
Beside me singing in the wilderness —
Oh, wilderness were Paradise enow③!

20

And this delightful Herb④ whose tender Green
Fledges the River's Lip on which we lean —
Ah, lean upon it lightly! for who knows
From what once lovely Lip it springs unseen!

24

Ah, make the most of what we yet may spend,
Before we too into the Dust descend;
Dust into Dust, and under Dust, to lie,
Sans⑤ Wine, sans Song, sans Singer, and — sans End!

29

Into this Universe, and why not knowing,
Nor whence, like Water willy-nilly⑥ flowing:
And out of it, as Wind along the Waste,
I know not whither, willy-nilly blowing.

---

① 译文参见本书第 233 至 234 页。

② thou [θaʊ] *pron.* 你。

③ enow: enough.

④ Herb [hɜːb] *n.* aromatic plants used especially in medicine or as seasoning (药草;芳草)。

⑤ sans: without.

⑥ willy-nilly: a modified form of an older phrase that is variously expressed as *will I*, *nill I* or *will ye*, *nill ye*, which means "be I willing, be I unwilling".

35

Then to this earthen Bowl did I adjourn
My Lip the secret Well of Life to learn:
And Lip to Lip it murmur'd — "While you live
Drink! — for once dead you never shall return."

36

I think the Vessel, that with fugitive
Articulation answer'd, once did live,
And merry-make; and the cold Lip I kiss'd
How many Kisses might it take — and give!

37

For in the Market-place, one Dusk of Day,
I watch'd the Potter thumping his wet Clay:
And with its all obliterated Tongue
It murmur'd — "Gently, Brother, gently, pray!"

38

And has not such a story from of Old
Down Man's successive generations rolled
Of such a clod of saturated Earth
Cast by the Maker into Human mold[①]?

Tr. by Edward J. Fitzgerald

Ⅵ. Arabian Tales

This large collection of *Arabian Nights* or *The Thousand and One Nights* consists of clever stories, fables, fairy tales, romances, legends, parables, anecdotes, morality tales, adventure stories, etc. The earliest extant manuscript fragment dates back to the ninth century, but the tales having Indian, Persian, and Arabic roots probably have a longer history. While quite uneven in quality and at times unpolished, crude, cruel, or politically incorrect, the stories offer a great deal of entertainment as well as detailed and uncensored glimpses of medieval Arabic life. They have been the inspiration for many works of art through the centuries, including other literary works.

① mold [məuld] *n.* frame or model on which something is formed or shaped (模子;铸模)。

The technique this collection uses is so called "frame story" or "story within story",

In the Prologue of this frame story, the Vizier's daughter, Sharazad, volunteers to entertain and distract the cruel Sassanid king by telling him stories. She drags these out over 1001 nights, in order to prevent him from killing more of the virgins of the realm (a rampage he began after killing his wife for adultery).

The Arabian Nights can be viewed as a valuable source of Middle Eastern social history, being composed of the most extensive and intimate recordings of the medieval Islamic period. Generations of Arabic readers have appreciated the imaginative use of Arabic and the mixture of the classical and colloquial language in many of the stories.

In this collection, Ali Baba *and the Forty Thieves* and Sinbad the Sailor are two of the most popular stories. In the story of Ali Baba *and the Forty Thieves*, Ali Baba, a poor woodcutter, discovered the secret hiding place where a band of robbers kept their stolen treasures. He became rich because of his poor slave-girl Morgiana's cleverishness. It is through her quick wittedness she saved Ali's life many times and eventually killed his worst enemy, the leader of the Forty Thieves. As reward, Ali freed her and Morgiana married Ali's son at the end of the story. In the story of *Sinbad the Sailor*, wisdom is seen as a powerful if not invincible tool. On every journey, Sinbad reaches a crisis as he braves a dangerous creature or an evil tyrant but he always finds a solution by using his ingenuity and wisdom.

Ali Baba and the Forty Thieves

In a town in Persia there dwelt two brothers, one named Cassim, the other Ali Baba. Cassim was married to a rich wife and lived in plenty, while Ali Baba had to maintain his wife and children by cutting wood in a neighboring forest and selling it in the town.

One day, when Ali Baba was in the forest, he saw a troop of men on horseback, coming toward him in a cloud of dust. He was afraid they were robbers, and climbed into a tree for safety. When they came up to him and dismounted①, he counted forty of them. They unbridled② their horses and tied them to trees.

The finest man among them, whom Ali Baba took to be their captain, went a little way among some bushes, and said, "Open, Sesame③!" so plainly that Ali Baba heard him.

A door opened in the rocks, and having made the troop go in, he followed them, and the door shut again of itself. They stayed some time inside, and Ali Baba, fearing they might come out and catch him, was forced to sit patiently in the tree. At last the door opened again, and the Forty Thieves came out. As the Captain went in last he came out

---

① dismount [dɪs'maʊnt] *v.* to get off or down, as from a horse or vehicle (下马)。

② unbridle [ʌn'braɪdl] *vt.* to free from a bridle (放松缰绳)。

③ sesame ['sesəmi] *n.* 芝麻。

first, and made them all pass by him; he then closed the door, saying, "Shut, Sesame!"

Every man bridled his horse and mounted, the Captain put himself at their head, and they returned as they came.

Then Ali Baba climbed down and went to the door concealed among the bushes, and said, "Open, Sesame!" and it flew open.

Ali Baba, who expected a dull, dismal place, was greatly surprised to find it large and well lighted, hollowed by the hand of man in the form of a vault, which received the light from an opening in the ceiling. He saw rich bales① of merchandise — silk, stuff-brocades②, all piled together, and gold and silver in heaps, and money in leather purses. He went in and the door shut behind him. He did not look at the silver, but brought out as many bags of gold as he thought his asses, which were browsing outside, could carry, loaded them with the bags, and hid it all with fagots③.

Using the words, "Shut, Sesame!" he closed the door and went home.

Then he drove his asses into the yard, shut the gates, carried the money-bags to his wife, and emptied them out before her. He bade her keep the secret, and he would go and bury the gold.

"Let me first measure it," said his wife. "I will go borrow a measure of someone, while you dig the hole."

So she ran to the wife of Cassim and borrowed a measure. Knowing Ali Baba's poverty, the sister was curious to find out what sort of grain his wife wished to measure, and artfully put some suet④ at the bottom of the measure. Ali Baba's wife went home and set the measure on the heap of gold, and filled it and emptied it often, to her great content. She then carried it back to her sister, without noticing that a piece of gold was sticking to it, which Cassim's wife perceived directly her back was turned.

She grew very curious, and said to Cassim when he came home, "Cassim, your brother is richer than you. He does not count his money, he measures it."

He begged her to explain this riddle, which she did by showing him the piece of money and telling him where she found it. Then Cassim grew so envious that he could not sleep, and went to his brother in the morning before sunrise. "Ali Baba," he said, showing him the gold piece, "you pretend to be poor and yet you measure gold."

By this Ali Baba perceived that through his wife's folly, Cassim and his wife knew their secret, so he confessed all and offered Cassim a share.

"That I expect," said Cassim, "but I must know where to find the treasure, otherwise I will discover all, and you will lose all."

---

① bale [beɪl] *n.* a large package (大包;大捆)。

② brocade [brəˈkeɪd] *n.* a heavy fabric interwoven with a rich, raised design (织锦;锦缎)。

③ fagot [ˈfæɡət] *n.* a bundle of twigs, sticks, or branches bound together (柴把;柴捆)。

④ suet [ˈsjuɪt] *n.* the hard fatty tissues around the kidneys of cattle and sheep (牛羊腰部的板油)。

Ali Baba, more out of kindness than fear, told him of the cave, and the very words to use. Cassim left Ali Baba, meaning to be beforehand with him and get the treasure for himself. He rose early next morning, and set out with ten mules① loaded with great chests. He soon found the place and the door in the rock.

He said, "Open, Sesame!" and the door opened and shut behind him. He could have feasted his eyes all day on the treasures, but he now hastened to gather together as much of it as possible; but when he was ready to go he could not remember what to say for thinking of his great riches. Instead of "Sesame," he said, "Open, Barley②!" and the door remained fast. He named several different sorts of grain, all but the right one, and the door still stuck fast. He was so frightened at the danger he was in that he had as much forgotten the word as if he had never heard it.

About noon the robbers returned to their cave, and saw Cassim's mules roving about with great chests on their backs. This gave them the alarm; they drew their sabers, and went to the door, which opened on their Captain's saying, "Open, Sesame!"

Cassim, who had heard the trampling of their horses' feet, resolved to sell his life dearly, so when the door opened he leaped out and threw the Captain down. In vain, however, for the robbers with their sabers soon killed him. On entering the cave they saw all the bags laid ready, and could not imagine how anyone had got in without knowing their secret. They cut Cassim's body into four quarters, and nailed them up inside the cave, in order to frighten anyone who should venture in, and went away in search of more treasure.

As night drew on Cassim's wife grew very uneasy, and ran to her brother-in-law, and told him where her husband had gone. Ali Baba did his best to comfort her, and set out to the forest in search of Cassim. The first thing he saw on entering the cave was his dead brother. Full of horror, he put the body on one of his asses, and bags of gold on the other two, and, covering all with some fagots, returned home. He drove the two asses laden with gold into his own yard, and led the other to Cassim's house.

The door was opened by the slave Morgiana, whom he knew to be both brave and cunning. Unloading the ass, he said to her, "This is the body of your master, who has been murdered, but whom we must bury as though he had died in his bed. I will speak with you again, but now tell your mistress I am come."

The wife of Cassim, on learning the fate of her husband, broke out into cries and tears, but Ali Baba offered to take her to live with him and his wife if she would promise to keep his counsel and leave everything to Morgiana; whereupon she agreed, and dried her eyes.

---

① mule [mjuːl] *n.* 骡。

② barley [ˈbɑːli] *n.* 大麦。

Morgiana, meanwhile, sought an apothecary[①] and asked him for some lozenges[②]. "My poor master," she said, "can neither eat nor speak, and no one knows what his distemper is." She carried home the lozenges and returned next day weeping, and asked for an essence only given to those just about to die.

Thus, in the evening, no one was surprised to hear the wretched shrieks and cries of Cassim's wife and Morgiana, telling everyone that Cassim was dead.

The day after Morgiana went to an old cobbler near the gates of the town who opened his stall early, put a piece of gold in his hand, and bade him follow her with his needle and thread. Having bound his eyes with a handkerchief, she took him to the room where the body lay, pulled off the bandage, and bade him sew the quarters together, after which she covered his eyes again and led him home. Then they buried Cassim, and Morgiana followed him to the grave, weeping and tearing her hair, while Cassim's wife stayed at home uttering lamentable cries. Next day she went to live with Ali Baba, who gave Cassim's shop to his eldest son.

The Forty Thieves, on their return to the cave, were much astonished to find Cassim's body gone and some of their money-bags.

"We are certainly discovered," said the Captain, "and shall be undone if we cannot find out who it is that knows our secret. Two men must have known it; we have killed one, we must now find the other. To this end one of you who is bold and artful must go into the city dressed as a traveller, and discover whom we have killed, and whether men talk of the strange manner of his death. If the messenger fails he must lose his life, lest we be betrayed."

One of the thieves started up and offered to do this, and after the rest had highly commended him for his bravery he disguised himself, and happened to enter the town at daybreak, just by Baba Mustapha's stall. The thief bade him good-day, saying, "Honest man, how can you possibly see to stitch[③] at your age?"

"Old as I am," replied the cobbler, "I have very good eyes, and will you believe me when I tell you that I sewed a dead body together in a place where I had less light than I have now."

The robber was overjoyed at his good fortune, and, giving him a piece of gold, desired to be shown the house where he stitched up the dead body. At first Mustapha refused, saying that he had been blindfolded; but when the robber gave him another piece of gold he began to think he might remember the turnings if blindfolded as before. This means succeeded; the robber partly led him, and was partly guided by him, right in front of Cassim's house, the door of which the robber marked with a piece of chalk. Then, well

---

① apothecary [əˈpɔθɪkəri] *n.* pharmacist (药剂师;药师)。

② lozenge [ˈlɔzɪndʒ] *n.* a small, medicated candy (药糖块;止咳糖)。

③ stitch [stɪtʃ] *n.* a mode of arranging the threads in sewing (针脚;缝针法)。

pleased, he bade farewell to Baba Mustapha and returned to the forest. By and by Morgiana, going out, saw the mark the robber had made, quickly guessed that some mischief was brewing, and fetching a piece of chalk marked two or three doors on each side, without saying anything to her master or mistress.

The thief, meantime, told his comrades of his discovery. The Captain thanked him, and bade him show him the house he had marked. But when they came to it they saw that five or six of the houses were chalked in the same manner. The guide was so confounded that he knew not what answer to make, and when they returned he was at once beheaded for having failed.

Another robber was dispatched, and, having won over Baba Mustapha, marked the house in red chalk; but Morgiana being again too clever for them, the second messenger was put to death also.

The Captain now resolved to go himself, but, wiser than the others, he did not mark the house, but looked at it so closely that he could not fail to remember it. He returned, and ordered his men to go into the neighboring villages and buy nineteen mules, and thirty-eight leather jars, all empty except one, which was full of oil. The Captain put one of his men, fully armed, into each, rubbing the outside of the jars with oil from the full vessel. Then the nineteen mules were loaded with thirty-seven robbers in jars, and the jar of oil, and reached the town by dusk.

The Captain stopped his mules in front of Ali Baba's house, and said to Ali Baba, who was sitting outside for coolness, "I have brought some oil from a distance to sell at tomorrow's market, but it is now so late that I know not where to pass the night, unless you will do me the favor to take me in."

Though Ali Baba had seen the Captain of the robbers in the forest, he did not recognize him in the disguise of an oil merchant. He bade him welcome, opened his gates for the mules to enter, and went to Morgiana to bid her prepare a bed and supper for his guest. He brought the stranger into his hall, and after they had supped went again to speak to Morgiana in the kitchen, while the Captain went into the yard under pretense of seeing after his mules, but really to tell his men what to do.

Beginning at the first jar and ending at the last, he said to each man, "As soon as I throw some stones from the window of the chamber where I lie, cut the jars open with your knives and come out, and I will be with you in a trice①."

He returned to the house, and Morgiana led him to his chamber. She then told Abdallah, her fellow slave, to set on the pot to make some broth for her master, who had gone to bed. Meanwhile her lamp went out, and she had no more oil in the house.

"Do not be uneasy," said Abdallah, "go into the yard and take some out of one of those jars."

---

① trice [traɪs] *n.* a very short period of time; an instant (一刹那)。

Morgiana thanked him for his advice, took the oil pot, and went into the yard. When she came to the first jar the robber inside said softly, "Is it time?"

Any other slave but Morgiana, on finding a man in the jar instead of the oil she wanted, would have screamed and made a noise; but she, knowing the danger her master was in, bethought herself of a plan, and answered quietly, "Not yet, but presently."

She went to all the jars, giving the same answer, till she came to the jar of oil. She now saw that her master, thinking to entertain an oil merchant, had let thirty-eight robbers into his house. She filled her oil pot, went back to the kitchen, and, having lit her lamp, went again to the oil jar and filled a large kettle full of oil. When it boiled she went and poured enough oil into every jar to stifle and kill the robber inside. When this brave deed was done she went back to the kitchen, put out the fire and the lamp, and waited to see what would happen.

In a quarter of an hour the Captain of the robbers awoke, got up, and opened the window. As all seemed quiet, he threw down some little pebbles which hit the jars. He listened, and as none of his men seemed to stir he grew uneasy, and went down into the yard. On going to the first jar and saying, "Are you asleep?" he smelt the hot boiled oil, and knew at once that his plot to murder Ali Baba and his household had been discovered. He found all the gang was dead, and, missing the oil out of the last jar, became aware of the manner of their death. He then forced the lock of a door leading into a garden, and climbing over several walls made his escape. Morgiana heard and saw all this, and, rejoicing at her success, went to bed and fell asleep.

At daybreak Ali Baba arose, and, seeing the oil jars still there, asked why the merchant had not gone with his mules. Morgiana bade him look in the first jar and see if there was any oil. Seeing a man, he started back in terror. "Have no fear," said Morgiana, "the man cannot harm you; he is dead."

Ali Baba, when he had recovered somewhat from his astonishment, asked what had become of the merchant.

"Merchant!" said she, "he is no more a merchant than I am!" and she told him the whole story, assuring him that it was a plot of the robbers of the forest, of whom only three were left, and that the white and red chalk marks had something to do with it. Ali Baba at once gave Morgiana her freedom, saying that he owed her his life. They then buried the bodies in Ali Baba's garden, while the mules were sold in the market by his slaves.

The Captain returned to his lonely cave, which seemed frightful to him without his lost companions, and firmly resolved to avenge them by killing Ali Baba. He dressed himself carefully, and went into the town, where he took lodgings in an inn. In the course of a great many journeys to the forest he carried away many rich stuffs and much fine linen, and set up a shop opposite that of Ali Baba's son. He called himself Cogia Hassan, and as he was both civil and well dressed he soon made friends with Ali Baba's son, and through him with Ali Baba, whom he was continually asking to sup with him.

Ali Baba, wishing to return his kindness, invited him into his house and received him smiling, thanking him for his kindness to his son.

When the merchant was about to take his leave Ali Baba stopped him, saying, "Where are you going, sir, in such haste? Will you not stay and sup with me?"

The merchant refused, saying that he had a reason; and, on Ali Baba's asking him what that was, he replied, "It is, sir, that I can eat no victuals that have any salt in them."

"If that is all," said Ali Baba, "let me tell you that there shall be no salt in either the meat or the bread that we eat to-night."

He went to give this order to Morgiana, who was much surprised.

"Who is this man," she said, "who eats no salt with his meat?"

"He is an honest man, Morgiana," returned her master, "therefore do as I bid you."

But she could not withstand a desire to see this strange man, so she helped Abdallah to carry up the dishes, and saw in a moment that Cogia Hassan was the robber Captain, and carried a dagger under his garment.

"I am not surprised," she said to herself, "that this wicked man, who intends to kill my master, will eat no salt with him; but I will hinder his plans."

She sent up the supper by Abdallah, while she made ready for one of the boldest acts that could be thought on. When the dessert had been served, Cogia Hassan was left alone with Ali Baba and his son, whom he thought to make drunk and then to murder them. Morgiana, meanwhile, put on a headdress① like a dancing-girl's, and clasped a girdle round her waist, from which hung a dagger with a silver hilt, and said to Abdallah, "Take your tabor, and let us go and divert our master and his guest."

Abdallah took his tabor and played before Morgiana until they came to the door, where Abdallah stopped playing and Morgiana made a low courtesy.

"Come in, Morgiana," said Ali Baba, "and let Cogia Hassan see what you can do." and, turning to Cogia Hassan. He said, "She's my slave and my housekeeper."

Cogia Hassan was by no means pleased, for he feared that his chance of killing Ali Baba was gone for the present; but he pretended great eagerness to see Morgiana, and Abdallah began to play and Morgiana to dance. After she had performed several dances she drew her dagger and made passes with it, sometimes pointing it at her own breast, sometimes at her master's, as if it were part of the dance. Suddenly, out of breath, she snatched the tabor from Abdallah with her left hand, and, holding the dagger in her right hand, held out the tabor to her master. Ali Baba and his son put a piece of gold into it, and Cogia Hassan, seeing that she was coming to him, pulled out his purse to make her a present, but while he was putting his hand into it Morgiana plunged the dagger into his

---

① headdress [ˈheddres] *adj.* a covering or an ornament for the head (头巾;头饰)。

heart.

"Unhappy girl!" cried Ali Baba and his son, "what have you done to ruin us?"

"It was to preserve you, master, not to ruin you," answered Morgiana. "See here," opening the false merchant's garment and showing the dagger, "see what an enemy you have entertained! Remember, he would eat no salt with you, and what more would you have? Look at him! He is both the false oil merchant and the Captain of the Forty Thieves."

Ali Baba was so grateful to Morgiana for thus saving his life that he offered her to his son in marriage, who readily consented, and a few days after the wedding was celebrated with greatest splendor.

At the end of a year Ali Baba, hearing nothing of the two remaining robbers, judged they were dead, and set out to the cave. The door opened on his saying, "Open Sesame!" He went in, and saw that nobody had been there since the Captain left it. He brought away as much gold as he could carry, and returned to town. He told his son the secret of the cave, which his son handed down in his turn, so the children and grandchildren of Ali Baba were rich to the end of their lives.

Retold by Andrew Lang

Chapter Three Renaissance Literature

Ⅰ. Introduction

The Renaissance is a series of ideological and cultural movements from the 14th to the mid-17th century, which happened in Italy and eventually expanded into Germany, France, England, and other parts of Europe.

The aim of these movements was to resist feudalism, ecclesiasticism and asceticism. Participants studied the great civilizations of ancient Greece and Rome and came to the conclusion that their own cultural achievements rivaled those of antiquity.

The word "renaissance" means rebirth. The idea of rebirth originated when Europeans rediscovered the superiority of the Greek and Roman civilization of the feudalist rules. The preceding era, which began with the collapse of the Roman Empire around the 5th century, became known as the Middle Ages to indicate its position between the classical and the modern world.

The dominant idea of the Renaissance is the concept of humanism, which includes four basic aspects.

1. It emphasizes the dignity of the individual and uses the humanity to oppose the divine authority. Because the Renaissance humanists "discovered" the "human being", the basic theme of the Renaissance poetry is to praise the humanity and the worth of human beings.

2. It focuses on the liberation of individuality to resist ecclesiasticism and asceticism. The Renaissance humanists thought that the happiness of the real world was most important, and that the aim of the human beings in this world was to enjoy the present life and to pursue freedom.

3. It opposes obscurantism with the idea of reason. The humanists alleged that reason was the nature of man, and that the knowledge was the power and headspring of happiness. They believed it was possible to improve human society through classical education. This education relied on teachings from ancient texts and emphasized a range of disciplines, including poetry, history, rhetoric (rules for writing influential prose or speeches), and moral philosophy. Renaissance humanism was complex, with few unifying features beyond a common belief that humanity and society could be improved through a

new kind of education based on a study of the classics. Humanists varied widely in the ways they applied these ideas to areas that interested them. Some humanists were mainly interested in rhetoric and Latin prose style, while others analyzed ancient texts to determine exact meanings. One group focused on ways to improve society in general, while Christian humanism applied the techniques of humanist scholarship to the study of church documents, particularly the Bible.

4. The humanists supported the centralization of authority, and opposed the feudal separation. Their political desire was to establish the centralized unified state.

In sum, humanism is based on such a conception that man is measure of all beings. By emphasizing the dignity of human beings and the importance of the earthly life, humanists voiced their beliefs that man not only has the right to enjoy the beauty of this life but had the ability to develop himself in the direction of perfection. Its essential contribution to the modern world was not its concern with antiquity, but its flexibility and openness to all the possibilities of life.

The achievements of the Renaissance literature represented in Italy, France and England. The Renaissance writers focused on the exhibition of human nature, such as human feelings and passions. The innermost being became the objects for many writers to explore. Besides, they liked to use the plain style and the simple language in order to make the literature close to human life.

Ⅱ. Francis Petrarch

Francis Petrarch (1304～1374) is generally regarded as the first great humanist in the history of culture of Western Europe. He was born near Florence and spent much of his life in the cities of Italy. His perfection of the sonnet form later influenced such English poets as Geoffrey Chaucer, William Shakespeare, and Edmund Spenser. His wide knowledge of the classical authors and his restoration of the classical Latin language earned him his reputation as the first great humanist in Western Europe; but he also played an important role in the development of Italian as a literary language.

Petrarch's *Songbook* is a collection of sonnets and odes that declare his deep love for a woman named Laura with whom he fell deeply in love, even though she was already married and did not return his affections.

The collection *Songbook* includes 317 sonnets. The form of these poems is called the Petrarchan sonnet, or Italian sonnet. This probably developed from the stanza form of Italian folk songs. The Petrarchan sonnet consists of an octave (eight-line stanza) and a sestet (six-line stanza). The octave has two quatrains, rhyming *a b b a*, *a b b a*, but avoiding a couplet; the first quatrain presents the theme, and the second develops it. The sestet is built on two or three different rhymes, arranged *c d e c d e*, or *c d c d c d*, or *c d e d c e*; the first three lines exemplify or reflect on the theme, and the last three lines bring the whole poem to a unified close.

His famous poem "Love's Inconsistency" is characteristic for the technique of paradox. There are contradicting images or statements almost in every line of the poem, and these contradictions sharply express the exact psychological conflicts and the true inner world of the lyrical hero.

Love's Fidelity①

Set me whereas the sun doth② parch the green,
Or where his beams do not dissolve the ice:
In temperate heat, where he is felt and seen;
In presence prest of people mad or wise;

Set me in high, or yet in low degree;
In longest night, or in the shortest day;
In clearest sky, or where the clouds thickest be;
In lusty youth, or when my hairs are grey:

Set me in heaven, in earth, or else in hell,
In hill or dale, or in the foaming flood;
Thrall③, or at large④, alive whereso I dwell,

Sick or in health, in evil fame or good,
Hers will I be; and only with this thought
Content myself although my chance be nought.

Tr. by Henry Howard, Earl of Surrey

Love's Inconsistency⑤

I find no peace, and all my war is done;
I fear hope, I burn and freeze likewise;
I fly above the wind, yet cannot rise;
And nought I have, yet all the world I seize on;

① 译文参见本书第 234 页。

② doth [dʌθ]：古英语中动词 do 的第三人称单数现在式。在此是用于强调。

③ thrall [θrɔːl] *n.* the station of being enslaved or be held in bondage (奴役)。

④ at large: be free.

⑤ 译文参见本书第 234 至 235 页。

That looseth, nor locketh, holdeth① me in prison,
And holds me not, yet can I 'scape② no wise;
Nor lets me live, nor die, at my devise,
And yet of death it giveth none occasion,

Without eyes I see, and without tongue I plain;
I wish to perish③, yet I ask for health;
I love another, and yet I hate myself;

I feed in sorrow, and laugh in all my pain;
Lo, thus displeaseth④ me both death and life,
And my delight is causer of my grief.

Tr. by Sir Thomas Wyatt

Ⅲ. Giovanni Boccaccio

Giovanni Boccaccio (1313～1375) was an important Renaissance humanist and the author of a number of notable works including *The Decameron* and *On Famous Women*.

The Decameron is his representative work. It is an entertaining series of stories written in the wake of the Black Death and the technique the author used is the frame tale or story within stories. The book consists of one hundred stories — each member of the group, three noblemen and seven girls who are seeking to escape the ravages of the plague, tells one story every day over ten days. What we select here is the first story from the fourth day.

Boccaccio is a master of drama. His works vividly portrays people from almost all aspects of life, with plots that revel in a bewildering variety of human behaviours.

The Decameron⑤

(Excerpt)

Tancred, Prince of Salerno⑥, a lord most humane and kind of heart, but that in his old age he imbrued his hands in the blood of a lover, had in the whole course of his life but

① looseth, locketh, holdeth 分别为动词 loose, lock, hold 的第三人称单数现在式。
② 'scape: escape.
③ perish [ˈperɪʃ] *vi.* to pass from existence; disappear (毁灭;死亡)。
④ displeaseth: 动词 displease 的第三人称单数现在式。
⑤ 译文参见本书第 235 至 238 页。
⑥ Salerno [səˈlɜːnəʊ] *n.* 萨勒诺。

one daughter; and had he not had her, he had been more fortunate. Never was daughter more tenderly beloved of father than she of the Prince, who, for that cause not knowing how to part with her, kept her unmarried for many a year after she had come of marriageable age: then at last he gave her to a son of the Duke of Capua, with whom she had lived but a short while, when he died and she returned to her father.

Most lovely was she of form and feature, and young and light of heart, and more knowing, perchance①, than beseemed a woman. Dwelling thus with her loving father, as a great lady, in no small luxury, nor failing to see that the Prince, for the great love he bore her, was at no pains to provide her with another husband, and deeming it unseemly on her part to ask one of him, she cast about how she might come by a gallant to be her secret lover.

And seeing at her father's court not a few men, both gentle and simple, that resorted thither, as we know men use to frequent courts, and closely scanning their mien and manners, she preferred before all others the Prince's page, Guiscardo by name, a man of very humble origin, but pre-eminent for native worth and noble bearing; of whom, seeing him frequently, she became hotly enamoured②, hourly extolling his qualities more and more highly. The young man, who for all his youth by no means lacked shrewdness, read her heart, and gave her his own on such wise that his love for her engrossed his mind to the exclusion of almost everything else.

While thus they burned in secret for one another, the lady, desiring of all things a meeting with Guiscardo, but being shy of making any her confidant, hit upon a novel expedient to concert the affair with him. She wrote him a letter containing her commands for the ensuing day, and thrust it into a cane in the space between two of the knots, which cane she gave to Guiscardo, saying: "Thou canst let thy servant have it for a bellows to blow thy fire up to night."

Guiscardo took it, feeling sure that 'twas not unadvisedly that she made him such a present, accompanied with such words, hied him straight home, where, carefully examining the cane, he observed that it was cleft, and, opening it, found the letter; which he had no sooner read, and learned what he was to do, then, pleased as ne'er another, he fell to devising how to set all in order that he might not fail to meet the lady on the following day, after the manner she had prescribed.

Now hard by the Prince's palace was a grotto③, hewn in days of old in the solid rock, and now long disused, so that an artificial orifice④, by which it received a little light, was

---

① perchance [pə'tʃɑːns] *adv.* 偶然;恐怕。

② enamour [ɪ'næmə] *vt.* 迷住;使迷恋。

③ grotto ['grɔtəʊ] *n.* a small cave or cavern (洞穴;岩穴)。

④ orifice ['ɔrɪfɪs] *n.* 孔;通口。

all but choked with brambles[①] and plants that grew about and overspread it. From one of the ground-floor rooms of the palace, which room was part of the lady's suite, a secret stair led to the grotto, though the entrance was barred by a very strong door.

This stair, having been from time immemorial disused, had passed out of mind so completely that there was scarce any that remembered that it was there: but Love, whose eyes nothing, however secret, may escape, had brought it to the mind of the enamoured lady.

For many a day, using all secrecy, that none should discover her, she had wrought with her tools, until she had succeeded in opening the door; which done, she had gone down into the grotto alone, and having observed the orifice, had by her letter apprised Guiscardo of its apparent height above the floor of the grotto, and bidden him contrive[②] some means of descending thereby.

Eager to carry the affair through, Guiscardo lost no time in rigging up a ladder of ropes, whereby he might ascend and descend; and having put on a suit of leather to protect him from the brambles, he hied him the following night (keeping the affair close from all) to the orifice, made the ladder fast by one of its ends to a massive trunk that was rooted in the mouth of the orifice, climbed down the ladder, and awaited the lady.

On the morrow, making as if she would fain sleep, the lady dismissed her damsels, and locked herself into her room: she then opened the door of the grotto, hied her down, and met Guiscardo, to their marvellous mutual satisfaction. The lovers then repaired to her room, where in exceeding great joyance they spent no small part of the day.

Nor were they neglectful of the precautions needful to prevent discovery of their amour; but in due time Guiscardo returned to the grotto; whereupon the lady locked the door and rejoined her damsels. At nightfall Guiscardo reascended his ladder, and, issuing forth of the orifice, hied him home; nor, knowing now the way, did he fail to revisit the grotto many a time thereafter.

But Fortune, noting with envious eye a happiness of such degree and duration, gave to events a dolorous turn, whereby the joy of the two lovers was converted into bitter lamentation.

'Twas Tancred's custom to come from time to time quite alone to his daughter's room, and tarry talking with her a while.

Whereby it so befell that he came down there one day after breakfast, while Ghismonda — such was the lady's name — was in her garden with her damsels; so that none saw or heard him enter; nor would he call his daughter, for he was minded that she should not forgo her pleasure. But, finding the windows closed and the bed-curtains drawn

---

① bramble [ˈbræmbl] *n.* 荆棘；树莓。

② contrive [kənˈtraɪv] *v.* to invent; to plan（发明；设计）。

down, he seated himself on a divan[①] that stood at one of the corners of the bed, rested his head on the bed, drew the curtain over him, and thus, hidden as if of set purpose, fell asleep.

As he slept Ghismonda, who, as it happened, had caused Guiscardo to come that day, left her damsels in the garden, softly entered the room, and having locked herself in, unwitting that there was another in the room, opened the door to Guiscardo, who was in waiting. Straightway they got them to bed, as was their wont; and, while they there solaced and disported them together, it so befell that Tancred awoke, and heard and saw what they did: whereat he was troubled beyond measure, and at first was minded to upbraid[②] them; but on second thoughts he deemed it best to hold his peace, and avoid discovery, if so he might with greater stealth and less dishonour carry out the design which was already in his mind.

The two lovers continued long together, as they were wont[③], all unwitting[④] of Tancred; but at length they saw fit to get out of bed, when Guiscardo went back to the grotto, and the lady hied her forth of the room.

Whereupon Tancred, old though he was, got out at one of the windows, clambered down into the garden, and, seen by none, returned sorely troubled to his room.

By his command two men took Guiscardo early that same night, as he issued forth of the orifice accoutred in his suit of leather, and brought him privily[⑤] to Tancred; who, as he saw him, all but wept, and said:

"Guiscardo, my kindness to thee is ill requited by the outrage and dishonour which thou hast done me in the person of my daughter, as to-day I have seen with my own eyes."

To whom Guiscardo could answer nought but: "Love is more potent[⑥] than either you or I."

Tancred then gave order to keep him privily under watch and ward in a room within the palace; and so 'twas done. Next day, while Ghismonda wotted nought of these matters, Tancred, after pondering divers novel expedients, hied him after breakfast, according to his wont, to his daughter's room, where, having called her to him and locked himself in with her, he began, not without tears, to speak on this wise:

"Ghismonda, conceiving that I knew thy virtue and honour, never, though it had been reported to me, would I have credited, had I not seen with my own eyes, that thou wouldst so much as in idea, not to say fact, have ever yielded thyself to any man but thy

---

① divan [dɪˈvæn] *n.* a long backless sofa (长沙发椅)。

② upbraid [ʌpˈbreɪd] *v.* reproach (责备)。

③ wont [wəunt] *adj./n.* inclined to do sth.; customary practice; usage (习惯于……;惯例)。

④ unwitting [ʌnˈwɪtɪŋ] *adj.* not knowing; unaware (不知情的)。

⑤ privily [ˈprɪvɪli] *adv.* in a privy manner; secretly (暗中;秘密地)。

⑥ potent [ˈpəutənt] *adj.* powerful (有力的;有效的)。

husband; wherefore, for the brief residue of life that my age has in store for me, the memory of thy fall will ever be grievous to me.

"And would to God, as thou must needs demean thyself to such dishonour, thou hadst taken a man that matched thy nobility; but of all the men that frequent my court, thou must needs choose Guiscardo, a young man of the lowest condition, a fellow whom we brought up in charity from his tender years; for whose sake thou hast plunged me into the abyss of mental tribulation, insomuch that I know not what course to take in regard of thee.

"As to Guiscardo, whom I caused to be arrested last night as he issued from the orifice, and keep in durance①, my course is already taken, but how I am to deal with thee, God knows, I know not.

"I am distraught② between the love which I have ever borne thee, love such as no father ever bare to daughter, and the most just indignation evoked in me by thy signal folly; my love prompts me to pardon thee, my indignation bids me harden my heart against thee, though I do violence to my nature. But before I decide upon my course, I would fain hear what thou hast to say to this."

So saying, he bent his head, and wept as bitterly as any child that had been soundly thrashed③.

Her father's words, and the tidings they conveyed that not only was her secret passion discovered, but Guiscardo taken, caused Ghismonda immeasurable grief, which she was again and again on the point of evincing, as most women do, by cries and tears; but her high spirit triumphed over this weakness; by a prodigious④ effort she composed her countenance, and taking it for granted that her Guiscardo was no more, she inly⑤ devoted herself to death rather than a single prayer for herself should escape her lips.

Wherefore, not as a woman stricken with grief or chidden for a fault, but unconcerned and unabashed, with tearless eyes, and frank and utterly dauntless mien, thus answered she her father:

"Tancred, your accusation I shall not deny, neither will I cry you mercy, for nought should I gain by denial, nor aught would I gain by supplication: nay more; there is nought I will do to conciliate thy humanity and love; my only care is to confess the truth, to defend my honour by words of sound reason, and then by deeds most resolute to give effect to the promptings of my high soul.

"True it is that I have loved and love Guiscardo, and during the brief while I have yet

---

① durance [ˈdjʊərəns] *n.* imprisonment (禁锢;监禁)。

② distraught [disˈtrɔːt] *adj.* mad; insane (发狂的)。

③ thrash [θræʃ] *vt.* to beat someone violently in order to punish them (用棍、鞭等痛打)。

④ prodigious [prəˈdɪdʒəs] *adj.* enormous (巨大的)。

⑤ inly [ˈɪnli] *adv.* in an inward manner; inwardly (在内心中;衷心地)。

to live shall love him, nor after death, so there be then love, shall I cease to love him; but that I love him, is not imputable to my womanly frailty so much as to the little zeal thou shewedst for my bestowal in marriage, and to Guiscardo's own worth.

"It should not have escaped thee, Tancred, creature of flesh and blood as thou art, that thy daughter was also a creature of flesh and blood, and not of stone or iron; it was, and is, thy duty to bear in mind (old though thou art) the nature and the might of the laws to which youth is subject; and, though thou hast spent part of thy best years in martial exercises, thou shouldst nevertheless have not been ignorant how potent is the influence even upon the aged — to say nothing of the young — of ease and luxury.

"And not only am I, as being thy daughter, a creature of flesh and blood, but my life is not so far spent but that I am still young, and thus doubly fraught with fleshly appetite, the vehemence① whereof is marvellously enhanced by reason that, having been married, I have known the pleasure that ensues upon the satisfaction of such desire.

"Which forces being powerless to withstand, I did but act as was natural in a young woman, when I gave way to them, and yielded myself to love. Nor in sooth did I fail to the utmost of my power so to order the indulgence② of my natural propensity that my sin should bring shame neither upon thee nor upon me.

"To which end Love in his pity, and Fortune in a friendly mood, found and discovered to me a secret way, whereby, none witting, I attained my desire: this, from whomsoever thou hast learned it, howsoever thou comest to know it, I deny not.

"'Twas not at random, as many women do, that I loved Guiscardo; but by deliberate choice I preferred him before all other men, and of determinate forethought I lured him to my love, whereof, through his and my discretion and constancy, I have long had joyance.

"Whereint' would seem that thou, following rather the opinion of the vulgar than the dictates of truth, find cause to chide③ me more severely than in my sinful love, for, as if thou wouldst not have been vexed, had my choice fallen on a nobleman, thou complainest that I have forgathered with a man of low condition; and dost not see that therein thou censurest not my fault but that of Fortune, which not seldom raises the unworthy to high place and leaves the worthiest in low estate.

"But leave we this: consider a little the principles of things: thou seest that in regard of our flesh we are all moulded of the same substance, and that all souls are endowed by one and the same Creator with equal faculties, equal powers, equal virtues.

"'Twas merit that made the first distinction between us, born as we were, nay, as we are, all equal, and those whose merits were and were approved in act the greatest were called noble, and the rest were not so denoted. Which law, albeit overlaid by the contrary

---

① vehemence [ˈviːɪməns] *n.* 热烈;激烈。

② indulgence [ɪnˈdʌldʒəns] *n.* the act of indulging in something (放任)。

③ chide [tʃaɪd] *v.* to scold mildly (斥责;责骂)。

usage of after times, is not yet abrogated, nor so impaired but that it is still traceable in nature and good manners; for which cause whoso with merit acts, does plainly shew himself a gentleman; and if any denote him otherwise, the default is his own and not his whom he so denotes.

"Pass in review all thy nobles, weigh their merits, their manners and bearing, and then compare Guiscardo's qualities with theirs: if thou wilt judge without prejudice, thou wilt pronounce him noble in the highest degree, and thy nobles one and all churls. As to Guiscardo's merits and worth I did but trust the verdict which thou thyself didst utter in words, and which mine own eyes confirmed.

"Of whom had he such commendation as of thee for all those excellences whereby a good man and true merits commendation? And in sooth thou didst him but justice; for, unless mine eyes have played me false, there was nought for which thou didst commend him but I had seen him practise it, and that more admirably than words of thine might express; and had I been at all deceived in this matter, 'twould have been by thee.

"Wilt thou say then that I have forgathered with a man of low condition? If so, thou wilt not say true.

"Didst thou say with a poor man, the impeachment might be allowed, to thy shame, that thou so ill hast known how to requite a good man and true that is thy servant; but poverty, though it take away all else, deprives no man of gentilesse. Many kings, many great princes, were once poor, and many a ditcher or herdsman has been and is very wealthy.

"As for thy last perpended doubt, to wit, how thou shouldst deal with me, banish it utterly from thy thoughts. If in thy extreme old age thou art minded to manifest a harshness unwonted in thy youth, wreak thy harshness on me, resolved as I am to cry thee no mercy, prime cause as I am that this sin, if sin it be, has been committed; for of this I warrant thee, that as thou mayst have done or shalt do to Guiscardo, if to me thou do not the like, I with my own hands will do it.

"Now get thee gone to shed thy tears with the women, and when thy melting mood is over, ruthlessly destroy Guiscardo and me, if such thou deem our merited doom, by one and the same blow."

The loftiness of his daughter's spirit was not unknown to the Prince; but still he did not credit her with a resolve quite as firmly fixed as her words implied, to carry their purport into effect. So, parting from her without the least intention of using harshness towards her in her own person, he determined to quench the heat of her love by wreaking his vengeance on her lover, and bade the two men that had charge of Guiscardo to strangle him noiselessly that same night, take the heart out of the body, and send it to him.

The men did his bidding: and on the morrow the Prince had a large and beautiful cup of gold brought to him, and having put Guiscardo's heart therein, sent it by the hand of one of his most trusted servants to his daughter, charging the servant to say, as he gave it to her: "Thy father sends thee this to give thee joy of that which thou lovest best, even as thou hast given him joy of that which he loved best."

Now when her father had left her, Ghismonda, wavering not a jot in her stern resolve, had sent for poisonous herbs and roots, and therefrom had distilled a water, to have it ready for use, if that which she apprehended should come to pass.

And when the servant appeared with the Prince's present and message, she took the cup unblenchingly, and having lifted the lid, and seen the heart, and apprehended the meaning of the words, and that the heart was beyond a doubt Guiscardo's, she raised her head, and looking straight at the servant, said:

"Sepulture less honourable than of gold had ill befitted heart such as this: herein has my father done wisely."

Which said, she raised it to her lips, and kissed it, saying: "In all things and at all times, even to this last hour of my life, have I found my father most tender in his love, but now more so than ever before; wherefore I now render him the last thanks which will ever be due from me to him for this goodly present."

So she spoke, and straining the cup to her, bowed her head over it, and gazing at the heart, said: "Ah! sojourn most sweet of all my joys, accursed be he by whose ruthless act I see thee with the bodily eye: 'twas enough that to the mind's eye thou wert hourly present.

"Thou hast run thy course; thou hast closed the span that Fortune allotted thee; thou hast reached the goal of all; thou hast left behind thee the woes and weariness of the world; and thy enemy has himself granted thee sepulture accordant with thy deserts.

"No circumstance was wanting to duly celebrate thy obsequies, save the tears of her whom, while thou livedst, thou didst so dearly love; which that thou shouldst not lack, my remorseless father was prompted of God to send thee to me, and, albeit my resolve was fixed to die with eyes unmoistened and front all unperturbed by fear, yet will I accord thee my tears; which done, my care shall be forthwith by thy means to join my soul to that most precious soul which thou didst once enshrine."

"And is there other company than hers, in which with more of joy and peace I might fare to the abodes unknown? She is yet here within, I doubt not, contemplating the abodes of her and my delights, and — for sure I am that she loves me — awaiting my soul that loves her before all else."

Having thus spoken, she bowed herself low over the cup; and, while no womanish cry escaped her, 'twas as if a fountain of water were unloosed within her head, so wondrous a flood of tears gushed from her eyes, while times without number she kissed the dead heart.

Her damsels that stood around her knew not whose the heart might be or what her words might mean, but melting in sympathy, they all wept, and compassionately, as vainly, enquired the cause of her lamentation, and in many other ways sought to comfort her to the best of their understanding and power.

When she had wept her fill, she raised her head, and dried her eyes. Then: "O heart," said she, "much cherished heart, discharged is my every duty towards thee; nought now remains for me to do but to come and unite my soul with thine."

So saying, she sent for the vase that held the water which the day before she had distilled, and emptied it into the cup where lay the heart bathed in her tears; then, nowise afraid, she set her mouth to the cup, and drained it dry, and so with the cup in her hand she got her upon her bed, and having there disposed her person in guise as seemly as she might, laid her dead lover's heart upon her own, and silently awaited death.

Meanwhile the damsels, seeing and hearing what passed, but knowing not what the water was that she had drunk, had sent word of each particular to Tancred; who, apprehensive of that which came to pass, came down with all haste to his daughter's room, where he arrived just as she got her upon her bed, and, now too late, addressed himself to comfort her with soft words, and seeing in what plight she was, burst into a flood of bitter tears.

To whom the lady: "Reserve thy tears, Tancred, till Fortune send thee hap less longed for than this: waste them not on me who care not for them. Whoever yet saw any but thee bewail the consummation of his desire? But, if of the love thou once didst bear me any spark still lives in thee, be it thy parting grace to me, that, as thou brookedst not that I should live with Guiscardo in privity and seclusion, so wherever thou mayst have caused Guiscardo's body to be cast, mine may be united with it in the common view of all."

The Prince replied not for excess of grief; and the lady, feeling that her end was come, strained the dead heart to her bosom, saying: "Fare ye well; I take my leave of you;" and with eyelids drooped and every sense evanished departed this life of woe.

Such was the lamentable end of the loves of Guiscardo and Ghismonda; whom Tancred, tardily① repentant② of his harshness, mourned not a little, as did also all the folk of Salerno, and had honourably interred side by side in the same tomb.

Tr. by J.M. Rigg

Ⅳ. Miguel de Cervantes

Miguel de Cervantes (1547～1616) is considered one of the greatest Spanish writers, whose novel *Don Quixote* is regarded as the entire spanish literary canon and a founding work of modern literature.

---

① tardily [ˈtɑːdɪli] *adv.* slowly (缓慢)。

② repentant [rɪˈpentənt] *adj.* penitent (后悔的；悔改的)。

Cervantes was born in Alcala de Henares. In 1568, when he was a student, a number of his poems were published. In 1569, Cervantes went to Rome, and joined a Spanish military regiment in Naples. He fought in 1571 against the Turks in the Battle of Lepanto, in which he lost the use of his left hand. While returning to Spain in 1575, he was captured by Barbary pirates, and was taken to Algeria as a slave and held there for ransom. During the next five years he made several unsuccessful attempts to escape before he was finally ransomed in 1580 by his family and friends.

Returning to Spain at the age of 33, Cervantes, despite his wartime service and misfortunes in Algeria, was unable to obtain employment with a noble family. Deciding to become a writer, he produced poems and plays at a prodigious rate between 1582 and 1585, but few of these works have survived.

In his famous novel *Don Quixote*, Miguel de Cervantes' tale of the deranged gentleman who turns knight-errant, tilts at windmills and battles with sheep in the service of the lady of his dreams, has fascinated generations of readers, and inspired other creative artists such as Flaubert, Picasso and Richard Strauss. The thin knight and his squire Sancho have found their way into films, cartoons and even computer games. As a parody of the most popular escapist fiction of the day, the book is not only a spoof of the chivalric romance literature but also a sophisticated, comic account of the contradictions of human nature.

On his "heroic" journey Don Quixote meets characters of every class and condition, from the prostitute Maritornes, who is commended for her Christian charity, to the Knight of the Green Coat, who seems to embody some of the constraints of virtue.

Cervantes' greatest work can be enjoyed on many levels, and suffused with a subtle irony that reaches out to encompass the reader, and does not leave the author outside its circle.

Next passage is selected from Chapter Ⅷ of the novel. It described the story of fighting windmills.

"Fighting windmills" or "tilting at windmills" becomes an English idiom which means attacking imaginary enemies, or fighting unwinnable or futile battles. The word "tilt", in this context, comes from jousting.

Don Quixote①

(Excerpt)

At this point they came in sight of thirty or forty windmills that are on that plain②.

① 译文参见本书第 238 至 239 页。

② plain [pleɪn] *n.* an extensive, level, usually treeless area of land (平原;旷野)。

"Fortune," said Don Quixote to his squire[①], as soon as he had seen them, "is arranging matters for us better than we could have hoped. Look there, friend Sancho Panza, where thirty or more monstrous giants rise up, all of whom I mean to engage in battle and slay, and with whose spoils we shall begin to make our fortunes. For this is righteous warfare, and it is God's good service to sweep so evil a breed from off the face of the earth."

"What giants?" said Sancho Panza.

"Those you see there," answered his master, "with the long arms, and some have them nearly two leagues[②] long."

"Look, your worship," said Sancho. "What we see there are not giants but windmills, and what seem to be their arms are the vanes[③] that turned by the wind make the millstone go."

"It is easy to see," replied Don Quixote, "that you are not used to this business of adventures. Those are giants, and if you are afraid, away with you out of here and betake yourself to prayer, while I engage them in fierce and unequal combat."

So saying, he gave the spur[④] to his steed[⑤] Rocinante, heedless of the cries his squire Sancho sent after him, warning him that most certainly they were windmills and not giants he was going to attack. He, however, was so positive they were giants that he neither heard the cries of Sancho, nor perceived, near as he was, what they were.

"Fly not, cowards and vile beings," he shouted, "for a single knight attacks you."

A slight breeze at this moment sprang up, and the great vanes began to move.

"Though ye flourish more arms than the giant Briareus[⑥], ye have to reckon with me!" exclaimed Don Quixote, when he saw this.

So saying, he commended himself with all his heart to his lady Dulcinea[⑦], imploring her to support him in such a peril[⑧]. With lance braced and covered by his shield, he charged at Rocinante's fullest gallop and attacked the first mill that stood in front of him. But as he drove his lance-point into the sail, the wind whirled it around with such force that it shivered the lance to pieces. It swept away with it horse and rider, and they were sent rolling over the plain, in sad condition indeed.

Sancho hastened to his assistance as fast as the ass could go. When he came up and

---

① squire [ˈskwaɪə] *n.* servant of the knight; an English country gentleman (骑士侍从;乡绅)。

② two leagues: several miles.

③ vane [veɪn] *n.* a blade in a turbine or a sail on a windmill (风车、螺旋桨等的翼;叶片)。

④ spur [spɜː] *n.* a short spike or spiked wheel that attaches to the heel of a rider's boot and is used to urge a horse forward (马刺;刺激)。

⑤ steed [stiːd] *n.* a horse, especially a spirited one (骏马;战马)。

⑥ Briareus [braɪˈeəriəs] *n.* a hundred-armed giant from Greek mythology (布里亚柔斯)。

⑦ Dulcinea [ˌdʌlsɪˈniə] *n.* 达西妮亚(堂吉诃德心目中的情人,现已转义为理想中的爱人)。

⑧ peril [ˈperɪl] *n.* great danger (巨大的危险)。

found Don Quixote unable to move, with such an impact had Rocinante fallen with him.

"God Bless me!" said Sancho, "did I not tell your worship to watch what you were doing, because they were only windmills? No one could have made any mistake about it unless he had something of the same kind in his head."

"Silence, friend Sancho," replied Don Quixote. "The fortunes of war more than any other are liable to frequent fluctuations. Moreover I think, and it is the truth, that the same sage Frestón who carried off my study and books, has turned these giants into mills in order to rob me of the glory of vanquishing them, such is the enmity he bears me. But in the end his wicked arts will avail but little against my good sword."

"God's will be done," said Sancho Panza, and helping him to rise got him again on Rocinante, whose shoulder was half dislocated. Then, discussing the adventure, they followed the road to Puerto Lápice, for there, said Don Quixote, they could not fail to find adventures in abundance and variety, as it was a well-traveled thoroughfare①. For all that, he was much grieved at the loss of his lance, and said so to his squire.

"I remember having read," he added, "how a Spanish knight, Diego Pérez de Vargas by name, having broken his sword in battle, tore from an oak a ponderous bough or branch. With it he did such things that day, and pounded so many Moors, that he got the surname of Machuca② and his descendants from that day forth are called Vargas y Machuca. I mention this because from the first oak I see I mean to tear a branch, large and stout. I am determined and resolved to do such deeds with it that you may deem yourself very fortunate in being found worthy to see them and be an eyewitness of things that will scarcely be believed."

"Be that as God wills," said Sancho, "I believe it all as your worship says it. But straighten yourself a little, for you seem to be leaning to one side, maybe from the shaking you got when you fell."

"That is the truth," said Don Quixote, "and if I make no complaint of the pain it is because knights-errant③ are not permitted to complain of any wound, even though their bowels be coming out through it."

"If so," said Sancho, "I have nothing to say. But God knows I would rather your worship complained when anything ailed you. For my part, I confess I must complain however small the ache may be, unless this rule about not complaining applies to the squires of knights-errant also."

Don Quixote could not help laughing at his squire's simplicity, and assured him he might complain whenever and however he chose, just as he liked. So far he had never read of anything to the contrary in the order of knighthood.

---

① thoroughfare [ˈθʌrəfeə] *n.* a main road or public highway (通路;大道)。

② Machuca: he who crushes.

③ knights-errant: 游侠骑士。

Sancho reminded him it was dinner time, to which his master answered that he wanted nothing himself just then, but that Sancho might eat when he had a mind. With this permission Sancho settled himself as comfortably as he could on his beast, and taking out of the saddlebags what he had stowed away in them, he jogged along behind his master munching slowly. From time to time he took a pull at the wineskin with all the enjoyment that the thirstiest tavern-keeper in Málaga might have envied. And while he went on in this way, between gulps, he never gave a thought to any of the promises his master had made him, nor did he rate it as hardship but rather as recreation going in quest of adventures, however dangerous they might be.

Finally they settled down for the night among some trees. From one of them Don Quixote plucked a dry branch to serve as a lance, fixing on it the head he had removed from the broken one. All that night Don Quixote lay awake thinking of his lady Dulcinea, in conformity with what he had read in his books, how many a night in the forests and deserts knights used to lie sleepless, borne up by the memory of their mistresses.

Sancho Panza spent it thus: having his stomach full of something stronger than chicory① water he slept straight through. If his master had not called him, neither the rays of the sun beating on his face nor all the cheery notes of the birds welcoming the approach of day would have had power to waken him.

Tr. by John Ormsby

Ⅴ. William Shakespeare

William Shakespeare (1564～1616), one of the remarkable English playwrights and poets, is regarded in much of the world as the greatest of all writers. Ben Jonson assured us that Shakespeare was "not of an age but for all time".

A complete, authoritative account of William Shakespeare's life is absent, and thus much supposition surrounds relatively few facts. It is commonly accepted that he was born in Stratford-upon-Avon. As the third of eight children, he was probably educated at the local grammar school. As the eldest surviving son, William Shakespeare ordinarily would have been apprenticed to his father's shop so that he could learn and eventually take over the business, but according to one account he was apprenticed to a butcher because of declines in his father's financial situation. In 1582, William Shakespeare married Anne Hathaway, the daughter of a farmer. He is supposed to have left Stratford after he had three children.

Shakespeare apparently arrived in London about 1588 and by 1592 had attained success as an actor and a playwright. The publication of Shakespeare's two fashionably

① chicory [ˈtʃɪkəri] *n.* 菊苣。

erotic narrative poems *Venus and Adonis* (1593) and *The Rape of Lucrece* (1594) and his *Sonnets* (published in 1609) established his reputation as the most gifted and popular poet of the Renaissance. Harold Bloom asserted, "Shakespeare wrote the best poetry ... in English, or perhaps in any Western language." ①

William Shakespeare's famous collection of *Sonnets* consists of 154 poems. Thought to be written between 1595 and 1599, when he was still a comic playwright, this collection is considered one of the supreme achievements in this form in all of English literature.

The sonnets describe the devotion of a person, often identified as Shakespeare himself, to a young man whose beauty and virtue he praises and to a mysterious and faithless "Dark Lady" with whom the poet is infatuated. In several sonnets the poet accuses his patron of deserting him for a rival poet or charges him with stealing the poet's mistress, the "Dark Lady". The ensuing triangular situation, resulting from the attraction of the poet's friend to the "Dark Lady", is treated with passionate intensity and psychological insight.

The sonnets are grouped in a rough pattern, loosely linked by subject matter. The first 126 sonnets are addressed to the young nobleman. In the first 17 sonnets the poet urges the young man to marry and beget children before his youth fades. Then the poet thought that his poetry could keep the young man's beauty. Sonnets 100 to 126 are addressed to him again after an interval of two or three years. Sonnets 127 to 152 are miscellaneous but are mostly addressed to the "Dark Lady", who has already appeared in some of the earlier sonnets.

While some readers accept the sonnets as a literal account of events that actually happened to Shakespeare, most critics view them as semiautobiographical evidence that has yet to be satisfactorily proven.

The form generally regarded as Shakespeare used in his *Sonnets* is called English sonnet or Shakespearean sonnet. It developed as an adaptation to a language less rich in rhymes than that of Italian. This form differs from the Petrarchan sonnet in being divided into three quatrains, each rhymed differently, with a final, independently rhymed couplet that makes an effective, unifying climax to the whole. The rhyme scheme is *a b a b*, *c d c d*, *e f e f*, *g g*.

The tragedy *Hamlet* is generally regarded as Shakespeare's greatest play for its combination of adroit plot constructions, splendid language, fierce emotional conflicts and a philosophical exploration into life and death. It is written in a kind of "blank verse". Prince Hamlet is a humanist of the Renaissance. He devotes himself to avenging his father's death. However, because he is contemplative and thoughtful by nature, he delays, entering into a deep melancholy and even apparent madness. At the end of the

---

① Harold Bloom. *Shakespeare: The Invention of the Human*, New York: Riverhead-Penguin Putnam, 1998, p. xviii.

tragedy, Hamlet dies immediately after achieving his revenge.

Sonnets[①]

Sonnet 18

Shall I compare thee[②] to a summer's day?
Thou art more lovely and more temperate.
Rough winds do shake the darling buds of May,
And summer's lease hath all too short a date.
Sometime[③] too hot the eye of heaven[④] shines,
And often is his gold complexion dimm'd,
And every fair from fair[⑤] sometime declines,
By chance or nature's changing course untrimm'd[⑥].
But thy eternal summer shall not fade,
Nor lose possession of that fair thou ow'st[⑦],
Nor shall Death brag thou wander'st in his shade
When in eternal lines to time thou grow'st.
So long as men can breathe, or eyes can see,
So long lives this, and this gives life to thee.

Sonnet 66

Tired with all these, for restful death I cry,
As, to behold desert a beggar born[⑧],
And needy nothing trimm'd in jollity,
And purest faith unhappily forsworn,
And gilded honor shamefully misplaced,

---

① 译文参见本书第 240 页。

② thee: you。在英国伊丽莎白时代,第二人称单数形式代词多用 thou,其宾格形式为 thee。下文中的 thy 是所有格,等于 your。

③ sometime: sometimes.

④ the eye of heaven: sun.

⑤ every fair from fair: 此处两个 fair 意思并不相同,前者指具体的美人或美的事物,后者指美貌。此处的内涵是:Everyone who is fair (Everything that is fair) loses the beauty, by chance or in the course of changing nature.

⑥ untrimm'd: stripped of trimmings.

⑦ ow'st 以及下文的 grow'st 是第二人称单数动词词尾形式。ow'st 在此处等于 ownest。动词与 thou 搭配,词尾需加-est,-st 或-t。上文中的 art 也属这种形式。fair thou ow'st: beauty you own。

⑧ 此处的 beggar born 以及下文的 needy nothing 等用的是头韵(Alliteration)。头韵一般是指同一诗行或不同的诗行中,两个以上的词首辅音、元音或辅音组合相同。

And maiden virtue rudely strumpeted,
And right perfection wrongfully disgraced,
And strength by limping sway disabled,
And art made tongue-tied by authority,
And folly, doctor-like, controlling skill,[①]
And simple truth miscall'd simplicity,
And captive good attending captain ill.[②]
Tired with all these, from these would I be gone,
Save that, to die I leave my love alone.

Sonnet 73

That time of year thou mayst in me behold[③]
When yellow leaves, or none, or few, do hang
Upon those boughs which shake against the cold,
Bare ruin'd choirs where late the sweet birds sang.
In me thou see'st the twilight of such day
As after sunset fadeth in the west,
Which by and by black night doth take away,
Death's second self[④], that seals up all in rest.
In me thou see'st the glowing of such fire
That on the ashes of his youth doth lie,
As the death-bed whereon it must expire,
Consumed with that which it was nourished by.
This thou percev'st, which makes thy love more strong,
To love that well which thou must leave ere long[⑤].

Sonnet 116

Let me not to the marriage of true minds

---

① 诗人用 doctor-like 来修饰 folly,下文中使用 captive 来修饰 good,用 captain 来修饰 ill,这些词语的搭配,看上去似乎有悖常情,却体现了相反相成的艺术效果。

② 从第 2 行到第 12 行中,每一行都有转喻(Metonymy)的或拟人化的抽象名词,如 desert、nothing、faith、honour、virtue、perfection、strength、art、folly、skill、truth 等。同时,这首诗中前 12 行是一个整句,核心部分为 I cry for restful death, being tired of beholding ... 在 behold 之后,接着出现 desert、nothing 等 11 个宾语。

③ 此处为倒装结构,正常的语序为 thou mayst behold in me that time of year, 下面由 when 引导的从句用来限定 that time of year。

④ Death's second self: 指黑夜。

⑤ ere long: before long.

Admit impediments. Love is not love[①]
Which alters when it alteration finds,
Or bends with the remover to remove[②].
Oh no! It is an ever-fixed mark
That looks on tempests and is never shaken.
It is the star to every wandering bark[③],
Whose worth's unknown although his height[④] be taken.
Love's not Time's fool, though rosy lips and cheeks
Within his bending sickle's compass come.
Love alters not with his brief hours and weeks,
But bears[⑤] it out even to the edge of doom.
  If this be error and upon me proved,
  I never writ[⑥], nor no man ever loved.

Sonnet 130

  My mistress' eyes are nothing like the sun;
Coral is far more red than her lips' red;
If snow be white, why then her breasts are dun[⑦];
If hairs be wires, black wires grow on her head.[⑧]
I have seen roses damasked, red and white,
But no such roses see I in her cheeks;
And in some perfumes is there more delight
Than in the breath that from my mistress reeks.
I love to hear her speak, yet well I know
That music hath a far more pleasing sound;
I grant I never saw a goddess go;
My mistress, when she walks, treads on the ground.
  And yet, by heav'n, I think my love as rare
  As any she[⑨] belied with false compare.

---

① Love is not love: That kind of love which ... is not love.

② Or bends with the remover to remove: Or changes when one of them changes.

③ bark [bɑːk] *n.* ship.

④ height: altitude.

⑤ bears: lasts.

⑥ writ: wrote.

⑦ dun: dull brown.

⑧ 此诗是写 Dark Lady 的，因此，诗中的 breasts are dun 和 black wires 等暗示了女郎的褐色皮肤、黑色头发。

⑨ as rare as any she: as rare as any woman.

Hamlet[①]

(Excerpt)

[*Enter King Claudius, Queen Gertrude, Polonius, Ophelia, Rosencrantz, and Guildenstern.*]

King Claudius.

And can you, by no drift of circumstance,
Get from him why he puts on this confusion,
Grating so harshly all his days of quiet
With turbulent and dangerous lunacy[②]?

Rosencrantz.

He does confess he feels himself distracted;
But from what cause he will by no means speak.

Guildenstern.

Nor do we find him forward to be sounded,
But, with a crafty madness, keeps aloof[③],
When we would bring him on to some confession
Of his true state.

Queen Gertrude.

Did he receive you well?

Rosencrantz.

Most like a gentleman.

Guildenstern.

But with much forcing of his disposition.

Rosencrantz.

Niggard of question; but, of our demands,
Most free in his reply.

Queen Gertrude.

Did you assay him
To any pastime?

Rosencrantz.

Madam, it so fell out, that certain players
We o'er-raught on the way: of these we told him;
And there did seem in him a kind of joy

---

① 选自第三幕第一场，译文参见本书第 241 至 243 页。

② lunacy [ˈljuːnəsi] *n.* insanity (精神失常)。

③ aloof [əˈluːf] *adv.* at a distance but within view; apart (避开；远离)。

To hear of it: they are about the court,
And, as I think, they have already order
This night to play before him.

Lord Polonius.

'Tis most true:
And he beseech'd[1] me to entreat your majesties
To hear and see the matter.

King Claudius.

With all my heart; and it doth much content me
To hear him so inclined.
Good gentlemen, give him a further edge,
And drive his purpose on to these delights.

Rosencrantz.

We shall, my lord.
[*Exeunt Rosencrantz and Guildenstern.*]

King Claudius.

Sweet Gertrude, leave us too;
For we have closely sent for Hamlet hither,
That he, as'twere by accident, may here
Affront Ophelia:
Her father and myself, lawful espials[2],
Will so bestow ourselves that, seeing, unseen,
We may of their encounter frankly judge,
And gather by him, as he is behaved,
If 't be the affliction of his love or no
That thus he suffers for.

Queen Gertrude.

I shall obey you.
And for your part, Ophelia, I do wish
That your good beauties be the happy cause
Of Hamlet's wildness: so shall I hope your virtues
Will bring him to his wonted way again,
To both your honours.

Ophelia.

Madam, I wish it may.
[*Exit Queen Gertrude.*]

---

① beseech [bɪ'siːtʃ] *v.* to request earnestly; beg for (恳求;哀求)。

② espial [ɪs'paɪəl] *n.* the act of watching or observing (密探;侦探)。

Lord Polonius.

Ophelia, walk you here. Gracious, so please you,
We will bestow ourselves.
[*To Ophelia*]
Read on this book;
That show of such an exercise may colour
Your loneliness. We are oft to blame in this, —
'Tis too much proved — that with devotion's visage
And pious action we do sugar o'er
The devil himself.

King Claudius.

[*Aside*] O, 'tis too true!
How smart a lash that speech doth give my conscience!
The harlot's① cheek, beautied with plastering art,
Is not more ugly to the thing that helps it
Than is my deed to my most painted word:
O heavy burthen!

Lord Polonius.

I hear him coming: let's withdraw, my lord.
[*Exeunt King Claudius and Polonius.*]
[*Enter Hamlet.*]

Hamlet.

To be, or not to be: that is the question:
Whether 'tis nobler in the mind to suffer
The slings② and arrows of outrageous fortune,
Or to take arms against a sea of troubles,
And by opposing end them? To die: to sleep;
No more; and by a sleep to say we end
The heart-ache and the thousand natural shocks
That flesh is heir to, 'tis a consummation③
Devoutly to be wish'd. To die, to sleep;
To sleep: perchance to dream: ay, there's the rub④;
For in that sleep of death what dreams may come
When we have shuffled off this mortal coil,

---

① harlot [ˈhɑːlət] *n.* a prostitute (妓女)。

② sling [slɪŋ] *n.* a slingshot (弹弓;投掷)。

③ consummation [ˌkɔnsʌˈmeɪʃən] *n.* fulfillment (圆满成功;成就)。

④ rub [rʌb] *n.* an unforeseen obstacle (障碍)。

Must give us pause: there's the respect
That makes calamity of so long life;
For who would bear the whips and scorns of time,
The oppressor's wrong, the proud man's contumely[①],
The pangs of despised love, the law's delay,
The insolence of office and the spurns
That patient merit of the unworthy takes,
When he himself might his quietus make
With a bare bodkin? who would fardels bear,
To grunt and sweat under a weary life,
But that the dread of something after death,
The undiscover'd country from whose bourn
No traveller returns, puzzles the will
And makes us rather bear those ills we have
Than fly to others that we know not of?
Thus conscience does make cowards of us all;
And thus the native hue of resolution
Is sicklied o'er with the pale cast of thought,
And enterprises of great pith and moment
With this regard their currents turn awry,
And lose the name of action. — Soft you now!
The fair Ophelia! Nymph, in thy orisons
Be all my sins remember'd.

Ophelia.

Good my lord,
How does your honour for this many a day?

Hamlet.

I humbly thank you; well, well, well.

Ophelia.

My lord, I have remembrances of yours,
That I have longed long to re-deliver;
I pray you, now receive them.

Hamlet.

No, not I;
I never gave you aught[②].

---

① contumely [ˈkɔntjumli] *n.* insolence; rudeness (傲慢;侮辱)。

② aught [ɔːt] *n.* anything whatever (任何事物)。

Ophelia.

My honour'd lord, you know right well you did;
And, with them, words of so sweet breath composed
As made the things more rich: their perfume lost,
Take these again; for to the noble mind
Rich gifts wax poor when givers prove unkind.
There, my lord.

Hamlet.

Ha, ha! are you honest?

Ophelia.

My lord?

Hamlet.

Are you fair?

Ophelia.

What means your lordship?

Hamlet.

That if you be honest and fair, your honesty should admit no discourse to your beauty.

Ophelia.

Could beauty, my lord, have better commerce than with honesty?

Hamlet.

Ay, truly; for the power of beauty will sooner transform honesty from what it is to a bawd① than the force of honesty can translate beauty into his likeness: this was sometime a paradox, but now the time gives it proof. I did love you once.

Ophelia.

Indeed, my lord, you made me believe so.

Hamlet.

You should not have believed me; for virtue cannot so inoculate② our old stock but we shall relish of it: I loved you not.

Ophelia.

I was the more deceived.

Hamlet.

Get thee to a nunnery③: why wouldst thou be a breeder④ of sinners? I am myself indifferent honest; but yet I could accuse me of such things that it were better my

---

① bawd [bɔːd] *n.* a woman who keeps a brothel (鸨母;娼主)。

② inoculate [ɪ'nɔkjʊleɪt] *vt.* to engraft (嫁接)。

③ nunnery ['nʌnəri] *n.* a convent of nuns (女修道院;尼姑庵)。

④ breeder ['briːdə] *n.* a person who breeds animals or plants (饲养动物者;培育植物者)。

mother had not borne me: I am very proud, revengeful, ambitious, with more offences at my beck than I have thoughts to put them in, imagination to give them shape, or time to act them in. What should such fellows as I do crawling between earth and heaven? We are arrant① knaves, all; believe none of us. Go thy ways to a nunnery. Where's your father?

Ophelia.

At home, my lord.

Hamlet.

Let the doors be shut upon him, that he may play the fool no where but in's own house. Farewell.

Ophelia.

O, help him, you sweet heavens!

Hamlet.

If thou dost marry, I'll give thee this plague for thy dowry: be thou as chaste as ice②, as pure as snow, thou shalt not escape calumny③. Get thee to a nunnery, go: farewell. Or, if thou wilt needs marry, marry a fool; for wise men know well enough what monsters you make of them. To a nunnery, go, and quickly too. Farewell.

Ophelia.

O heavenly powers, restore him!

Hamlet.

I have heard of your paintings too, well enough; God has given you one face, and you make yourselves another: you jig, you amble, and you lisp, and nick-name God's creatures, and make your wantonness④ your ignorance. Go to, I'll no more on't; it hath made me mad. I say, we will have no more marriages: those that are married already, all but one, shall live; the rest shall keep as they are. To a nunnery, go. [*Exit.*]

Ophelia.

O, what a noble mind is here o'erthrown!
The courtier's, soldier's, scholar's, eye, tongue, sword;
The expectancy and rose of the fair state,
The glass of fashion and the mould of form,
The observed of all observers, quite, quite down!
And I, of ladies most deject and wretched,
That suck'd the honey of his music vows,

---

① arrant [ˈærənt] *adj.* completely such; thoroughgoing (彻头彻尾的)。

② as chaste as ice: 像冰一样坚贞。

③ calumny [ˈkæləmni] *n.* slander; a false statement (诽谤)。

④ wantonness [ˈwɔntənɪs] *n.* frolic; lewdness (嬉戏;淫荡)。

Now see that noble and most sovereign reason,
Like sweet bells jangled, out of tune and harsh;
That unmatch'd form and feature of blown youth
Blasted with ecstasy: O, woe is me,
To have seen what I have seen, see what I see!
[*Re-enter King Claudius and Polonius.*]

King Claudius.

Love! his affections do not that way tend;
Nor what he spake, though it lack'd form a little,
Was not like madness. There's something in his soul,
O'er which his melancholy sits on brood;
And I do doubt the hatch and the disclose
Will be some danger: which for to prevent,
I have in quick determination
Thus set it down: he shall with speed to England,
For the demand of our neglected tribute
Haply the seas and countries different
With variable objects shall expel
This something-settled matter in his heart,
Whereon his brains still beating puts him thus
From fashion of himself. What think you on't?

Lord Polonius.

It shall do well: but yet do I believe
The origin and commencement① of his grief
Sprung from neglected love. How now, Ophelia!
You need not tell us what Lord Hamlet said;
We heard it all. My lord, do as you please;
But, if you hold it fit, after the play
Let his queen mother all alone entreat② him
To show his grief: let her be round with him;
And I'll be placed, so please you, in the ear
Of all their conference. If she find him not,
To England send him, or confine③ him where
Your wisdom best shall think.

---

① commencement [kə'mensmənt] *n.* a beginning; a start (开端;开始)。

② entreat [ɪn'triːt] *v.* to ask for earnestly (恳求;乞求)。

③ confine ['kɔnfaɪn] *vt.* to shut or keep in, especially to imprison (关闭;禁闭)。

King Claudius.

It shall be so:
Madness in great ones must not unwatch'd go.
[*Exeunt.*]

Chapter Four 17th-Century Literature

Ⅰ. Introduction

The main achievements of 17th-century literature include the following four types:

1. Neoclassical literature, which was popular in France. The writers of neoclassical literature attempted to view the world objectively and initiate a new emphasis on subjectivity. Based on rationalism, neoclassicists held that natural passions must be subordinated to reason. In France, drama, especially tragedy, is one of the basic achievements of neoclassical literature.

2. English revolutionary literature. The representative writer is the Puritan poet John Milton, whose representative works are *Paradise Lost* and *Paradise Regained*.

3. The Spanish poetry of the baroque period and English metaphysical poetry. It was at this time that Gongorism flourished in Spain and the witty "conceits" of the metaphysical poets were popular in England.

4. The Haiku of Japanese poetry.

Among the four types, neoclassical literature and metaphysical poetry are the two most important in this period.

Neoclassical Literature

The neoclassical period is a time when society was undergoing great changes. The middle class was rising in power and prestige. The creation of new wealth through trade was challenging established hierarchies. And the idea of the "divine right of kings" (that kings were authorized to rule as God's representatives on the earth) was losing its hold. In 1649, Charles Ⅰ, King of England, was beheaded and his throne was replaced by the Commonwealth under Oliver Cromwell. Moreover, the end of the neoclassical period witnessed American and French revolutions.

The main element of neoclassical literature is the emphasis on reason. To neoclassicists, reason should be the final cause of any human thought and activity. The important idea in this century is the Cartesian Revolution, as Descartes writes, "I think, therefore I am," which brings into question any attempt to view the world objectively and initiates a new emphasis on subjectivity. To neoclassical minds, natural passions are not necessarily good; they must be subordinated to social needs and strictly controlled, and social needs are more important than individual needs.

Another characteristic of neoclassical literature is the emphasis on forms, especially the so called "three unities". The three unities or classical unities are rules for drama derived from Aristotle's *Poetics*. In their neoclassical form they are as follows:

1. The unity of action: a play should have one main action that it follows, with no or few subplots.

2. The unity of place: a play should cover a single physical space and should not attempt to compress geography, nor should the stage represent more than one place.

3. The unity of time: a play should represent an action that takes approximately the same amount of time as the play; years should not pass during the hours a play takes.

In sum, the hallmark of neoclassicism includes restraint in emotion and refinement in diction.

Metaphysical Poetry

The term "metaphysical poetry" is used to name the work of the 17th-century poets who wrote under the influence of John Donne (1572～1631). Although in no sense a school or movement proper, they share common characteristics of wit, inventiveness, and passion for elaborate stylistic manoeuvres.

Metaphysical concerns are the common subject of metaphysical poetry, which investigates the world by rational discussion of its phenomena rather than by intuition or mysticism. Dryden was the first to apply the term to 17th-century poetry when, in 1693, he criticized Donne: "He affects the Metaphysics ... in his amorous verses, where nature only should reign; and perplexes the minds of the fair sex with nice speculations of philosophy, when he should engage their hearts." He disapproved of Donne's stylistic excesses, particularly his extravagant conceits (or witty comparisons) and his tendency towards hyperbolic abstractions. Johnson consolidated the argument in *The Lives of the Poets*, where he noted (with reference to Cowley) that "about the beginning of the seventeenth century appeared a race of writers that may be termed the metaphysical poets". He went on to describe the far-fetched nature of their comparisons as "a combination of dissimilar images, or discovery of occult resemblances in things apparently unlike". Examples of the practice include the extended comparison of love with astrology (by Donne) and the soul with a drop of dew (by Marvell).

Reacting against the deliberately smooth and sweet tones of much 16th-century verse, the metaphysical poets adopted a style that is energetic, uneven, and rigorous. (Johnson decried its roughness and violation of decorum, the deliberate mixture of different styles.) It has also been labelled the "poetry of strong lines". In his important essay, "The Metaphysical Poets" (1921), which helped bring the poetry of Donne and his contemporaries back into favour, T. S. Eliot argued that their work shows a fusion of reason and passion and a unification of thought and feeling which later became separated into a "dissociation of sensibility".

Ⅱ. John Donne

John Donne (1572～1631) was born in London into a Roman Catholic family. He is known as the most important poet of the metaphysical school of poetry.

John Donne studied at both Oxford and Cambridge in his early teen years. He wrote most of his love lyrics, erotic verse, and some sacred poems in the 1590's, creating two major volumes of work: *Satires*, and *Songs and Sonnets*.

In 1598, after returning from a two-year naval expedition against Spain, John Donne was appointed private secretary to Sir Thomas Egerton. While sitting on Queen Elizabeth's last Parliament in 1601, Donne secretly married Anne More, the sixteen-year-old niece of Lady Egerton. Donne's father-in-law disapproved of the marriage.

John Donne continued to write poems and published the *Divine Poems* in 1607. In 1615, James Ⅰ pressured him to enter the Anglican Ministry by declaring that Donne could not be employed outside of the Church. He was appointed Royal Chaplain later that year. The *Holy Sonnets* are also attributed to this phase of his life.

In 1621 he became dean of Saint Paul's Cathedral. In his later years, Donne's writing reflected his fear of his inevitable death. He wrote his private prayers, *Devotions upon Emergent Occasions*, during a period of severe illness and published them in 1624. His learned, charismatic and inventive preaching made him a highly influential presence in London.

The typical characteristic of John Donne's poetry is the remarkable combination of intellectuality and feeling. He was apt at drawing the materials of his figures of speech from highly unpoetical sources, not only from the activities of everyday life, but also from all the sciences and school-knowledge of the seventeenth century, such as the image of compasses in his famous poem "The Good-Morrow".

The Good-Morrow①

I wonder by my troth, what thou and I
Did, till we loved; were we not wean'd till then?
But suck'd on country pleasures, childishly?
Or snorted we in the Seven Sleepers' den?
'Twas so; but this, all pleasures fancies be;
If ever any beauty I did see,
Which I desired, and got, 'twas but a dream of thee.

---

① 译文参见本书第 243 页。

And now good-morrow to our waking souls,
Which watch not one another out of fear;
For love, all love of other sights controls,
And makes one little room, an everywhere.
Let sea-discoverers to new worlds have gone;
Let maps to other, worlds on worlds have shown,
Let us possess one world; each hath one, and is one.

My face in thine eye, thine in mine appears,
And true plain hearts do in the faces rest;
Where can we find two better hemispheres
Without sharp North, without declining West?
Whatever dies, was not mix'd equally;
If our two loves be one, or thou and I
Love so alike that none can slacken①, none can die.

A Valediction: Forbidding Mourning②

As virtuous men pass mildly away,
　And whisper to their souls to go,
Whilst some of their sad friends do say,
　"The breath goes now," and some say, "No,"

So let us melt, and make no noise,
　No tear-floods, nor sigh-tempests move;
'Twere profanation of our joys
　To tell the laity our love.

Moving of the earth brings harms and fears;
　Men reckon what it did and meant:
But trepidation of the spheres,
　Though greater far, is innocent.

Dull súblunary lovers' love
　(Whose soul is sense) cannot admit
Absence, because it doth remove

① slacken [ˈslækən] *v.* slow down（减弱；减少）。
② 译文参见本书第 243 页。

Those things which elemented it.

But we, by a love so much refined
That our selves know not what it is,
Inter-assured of the mind,
Care less, eyes, lips, and hands to miss.

Our two souls therefore, which are one,
Though I must go, endure not yet
A breach, but an expansion.
Like gold to airy thinness beat.

If they be two, they are two so
As stiff twin compasses are two:
Thy soul, the fixed foot, makes no show
To move, but doth, if the other do;

And though it in the centre sit,
Yet when the other far doth roam,
It leans, and hearkens after it,
And grows erect, as that comes home.

Such wilt thou be to me, who must,
Like the other foot, obliquely run:
Thy firmness makes my circle just,
And makes me end where I begun.

Ⅲ. Andrew Marvell

Andrew Marvell (1621～1678) was educated at the Hull Grammar School, and in 1633 he matriculated as a Sizar of Trinity College, Cambridge. In 1638 Marvell was admitted a Scholar of Trinity College, and took his B. A. degree in the same year.

In 1650, Marvell became the tutor of twelve-year-old Mary Fairfax (later Duchess of Buckingham), daughter of Sir Thomas Fairfax, retired Lord General of the parliamentary forces. Here, over a period of about three years, Marvell seems to have written most of his non-satiric English poems, and the sojourn provided material for Marvell's most profound poem "Upon Appleton House", a poem crucial to his development both as man and as poet. In this poem he examines the competing claims of public service and the search for personal insight. To the same period probably belong Marvell's "To His Coy Mistress" and "The Definition of Love".

In September, 1657, Marvell was appointed assistant to John Milton, Latin Secretary for the Commonwealth. During his last twenty years of life, Marvell was engaged in political activities, taking part in embassies to Holland and Russia and writing political pamphlets and satires.

Marvell' famous poem "To His Coy Mistress" is a dramatic monologue. It presents the popular theme of English metaphysical poetry — seize the day. The poet adopted logical argument or syllogism in this poem to emphasize the significance of grasping the chance and enjoying the pleasure of real life.

To His Coy Mistress①

Had we but world enough, and time,
This coyness, lady, were no crime.
We would sit down and think which way
To walk, and pass our long love's day;
Thou by the Indian Ganges'② side
Shouldst rubies find; I by the tide
Of Humber③ would complain. I would
Love you ten years before the Flood;
And you should, if you please, refuse
Till the conversion of the Jews.
My vegetable love should grow
Vaster than empires, and more slow.
An hundred years should go to praise
Thine eyes, and on thy forehead gaze;
Two hundred to adore each breast,
But thirty thousand to the rest;
An age at least to every part,
And the last age should show your heart.
For, lady, you deserve this state,
Nor would I love at lower rate.

But at my back I always hear

---

① 译文参见本书第 244 页。
② Ganges [ˈgændʒiːz] *n.* 恒河(在印度北境)。
③ Humber [ˈhʌmbə] *n.* 洪泊河(英格兰东北部的河流)。

Time's winged chariot hurrying near;
And yonder all before us lie
Deserts of vast eternity.
Thy beauty shall no more be found,
Nor, in thy marble vault, shall sound
My echoing song; then worms shall try
That long preserv'd virginity,
And your quaint honour turn to dust,
And into ashes all my lust.
The grave's a fine and private place,
But none I think do there embrace.

Now therefore, while the youthful hue
Sits on thy skin like morning dew,
And while thy willing soul transpires
At every pore with instant fires,
Now let us sport us while we may;
And now, like am'rous birds of prey,
Rather at once our time devour,
Than languish in his slow-chapp'd power.
Let us roll all our strength, and all
Our sweetness, up into one ball;
And tear our pleasures with rough strife
Thorough the iron gates of life.
Thus, though we cannot make our sun
Stand still, yet we will make him run.

The Definition of Love①

My Love is of a birth as rare
  As 'tis, for object, strange and high:
It was begotten by Despair,
  Upon Impossibility.

Magnanimous② Despair alone
  Could show me so divine a thing,

---

① 译文参见本书第 244 至 245 页。

② magnanimous [mæg'nænɪməs] *adj.* generous in forgiving（宽宏大量的）。

Where feeble Hope could ne'er① have flown,
  But vainly flapped its tinsel wing.

And yet I quickly might arrive
  Where my extended soul is fixed;
But Fate does iron wedges drive,
  And always crowds itself betwixt②.

For Fate with jealous eye does see
  Two perfect loves, nor lets them close:
Their union would her ruin be,
  And her tyrannic power depose.

And therefore her decrees of steel
  Us as the distant poles have placed,
(Though Love's whole World on us doth wheel)
  Not by themselves to be embraced,

Unless the giddy③ heaven fall,
  And earth some new convulsion tear;
And, us to join, the world should all
  Be cramp'd into a planisphere④.

As lines, so love's oblique, may well
  Themselves in every angle greet:
But ours, so truly parallel,
  Though infinite, can never meet.

Therefore the love which us doth bind,
  But Fate so enviously debars,
Is the conjunction of the Mind,
  And opposition of the stars.

---

① ne'er: never.

② betwixt: between.

③ giddy [ˈgɪdi] *adj*. dizzy（眼花缭乱的）。

④ planisphere [ˈplænɪsfɪə] *n*. a representation of a sphere or part of a sphere on a plane surface（平面天体图;星座图）。

Ⅳ. John Milton

John Milton (1608 ~1674) was born in London into a rich family. He was educated at St Paul's School and then at Christ's College, Cambridge. During his Cambridge period, while considering himself destined for the ministry, he began to write poetry in Latin, Italian, and English.

Milton is best known for his *Paradise Lost* (1667), an epic poem in blank verse. The poem is built upon the stories and myths in the Bible and in the classical tradition, which concerns the Christian story of the Fall of Man: the temptation of Adam and Eve by the fallen angel Satan and their expulsion from the Garden of Eden.

Milton worked very hard on his epic poems although his eyesight was not in good condition. Approximately during the mid-1640s, he began to notice the deterioration of his eyesight, and at the beginning of (the) 1650s this decay continued until he was completely blind. But blindness helped to stimulate his verbal richness, and he is remembered as a true poet of English language.

"Methought I Saw ..."①

Methought I saw my late espousèd saint②
Brought to me, like Alcestis③, from the grave,
Whom Jove's great son to her glad husband gave,
Rescu'd from death by force, though pale and faint.
Mine, as whom wash'd from spot of child-bed taint
Purification in the old Law did save,
And such as yet once more I trust to have
Full sight of her in Heaven without restraint,
Came vested all in white, pure as her mind;
Her face was veil'd, yet to my fancied sight
Love, sweetness, goodness, in her person shin'd
So clear as in no face with more delight.
But Oh! as to embrace me she inclin'd,

---

① 译文参见本书第 245 页。

② my late espoused saint: Katharine Woodcock, Milton's second wife, whom he married in 1656, when he had already been blind. She gave birth to a daughter in October, 1657 (who also died), and she died in February, 1658. Saint bears witness to her piety and gentleness.

③ Alcestis: In the *Alcestis* of Euripides, the heroine dies but is rescued from the lower world and restored to Admetus ("her glad husband") by Hercules, the son of Zeus ("Jove's great son").

I wak'd, she fled, and day brought back my night[①].

Ⅴ. Molière

Molière is the stage name of Jean-Baptiste Poquelin (1622～1673). He was a French playwright and actor who is considered one of the greatest masters of comedy in Western literature. *Tartuffe* or *The Hypocrite* is his best-known drama, one of the comic monuments of dramatic literature.

The main character of this play is Tartuffe, an odious hypocrite. When he has been taken into Orgon's home because of his apparent piety, both Orgon and his mother Madame Pernelle believe that Tartuffe's pious example will be good for the other members of the family. But everyone else in the family, including even the outspoken servant Dorine, is perceptive and wise enough to see the matter of fact.

But Orgon determines that his daughter Mariane shall marry Tartuffe, although she is in love with a young man named Valere. When Orgon's wife Elmire seeks out Tartuffe to beg him to refuse Mariane's hand, he attempts to seduce her. Orgon's son Damis has heard what Tartuffe said to his mother, and denounces him, but Orgon reacts by banishing his son rather than his guest and by signing over his entire property to Tartuffe.

Realizing the futility of reasoning with either Tartuffe or her husband, Elmire devises a way to expose the hypocrite to Orgon. She persuades Orgon to conceal himself under a table while she speaks to Tartuffe, and her husband is thus a witness to the impostor's advances to her.

Orgon's eyes are opened a little too late, for he has already assigned all he owns to Tartuffe. When Tartuffe realizes his hypocrisy has been discovered, he promptly turns the family out of the house. Then by reporting to the authorities that Orgon possesses a strongbox containing the papers of an exiled friend, Tartuffe contrives to have his former host arrested. But by order of the King, the arresting officer apprehends Tartuffe instead, and the impostor is hauled off to prison for his treacherous behavior.

The following selection is from Act Ⅰ, Scene Ⅰ of the play.

Tartuffe[②]

(Excerpt)

[*Madame Pernelle and her servant Flipote, Elmire, Mariane, Dorine, Damis, Cleante*]

---

① day brought back my night: the night of his blindness as well as of his loss.

② 译文参见本书第 245 至 246 页。

Mme. Pernelle.

Let's go, Flipote, let's go. I hate this place.

Elmire.

I can't keep up[①], you rush at such a pace.

Mme. Pernelle.

Peace, my dear, peace; come no farther.
I don't wish to cause you any bother.

Elmire.

What duty demands, I insist on giving.
But, mother, what has caused your hasty leaving?

Mme. Pernelle.

I just can't stand the way your household runs ...
And no one cares what I wish to have done.
Oh, yes, I leave your household quite dissatisfied
For all my wise advice has been defied ...
And nobody respects me, and everybody shouts,
And truly this is a home for the king of louts!

Dorine.

If ...

Mme. Pernelle.

You, my dearie, are a bold lassy[②],
A little brazen[③] and very sassy[④],
You butt into everything to speak your mind.
Damis.
But ...

Mme. Pernelle.

You, grandson, are a fool of the worst kind.
It is I, your grandmother, that pronounce this edict
And to my son, your father, I have oft predicted
That you'll turn out to be a worthless wastrel[⑤],
And give him in life a foretaste of Hell.

Mariane.

I think ...

---

① keep up：跟得上。

② lassy [ˈlæsi] *n.* a young woman or girl（少女）。

③ brazen [ˈbreɪzn] *adj.* made of brass; impudent（黄铜制的；厚颜无耻的）。

④ sassy [ˈsæsi] *adj.* disrespectful; shameless（无礼的；厚脸皮的）。

⑤ wastrel [ˈweɪstrəl] *n.* one who wastes, a profligate（废物；放荡者）。

Mme. Pernelle.

My lord, his sister! You seem so discreet[①]
And so untainted, so very sweet,
But the stillest waters are filled with scum[②],
And your sly ways earn my revulsion[③].

Elmire.

But ...

Mme. Pernelle.

Daughter, my views may make you mad,
But your conduct in all things is all bad.
In your family's eyes you should be an example-setter;
In that respect their late mother did far better.
You are extravagant[④], and it wounds me, I guess,
To see you sashay[⑤] about dressed like a princess.
A woman who wishes only to please her mate,
Dear daughter, need not primp and undulate.

Cleante.

Madam, after all ...

Mme. Pernelle.

And her brother, as for you,
I respect you, love you, and revere you, too,
But finally, if I were my son, her spouse,
I would at once beg you to leave this house.
Without cease you teach your rules and mottos
Which decent people should never follow.
I now speak frankly, but it is my part;
I never spare the words that stir my heart.

Damis.

Your man Tartuffe is satisfied, no fear ...

Mme. Pernelle.

He is a holy man whom all should hear,

---

① discreet [dɪsˈkriːt] *adj.* circumspect; showing prudence and wise self-restraint in speech and behavior (言行慎重的;小心的)。

② scum [skʌm] *n.* a filmy layer of extraneous or impure matter that forms on or rises to the surface of a liquid or body of water (浮渣;浮垢)。

③ revulsion [rɪˈvʌlʃən] *n.* a feeling of violent disgust or loathing (嫌恶;反感)。

④ extravagant [ɪksˈtrævəgənt] *adj.* given to lavish or imprudent expenditure (奢侈的;浪费的)。

⑤ sashay [sæˈʃeɪ] *vi.* to walk or proceed in an easy or casual manner (走动;漫不经心地行走)。

And I cannot bear, without great rue[①],
To hear him mocked by a fool like you.

Damis.

What? Am I myself to bear a carping[②] critic,
A base usurper[③] with a power tyrannic,
Such that we can do nothing for diversion
Without hearing about that creep's aversion?

Dorine.

If we were to hear and obey his whims,
We couldn't do anything without sins
For he forbids all, this false Capuchin.

Mme. Pernelle.

And everything he forbids is well forbidden.
He strives to guide you on the road to heaven,
And it's my son's duty to make you love him.

Damis.

No, grandma, neither dad nor anyone else
Can oblige me to wish for his good health.
I'd be false to myself if I didn't say this:
When I see him around, I begin to get pissed.
I can smell the outcome, and soon this coot,
And I will find ourselves in a grand dispute.

Dorine.

It's certainly a clear cause for remark
When a nobody acts like a patriarch[④],
A beggar who was barefoot when he came hence
And whose whole wardrobe wasn't worth two cents!
And he's gone so far as to forget his past for
He opposes everything and plays the master.

Mme. Pernelle.

Ah! mercy on me! Things would be better,
If you'd only follow his holy orders.

Dorine.

He passes for a saint in your fantasy,

---

① rue [ruː] *n.* to feel regret, remorse, or sorrow for (悲叹;悔恨)。

② carping [ˈkɑːpiŋ] *adj.* naggingly critical or complaining (吹毛求疵的)。

③ usurper [ju(ː)ˈzɜːpə] *n.* one who takes over or occupies without right (篡夺者;侵占者)。

④ patriarch [ˈpeɪtrɑːk] *n.* a man who rules a family or clan (家长;族长)。

But, I swear, he acts with hypocrisy[①].

Mme. Pernelle.

Watch your tongue!

Dorine.

Not to him nor his man Laurent
Would I trust my honor without good warrant.

Mme. Pernelle.

I don't know what his servant's like at heart,
But for the man himself, I'll guarantee his part.
You only treat him with hate and aversion
Because he truly strives for your conversion.
He hurls his heart up against each sin
And the glory of God is all he hopes to win.

Dorine.

Yes. But why, especially during some
Time past, must he ban all guests from our home?
Can a courtesy call offend Heaven
Enough to merit a huge commotion?
Would you like it explained, just between us?
[*Gesturing toward Elmire.*]
Of Madam there, on my oath, he's jealous!

Mme. Pernelle.

Be quiet, and think before you speak.
Others, too, condemn the company you keep.
All this bustle from the people who arrive,
The carriages ceaselessly parking at curb-side,
And the servants in a circle chattering,
Make noise that your neighbors find nerve-shattering.
I'd like to think there's no harm meant,
But when gossips talk, they're malevolent[②].

Cleante.

How can you hope to stop people talking?
It would truly be most irritating
If, for the sake of idle, foolish chatter,
We must renounce the friends that really matter.
And even if we could resolve to do it,

---

① hypocrisy [hɪˈpɔkrəsi] *n.* falseness (伪善)。

② malevolent [məˈlevələnt] *adj.* having or exhibiting ill will; malicious (幸灾乐祸的)。

How could you hope to keep the whole world quiet?
No castle wall can defend against lies,
So let's ignore the fools who criticize,
And strive to live in innocence and ease,
Letting gossips gossip as they please.

Dorine.

Daphne, our neighbor, and her petty spouse —
Weren't they the ones who slandered this house?
Those whom the whole world finds ridiculous
Are always first in line to stick it to us.
They never fail to sniff out and swiftly share
The earliest rumor of a love affair,
Sowing seeds of scandal with eager expedition
And twisting truth past all recognition.
In their own colors, they paint all others,
Brazenly calling all men their brothers;
In the faint hope of finding some resemblance,
They try to give a gloss of innocence
To their schemes or to make others share
The burden of blame that is only theirs.

Mme. Pernelle.

All this hair-splitting① is off the subject.
Orante lives a life that is perfect
With all her thoughts on heaven, and I hear
That she deeply mourns the way you live here.

Dorine.

The lady herself is quite an example!
You want a chaste life? She's a nice sample.
But old age has stuck her in this zealous mood,
And everyone knows she's a reluctant prude②.
'Cause as long as she could snare③ a man's heart,
She was more than willing to play her part.
But now that her eyes have lost their luster,
She leaves the world that already left her

① hair-splitting：过于讲究细微差别的；吹毛求疵的。

② prude [pruːd] *n.* one who is excessively concerned with being or appearing to be proper, modest, or righteous (装成规矩的女人)。

③ snare [sneə] *v.* to trap (诱捕)。

And uses a pompous[①] veil of phony wisdom
To hide the fact that her looks are gone.
It's the last resort of the aging flirt,
So peeved at having no man at her skirt
That, alone and abandoned to solitude,
Her only recourse is to become a prude.

Tr. by Jeffrey D. Hoeper

Ⅵ. Luis de Gongora

Luis de Gongora (1561～1627) was a famous Spanish poet of the Baroque period. He wrote many simple and beautiful lyrics and ballads in the popular style, composed some very abstruse poems replete with mythological and historical allusions in a language of images which was unique, and left a series of sonnets that are among the finest in the history of Spanish literature.

The themes of Gongora's poems are various. His poetry speaks of the hardships of love, current events, friendship, the trials of life at court, and the beauties of his beloved Córdoba.

Vastly popular in the seventeenth century and during the first half of the eighteenth century, Gongora's poetry began to fall into neglect, and it even became difficult to make sense out of many of his compositions.

The French symbolists and some perceptive Spanish writers "rediscovered" Congora at the end of the nineteenth century, and the Generation of 1927 in Spain chose Congora as the symbol of their group, which consisted of Lorca, Alberti, Aleixandre, and others. Today Gongora is widely considered to be Spain's greatest poet. Famous for intricate metaphors in baroque style and syntax, Gongora has even been immortalized as a literary term: a "gongorism".

The sonnet like "While to Contend in Brightness with Thy Hair" is one of the best expressions in Spanish of the *Carpe Diem* (enjoy this day) theme, which was made famous by the Roman poet Horace and was very popular among the Renaissance poets of Spain.

While to Contend in Brightness with Thy Hair[②]

While to contend[③] in brightness with thy hair

---

① pompous [ˈpɔmpəs] *adj.* full of high-sounding phrases; bombastic (华而不实的)。

② 译文参见本书第 247 页。

③ contend [kənˈtend] *vi.* to strive in opposition or against difficulties; struggle (斗争;竞争)。

Sunlight on burnished gold may strive in vain,
While thy proud forehead's whiteness may disdain
The lilies of the field, which bloom less fair,

While each red lip at once more eyes will snare
Than the perfumed carnation[①] bud new born,
And while thy graceful neck with queenly scorn
Outshines bright crystal on the morning air:

Enjoy thy hour, neck, ringlets, lips and brow,
Before the glories of this age of gold:
Earth's precious ore[②], sweet flowers, and crystal bright

Turn pale and dim; and Time with Fingers cold
Rifle[③] the bud and bloom; and they, and thou
Become but ash, smoke, shadow, dust and night.

Tr. by Edward Churton

Pride of the Fourth and Liquid Element[④]

Pride of the fourth and liquid element,
Sweet brook whose waters with soft music pass,
Stretching, pellucid[⑤] and preeminent,
Their ribbon of bright silver through the grass,
Since Cupid on your smooth and quiet stream,
As she looks into it, portrays the snow
And scarlet of her face, for whom I seem
At times to freeze, at other times to glow,

Watch how you move; be careful to keep taut
The crystal bridle's wavy rein with which
You curb your current's striving to run faster.
It would be wrong if beauty should be caught,
Confused, in that deep breast, beauty so rich,

---

① carnation [kɑːˈneɪʃən] *n.* 康乃馨。
② ore [ɔː(r)] *n.* 矿石;含有金属的岩石。
③ rifle [ˈraɪfl] *vt.* to rob; to ransack (抢夺;掠夺)。
④ 译文参见本书第 247 页。
⑤ pellucid [pəˈljuːsɪd] *adj.* transparent; clear (透明的;澄清的)。

Caught by the watery trident's mighty master.

Tr. by J. M. Cohen

Ⅶ. Matsuo Bashō

Matsuo Bashō (1644～1694) was the most famous poet of the Edo period in Japan. Bashō took his name from the Japanese word for "banana tree".

He is recognized as a master of brief and clear haiku. He is the most significant writer in haiku history.

Haiku is considered the world's shortest form of poetry, consisting of 17 syllables arranged in a sequence of 5-7-5.

"Old Pond" is Bashō's most quoted haiku poem. It is characteristic for the fusion of the paradox: silence with voice and it implies the "awakening" in Zen Buddhism.

Old Pond[①]

An old silent pond ...
A frog jumps into the pond,
Splash! Silence again.

Tr. by Harry Behn

① 译文参见本书第 247 页。

Chapter Five 18th-Century Literature

Ⅰ. Introduction

The dominant trend of the eighteenth century is the intellectual movement called the Enlightenment. This is one of those rare historical movements which in fact named itself. The enlighteners bent themselves to enlightening the whole world with the light of rationality. They believed that human reason could be used to combat ignorance, superstition, and tyranny in order to build a better world. Their principal targets were to reorder religion and society by a hereditary aristocracy.

The main achievements of literature of this century are represented by the literary works of Sentimentalism in England, Germany and Russia, the literature of Storm and Stress in Germany, and the literature of pre-romanticism, to which Robert Burns and William Blake are often linked. William Blake is ranked as one of the great poets of the century, although he broke with much of neoclassicism of the earlier part of the century. He began with *Poetical Sketches*, then published *Songs of Innocence* and *Songs of Experience* in the end of the century, which are considered by some critics as the first signs of Romantic poetry in some sense.

Sentimentalism

During the eighteenth century, the apparent absence of feeling in neoclassical literature began to be perceived as a fault, and a new trend developed around the desire to reform this aspect of neoclassical practice. The new tendency, called "sentimentalism" by literary historians, sought to place feelings on a par with intellect and morality. The rise of sentimentalism is closely associated with the increasing legitimacy of prose as a medium of literary expression.

In the history of English literature, Laurence Sterne (1713～1768) was the most prominent and the most typical of the sentimental tradition among English novelists and among English writers of the 18th century. And his novel *A Sentimental Journey* is regarded as the representative work of the English sentimentalism.

The master of sentimentalism in Russia is Karamzin (1766～1826). He established himself as the first major short-story writer in Russia. He wrote more than a dozen stories. All were in the sentimentalist style and most were extremely popular. The best remembered is *Poor Liza* (1792). And critics think that *Poor Liza* and several other novellas written by Karamzin remained the favorite native prose works among Russian readers until the appearance of Pushkin's and Gogol's stories in the 1830s.

Storm and Stress

Storm and Stress (Sturm und Drang) is a literary movement in German literature that flourished from 1770s to 1780s. It takes its name from a play by F. M. von Klinger, *Storm and Stress* (1776).

Owing to Storm and Stress, German authors became cultural leaders of Europe, whose literature was revolutionary in its emphasis on subjectivity and on the unease of man in contemporary society. The movement was distinguished also by the intensity with which it developed the theme of youthful genius in rebellion against accepted standards, by its enthusiasm for nature, and by its rejection of the rules of the 18th-century neoclassical style.

The great figure of the movement was Goethe, whose most sensational and representative novel is *The Sorrows of Young Werther* (1774). The works of the Storm and Stress movement writers can be considered as a prelude to Romanticism.

Pre-Romanticism

Pre-Romanticism was largely contemporaneous with neoclassicism, and provided a complementary perspective. Pre-Romantic tendencies became dominant towards the second half of the eighteenth century.

Pre-Romanticism is a term that is greatly contested. The ideas of pre-Romanticism and romanticism are essentially the same so some argue that pre-Romanticism is merely early Romanticism.

English novelist Daniel Defoe and German writer Johann Wolfgang von Goethe are two important figures of this period. Defoe's *Robinson Crusoe* is considered the first novel in English, while Goethe's novel *The Sorrows of Young Werther* and the poetic drama *Faust* are literary landmarks of that period.

Ⅱ. Robert Burns

Born in Alloway, Scotland, Robert Burns (1759～1796) was the first of William and Agnes Burns' seven children. At the age of fifteen, Burns pursued both love and poetry with uncommon zeal.

Between 1784 and 1785, Robert Burns wrote many of the poems collected in his first book, *Poems, Chiefly in the Scottish Dialect*, which was published in 1786. This collection, written in the Scottish dialect of the English language, was an immediate success, making Burns celebrated throughout England and Scotland as a great "peasant-poet". Besides making original compositions, Robert Burns also collected folk songs from across Scotland, often revising or adapting them. His poem "A Red, Red Rose", adapted from a folk song, remains well-known across the world today.

A Red, Red Rose①

O my luve's② like a red, red rose,
That's newly sprung in June;
O my luve's like the melodie
That's sweetly played in tune③.

As fair art thou, my bonnie lass④,
So deep in luve am I;
And I will luve thee still, my dear,
Till a' the seas gang dry⑤.

Till a' the seas gang dry, my dear,
And the rocks melt wi' the sun⑥:
O I will love thee still, my dear,
While the sands o' life⑦ shall run.

And fare thee weel⑧, my only luve,
And fare thee weel awhile!
And I will come again, my luve,
Though it were ten thousand mile.

My Heart's in the Highlands⑨

My heart's in the Highlands⑩, my heart is not here;

---

① 译文参见本书第 247 页。
② my luve's: my love is.
③ in tune: harmoniously.
④ my bonnie lass: my pretty girl.
⑤ Till a' the seas gang dry: Till all the seas go dry.
⑥ wi' the sun: with the sun.
⑦ sands o' life: sands of life. sands 指古代用沙漏计时的沙,代表时间。
⑧ weel: well. fare thee weel: fare you well, which means "good-bye to you".
⑨ 译文参见本书第 247 至 248 页。
⑩ the Highlands: a mountainous region of central and northern Scotland (苏格兰高地)。

My heart's in the Highlands a-chasing[①] the deer;
A-chasing the wild deer and following the roe —
My heart's in the Highlands, wherever I go!

Farewell to the Highlands, farewell to the North,
The birthplace of Valour, the country of Worth!
Wherever I wander, wherever I rove,
The hills of the Highlands for ever I love.

Farewell to the mountains high cover'd with snow;
Farewell to the straths[②] and green valleys below;
Farewell to the forests and wild-hanging woods;
Farewell to the torrents and loud-pouring floods!

My heart's in the Highlands, my heart is not here;
My heart's in the Highlands a-chasing the deer;
A-chasing the wild deer and following the roe —
My heart's in the Highlands, wherever I go!

Ⅲ. William Blake

William Blake (1757～1827) was born in London. From early childhood, Blake spoke of having visions — at four he saw God "put his head to the window"; around age nine, he saw a tree filled with angels while walking through the countryside. Although his parents tried to discourage him from "lying", they did observe that he was different from his peers and therefore did not force him to attend conventional school. He learned to read and write at home. At age ten, Blake expressed a wish to become a painter, so his parents sent him to drawing school. Two years later, Blake began writing poetry. When he turned fourteen, he apprenticed with an engraver because art school proved too costly. After his seven-year term ended, he studied briefly at the Royal Academy.

Blake's first printed work, *Poetical Sketches* (1783), is a collection of apprentice verse, mostly imitating classical models. He published his most popular collection, *Songs of Innocence*, in 1789 and followed it, in 1794, with *Songs of Experience*.

William Blake' poetry is characteristic for its ambiguity, because he liked to use the symbol in his poems. A symbol is an image that suggests something else, as Robert Frost

① a-chasing: chasing.

② strath [stræθ] *n.* a wide, flat river valley (宽广的山谷;平底河谷)。

once said: "A symbol is like a little thing that touches a larger thing."[①] So the central image of tiger in some of his poems transcends its literal meaning and could stand for the creativity and the resplendence of human invention or artistic imagination.

The Tyger[②]

Tyger[③]! Tyger! burning bright
In the forests of the night,
What immortal hand or eye
Could frame thy fearful symmetry?

In what distant deeps[④] or skies
Burnt the fire of thine eyes?
On what wings dare he aspire?
What the hand, dare sieze the fire?

And what shoulder, & what art,
Could twist the sinews[⑤] of thy heart?
And when thy heart began to beat,
What dread hand, & what dread feet?

What the hammer? what the chain?
In what furnace was thy brain?
What the anvil? what dread grasp
Dare its deadly terrors clasp?

When the stars threw down their spears,
And water'd heaven with their tears,
Did he smile his work to see?
Did he who made the Lamb make thee?

Tyger! Tyger! burning bright
In the forests of the night,

---

① Laurie G. Kirszner & Stephen R. Mandell eds. *Literature: Reading, Reacting, Writing*, *Thomson Learning*, 2004, p. 1013.

② 译文参见本书第 248 页。

③ tyger: tiger.

④ deeps: seas.

⑤ sinew ['sɪnjuː] *n.* vigorous strength; muscular power (充沛的力量;精力)。

What immortal hand or eye
Dare frame thy fearful symmetry?

A Poison Tree[①]

I was angry with my friend:
I told my wrath, my wrath[②] did end.
I was angry with my foe:
I told it not, my wrath did grow.

And I watered it in fears
Night and morning with my tears,
And I sunned it with smiles
And with soft deceitful wiles.

And it grew both day and night,
Till it bore an apple bright,
And my foe beheld it shine,
And he knew that it was mine, —

And into my garden stole
When the night had veiled the pole;
In the morning, glad, I see
My foe outstretched beneath the tree.

Ⅳ. Daniel Defoe

Daniel Defoe (1660～1731), an English novelist and journalist, was born in London. His novels include *Robinson Crusoe* (1719), *Captain Singleton* (1720), *A Journal of the Plague Year* (1722), *Captain Jack* (1722), *Moll Flanders* (1722) and *Roxada* (1724). Along with Samuel Richardson, Defoe is considered the founder of the English novel.

He is most famous as the author of *Robinson Crusoe* (1719), a story of a man shipwrecked alone on an island and his subsequent adventures. The book is a fictional autobiography of the title character — a castaway who spends 27 years on a remote tropical

① 译文参见本书第 248 页。
② wrath [ræθ] *n.* extreme anger (愤怒)。

island, encountering Native Americans, captives, and mutineers before being rescued.

The following expert is selected from the third part of the novel.

Robinson Crusoe①

(Excerpt)

This at length put me upon thinking, whether it was not possible to make my self a *Canoe*②, or *Periagua*③, such as the Natives of those Climates make, even without Tools, or, as I might say, without Hands, *viz.* ④ of the Trunk of a great Tree. This I not only thought possible, but easy, and pleas'd my self extremly with the Thoughts of making it, and with my having much more Convenience for it than any of the *Negroes* or *Indians*; but not at all considering the particular Inconveniences which I lay under, more than the Indians did, *viz.* want of Hands to move it, when it was made, into the Water, a Difficulty much harder for me to surmount, than all the Consequences of Want of Tools could be to them; for what was it to me, That when I had chosen a vast Tree in the Woods, I might with much Trouble cut it down, if after I might be able with my Tools to hew and dub the Out-side into the proper Shape of a Boat, and burn or cut out the In-side to make it hollow, so to make a Boat of it: If after all this, I must leave it just there where I found it, and was not able to launch it into the Water.

One would have thought, I could not have had the least Reflection upon my Mind of my Circumstance, while I was making this Boat; but I should have immediately thought how I should get it into the Sea; but my Thoughts were so intent upon my Voyage over the Sea in it, that I never once consider'd how I should get it off of the Land; and it was really in its own Nature more easy for me to guide it over forty five Miles of Sea, than about forty five Fathom⑤ of Land, where it lay, to set it a float in the Water.

I went to work upon this Boat, the most like a Fool, that ever Man did, who had any of his Senses awake. I pleas'd my self with the Design, without determining whether I was ever able to undertake it; not but that the Difficulty of launching my Boat came often into my Head; but I put a stop to my own Enquiries into it, by this foolish Answer which I gave my self, *Let's first make it, I'll warrant I'll find some Way or other to get it along, when 'tis done.*

This was a most preposterous Method; but the Eagerness of my Fancy prevail'd, and

---

① 译文参见本书第 248 至 249 页。

② canoe [kə'nuː] *n.* a light, slender boat (独木舟;轻舟)。

③ periagua: a dugout canoe.

④ viz. [vɪz] (拉丁语)即;就是 (读做 namely)。

⑤ fathom ['fæðəm] *n.* a unit of length equal to 6 feet or 1.8 meters (寻,长度单位,等于 6 英尺或 1.8 米)。

to work I went. I fell'd a Cedar① Tree: I question much whether *Solomon* ever had such a One for the Building of the Temple at *Jerusalem*. It was five Foot ten Inches Diameter at the lower Part next the Stump, and four Foot eleven Inches Diameter at the End of twenty two Foot, after which it lessen'd for a while, and then parted into Branches: It was not without infinite Labour that I fell'd this Tree: I was twenty Days hacking and hewing at it at the Bottom. I was fourteen more getting the Branches and Limbs, and the vast spreading Head of it, cut off, which I hack'd and hew'd through with Axe and Hatchet, and inexpressible Labour: After this, it cost me a Month to shape it, and dub it to a Proportion, and to something like the Bottom of a Boat, that it might swim upright as it ought to do. It cost me near three Months more to clear the In-side, and work it out so, as to make an exact Boat of it: This I did indeed without Fire, by meer Malett and Chisel, and by the dint of hard Labour, till I had brought it to be a very handsome *Periagua*, and big enough to have carry'd six and twenty Men, and consequently big enough to have carry'd me and all my Cargo.

When I had gone through this Work, I was extremely delighted with it. The Boat was really much bigger than I ever saw a Canoe, or Periagua, that was made of one Tree, in my Life. Many a weary Stroke it had cost, you may be sure; and there remain'd nothing but to get it into the Water; and had I gotten it into the Water, I make no question but I should have began the maddest Voyage, and the most unlikely to be perform'd, that ever was undertaken.

But all my Devices to get it into the Water fail'd me; tho' they cost me infinite Labour too. It lay about one hundred Yards from the Water, and not more: But the first Inconvenience was, it was up Hill towards the Creek; well, to take away this Discouragement, I resolv'd to dig into the Surface of the Earth, and so make a Declivity: This I begun, and it cost me a prodigious② deal of Pains; but who grutches Pains, that have their Deliverance in View: But then this was work'd through, and this Difficulty manag'd, it was still much at one; for I could no more stir the *Canoe*, than I could the other Boat.

Then I measure'd the Distance of Ground, and resolv'd to cut a Dock, or Canal, to bring the Water up to the *Canoe*, seeing I could not bring the *Canoe* down to the Water: Well, I began this Work, and when I began to enter into it, and calculate how deep it was to be dug, how broad, how the Stuff to be thrown out, I found, That by the Number of Hands I had, being none but my own, it must have been ten or twelve Years before I should have gone through with it; for the Shore lay high, so that at the upper End, it must have been at least twenty Foot Deep; so at length, tho' with great Reluctancy, I gave this Attempt over also.

This griev'd me heartily, and now I saw, tho' too late, the Folly of beginning a Work

① cedar [ˈsiːdə] *n.* 雪松。

② prodigious [prəˈdɪdʒəs] *adj.* impressively great in size, force, or extent; enormous (巨大的)。

before we count the Cost; and before we judge rightly of our own Strength to go through with it.

Ⅴ. Johann Wolfgang von Goethe

Goethe (1749～1832), the great German writer, is regarded as one of the most important figures in the history of world literature.

At the early age of eight Goethe had already acquired some knowledge of Greek, Latin, French and Italian. Goethe's early education was somewhat irregular and informal. When he was about 16, he was sent to Leipzig, ostensibly to study law. He apparently studied more life than law and put in his time expressing his reactions through some form of writing. On at least two occasions, this form was dramatic.

Finally, in 1770 Goethe went to Strassburg, this time really intent on passing his preliminary examinations in law. Along with his study of law, he studied art, music, anatomy and chemistry.

In 1771 Goethe returned to Frankfurt, nominally to practice law, but he was soon deep in working on his five-act tragedy *Götz von Berlichingen*, which brought him recognition.

In 1775, Goethe went to live in Weimar, becoming the Duke's chief adviser. Interested in various other activities, he didn't do much actual writing for a period of nearly ten years.

In the late 18th and the early 19th century, Goethe was one of the key figures of the movement of Weimar Classicism.

In literature Goethe gained fame early with *The Sorrows of Young Werther* as well as his lyrical poems, but his most famous work was the poetic drama, *Faust*.

Goethe's famous short novel *The Sorrows of Young Werther*, published in 1774, recounts an unhappy romantic love story that ends in suicide. The short novel has been translated into dozens of languages and its influence is enormous. The protagonist of the short novel, the young Werther, as an obsessive figure driven to despair and destruction by his unrequited love for the young Lotte, has become a pervasive literary archetype. The tragic fate of his life originated from both the internal contradiction and the external social context and the external world serves as the typical setting to express his internal conflicts.

The writing of *Faust*, however, extended over practically the whole of Goethe's literary life, a period of 57 years. It was finished when Goethe was 81. *Faust* is in reality a dramatic poem rather than a piece for the stage. Although based on the same legend as Marlowe's *Dr. Faustus*, it far transcends both its legendary source and the English play, and it is regarded as the summing-up of the spiritual exploring of the intellectuals since the

Renaissance.

The Hunter's Even-Song[①]

The plain with still and wand'ring feet,
And gun full-charged, I tread,
And hov'ring see thine image sweet,
Thine image dear, o'er head.

In gentle silence thou dost fare
Through field and valley dear;
But doth my fleeting image ne'er
To thy mind's eye appear?

His image, who, by grief oppress'd,
Roams through the world forlorn,
And wanders on from east to west,
Because from thee he's torn?

When I would think of none but thee,
Mine eyes the moon survey;
A calm repose then steals o'er me,
But how, 'twere hard to say.

Tr. by Edgar Alfred Bowring

The Wanderer's Night-Song[②]

Hush'd on the hill
Is the breeze;
Scarce by the zephyr[③]
The trees
Softly are press'd;
The woodbird's asleep on the bough.
Wait, then, and thou
Soon wilt find rest.

Tr. by Edgar Alfred Bowring

---

① 译文参见本书第 249 页。
② 译文参见本书第 249 至 250 页。
③ zephyr ['zefə] *n.* the west wind; gentle breeze (西风;和风)。

The Sorrows of Young Werther[①]

(Excerpt)

MAY 10.

A wonderful serenity has taken possession of my entire soul, like these sweet mornings of spring which I enjoy with my whole heart. I am alone, and feel the charm of existence in this spot, which was created for the bliss of souls like mine. I am so happy, my dear friend, so absorbed in the exquisite[②] sense of mere tranquil existence, that I neglect my talents. I should be incapable of drawing a single stroke at the present moment; and yet I feel that I never was a greater artist than now. When, while the lovely valley teems with vapour around me, and the meridian[③] sun strikes the upper surface of the impenetrable foliage of my trees, and but a few stray gleams steal into the inner sanctuary, I throw myself down among the tall grass by the trickling stream; and, as I lie close to the earth, a thousand unknown plants are noticed by me: when I hear the buzz of the little world among the stalks, and grow familiar with the countless indescribable forms of the insects and flies, then I feel the presence of the Almighty, who formed us in his own image, and the breath of that universal love which bears and sustains us, as it floats around us in an eternity of bliss; and then, my friend, when darkness overspreads my eyes, and heaven and earth seem to dwell in my soul and absorb its power, like the form of a beloved mistress, then I often think with longing, Oh, would I could describe these conceptions, could impress upon paper all that is living so full and warm within me, that it might be the mirror of my soul, as my soul is the mirror of the infinite God! O my friend — but it is too much for my strength — I sink under the weight of the splendour of these visions!

JULY 16.

How my heart beats when by accident I touch her finger, or my feet meet hers under the table! I draw back as if from a furnace; but a secret force impels me forward again, and my senses become disordered. Her innocent, unconscious heart never knows what agony these little familiarities inflict[④] upon me. Sometimes when we are talking she lays her hand upon mine, and in the eagerness of conversation comes closer to me, and her balmy breath reaches my lips, — when I feel as if lightning had struck me, and that I could sink into the earth. And yet, Wilhelm, with all this heavenly confidence, — if I

---

① 译文参见本书第 250 至 251 页。

② exquisite [ˈekswɪzɪt] *adj.* excellent; flawless (优美的;精致的)。

③ meridian [məˈrɪdiən] *n./adj.* either half of such a great circle from pole to pole; relating to, or constituting the highest point (子午线;子午线的)。

④ inflict [ɪnˈflɪkt] *v.* to impose (造成)。

know myself, and should ever dare — you understand me. No, no! my heart is not so corrupt, it is weak, weak enough but is not that a degree of corruption?

She is to me a sacred being. All passion is still in her presence: I cannot express my sensations when I am near her. I feel as if my soul beat in every nerve of my body. There is a melody which she plays on the piano with angelic skill, — so simple is it, and yet so spiritual! It is her favourite air; and, when she plays the first note, all pain, care, and sorrow disappear from me in a moment.

I believe every word that is said of the magic of ancient music. How her simple song enchants me! Sometimes, when I am ready to commit suicide, she sings that air; and instantly the gloom and madness which hung over me are dispersed, and I breathe freely again.

AUGUST 21.

In vain do I stretch out my arms toward her when I awaken in the morning from my weary slumbers. In vain do I seek for her at night in my bed, when some innocent dream has happily deceived me, and placed her near me in the fields, when I have seized her hand and covered it with countless kisses. And when I feel for her in the half confusion of sleep, with the happy sense that she is near, tears flow from my oppressed heart; and, bereft[①] of all comfort, I weep over my future woes.

NOVEMBER 21.

She does not feel, she does not know, that she is preparing a poison which will destroy us both; and I drink deeply of the draught which is to prove my destruction. What mean those looks of kindness with which she often — often? no, not often, but sometimes, regards me, that complacency with which she hears the involuntary sentiments which frequently escape me, and the tender pity for my sufferings which appears in her countenance?

Yesterday, when I took leave she seized me by the hand, and said, "Adieu, dear Werther." Dear Werther! It was the first time she ever called me dear: the sound sunk deep into my heart. I have repeated it a hundred times; and last night, on going to bed, and talking to myself of various things, I suddenly said, "Good night, dear Werther!" and then could not but laugh at myself.

Tr. by R. D. Boylan

---

① bereft [bɪ'reft] *adj.* deprived of (被剥夺的)。

Chapter Six Romantic Literature

Ⅰ. Introduction

The literary movement of the early part of the 19th century was Romanticism, a movement in art and literature in revolt against the neoclassical reason prevailing in the previous centuries. It is the usual idea that the Romantic literature began in English poetry with the publication of William Wordsworth and Samuel Taylor Coleridge's *Lyrical Ballads* in 1798. Moreover, although it is true that the French Revolution of 1789 and the Industrial Revolution were two main political and social factors affecting the Romantic poets in early 19th-century England, many characteristics of Romanticism in literature sprang from literary or philosophical sources.

A philosophical background was provided in the 18th century chiefly by Rousseau, whose emphasis on the individual, nature and the power of inspiration influenced Wordsworth and many other Romantic writers. Positive as it was, the influence of Rousseau must also be seen as a partly negative reaction against 18th-century rationalism with its emphasis on intellect.

Belief in self-knowledge was, indeed, a principal article of Romantic faith. The Romantic writers believed that the real truth of things could be explained only through examination of their own emotions in the context of the universe. Because of the emphasis on inspiration, a poet came to assume a central role that of seer and visionary. Simultaneously, such formal conventions as imitation of the classics were rejected as binding rules. A new directness of the poet's role emphasized the language of the heart and of ordinary men, and Wordsworth even tried to invent a new simplified diction. Poetry became divorced from its 18th-century social context, and a poet was answerable only to the ultimate truth and himself. Two classic poses of the Romantic poets were the mystic visionary of Keats and the superman of Byron. Besides, satirizing of the Byronic hero was to become a theme of some Russian writers.

The early and middle 19th century was an era of poetry and prose rather than of drama. The Romantic style in poetry was seen everywhere in Europe at that time.

The impetus of the Romantic poetry began to slacken after about 1830 and gave way to some more objective styles, although many of its themes and devices continued to be employed.

The particular characteristics of the Romantic poetry include: (a) subjectivity and individualism; (b) glorification of feelings and emotions; (c) superiority of imagination over reason; and (d) worship of nature and devotion to beauty of nature.

Ⅱ. William Wordsworth

William Wordsworth (1770～1850) was one of the poets that came under the influence of the French Revolution in their impressionable years. He was born in a small village in the Lake District. He was educated at Cambridge. In 1790 he took a walking tour on the Continent, when the French Revolution was in progress.

In 1798 Wordsworth and his friend Samuel Taylor Coleridge produced a little volume of poems entitled *Lyrical Ballads*. In 1799 Wordsworth retired to his native mountains in the Lake District where he wrote poems and spent his long and uneventful life there.

In his "Preface to Lyrical Ballads" (1800), which is viewed as an important work of Romantic literary theory, Wordsworth defines poetry as the "spontaneous overflow of powerful feelings arising from emotion recollected in tranquility" and this definition about romantic poetry is well known to modern readers.

Wordsworth' famous poem "I Wandered Lonely as a Cloud", commonly known as "The Daffodils", consists of four six-line stanzas, in iambic tetrameter and an ABABCC rhyme scheme. It describes the beauty of nature and the reconciliation of man with his environment. While in the poem "We Are Seven" we can see Wordsworth's adoration of childlike innocence.

I Wandered Lonely as a Cloud[①]

I wandered lonely as a cloud
That floats on high o'er vales and hills,
When all at once I saw a crowd,
A host, of golden daffodils;
Beside the lake, beneath the trees,
Fluttering and dancing in the breeze.

Continuous as the stars that shine
And twinkle on the milky way,
They stretched in never-ending line

① 译文参见本书第 251 页。

Along the margin of a bay:
Ten thousand saw I at a glance,
Tossing their heads in sprightly[①] dance.

The waves beside them danced; but they
Out-did the sparkling waves in glee[②]:
A poet could not but be gay,
In such a jocund[③] company:
I gazed — and gazed — but little thought
What wealth the show to me had brought:

For oft, when on my couch I lie
In vacant or in pensive mood,
They flash upon that inward eye
Which is the bliss of solitude;
And then my heart with pleasure fills,
And dances with the daffodils.

We Are Seven[④]

— A simple Child,
That lightly draws its breath,
And feels its life in every limb,
What should it know of death?

I met a little cottage Girl:
She was eight years old, she said;
Her hair was thick with many a curl
That clustered round her head.

She had a rustic, woodland air,
And she was wildly clad[⑤]:
Her eyes were fair, and very fair;
— Her beauty made me glad.

---

① sprightly [ˈspraɪtli] *adj.* lively; brisk (轻快的)。

② glee [gliː] *n.* jubilant delight; joy (欢乐)。

③ jocund [ˈdʒɔkənd] *adj.* sprightly and lighthearted; jolly (欢乐的;高兴的)。

④ 译文参见本书第 251 至 252 页。

⑤ clad [klæd] *v.* 动词 clothe 的过去式和过去分词。

"Sisters and brothers, little Maid,
How many may you be?"
"How many? Seven in all," she said
And wondering looked at me.

"And where are they? I pray you tell."
She answered, "Seven are we;
And two of us at Conway dwell,
And two are gone to sea.

"Two of us in the church-yard lie,
My sister and my brother;
And, in the church-yard cottage, I
Dwell near them with my mother."

"You say that two at Conway dwell,
And two are gone to sea,
Yet ye are seven! I pray you tell,
Sweet Maid, how this may be."

Then did the little Maid reply,
"Seven boys and girls are we;
Two of us in the church-yard lie,
Beneath the church-yard tree."

"You run about, my little Maid,
Your limbs they are alive;
If two are in the church-yard laid,
Then ye are only five."

"Their graves are green, they may be seen,"
The little Maid replied,
"Twelve steps or more from my mother's door,
And they are side by side.

"My stockings there I often knit,
My kerchief there I hem;
And there upon the ground I sit,

And sing a song to them.

"And often after sun-set, Sir,
When it is light and fair,
I take my little porringer[①],
And eat my supper there.

"The first that died was sister Jane;
In bed she moaning lay,
Till God released her of her pain;
And then she went away.

"So in the church-yard she was laid;
And, when the grass was dry,
Together round her grave we played,
My brother John and I.

"And when the ground was white with snow,
And I could run and slide,
My brother John was forced to go,
And he lies by her side."

"How many are you, then," said I,
"If they two are in heaven?"
Quick was the little Maid's reply,
"O Master! we are seven."

"But they are dead; those two are dead!
Their spirits are in heaven!"
'Twas throwing words away; for still
The little Maid would have her will,
And said, "Nay[②], we are seven!"

---

① porringer [ˈpɔrɪndʒə] *n.* a shallow cup or bowl with a handle（粥碗；小汤碗）。

② nay [neɪ] *adv.*（古）否；不。

Ⅲ. George Gordon Byron

George Byron (1788～1824) was born into a Scottish aristocratic family. He was born with a clubbed foot, with which he suffered throughout his life. Byron's father had married his mother for her money, which he soon squandered, and then, he fled to France where he died in 1791.

When Byron was one year old, he and his mother moved to Aberdeen, Scotland, where Byron spent his childhood. Upon the death of his great uncle in 1798, Byron became the sixth Baron Byron of Rochdale and inherited the ancestral home, Newstead Abbey in Nottingham. He attended Harrow School from 1801 to 1805 and then Trinity College at Cambridge University until 1808, when he received a master's degree. When he turned twenty-one in 1809, Byron was entitled to a seat in the House of Lords, and he attended several sessions of Parliament that year. In July, however, he left England on a journey through Greece and Turkey. He recorded his experiences in poetic form in several works, most importantly in *Childe Harold's Pilgrimage* (1812～18). He returned to England in 1811 and once again took his seat in Parliament.

The publication of the first two cantos of *Childe Harold* in 1812 met with great acclaim. Around this time he engaged in a tempestuous affair with Lady Caroline Lamb, who characterized Byron as "mad — bad — and dangerous to know". Throughout his life Byron conducted numerous affairs and fathered several illegitimate children. For several years since 1817, Byron lived in a variety of Italian cities, composing a major portion of his masterpiece *Don Juan* (1819～24) as well as other poems.

In one of his most famous lyrical poems "She Walks in Beauty", adopting the conventional meters and manner of convivial songs, Byron praised the extraordinary beauty of a young lady, Mrs Wilmont, both physical and spiritual.

She Walks in Beauty[①]

She walks in Beauty, like the night
    Of cloudless climes and starry skies;
And all that's best of dark and bright
    Meet in her aspect and her eyes:
Thus mellow'd to that tender light
    Which Heaven to gaudy day denies.

① 译文参见本书第252页。

One shade the more, one ray the less,
  Had half impair'd[1] the nameless grace
Which waves in every raven tress,
  Or softly lightens o'er her face;
Where thoughts serenely sweet express
  How pure, how dear their dwelling-place.

And on that cheek, and o'er that brow,
  So soft, so calm, yet eloquent,
The smiles that win, the tints that glow,
  But tell of days in goodness spent,
A mind at peace with all below,
  A heart whose love is innocent!

Ⅳ. Percy Bysshe Shelley

Percy Bysshe Shelley (1792～1822) was born in Sussex into a wealth family and as the heir of a rich estate acquired by his grandfather. In 1810 Shelley entered the Oxford University College. But he was expelled from the college the next year for publishing *The Necessity of Atheism*, which repudiates the existence of God. His father renounced Shelley's inheritance in favour of a small annuity, after he eloped with the 16-year-old Harriet Westbrook, the daughter of a London tavern owner. Shelly continued his nomadic life and published in 1813 his first important poem, the atheistic *Queen Mab*.

The poet's first marriage turned to be a failure. In 1814 Shelley travelled abroad with Mary Wollstonecraft Godwin, the daughter of the philosopher and anarchist William Godwin (1756～1836), and Mary's young stepsister Jane (Claire) Clairmont. Harriet drowned herself in the Serpentine in 1816, and in the same year Shelley married Mary Wollstonecraft.

During the summer of 1816 Shelley spent with Lord Byron at Lake Geneva, where Byron had an affair with Clairmont. Shelley composed some poems and Mary Wollstonecraft started her famous novel *Frankenstein*.

In 1818 the Shelleys and Clairmount moved to Italy where Byron was residing. In 1819 they went to Rome and in 1820 to Pisa. And on July 8, 1822, during the stormy return voyage to Lerici, the boat sank and Shelley drowned. The poet was buried in Rome. On his tombstone was inscribed "Persy Bysshe Shelley, Cor Cordium", with the meaning "the heart of all hearts".

---

① impair [ɪm'peə] *v.* to cause to diminish (削弱)。impair'd: impaired.

Shelley's important works include the lyrical drama *Prometheus Unbound* and the famous lyrical poems of nature such as *Ode to the West Wind* and *To a Skylark*.

To ...[1]

One word is too often profaned
  For me to profane it,
One feeling too falsely disdained
  For thee to disdain it;
One hope is too like despair
  For prudence to smother,
And pity from thee more dear
  Than that from another.

I can give not what men call love,
  But wilt thou accept not
The worship the heart lifts above
  And the Heavens reject not, —
The desire of the moth for the star,
  Of the night for the morrow,
The devotion to something afar
  From the sphere of our sorrow.

Ode to the West Wind[2]

I

O wild West Wind, thou breath of Autumn's being,
Thou, from whose unseen presence the leaves dead
Are driven, like ghosts from an enchanter fleeing,

Yellow, and black, and pale, and hectic[3] red,
Pestilence-stricken multitudes: O thou,
Who chariotest[4] to their dark wintry bed

---

① 译文参见本书第 252 至 253 页。
② 译文参见本书第 253 至 254 页。
③ hectic [ˈhektɪk] *adj.* feverish; flushed (脸上发红、发热的;狂热的)。
④ chariotest: chariot (战车)。

The winged seeds, where they lie cold and low,
Each like a corpse within its grave, until
Thine azure sister of the Spring shall blow

Her clarion[①] o'er the dreaming earth, and fill
(Driving sweet buds like flocks to feed in air)
With living hues and odours plain and hill:

Wild Spirit, which art moving everywhere;
Destroyer and preserver[②]; hear, oh hear!

Ⅱ

Thou on whose stream, mid[③] the steep sky's commotion,
Loose clouds like earth's decaying leaves are shed,
Shook from the tangled boughs of Heaven and Ocean,

Angels of rain and lightning: there are spread
On the blue surface of thine aery surge,
Like the bright hair uplifted from the head

Of some fierce Maenad[④], even from the dim verge
Of the horizon to the zenith's height,
The locks of the approaching storm. Thou dirge[⑤]

Of the dying year, to which this closing night
Will be the dome of a vast sepulchre,
Vaulted with all thy congregated might

Of vapours, from whose solid atmosphere
Black rain, and fire, and hail will burst: oh hear!

Ⅲ

Thou who didst[⑥] waken from his summer dreams

---

① clarion [ˈklæriən] *n.* a medieval trumpet with a shrill, clear tone (号角)。
② destroyer and preserver: it's Shelley's important metaphysical view towards the west wind.
③ mid: amid.
④ Maenad [ˈmiːnæd] *n.* 酒神 Bacchus 的女侍;狂女。
⑤ dirge [ˈdɜːdʒ] *n.* a funeral hymn or lament (挽歌)。
⑥ didst [dɪdst] *v.* (古英语中与 thou 一起使用)动词 do 的第二人称单数过去式。

The blue Mediterranean, where he lay,
Lull'd by the coil of his crystal line streams,

Beside a pumice[①] isle in Baiae's bay[②],
And saw in sleep old palaces and towers
Quivering within the wave's intenser day,

All overgrown with azure moss and flowers
So sweet, the sense faints picturing them! Thou
For whose path the Atlantic's level powers

Cleave themselves into chasms[③], while far below
The sea-blooms and the oozy[④] woods which wear
The sapless foliage of the ocean, know

Thy voice, and suddenly grow gray with fear,
And tremble and despoil themselves: oh hear!

Ⅳ

If I were a dead leaf thou mightest bear;
If I were a swift cloud to fly with thee;
A wave to pant beneath thy power, and share

The impulse of thy strength, only less free
Than thou, O uncontrollable! If even
I were as in my boyhood, and could be

The comrade of thy wanderings over Heaven,
As then, when to outstrip thy skiey speed
Scarce seemed a vision; I would ne'er have striven

As thus with thee in prayer in my sore need.
Oh! lift me as a wave, a leaf, a cloud!
I fall upon the thorns of life! I bleed!

---

① pumice [ˈpʌmɪs] *n.* a light, porous, glassy lava (浮石)。

② Baiae's Bay: Baiae was named after Baius, Odysseus's (Ulysses's) companion.

③ chasm [ˈkæzəm] *n.* a deep, steep-sided opening in the earth's surface (深坑;裂口)。

④ oozy [ˈuːzi] *adj.* exuding moisture (潮湿的)。

A heavy weight of hours has chain'd and bow'd
One too like thee: tameless, and swift, and proud.

V

Make me thy lyre, even as the forest is:
What if my leaves are falling like its own!
The tumult of thy mighty harmonies

Will take from both a deep, autumnal tone,
Sweet though in sadness. Be thou, Spirit fierce,
My spirit! Be thou me, impetuous① one!

Drive my dead thoughts over the universe
Like wither'd leaves to quicken a new birth!
And, by the incantation② of this verse,

Scatter, as from an unextinguish'd hearth
Ashes and sparks, my words among mankind!
Be through my lips to unawakened earth

The trumpet③ of a prophecy④! O Wind,
If Winter comes, can Spring be far behind?

V. Alexander Pushkin

Alexander Pushkin (1799～1837) holds a place in Russian literature perhaps even larger than that of Shakespeare in English. He is the forerunner of modern Russian literature and the Russian literary language as we know it today. Beloved of all Russians, it is Pushkin who found the Russian literary tradition in practically every genre.

Pushkin was born in Moscow into a noble family. He took particular pride in his great-grandfather Hannibal, a black general who served Peter the Great. Educated at the

---

① impetuous [ɪm'petjʊəs] *adj.* characterized by sudden and forceful energy or emotion; impulsive and passionate（冲动的；猛烈的）。

② incantation [ˌɪnkæn'teɪʃən] *n.* a formula used in ritual recitation; a spell（咒语）。

③ trumpet ['trʌmpɪt] *n.* a brass wind instrument; clarion（喇叭；号角）。

④ prophecy ['prʌfɪsi] *n.* a prediction of the future, made under divine inspiration（预言；先兆）。

Imperial Lyceum at Tsarkoye Selo, Petersburg, Pushkin demonstrated an early poetic gift. In 1817 Pushkin was taken into the ministry of foreign affairs in St. Petersburg; there he mingled in the social life of the capital and took part in an underground revolutionary group. In 1820 his "Ode to Liberty" came to the attention of the authorities, and the young poet was exiled to the Caucasus.

That same year Pushkin published his *Ruslan and Ludmila*, a long Romantic poem based on folklore, which brought him a reputation as one of Russia's most promising poetic talents. The influence of Lord Byron shows itself, along with Pushkin's own love of liberty, in his next major poems, *The Prisoner of the Caucasus* (1822), *The Fountain of Bakhchisarai* (1822), and *The Gypsies* (1823～1824). He began his most famous work, *Eugene Onegin*, in 1823; a love story with a realistic contemporary setting that has been described as the first of the great Russian novels (although in verse), it was not completed until 1831. In 1824 he was banished to his mother's estate near Pskov. There he wrote *Boris Godunov*, a Russian historical tragedy in the Shakespearean tradition, published six years later. Recognizing his enormous popularity, Tsar Nicholas Ⅰ, pardoned him in 1826. Pushkin continued to draw upon Russian history in two long poems, *Poltava* and *The Bronze Horseman*, and in his novel of the Pugachev's rebellion, *The Captain's Daughter*. He also wrote short stories, among which the best known is *The Queen of Spades*. Pushkin died from wounds that he suffered in a duel which he had fought in St. Petersburg.

Pushkin provided a literary heritage for Russians, whose native language had hitherto been considered unfit for literature. He was also a versatile writer of great vigor and optimism who understood the many facets of the Russian character.

Pushkin's "To ..." is one of the most famous poems in the Russian literary tradition. It was written during his exile in Mikhaylovskoye in Pskov Province. This poem is addressed to Kern, a girl from St. Petersburg. The night before Kern left Pskov for St. Petersburg, Pushkin gave her a manuscript of Chapter Ⅱ of *Eugene Onegin*. Stuck within its pages was this famous lyric. In this poem, we can feel the magic of love for the recuperation of creativity and vitality.

The Station-master is regarded as one of the finest short stories in Russian literature. Pushkin described in this story the conflict among social classes as well as the ambiguity of human existence. The main character Vyrin, the stationmaster, became the typical representative of low-born "small man" in the history of Russian literature.

To ...[①]

I still remember that amazing moment

---

① 译文参见本书第 254 页。

You have appeared before my sight
As though a brief and fleeting omen,
Pure phantom[①] in enchanting light.

Locked in depression's hopeless captive,
In haste of clamorous[②] processions,
I heard your voice — soft and attractive.
And dreamt of your beloved expressions.

Time passed. In gusts[③], rebellious and active,
A tempest scattered my affections
And I forgot your voice attractive,
Your sacred and divine expressions.

Detained[④] in darkness, isolation,
My days would slowly drag in strife.
With lack of faith and inspiration,
With lack of tears, and love and life.

My soul attained its waking moment:
You re-appeared before my sight,
As though a brief and fleeting omen,
Pure phantom in enchanting light.

And now, my heart, in fascination
Beats rapidly and finds revived:
Devout[⑤] faith and inspiration,
And tender tears and love and life.

If by Life You Were Deceived[⑥]

If by life you were deceived,

---

① phantom [ˈfæntəm] *n.* something apparently seen, heard, or sensed, but having no physical reality; a ghost or an apparition（幻影）。

② clamorous [ˈklæmərəs] *adj.* making or marked by loud outcry（喧嚷的）。

③ gust [gʌst] *n.* an abrupt rush of wind; an outburst of emotion（阵风；情感爆发）。

④ detain [dɪˈteɪn] *vt.* to keep in custody or temporary confinement; to delay（拘留；留住）。

⑤ devout [dɪˈvaʊt] *adj.* religious; earnest（虔敬的；诚恳的）。

⑥ 译文参见本书第 254 页。

Don't be dismal[①], don't be wild!
In the day of grief, be mild
Merry days will come, believe.

Heart is living in tomorrow;
Present is dejected[②] here;
In a moment, passes sorrow;
That which passes will be dear.

The Station-master[③]

Here's a collegiate registrator,
Of posting stations the dictator.

Prince Viazemsky

Who has not cursed the superintendents[④] of posting stations? Who has not quarrelled with them? Who in a moment of anger has not demanded from them the fatal book to write in it his useless complaint of injustice, rudeness, and inefficiency? Who does not regard them as human monsters, as bad as the attorneys[⑤] of the old days or at any rate as the Murom highwaymen[⑥]? Let us be just, however, let us try to consider their position, and perhaps we shall feel more kindly towards them. What is a station-master? A true martyr, whose low rank in the civil service protects him only from blows, and that not always (I appeal to my readers' conscience). What sort of life has this "dictator", as Prince Viazemsky jokingly calls him? The life of a galley-slave[⑦]. He has no rest either by day or by night. Travellers vent upon him all the annoyance accumulated during their tedious[⑧] journey: the weather is unbearable, the roads are bad, the driver is obstinate, the horses don't go — and it is all the station-master's fault. Coming into his poor dwelling, the traveller looks upon him as an enemy; he is lucky if he can soon get rid of his unwelcome visitor; but if there happen to be no horses? ...Goodness, what abuse, what threats are showered upon him! In rain and sleet he is forced to run about the village trying to find

---

① dismal [ˈdɪzməl] *adj.* gloomy; dreary (情绪低落的;凄凉的)。

② dejected [dɪˈjektɪd] *adj.* being in low spirits; depressed (沮丧的)。

③ 译文参见本书第 254 至 259 页。

④ superintendent [ˌsjuːpərɪnˈtendənt] *n.* a person who has the authority to supervise or direct (主管;负责人;管理者)。

⑤ attorney [əˈtɜːni] *n.* lawyer; agent (律师;法律事务上的代理人)。

⑥ highwayman [ˈhaɪweɪmən] *n.* a man who holds up and robs travelers on a road (拦路强盗)。

⑦ galley-slave: a slave or convict forced to ply an oar of a galley; a person assigned to perform tedious or menial tasks (划桨的奴隶;做苦工的人)。

⑧ tedious [ˈtiːdiəs] *adj.* boring (单调乏味的;沉闷的)。

horses; in the storm, and in the Epiiphanial frosts he has to go into the cold entry to have a minute's respite from the angry traveller's shouts and blows. A general arrives; the station-master, trembling, gives him his last troikas①, including the one for government messengers. The general drives off without saying: "Thank you." Five minutes later a bell is heard, and a government courier throws his order for horses on the table! Let us consider all this closely and, instead of indignation, our heart will be filled with genuine sympathy. A few words more: during twenty years in succession I have travelled up and down Russia in all directions; I have been on almost all the posting routes; I have known several generations of drivers; there are few station-masters whose faces are not familiar to me and with whom I have not had something to do; I hope to publish in the near future an interesting collection of my travelling impressions; meanwhile I shall only say that the class of station-masters has been grossly misrepresented to the public. Those officials, so cruelly maligned②, are, generally speaking, peaceable men, obliging by nature, of sociable disposition, modest in their ambitions, and not too grasping. Much that is interesting and instructive may be gathered from their conversation, which the travellers do wrong to despise. As for myself, I confess I prefer their talk to that of some important official of the sixth class travelling on government business.

It is not difficult to guess that I have friends among the honourable company of station-masters. In fact, the memory of one of them is precious to me. Circumstances drew us together once, and it is of him I now want to tell my kind readers.

In May 1816 I happened to go through the province of X. along a posting route that has since been done away with. Being of low rank in the service I travelled by post-stages and hired only two horses. In consequence station-masters did not stand on ceremony with me, and I often had to fight for what I regarded as my lawful due. Being young and hot-tempered I felt indignant at the station-master's meanness and cowardice when he gave to some gentleman of rank the troika intended for me. It took me just as long to get accustomed to being passed over by a discriminating flunkey handing dishes at a governor's dinner. Now both the one and the other seem to me in the natural order of things. What, indeed, would become of us if, instead of the convenient rule of precedence by rank, some other rule were introduced such as "precedence by intelligence"? What disputes there would be! and who would be first served at dinner? But I return to my story.

The day was hot. Three versts from the station N. I felt a few spots of rain; in another minute there was a regular downpour and I was drenched to the skin. When I arrived at the station the first thing I did was to change my clothes; the second, to ask for some tea.

---

① troika [ˈtrɔɪkə] *n.* a Russian carriage drawn by a team of three horses abreast（俄国的三驾马车）。

② malign [məˈlaɪn] *v.* to speak evil of（诽谤）。

"Dounia!" the station-master cried, "heat the samovar[①] and run for some cream."

At these words a girl of about fourteen came out from behind the partition and ran to the entry. I was struck by her beauty.

"Is that your daughter?" I asked the station-master.

"Yes, sir," he answered with an air of satisfied pride, "and such a good girl, and so quick, the very picture of her dead mother."

Thereupon he began copying out my pass, and I examined the pictures that adorned his humble but clean dwelling. They illustrated the story of the Prodigal Son: in the first, a venerable old man in a night-cap and dressing-gown was saying good-bye to the restless youth, who was hastily receiving his blessing and a purse of gold. Another vividly depicted the young man's dissolute conduct; he was sitting at the table surrounded by false friends and shameless women. Farther on, the young man, in a three-cornered hat and ragged clothes, was herding pigs and sharing their meal; his face expressed profound sorrow and penitence[②]. The last picture showed his return to his father: the kind old man in the same dressing-gown and night-cap was running to meet him; the prodigal[③] son was kneeling; in the background the cook could be seen killing the fatted calf, and the elder brother asking the servants about the reason for such rejoicing. Under each picture I read appropriate German verses. I remember it all to this day, as well as the clarkia[④] in pots, the bed with a gaily coloured curtain, and the other things in the room. I clearly see before me the himself, a vigorous and well-preserved man of about fifty, dressed in a long green coat with three medals attached to faded ribbons. I had scarcely had time to settle with my old driver when Dounia came in with the samovar. The little coquette[⑤] noticed at the second glance the impression she had made on me; she cast down her big blue eyes; I spoke to her; she answered me without any timidity, like a girl who had seen the world. I offered her father a glass of punch, gave Dounia a cup of tea, and we talked together, the three of us, as though we had known one another all our lives.

My horses had long been ready, but still I did not want to part with the station-master and his daughter. At last I bid them good-bye; the father wished me a pleasant journey, and the daughter saw me off to my vehicle. In the entry I stopped and asked if she would allow me to kiss her. Dounia consented. I can count many kisses, since the day I took up this pursuit, but not one of them left such a long and pleasant memory in my

---

① samovar [ˌsæməʊˈvɑː] *n.* a metal urn with a chimney, a vertical compartment for hot charcoal, and a spigot, used especially by Russians to boil water for tea (茶炊)。

② penitence [ˈpenɪtəns] *n.* the condition of being penitent; regret for wrongdoing (悔罪)。

③ prodigal [ˈprɔdɪgəl] *adj./n.* wastefully extravagant; one who is given to wasteful luxury or extravagance (浪费的;浪子)。

④ clarkia [ˈklɑːkjə] *n.* 山字草。

⑤ coquette [kəʊˈket] *n.* a seductive woman who uses her sexual appeal to exploit men; a flirt (卖弄风情的女子)。

mind.

Several years had passed, and circumstances brought me to the same posting route, to the same neighbourhood, once more. I recalled the old station-master's daughter, and was glad to think that I should see her again. "But perhaps there is some other man in the old station-master's place," I thought; "Dounia is probably already married." The thought that one or the other of them might have died also crossed my mind, and I approached the station N. with a sad foreboding.

The horses stopped by the station-house. Coming into the room I recognized at once the pictures illustrating the story of the Prodigal Son; the bed and the table stood in their old places, but there were no longer flowers in the windows, and everything around me looked worn and neglected. The station-master was sleeping under a sheepskin coat; my arrival woke him; he got up. ... It was he, Simeon Vyrin, indeed; but how he had aged! While he was preparing to copy out my pass, I gazed at his grey hair, at the deep lines of his unshaven face, at his stooping shoulders — and could not understand how three or four years could have transformed him into a decrepit① old man.

"Do you recognize me?" I asked, "You and I are old friends."

"Perhaps," he answered morosely②, "I live on the high road; many travellers have passed through my station."

"How is your Dounia?" I asked.

The old man frowned. "I really couldn't say," he answered.

"So then she is married?" I asked.

He pretended not to hear me, and went on reading my pass in a whisper. I did not question him any further, but asked to have a kettle put on the fire. I was beginning to feel curious and hoped that punch would untie my old friend's tongue.

I was not mistaken: the old man did not refuse the glass I offered him. I noticed that rum put him into a better humour. At the second glass he grew talkative; he remembered, or pretended to remember, who I was, and I heard from him a story which interested and touched me greatly at the time.

"So you knew my Dounia?" he began, "Every one knew her, indeed! Ah, Dounia, Dounia! What a fine girl she was! Whoever went by always praised her, no one found fault with her. Ladies would give her a kerchief and a pair of ear-rings. Gentlemen, driving past, would stop to have dinner or supper simply because they wanted to see more of her. However angry a man might be, he always calmed down when he saw her, and spoke to me kindly. Would you believe it, sir, government messengers and couriers used to stop for half an hour talking to her. She kept the house going: did all the cleaning and cooking, and managed everything. And I, old fool that I was, did nothing but delight in

---

① decrepit [dɪˈkrepɪt] *adj.* weakened（衰老的）。

② morosely [məˈrəʊsli] *adv.* gloomily（闷闷不乐地；忧郁地）。

her. How I loved my Dounia, how I cherished her! No girl could have had a happier life. But no, there is no keeping off misfortune; what is to be will be."

Then he told me the story of his trouble. Three years previously, on a winter night, when he was ruling out a new post book, and his daughter behind the partition was making herself a dress, a troika drove up, and a traveller wrapped up in a rug, wearing a Circassian① cap and a military uniform, came into the room asking for horses. There were no horses to be had. On hearing this, the traveller raised his voice and his whip; but Dounia, used to such scenes, ran out from behind the partition and amiably② asked the traveller if he would have something to eat. Dounia's appearance produced its usual effect. The traveller's anger cooled; he agreed to wait for the horses and ordered supper. When he had taken off his wet shaggy cap, unwrapped his rug and folded his overcoat, he proved to be a graceful young hussar③ with a small black moustache. He made himself at home, and began talking cheerfully to the station-master and his daughter. Supper was served. Meanwhile the horses had come back and the station-master gave orders that they were to be harnessed at once, without being fed, to the young man's covered sledge; but on coming back he found the young man lying almost senseless on the bench: he had been suddenly taken ill, his head ached, he could not go. ... What was to be done? The station-master gave up his bed to him, and it was decided that if the invalid was no better in the morning, they would send to S. for a doctor.

The following day the hussar was worse. His servant rode to the town to fetch a doctor. Dounia tied up his head with a handkerchief soaked in vinegar, and sat down by his bedside with her needlework. While the station-master was in the room the invalid groaned and hardly spoke a word, but he managed to drink two cups of coffee and, groaning, ordered some dinner. Dounia never left his side. He asked for a drink every minute and Dounia gave him the mug of lemonade she had prepared. The invalid moistened his lips in it, and every time he returned the mug he gratefully pressed Dounia's hand with his feeble fingers. The doctor arrived by dinnertime. He felt the invalid's pulse, talked to him in German, and declared in Russian that all he needed was rest, and that in a couple of days he would be able to go on with his journey. The hussar gave him twenty-five roubles for his visit, and invited him to share his dinner; the doctor agreed; both ate with much appetite, drank a bottle of wine, and parted very much pleased with each other.

Another day passed and the hussar recovered completely. He was extremely gay, joked all the time with Dounia and her father, whistled tunes, talked to the travellers, and copied out their passes into the post-book; the good old man took such a liking to him that on the morning of the third day he was quite sorry to part from his amiable lodger. It was

---

① Circassian [sɜːˈkæsɪən] *adj./n.* 切尔克斯的；切尔克斯人。

② amiably [ˈeɪmjəbli] *adv.* friendly（和蔼可亲地；亲切地）。

③ hussar [hʊˈzɑː] *n.* a member of a light cavalry unit（轻骑兵）。

a Sunday; Dounia was preparing to go to Mass. The hussar's sledge was brought. He said good-bye to the station-master, paying him generously for his board and lodging; he said good-bye to Dounia too, and offered to drive her as far as the church, which was at the end of the village. Dounia hesitated.

"What are you afraid of?" her father said. "His honour is not a wolf, he won't eat you. Have a lift to the church."

Dounia sat down in the sledge next to the hussar, the servant jumped on to the box, the driver whistled, and the horses galloped off.

Poor man, he could not understand how he could have allowed his Dounia to drive away with the hussar: he did not know how he could have been so blind, nor what could have become of his good sense. Before half an hour had passed his heart began to ache, and such anxiety possessed him that he could stand it no longer, and went to Mass himself. Coming up to the church he saw that people were already going home, but Dounia was neither in the churchyard, nor on the steps. He hastily entered the church; the priest was leaving, the sexton was blowing out the candles; two old women were still praying in a comer, but Dounia was not there. Her poor father could scarcely bring himself to ask the sexton whether Dounia had been to Mass. The sexton answered that she had not. The station-master went home more dead than alive. He had one hope left: with the thoughtlessness of youth Dounia might have decided to drive as far as the next station where her godmother lived. He waited in an agony of suspense for the return of the troika in which he had let her go. The driver was late; he returned at last in the evening, by himself, drunk, with the awful news that Dounia had gone on with the hussar from the next station.

The blow was too much for the old man; he was taken ill on the spot, and lay down in the same bed where the night before the young impostor had rested. Later on he guessed, putting all the circumstances together, that the hussar's illness had been a sham[①]. The station-master had brainfever, and was taken to S., while another man was temporarily appointed in his place. The same doctor who had come to the hussar, treated him. He assured the station-master that the young man had been perfectly well; he had guessed his evil intention at the time, but said nothing, fearing the hussar's whip. Whether the German spoke the truth or merely wanted to boast of his foresight, his words were not of the least comfort to the sick man. He had hardly recovered from his illness when he obtained a two months' leave from the S. postmaster and, not saying a word to any one about his intention, set out on foot in search of his daughter. He knew from the hussar's pass that Captain Minsky was travelling from Smolensk to Petersburg; the driver who had taken him said that Dounia wept all the way, though she seemed to have gone of her own will.

---

① sham [ʃæm] *n./adj.* a spurious imitation; fake (伪装;虚假的)。

"I may bring home my lost lamb," thought the station-master. With this idea he came to Petersburg, put up at the house of a retired sergeant, an old comrade of his in the service, and began his search. He soon learned that Captain Minsky was in Petersburg and lived in Demoute's Hotel: the station-master decided to go to him.

Early in the morning he came to his door and asked the servant to tell his honour that an old soldier wished to see him. The orderly, who was polishing boots, said that his master was asleep, and could not see any one till eleven o'clock. The station-master went away and came back at the appointed hour. Minsky in a dressing-gown and a red fez① came out to him.

"What do you want, brother?" he asked.

The old man's heart brimmed over, tears came into his eyes, and he could only bring out in a shaking voice: "Your honour! ... be so kind, I beg you! ..."

Minsky glanced at him quickly, flushed crimson, and taking him by the hand led him to his study, shutting the door after him.

"Your honour!" the old man went on, "it's no use crying over spilt milk, but give me back my poor Dounia. You have had your pleasure; don't ruin her for nothing."

"What is done cannot be undone," said the young man in extreme confusion. "I have wronged you, and am glad to ask your forgiveness; but don't think that I could ever abandon Dounia; she will be happy, I promise you on my honour. What do you want with her? She loves me; she has lost the habit of her old life. Neither you nor she could forget what has happened."

After that, thrusting something into the cuff② of the old man's sleeve, he opened the door, and the station-master did not remember how he found himself in the street.

He stood motionless for some time; then he saw a bundle of papers in the cuff of his sleeve; taking them out he unfolded several crumpled fifty-rouble notes. Tears came into his eyes again — tears of indignation! He crushed the notes into a ball, threw them down, stamped on them, and walked away ... After taking a few steps he stood still and thought ... and went back ... but the notes were no longer there. A well-dressed young man, catching sight of him, ran up to a cab, stepped in hastily, and shouted to the driver "Go!" ... The station-master did not follow him. He decided to go home, to his station, but before doing so he wanted to see his poor Dounia once more. With this end in view he called on Minsky again a couple of days later; but the orderly said to him sternly that his master was not seeing any one, and, almost pushing him out of the entry, banged the door in his face. The old man stood outside for a time and then walked home.

On the evening of that same day, after a service to Our Lady, "Joy of all the

---

① fez [fez] *n.* a man's felt cap (土耳其毡帽)。

② cuff [kʌf] *n.* the bottom of a sleeve (袖口)。

sorrowful", he was walking along the Liteyiny. Suddenly a smart-looking droshky[①] dashed past him, and he recognized Minsky. The droshky stopped at the front door of a house of three stories and the hussar ran up the steps. A happy thought struck the old man. He went back and, going up to the coachman, asked him:

"Whose horse is it? Minsky's, isn't it?"

"Yes, it is," the coachman answered. "Why do you ask?"

"Well, it's like this: your master told me to take a note to his Dounia, and as luck would have it, I've forgotten where Dounia lives."

"Why, here, on the first floor. You are late, brother, with your note; he is with her himself now."

"Never mind," the station-master answered with an indescribable feeling in his heart. "Thank you for telling me, I'll go and deliver the note." With these words he walked up the stairs.

The door was locked; he rang. He had a few seconds of painful expectation the key rattled; the door was opened.

"Does Avdotya Simeonovna live here?" he asked.

"Yes," a young maid-servant answered. "What do you want her for?"

Without answering the station-master walked into the hall.

"You can't see her!" the maid called after him. "She has visitors!"

But he walked on, not heeding her. The first two rooms were dark, in the third one there was a light. He walked up to the open door and stopped. Minsky, lost in thought, was sitting in the beautifully furnished room. Dounia, dressed in the height of fashion, sat on the arm of his chair like a rider on a side-saddle. She looked at Minsky tenderly, twisting his black curls round her white fingers. Poor station-master! Never had his daughter seemed to him more beautiful; he could not help admiring her.

"Who is there?" she asked without raising her head.

He said nothing. Not receiving an answer, Dounia looked up ... and fell down on the carpet with a cry. Minsky, terrified, rushed to lift her, but, suddenly seeing her father in the doorway, left Dounia and went up to him shaking with anger.

"What do you want?" he said to him, clenching his teeth. "Why do you steal after me everywhere like a brigand[②]? Do you want to murder me? Out with you!" and seizing the old man with a strong hand by the collar, he pushed him out on to the stairs.

The station-master walked back to his lodgings; his friend advised him to complain, but on thinking it over he decided to give up the whole thing. Two days later he went back to his station, and took up his duties there.

"It is over two years now," he concluded, "that I have lived without Dounia, knowing

① droshky [ˈdrɔʃki] *n.* an open four-wheeled horse-drawn carriage (无盖四轮马车)。

② brigand [ˈbrɪgənd] *n.* a robber or bandit, especially one of an outlaw band (土匪;强盗;歹徒)。

nothing whatever about her. God only knows whether she is still alive. All sorts of things happen. She is not the first or the last to have been seduced by a passer-by, kept for a while, and then abandoned. There are plenty of those silly girls in Petersburg, wearing satin and velvet one day, and sweeping the streets together with the riff-raff① from public-houses the next. When I think sometimes that my Dounia may have gone the same way I can't help wishing she were dead, sinner that I am! ..."

That was the story that my friend, the old station-master, told me, interrupting it more than once with tears which he picturesquely wiped with the skirt of his coat like the zealous Terentyitch in Dmitriev's beautiful ballad. Those tears were partly excited by punch, of which he drained five glasses in the course of his story — but, anyway, they greatly touched my heart. Long after parting from him I kept thinking of the station-master and of poor Dounia.

Not long ago, passing through the village of X., I remembered my old friend; I heard that the posting station he superintended had been closed. No one could give a satisfactory answer to my question whether the old station-master was still living. I decided to visit the place and, hiring some horses, went on to the village of N.

It was in the autumn. Grey clouds covered the sky; a cold wind blew from the harvested fields, snatching red and yellow leaves from the trees by the roadside. I arrived at the village at sunset, and stopped by the station-house. A fat woman came out into the entry (where poor Dounia had once kissed me); in answer to my questions she said that the station-master had died about a year ago, that the brewer was now living in his house, and that she was the brewer's wife. I regretted my useless journey, and the seven roubles I had spent on it.

"What did he die of?" I asked the woman. "Of drink, sir," she answered. "Where is he buried?" "Outside the village, next to his wife's grave." "Can someone take me there?" "Why not? Heigh, Vanka! You've played enough with the cat. Take the gentleman to the cemetery, and show him the station-master's grave."

At these words a ragged little boy, red-haired and blind in one eye, ran up to me and proceeded to take me to the cemetery.

"Did you know the old man?" I asked him on the way.

"Oh yes! He taught me to make whistles. When he went home from the public-house (God rest his soul!) we all ran after him crying, 'Granddad, granddad, give us some nuts!' and he would give some to each one. He was always playing with us."

"And do the travellers remember him?"

"There aren't many travellers now, the assessor② comes sometimes, but he has no thoughts to spare for the dead. But last summer a lady came who did ask for the old

① riff-raff [ˈrɪfræf] *n.* people regarded as disreputable or worthless (群氓;贱民)。

② assessor [əˈsesə] *n.* an official who evaluates property; an assistant to a judge(审核员;陪审官)。

station-master, and went to his grave, too."

"What lady?" I asked with interest.

"A lovely lady!" the boy answered. "She came in a carriage drawn by six horses, and had three children with her, and a wet-nurse, and a black lapdog, and when she heard that the old station-master was dead, she wept, and said to the children: 'You sit still, and I'll go to the cemetery.' I offered to take her, but she said: 'I know the way.' And she gave me five copecks in silver ... such a kind lady!"

We arrived at the cemetery' bare field, dotted about with wooden crosses, with no fence round it, and not a single tree. I never saw a more desolate cemetery.

"This is the old station-master's grave," said the boy, jumping on to a heap of sand with a black cross that had a brass ikon① fixed to it.

"And the lady came here?" I asked.

"Yes, she did," Vanka answered. "I watched her from a distance. She threw herself down on the grave and lay here for a long time. And then she walked to the village and called the priest, gave him some money, and went away, and gave me five copecks in silver ... a good lady!"

I, too, gave the boy five copecks, and no longer regretted my journey and the seven roubles I had spent.

Tr. by Natalie Duddington

Ⅵ. Mikhail Lermontov

Mikhail Lermontov (1814～1841), a Russian Romantic writer, sometimes called "the poet of the Caucasus", was the most important Russian poet after Alexander Pushkin's death. His influence on later Russian literature is still felt in modern times, not only through his poetry, but also through his prose. His poetry remains popular in Russia and the rest of world.

Lermontov was born in Moscow into a respectable noble family of the Tula Governorate. During his lifetime, he published only one slender collection of poems (1840). Three volumes were published a year after his death. His short poems range from patriotic indignation to the pantheistic glorification of living nature.

In the lyrical poem "The Sail", Lermontov used the technique of onomatopoeia to imitate the sounds of tempest and to express the solitary rebel's emotion.

---

① ikon [ˈaɪkɔn] *n.* variant of icon; an idol (圣像;画像)。

The Sail[①]

A lone white sail shows for an instant
Where gleams the sea, an azure streak.
What left it in its homeland distant?
In alien parts what does it seek?

The billows[②] play, the mast[③] bends, creaking,
The wind, impatient, moans and sighs ...
It is not joy that it is seeking,
Nor is't from happiness it flies.

The blue waves dance, they dance and tremble,
The sun's bright rays caress the seas.
And yet for storm it begs, the rebel,
As if in storm lurked[④] calm and peace! ...

Tr. by Irina Zheleznova

Ⅷ. Henry Wadsworth Longfellow

Henry Wadsworth Longfellow (1807～1882) was one of the most famous American poets. People love his poetry because they rhyme and sound like songs. Henry was born in Portland, Maine. He was very good at spelling and arithmetic. But he loved to write and eventually became a writer. Henry graduated from Bowdoin College at the age of 19. Then he travelled back to Europe to study.

Longfellow was given an honorary degree at Oxford and Cambridge. He was a chosen member of the Russian Academy and Spanish Academy. He died in 1882, but the sensation of his poetry is still with us.

Longfellow's style is notable for its simplicity and grace. His "The Song of Hiawatha" is a famous poem that records the picturesque traditions of the American Indian. His lyrical poem "The Arrow and the Song" represents the nature of friendship.

---

① 译文参见本书第 259 页。

② billow [ˈbɪləʊ] *n.* a large wave or swell of water (巨浪)。

③ mast [mɑːst] *n.* a tall vertical spar (桅;桅杆)。

④ lurk [lɜːk] *v.* to lie in wait; to move furtively (潜藏;潜伏)。

The Arrow and the Song[①]

I shot an arrow into the air,
It fell to earth, I knew not where;
For, so swiftly it flew, the sight
Could not follow it in its flight.

I breathed a song into the air,
It fell to earth, I knew not where;
For who has sight so keen and strong,
That it can follow the flight of song?

Long, long afterward, in an oak
I found the arrow, still unbroke;
And the song, from beginning to end,
I found again in the heart of a friend.

Ⅷ. Walt Whitman

Walt Whitman (1819～1892), known as the first important American poet, was born on a Long Island farm. He was taught in various Long Island schools and worked for several newspapers. He published some of his writings, but by his mid-thirties had still not displayed the slightest hint of his unique talent and vision. He published *Leaves of Grass* himself in 1855. The first edition was a slim volume of poems but it was quite a success. Ralph Waldo Emerson wrote a congratulatory letter to Whitman with the famous lines so many writers have since wished to hear: "I find it the most extraordinary piece of wit and wisdom that the America has yet contributed ... I greet you at the beginning of a great career." [②] Whitman published the ninth edition of *Leaves of Grass* before he died on March 26, 1892 in Camden, New Jersey.

Many writers have been called timeless, but Walt Whitman deserves this reputation in a special way. His poems were about himself, plain and simple, especially the ecstatic "Song of Myself", which celebrated the explosive joy of living inside a human body. His poems were as sexually frank as diary entries, and the rhythms of the words took "free

---

① 译文参见本书第259页。

② Aneetle T. Rubinstein. *American Literature Root and Flower*, Foreign Language Teaching and Research Press, 1968, p. 45.

verse" to a new threshold; it was as if meter and rhyme had never existed.

The influence of Walt Whitman on the modern world is significant. Professor Fernando Alegria at Stanford University has described Whitman's presence in Latin America: "Studying Whitman in the poetry of Hispanic America is like searching for the footprints of a ghost that can be felt everywhere but is nowhere to be seen." ①

Song of Myself②

I

I celebrate myself, and sing myself,
And what I assume you shall assume,
For every atom belonging to me as good belongs to you.

I loafe③ and invite my soul,
I lean and loafe at my ease observing a spear of summer grass.

My tongue, every atom of my blood, form'd from this soil, this air,
Born here of parents born here from parents the same, and their parents the same,
I, now thirty-seven years old in perfect health begin,
Hoping to cease not till death.

Creeds④ and schools in abeyance,
Retiring back a while sufficed at what they are, but never forgotten,
I harbor for good or bad, I permit to speak at every hazard⑤,
Nature without check with original energy.

II

Houses and rooms are full of perfumes, the shelves are crowded with perfumes,
I breathe the fragrance myself, and know it and like it,
The distillation⑥ would intoxicate me also, but I shall not let it.

---

① Ezra Greenspan ed. *The Cambridge Companion to Walt Whitman*, Cambridge University Press, 1997, p. 208.

② 译文参见本书第 259 至 261 页。

③ loafe: loaf.

④ creed [kriːd] *n.* a system of belief, principles, or opinions (信条)。

⑤ hazard [ˈhæzəd] *n.* a chance of being injured or harmed; danger (冒险;危险)。

⑥ distillation [ˌdɪstɪˈleɪʃən] *n.* the evaporation and subsequent collection of a liquid by condensation as a means of purification (蒸馏;精髓)。

The atmosphere is not a perfume, it has no taste of the distillation, it is odorless,
It is for my mouth forever, I am in love with it,
I will go to the bank by the wood and become undisguised and naked,
I am mad for it to be in contact with me.

The smoke of my own breath,
Echoes, ripples, and buzzed whispers, loveroot, silkthread, crotch and vine,
My respiration[①] and inspiration, the beating of my heart, the passing of blood and air through my lungs,
The sniff of green leaves and dry leaves, and of the shore and darkcolored sea-rocks, and of hay in the barn,
The sound of the belched words of my voice loosed to the eddies of the wind,

A few light kisses, a few embraces, reaching around of arms,
The play of shine and shade on the trees as the supple boughs wag,
The delight alone or in the rush of the streets, or along the fields and hill-sides,
The feeling of health, the full-noon trill, the song of me rising from bed and meeting the sun.

Have you reckoned a thousand acres much? Have you reckoned the earth much?
Have you practiced so long to learn to read?
Have you felt so proud to get at the meaning of poems?

Stop this day and night with me and you shall possess the origin of all poems,
You shall possess the good of the earth and sun (there are millions of suns left,)
You shall no longer take things at second or third hand, nor look through the eyes of the dead, nor feed on the specters in books,
You shall not look through my eyes either, nor take things from me,
You shall listen to all sides and filter them from yourself.

LIII

The spotted hawk swoops by and accuses me, he complains of my gab and my loitering.

I too am not a bit tamed, I too am untranslatable,

---

① respiration [ˌrespɪˈreɪʃən] *n.* the act or process of inhaling and exhaling; breathing (呼吸;呼吸作用)。

I sound my barbaric yawp[①] over the roofs of the world.

The last scud of day holds back for me,
It flings my likeness after the rest and true as any on the shadow'd wilds,
It coaxes me to the vapor and the dusk.

I depart as air, I shake my white locks at the runaway sun,
I effuse my flesh in eddies[②], and drift it in lacy jags.

I bequeath myself to the dirt to grow from the grass I love,
If you want me again look for me under your boot-soles.

You will hardly know who I am or what I mean,
But I shall be good health to you nevertheless,
And filter and fibre your blood.

Failing to fetch me at first keep encouraged,
Missing me one place search another,
I stop somewhere waiting for you.

---

① yawp [jɔːp; jɑːp] *n.* sharp cry（大声叫嚷）。

② eddy [ˈedi] *n.* a current, as of water or air, moving contrary to the direction of the main current（漩涡）。

Chapter Seven 19th-Century Literature (Ⅰ)

Ⅰ. Introduction

The 19th-century Western literature can be divided clearly into two periods: the Romantic period and the realistic period.

From about 1790 to 1830 was the Romantic period, and the basic achievement of literature is Romantic poetry. The major Romantics (Wordsworth, Coleridge, Keats, Shelley, Byron and Blake) shared an interest in the individual and the imagination, as well as having a heroic notion of the function of the poet.

The Realistic period (critical realism) began at about 1830, and lasted till the turn of the century. And the basic achievements of literature are prose works, including novels, novelettes and short stories.

Besides Romanticism and critical realism, 19th-century literature involves many other trends or schools, such as aestheticism and modernism in the fin-de-siecle world.

Just before the 20th century dawned, the aesthetic movement previewed many of the features of the modernism to come. They rejected the Victorian tradition, and adopted "art for art's sake" as their basic creed.

The main characteristics of critical realism are as follows:

1. Objectivity. One of the differences between Romantic literature and realistic literature is the subjectivity of the former and the objectivity of the latter in style of writing. Critical realists concentrated on faithful representation of social reality.

2. Characterization. The realistic writers paid attention to typical characters and put emphasis on psychological motivations. Characters in their novels are presented by the means of description, through their actions, speeches, thoughts and verisimilitude of details.

3. Typical social background. One of the aims of the critical realistic writers was the objective description of the representative characters under typical social circumstances.

4. Critical attitude. Critical realistic writers criticized the capitalist society from the humanistic perspective. They provided a vivid picture of the realistic world, exposed the social contradictions and sharply criticized the corruption and ugliness of the bourgeois world. At the same time, they were angry with the widespread misery, poverty and

injustice and showed profound sympathy for the masses.

The literary achievements of this period are mainly novels, represented by novelists in France, Russia, England and America. In this chapter, the literary achivements in France and Russia will be discussed.

French Literature

The 50 years between 1830 and 1880 witnessed enormous changes in the shape of the novel as it was molded by a succession of innovators. French literature of this period was represented by such great writers as Hugo, Stendhal, Balzac, and Zola.

Stendhal portrayed the dominant role of passion as a motivating force in life in his great novel, *The Red and the Black* (1830).

Victor Hugo, in his evocation of medieval Parisian life, *The Hunchback of Notre Dame* (1831), used the Romantic style. His *Les Misérables* (1862), recounting the redemption of a convict emerging from a low caste, successfully merged high drama with meditation on the social morality.

The colossus of the 19th-century French novelists, however, is Balzac, whose multivolume masterpiece, multivolume *Human Comedy* (1842～48), encompassing more than 2,000 characters from almost every walk of life and sweeping imaginatively over 40 years of French history, brilliantly delineates an age of tumultuous social upheavals. His genius for story-telling, together with his emphasis on details, bring out many a wonderful picture of man and society.

Russian Literature

The 19th century is the most important century for Russian literature. Several important events took place during this century in Russia. These events include:

1. The Patriotic War against Napoléon in 1812. The Patriotic War led to the formation of a strengthened national identity that would have great effect on Russian patriotism and the patriotic movement in the 19th century.

2. The uprising of the Decembrists in 1825. Decembrists, members of secret revolutionary societies, led the uprising of Dec. 1825, in St. Petersburg, to rebel against Czar Nicholas Ⅰ.

3. The serfdom reform in 1861. During the first half of the century, Russian peasants were still called "serfs", and treated as the property of their feudal masters. Russian serfs gained their freedom in 1861.

Even at the beginning of the 19th century, Russian literature still hopelessly lagged behind other Europe nations and it is during the 19th century that Russian literature developed rapidly and established itself as the peak of world literature. Many outstanding writers emerged, such as Alexander Pushkin, Ivan Turgenev, Leo Tolstoy, Fyodor Dostoyevsky and many others.

Ⅱ. Stendhal

Stendhal was the pen name of Marie-Henri Beyle (1783～1842), who was born in Grenoble, France. He was one of the most original French writers in the first half of the 19th century, who played a major role in the development of the modern novel.

Known for his acute analysis of his characters' psychology in his two novels *The Red and the Black* (1830) and *The Charterhouse of Parma* (1839), he is considered one of the earliest and foremost practitioners of realism.

Today, Stendhal's works attract attention due to their ironic and psychological and historical dimensions.

The novel *The Red and the Black* is considered as the first realistic novel in the history of French literature. It is a historical psychological novel in two volumes, depicting the attempts the romantic protagonist named Julien Sorel to rise socially beyond his humble origin with a combination of talent and hard work, deception and hypocrisy.

The Red and the Black[①]

(Excerpt)

An hour later, a footman[②] handed Julien a letter; it was nothing less than a declaration of love.

"The style is not unduly affected," he said to himself, seeking by literary observations to contain the joy that was contorting his features and forcing him to laugh in spite of himself.

"And so I," he suddenly exclaimed, his excitement being too strong to be held in check, "I, a poor peasant, have received a declaration of love from a great lady!

"As for myself, I have not done badly," he went on, controlling his joy as far as was possible, "I have succeeded in preserving the dignity of my character. I have never said that I was in love." He began to study the shapes of her letters; Mademoiselle de La Mole wrote in a charming little English hand. He required some physical occupation to take his mind from a joy which was bordering on delirium[③].

"Your departure obliges me to speak ... It would be beyond my endurance not to see you any more."

A sudden thought occurred to strike Julien as a discovery, interrupt the examination

---

① 选自《红与黑》第四十三章，译文参见本书第 261 至 262 页。

② footman [ˈfʊtmən] *n.* male servant (男仆)。

③ delirium [dɪˈlɪriəm] *n.* insanity (精神狂乱)。

that he was making of Mathilde's letter, and intensify his joy. "I am preferred to the Marquis de Croisenois," he cried, "I, who never say anything that is not serious! And he is so handsome! He wears moustaches, a charming uniform; he always manages to say, just at the right moment, something witty and clever."

It was an exquisite moment for Julien; he roamed about the garden, mad with happiness.

Later, he went upstairs to his office, and sent in his name to the Marquis de La Mole, who fortunately had not gone out. He had no difficulty in proving to him, by showing him various marked papers that had arrived from Normandy, that the requirements of his employer's lawsuits there obliged him to postpone his departure for Languedoc①.

"I am very glad you are not going," the Marquis said to him, when they had finished their business, "I like to see you." Julien left the room; this speech disturbed him.

"And I am going to seduce his daughter! To render impossible, perhaps, that marriage with the Marquis de Croisenois, which is the bright spot in his future: if he is not made Duke, at least his daughter will be entitled to a tabouret." Julien thought of starting for Languedoc in spite of Mathilde's letter, in spite of the explanation he had given the Marquis. This virtuous impulse soon faded.

"How generous I am," he said to himself; "I, a plebeian②, to feel pity for a family of such high rank! I, whom the Duc de Chaulnes calls a domestic! How does the Marquis increase his vast fortune? By selling national securities, when he hears at the Chateau that there is to be the threat of a Coup d' Etat next day. And I, cast down to the humblest rank by a stepmotherly Providence, I, whom Providence has endowed with a noble heart and not a thousand francs of income, that is to say not enough for my daily bread, literally speaking, not enough for my daily bread; am I to refuse a pleasure that is offered me? A limpid③ spring which wells up to quench my thirst in the burning desert of mediocrity④ over which I trace my painful course! Faith, I am no such fool; everyone for himself in this desert of selfishness which is called life."

And he reminded himself of several disdainful glances aimed at him by Madame de La Mole, and especially by the ladies, her friends.

The pleasure of triumphing over the Marquis de Croisenois completed the rout of this lingering trace of virtue.

"How I should love to make him angry!" said Julien; "with what assurance would I now thrust at him with my sword." And he struck a sweeping blow at the air. "Until now, I was a smug, basely profiting by a trace of courage. After this letter, I am his

---

① Languedoc [lɔŋgə'dɔk] *n.* 郎格多克（古时法国南部一省）。

② plebeian [plɪ'biən] *n.* common man（平民；庶民）。

③ limpid ['lɪmpɪd] *adj.* clear and transparent（清澈的）。

④ mediocrity [ˌmiːdɪ'ɔkrɪti] *n.* ordinariness; insignificance（平常；平庸）。

equal."

"Yes," he said to himself with an infinite delight, dwelling on the words, "our merits, the Marquis's and mine, have been weighed, and the poor carpenter from the Jura wins the day."

"Good!" he cried, "here is the signature to my reply ready found. Do not go and imagine, Mademoiselle de La Mole, that I am forgetting my station. I shall make you realise and feel that it is for the son of a carpenter that you are betraying a descendant of the famous Guy de Croisenois, who followed Saint Louis on his Crusade."

Julien was unable to contain his joy. He was obliged to go down to the garden. His room, in which he had locked himself up, seemed too confined a space for him to breathe in.

"I, a poor peasant from the Jura," he kept on repeating, "I, I condemned always to wear this dismal black coat! Alas, twenty years ago, I should have worn uniform like them! In those days a man of my sort was either killed, or a General at six and thirty." The letter, which he kept tightly clasped in his hand, gave him the bearing and pose of a hero. "Nowadays, it is true, with the said black coat, at the age of forty, a man has emoluments of one hundred thousand francs and the Blue Riband, like the Bishop of Beauvais."

"Oh, well!" he said to himself, laughing like Mephistopheles, "I have more sense than they; I know how to choose the uniform of my generation." And he felt an intensification① of his ambition and of his attachment to the clerical habit. "How many Cardinals② have there been of humbler birth than mine, who have risen to positions of government! My fellow-countryman Granvelle, for instance."

Tr. by C. K. Scott Moncrieff

Ⅲ. Honoré de Balzac

Honoré de Balzac (1799～1850), a great French novelist, was born in Tours into a family which had struggled to achieve respectability.

Balzac's huge production of novels and short stories are collected under the name *The Human Comedy*, originated from Dante's *Divine Comedy*, which presents a panorama of French life in the years after the fall of Napoléon Bonaparte in 1815.

Due to his keen observation of details and unfiltered representation of society, Balzac is regarded as one of the founders of critical realism in European literature. His writing

---

① intensification [ɪnˌtensɪfɪˈkeɪʃən] *n.* the action that makes something stronger or more extreme (激烈化)。

② cardinal [ˈkɑːdɪnəl] *n.* a high church official, ranking just below the pope (红衣主教)。

influenced many famous authors, including the novelists Marcel Proust, Émile Zola, Charles Dickens, and Gustave Flaubert.

Father Goriot (1835) is widely considered Balzac's representative work. It is a pessimistic study of the bourgeois society after the French Revolution. It tells the intertwined stories of Rastignac, an ambitious but penniless young man, and old Goriot, a father who sacrifices everything for his children.

Father Goriot①

(Excerpt)

"Oh! Is that her father?" the law student continued, aghast②.

"Yes, certainly; the old man had two daughters; he dotes on them, so to speak, though they will scarcely acknowledge him."

"Didn't the second daughter marry a banker with a German name?" the Vicomtesse③ asked, turning to Mme. de Langeais, "a Baron de Nucingen? And her name is Delphine, is it not? Isn't she a fair-haired woman who has a side-box at the Opera? She comes sometimes to the Bouffons, and laughs loudly to attract attention."

The Duchess smiled and said:

"I wonder at you, dear. Why do you take so much interest in people of that kind? One must have been as madly in love as Restaud was, to be infatuated with Mlle. Anastasie and her flour sacks. Oh! he will not find her a good bargain! She is in M. de Trailles' hands, and he will ruin her."

"And they do not acknowledge their father!" Eugene repeated.

"Oh! Well, yes, their father, the father, a father," replied the Vicomtesse, "a kind father who gave them each five or six hundred thousand francs, it is said, to secure their happiness by marrying them well; while he only kept eight or ten thousand livres a year for himself, thinking that his daughters would always be his daughters, thinking that in them he would live his life twice over again, that in their houses he should find two homes, where he would be loved and looked up to, and made much of. And in two years' time both his sons-in-law had turned him out of their houses as if he were one of the lowest outcasts."

Tears came into Eugene's eyes. He was still under the spell of youthful beliefs, he had just left home, pure and sacred feelings had been stirred within him, and this was his first day on the battlefield of civilization in Paris. Genuine feeling was so infectious that for a moment the three looked at each other in silence.

---

① 译文参见本书第 262 至 263 页。

② aghast[əˈɡɑːst] *adj.* struck by shock, terror, or amazement (惊骇的;恐怖的)。

③ vicomtesse [vɪˈktes] *n.* 子爵夫人。

"*Eh, mon Dieu*!" said Mme. de Langeais; "yes, it seems very horrible, and yet we see such things every day ... I can explain how it all came about in the old vermicelli maker's case. I think I recollect that Foriot —"

"Goriot, madame."

"Yes, that Moriot was once President of his Section during the Revolution. He was in the secret of the famous scarcity of grain, and laid the foundation of his fortune in those days by selling flour for ten times its cost. He had as much flour as he wanted. My grandmother's steward sold him immense quantities. No doubt Noriot shared the plunder with the Committee of Public Salvation, as that sort of person always did ... He settled one of his daughters under Restaud's roof, and grafted the other into the Nucingen family tree, the Baron de Nucingen being a rich banker who had turned Royalist ... As for me, dear, I believe that love has second-sight: poor Ninety-three; his heart must have bled. He saw that his daughters were ashamed of him, that if they loved their husbands his visits must make mischief. So he immolated himself. He made the sacrifice because he was a father; he went into voluntary exile. His daughters were satisfied, so he thought that he had done the best thing he could ... Their father had given them all he had. For twenty years he had given his whole heart to them; then, one day, he gave them all his fortune too. The lemon was squeezed; the girls left the rest in the gutter."

"The world is very base," said the Vicomtesse, plucking at the threads of her shawl. She did not raise her head as she spoke; the words that Mme. de Langeais had meant for her in the course of her story had cut her to the quick.

"Base? Oh, no," answered the Duchess, "the world goes its own way, that is all. If I speak in this way, it is only to show that I am not duped by it. I think as you do," she said, pressing the Vicomtesse's hand. "The world is a slough①; let us try to live on the heights above it."

She rose to her feet and kissed Mme. de Beauseant on the forehead as she said: "You look very charming today, dear. I have never seen such a lovely color in your cheeks before."

Then she went out with a slight inclination of the head to the cousin.

"Father Goriot is sublime!" said Eugene to himself, as he remembered how he had watched his neighbor work the silver vessel into a shapeless mass that night.

Mme. de Beauseant did not hear him; she was absorbed in her own thoughts. For several minutes the silence remained unbroken till the law student became almost paralyzed with embarrassment, and was equally afraid to go or stay or speak a word.

"The world is basely ungrateful and ill-natured," said the Vicomtesse at last. "No sooner does a trouble befall you than a friend is ready to bring the tidings and to probe your heart with the point of a dagger while calling on you to admire the handle. Epigrams

---

① slough [slau] *n.* a depression or hollow, usually filled with deep mud or mire (泥沼)。

and sarcasms already! Ah! I will defend myself!"

She raised her head like the great lady that she was, and lightnings flashed from her proud eyes.

"Ah!" she said, as she saw Eugene, "are you there?"

"Still," he said piteously.

"Well, then, M. de Rastignac, deal with the world as it deserves. You are determined to succeed? I will help you. You shall sound the depths of corruption in woman; you shall measure the extent of man's pitiful vanity. Deeply as I am versed in such learning, there were pages in the book of life that I had not read. Now I know all. The more cold-blooded your calculations, the further you will go. Strike ruthlessly; you will be feared. Men and women for you must be nothing more than post-horses; take a fresh relay, and leave the last to drop by the roadside; in this way you will reach the goal of your ambition. You will be nothing here, you see, unless a woman interests herself in you; and she must be young and wealthy, and a woman of the world. Yet, if you have a heart, lock it carefully away like a treasure; do not let any one suspect it, or you will be lost; you would cease to be the executioner, you would take the victim's place. And if ever you should love, never let your secret escape you! Trust no one until you are very sure of the heart to which you open your heart. Learn to mistrust every one; take every precaution for the sake of the love which does not exist as yet ..."

Tr. by Ellen Marriage

Ⅳ. Guy de Maupassant

Guy de Maupassant (1850～1893) is considered one of the fathers of the modern short story.

In 1869, Maupassant started to study law in Paris, but soon, at the age of 20, he volunteered to serve in the army during the Franco-Prussian War. Between the year 1872 and 1880 Maupassant became a civil servant, first at the ministry of maritime affairs, then at the ministry of education.

In 1880 he published what is considered his first masterpiece, *Boule de Suif* (*Ball of Fat*), which met with an instant and tremendous success. Flaubert characterized it as "a masterpiece that will endure".

During the 1880s Maupassant created nearly three hundred short stories, six novels, three travel books, and one volume of verse. His tales are marked by objectivity, highly controlled style, and sometimes by sheer comedy. Usually they are built by simple episodes from everyday life, which reveal the weaknesses of human nature.

The Necklace is one of Maupassant's best short stories. It's famous for its tight plotting, wealth of details, keen social commentary, and surprising ending.

The Necklace[①]

The girl was one of those pretty and charming young creatures who sometimes are born, as if by a slip of fate, into a family of clerks. She had no dowry[②], no expectations, no way of being known, understood, loved, married by any rich and distinguished man; so she let herself be married to a little clerk of the Ministry of Public Instruction.

She dressed plainly because she could not dress well, but she was unhappy as if she had really fallen from a higher station; since with women there is neither caste nor rank, for beauty, grace and charm take the place of family and birth. Natural ingenuity, instinct for what is elegant, a supple mind are their sole hierarchy, and often make of women of the people the equals of the very greatest ladies.

Mathilde suffered ceaselessly, feeling herself born to enjoy all delicacies and all luxuries. She was distressed at the poverty of her dwelling, at the bareness of the walls, at the shabby chairs, the ugliness of the curtains. All those things, of which another woman of her rank would never even have been conscious, tortured her and made her angry. The sight of the little Breton peasant who did her humble housework aroused in her despairing regrets and bewildering dreams. She thought of silent antechambers[③] hung with Oriental tapestry[④], illumined by tall bronze candelabra[⑤], and of two great footmen in knee breeches who sleep in the big armchairs, made drowsy by the oppressive heat of the stove. She thought of long reception halls hung with ancient silk, of the dainty cabinets containing priceless curiosities and of the little coquettish perfumed reception rooms made for chatting at five o'clock with intimate friends, with men famous and sought after, whom all women envy and whose attention they all desire.

When she sat down to dinner, before the round table covered with a tablecloth in use three days, opposite her husband, who uncovered the soup tureen and declared with a delighted air, "Ah, the good soup! I don't know anything better than that," she thought of dainty dinners, of shining silverware, of tapestry that peopled the walls with ancient personages and with strange birds flying in the midst of a fairy forest; and she thought of delicious dishes served on marvellous plates and of the whispered gallantries to which you listen with a sphinxlike smile while you are eating the pink meat of a trout[⑥] or the wings of

---

① 译文参见本书第 263 至 266 页。

② dowry [ˈdaʊəri] *n.* money or property brought by a bride to her husband at marriage (嫁妆)。

③ antechamber [ˈæntɪtʃeɪmbə] *n.* a smaller room serving as an entryway into a larger room (接待室；前厅)。

④ tapestry [ˈtæpɪstri] *n.* a heavy cloth woven with rich, often varicolored designs or scenes, usually hung on walls for decoration and sometimes used to cover furniture (织锦；挂毯)。

⑤ candelabra [ˌkændɪˈlɑːbrə] *n.* a candelabrum (枝状大烛台)。

⑥ trout [traʊt] *n.* 鲑鱼。

a quail.

She had no gowns, no jewels, nothing. And she loved nothing but that. She felt made for that. She would have liked so much to please, to be envied, to be charming, to be sought after.

She had a friend, a former schoolmate at the convent①, who was rich, and whom she did not like to go to see any more because she felt so sad when she came home.

But one evening her husband reached home with a triumphant air and holding a large envelope in his hand.

"There," said he, "there is something for you."

She tore the paper quickly and drew out a printed card which bore these words:

The Minister of Public Instruction and Madame Georges Ramponneau request the honor of M. and Madame Loisel's company at the palace of the Ministry on Monday evening, January 18th.

Instead of being delighted, as her husband had hoped, she threw the invitation on the table crossly, muttering:

"What do you wish me to do with that?"

"Why, my dear, I thought you would be glad. You never go out, and this is such a fine opportunity. I had great trouble to get it. Every one wants to go; it is very select, and they are not giving many invitations to clerks. The whole official world will be there."

She looked at him with an irritated② glance and said impatiently:

"And what do you wish me to put on my back?"

He had not thought of that. He stammered:

"Why, the gown you go to the theatre in. It looks very well to me."

He stopped, distracted, seeing that his wife was weeping. Two great tears ran slowly from the corners of her eyes toward the corners of her mouth.

"What's the matter? What's the matter?" he asked.

By a violent effort she conquered her grief and replied in a calm voice, while she wiped her wet cheeks:

"Nothing. Only I have no gown, and, therefore, I can't go to this ball. Give your card to some colleague whose wife is better equipped than I am."

He was in despair. He resumed:

"Come, let us see, Mathilde. How much would it cost, a suitable gown, which you could use on other occasions — something very simple?"

She reflected several seconds, making her calculations and wondering also what sum she could ask without drawing on herself an immediate refusal and a frightened exclamation from

---

① convent ['kɔnvənt] *n.* a community, especially of nuns, bound by vows to a religious life under a superior (女修道会;女修道院)。

② irritated ['ɪrɪteɪtɪd] *adj.* indignant; angry (恼怒的;生气的)。

the economical clerk.

Finally she replied hesitating:

"I don't know exactly, but I think I could manage it with four hundred francs."

He grew a little pale, because he was laying aside just that amount to buy a gun and treat himself to a little shooting next summer on the plain of Nanterre, with several friends who went to shoot larks there of a Sunday.

But he said:

"Very well. I will give you four hundred francs. And try to have a pretty gown."

The day of the ball drew near and Madame Loisel seemed sad, uneasy, anxious. Her frock was ready, however. Her husband said to her one evening:

"What is the matter? Come, you have seemed very queer these last three days."

And she answered:

"It annoys me not to have a single piece of jewelry, not a single ornament, nothing to put on. I shall look poverty-stricken. I would almost rather not go at all."

"You might wear natural flowers," said her husband. "They're very stylish at this time of year. For ten francs you can get two or three magnificent roses."

She was not convinced.

"No; there's nothing more humiliating[①] than to look poor among other women who are rich."

"How stupid you are!" her husband cried, "Go look up your friend, Madame Forestier, and ask her to lend you some jewels. You're intimate enough with her to do that."

She uttered a cry of joy:

"True! I never thought of it."

The next day she went to her friend and told her of her distress.

Madame Forestier went to a wardrobe with a mirror, took out a large jewel box, brought it back, opened it and said to Madame Loisel:

"Choose, my dear."

She saw first some bracelets, then a pearl necklace, then a Venetian gold cross set with precious stones, of admirable workmanship. She tried on the ornaments before the mirror, hesitated and could not make up her mind to part with them, to give them back. She kept asking:

"Haven't you any more?"

"Why, yes. Look further; I don't know what you like."

Suddenly she discovered, in a black satin box, a superb diamond necklace, and her heart throbbed with an immoderate desire. Her hands trembled as she took it. She fastened it round her throat, outside her high-necked waist, and was lost in ecstasy at her

---

① humiliating [hjuːˈmɪlieɪtɪŋ] *adj*. disgracing (羞辱性的)。

reflection in the mirror.

Then she asked, hesitating, filled with anxious doubt:

"Will you lend me this, only this?"

"Why, yes, certainly."

She threw her arms round her friend's neck, kissed her passionately, then fled with her treasure.

The night of the ball arrived. Madame Loisel was a great success. She was prettier than any other woman present, elegant, graceful, smiling and wild with joy. All the men looked at her, asked her name, sought to be introduced. All the attaches of the Cabinet wished to waltz with her. She was remarked by the minister himself.

She danced with rapture, with passion, intoxicated① by pleasure, forgetting all in the triumph of her beauty, in the glory of her success, in a sort of cloud of happiness comprised of all this homage, admiration, these awakened desires and of that sense of triumph which is so sweet to woman's heart.

She left the ball about four o'clock in the morning. Her husband had been sleeping since midnight in a little deserted anteroom with three other gentlemen whose wives were enjoying the ball.

He threw over her shoulders the wraps he had brought, the modest wraps of common life, the poverty of which contrasted with the elegance of the ball dress. She felt this and wished to escape so as not to be remarked by the other women, who were enveloping themselves in costly furs.

Loisel held her back, saying: "Wait a bit. You will catch cold outside. I will call a cab."

But she did not listen to him and rapidly descended the stairs. When they reached the street they could not find a carriage and began to look for one, shouting after the cabmen passing at a distance.

They went toward the Seine in despair, shivering with cold. At last they found on the quay one of those ancient night cabs which, as though they were ashamed to show their shabbiness during the day, are never seen round Paris until after dark.

It took them to their dwelling in the Rue des Martyrs, and sadly they mounted the stairs to their flat. All was ended for her. As to him, he reflected that he must be at the ministry at ten o'clock that morning.

She removed her wraps before the glass so as to see herself once more in all her glory. But suddenly she uttered a cry. She no longer had the necklace around her neck!

"What is the matter with you?" demanded her husband, already half undressed.

She turned distractedly toward him.

---

① intoxicated [ɪnˈtɔksɪkeɪtɪd] *adj.* excited by a chemical substance (especially alcohol); impassioned (陶醉的;极其兴奋的)。

"I have — I have — I've lost Madame Forestier's necklace," she cried.

He stood up, bewildered.

"What! — how? Impossible!"

They looked among the folds of her skirt, of her cloak, in her pockets, everywhere, but did not find it.

"You're sure you had it on when you left the ball?" he asked.

"Yes, I felt it in the vestibule① of the minister's house."

"But if you had lost it in the street we should have heard it fall. It must be in the cab."

"Yes, probably. Did you take his number?"

"No. And you — didn't you notice it?"

"No."

They looked, thunderstruck, at each other. At last Loisel put on his clothes.

"I shall go back on foot," said he, "over the whole route, to see whether I can find it."

He went out. She sat waiting on a chair in her ball dress, without strength to go to bed, overwhelmed, without any fire, without a thought.

Her husband returned about seven o'clock. He had found nothing.

He went to police headquarters, to the newspaper offices to offer a reward; he went to the cab companies — everywhere, in fact, whither he was urged by the least spark of hope.

She waited all day, in the same condition of mad fear before this terrible calamity②.

Loisel returned at night with a hollow, pale face. He had discovered nothing.

"You must write to your friend," said he, "that you have broken the clasp of her necklace and that you are having it mended. That will give us time to turn round."

She wrote at his dictation.

At the end of a week they had lost all hope. Loisel, who had aged five years, declared:

"We must consider how to replace that ornament."

The next day they took the box that had contained it and went to the jeweler whose name was found within. He consulted his books.

"It was not I, madame, who sold that necklace; I must simply have furnished the case."

Then they went from jeweler to jeweler, searching for a necklace like the other,

---

① vestibule [ˈvestɪbjuːl] *n.* a small entrance hall or passage between the outer door and the interior of a house or building (门廊;前厅)。

② calamity [kəˈlæmɪti] *n.* a disaster (灾难;不幸事件)。

trying to recall it, both sick with chagrin[①] and grief.

They found, in a shop at the Palais Royal, a string of diamonds that seemed to them exactly like the one they had lost. It was worth forty thousand francs. They could have it for thirty-six.

So they begged the jeweler not to sell it for three days yet. And they made a bargain[②] that he should buy it back for thirty-four thousand francs, in case they should find the lost necklace before the end of February.

Loisel possessed eighteen thousand francs which his father had left him. He would borrow the rest.

He did borrow, asking a thousand francs of one, five hundred of another, five louis here, three louis there. He gave notes, took up ruinous obligations, dealt with usurers[③] and all the race of lenders. He compromised all the rest of his life, risked signing a note without even knowing whether he could meet it; and, frightened by the trouble yet to come, by the black misery that was about to fall upon him, by the prospect of all the physical privations and moral tortures that he was to suffer, he went to get the new necklace, laying upon the jeweler's counter thirty-six thousand francs.

When Madame Loisel took back the necklace Madame Forestier said to her with a chilly manner:

"You should have returned it sooner; I might have needed it."

She did not open the case, as her friend had so much feared. If she had detected the substitution, what would she have thought, what would she have said? Would she not have taken Madame Loisel for a thief?

Thereafter Madame Loisel knew the horrible existence of the needy. She bore her part, however, with sudden heroism. That dreadful debt must be paid. She would pay it. They dismissed their servant; they changed their lodgings; they rented a garret[④] under the roof.

She came to know what heavy housework meant and the odious cares of the kitchen. She washed the dishes, using her dainty fingers and rosy nails on greasy pots and pans. She washed the soiled linen, the shirts and the dishcloths, which she dried upon a line; she carried the slops down to the street every morning and carried up the water, stopping for breath at every landing. And dressed like a woman of the people, she went to the fruiterer, the grocer, the butcher, a basket on her arm, bargaining, meeting with impertinence, defending her miserable money, sou[⑤] by sou.

---

① chagrin [ˈʃægrɪn] *n.* a keen feeling of mental unease（懊恼）。

② bargain [ˈbɑːgɪn] *n.* an agreement（契约；合同）。

③ usurer [ˈjuːʒərə] *n.* one who lends money at an exorbitant or unlawfully high rate（高利贷者）。

④ garret [ˈgærət] *n.* a room on the top floor of a house, typically under a pitched roof（阁楼）。

⑤ sou [suː] *n.* 苏（昔日法国之一种铜币）。

Every month they had to meet some notes, renew others, obtain more time.

Her husband worked evenings, making up a tradesman's accounts, and late at night he often copied manuscript for five sous a page.

This life lasted ten years.

At the end of ten years they had paid everything, everything, with the rates of usury and the accumulations of the compound interest.

Madame Loisel looked old now. She had become the woman of impoverished households — strong and hard and rough. With frowsy① hair, skirts askew② and red hands, she talked loud while washing the floor with great swishes of water. But sometimes, when her husband was at the office, she sat down near the window and she thought of that gay evening of long ago, of that ball where she had been so beautiful and so admired.

What would have happened if she had not lost that necklace? Who knows? who knows? How strange and changeful is life! How small a thing is needed to make or ruin us!

But one Sunday, having gone to take a walk in the Champs Elysees to refresh herself after the labors of the week, she suddenly perceived a woman who was leading a child. It was Madame Forestier, still young, still beautiful, still charming.

Madame Loisel felt moved. Should she speak to her? Yes, certainly. And now that she had paid, she would tell her all about it. Why not?

She went up.

"Good-day, Jeanne."

The other, astonished to be familiarly addressed by this plain good-wife, did not recognize her at all and stammered:

"But — madame! — I do not know — You must have mistaken."

"No. I am Mathilde Loisel."

Her friend uttered a cry.

"Oh, my poor Mathilde! How you are changed!"

"Yes, I have had a pretty hard life, since I last saw you, and great poverty — and that because of you!"

"Of me! How so?"

"Do you remember that diamond necklace you lent me to wear at the ministerial ball?"

"Yes. Well?"

"Well, I lost it."

"What do you mean? You brought it back."

"I brought you back another exactly like it. And it has taken us ten years to pay for

---

① frowsy [ˈfrauzi] *adj.* not neat and tidy (不整洁的)。

② askew [əˈskjuː] *adv.* to one side; awry (歪斜地)。

it. You can understand that it was not easy for us, for us who had nothing. At last it is ended, and I am very glad."

Madame Forestier had stopped.

"You say that you bought a necklace of diamonds to replace mine?"

"Yes. You never noticed it, then! They were very similar."

And she smiled with a joy that was at once proud and ingenuous①.

Madame Forestier, deeply moved, took her hands.

"Oh, my poor Mathilde! Why, my necklace was paste②! It was worth at most only five hundred francs!"

Ⅴ. Leo Tolstoy

Leo Tolstoy (1828～1910) was born at Yasnaya Polyana, his family's estate, in Russia's Tula Province.

Tolstoy was educated at home by German and French tutors. In 1844 he entered Kazan University. Planning on a diplomatic career, he entered the Faculty of Oriental Languages. Finding these studies too demanding, he switched two years later to studying law. He left the university in 1847 without taking his degree.

Tolstoy returned to Yasnaya Polyana, determined to become a model farmer. When he served in the army, he began to write the autobiographical sketch *Childhood* (1852), and it was published with a great success.

Leo Tolstoy is considered as one of Russia's greatest writers, best known for novels *War and Peace* (1869), *Anna Karenina* (1873— 1977), and *Resurrection* (1899).

War and Peace represents a high point in the history of world literature. Balls and battles, birth and death, all are described in amazing detail. In this book the European realistic novel, with its attention to social structures, exact description, and psychological rendering, finds its most complete expression.

The novel *Anna Karenina* was based partly on events that had occurred on a neighboring estate, where a nobleman's rejected mistress had thrown herself under a train. It tells parallel stories of an adulterous woman trapped by the conventions and falsities of society and of a landowner's philosophical and social search for reform.

The following selection is taken from Chapter 29, Book Two of the novel *Anna Karenina*.

---

① ingenuous [ɪnˈdʒenjuəs] *adj.* straightforward; frank (自然的；直率的)。

② paste [peɪst] *n.* artificial gem (人造宝石)。

Anna Karenina[①]

(Excerpt)

Everyone was loudly expressing disapprobation[②], everyone was repeating a phrase someone had uttered: "The lions and gladiators[③] will be the next thing," and everyone was feeling horrified; so that when Vronsky fell to the ground, and Anna moaned aloud, there was nothing very much out of the way in it. But afterward a change came over Anna's face which really went beyond decorum[④]. She utterly lost her head. She began fluttering like a caged bird, at one moment wanting to get up and move away, and at the next turning to Betsy.

"Let us go, let us go!" she said.

But Betsy did not hear her. She was bending down, talking to a general who had come up to her.

Alexei Alexandrovich went up to Anna and courteously[⑤] offered her his arm.

"Let us go, if you like," he said in French, but Anna was listening to the general and did not notice her husband.

"He's broken his leg too, so they say," the general was saying, "This surpasses everything."

Without answering her husband, Anna lifted her opera glass and gazed toward the place where Vronsky had fallen; but it was so far off, and there was such a crowd of people about it, that she could make out nothing. She put down the opera glass, and would have moved away, but at that moment an officer galloped[⑥] up and made some announcement to the Czar. Anna craned forward, listening.

"Stiva! Stiva!" she cried to her brother.

But her brother did not hear her. Again she would have moved away.

"Once more I offer you my arm if you want to be going," said Alexei Alexandrovich, reaching for her hand.

She drew back from him with aversion[⑦], and without looking at his face answered:

"No, no, leave me alone — I'll stay."

---

① 译文参见本书第 266 至 268 页。

② disapprobation [ˌdɪsæprəʊˈbeɪʃən] *n.* condemnation (非难)。

③ gladiator [ˈglædɪeɪtə] *n.* a person, usually a professional combatant, a captive, or a slave, trained to entertain the public by engaging in mortal combat with another person or a wild animal in the ancient Roman arena (古罗马角斗士;格斗者)。

④ decorum [dɪˈkɔːrəm] *n.* the conventions of polite behavior (礼貌;端庄)。

⑤ courteously [ˈkɜːtjəsli] *adv.* politely (有礼貌地;亲切地)。

⑥ gallop [ˈgæləp] *vi.* to move or progress swiftly (疾驰;飞奔)。

⑦ aversion [əˈvɜːʃən] *n.* a fixed, intense dislike (厌恶)。

She saw now that from the place of Vronsky's accident an officer was running across the course toward the pavilion. Betsy waved her handkerchief to him. The officer brought the news that the rider was not killed, but that the back of the horse had been broken.

On hearing this Anna sat down hurriedly, and hid her face in her fan. Alexei Alexandrovich saw that she was weeping, and could not control her tears, nor even the sobs that were shaking her bosom. Alexei Alexandrovich stood so as to screen her, giving her time to recover herself.

"For the third time I offer you my arm," he said to her after a short interval, turning to her. Anna gazed at him and did not know what to say. Princess Betsy came to her rescue.

"No, Alexei Alexandrovich; I brought Anna and I promised to take her home," put in Betsy.

"Excuse me, Princess," he said smiling courteously, but looking her very firmly in the face, "but I see that Anna's not very well, and I wish her to come home with me."

Anna looked about her in a frightened way, got up submissively①, and laid her hand on her husband's arm.

"I'll send to him and find out, and let you know," Betsy whispered to her.

As they left the pavilion, Alexei Alexandrovich, as always, talked to those he met, and Anna had, as always, to talk and answer; but she was utterly beside herself, and moved hanging on her husband's arm, as though in a dream.

"Is he killed or not? Is it true? Will he come or not? Shall I see him today?" she was thinking.

She took her seat in her husband's carriage in silence, and in silence drove out of the press of carriages. In spite of all he had seen, Alexei Alexandrovich still did not allow himself to consider his wife's real condition. He merely saw the outward symptoms. He saw that she was behaving unbecomingly②, and considered it his duty to tell her so. But it was very difficult for him not to say more, to tell her nothing but that. He opened his mouth to tell her she had behaved unbecomingly, but he could not help saying something utterly different.

"What an inclination we all have, though, for these cruel spectacles!" he said. "I observe ..."

"Eh? I don't understand," said Anna contemptuously.

He was offended, and at once began to say what he had meant to say.

"I am obliged to tell you ..." he began.

"So now we are to have it out," she thought, and she felt frightened.

"I am obliged to tell you that your behavior has been unbecoming today," he said to

① submissively [səbˈmɪsɪvli] *adv.* obediently（顺从地；服从地）。

② unbecomingly [ˈʌnbɪˈkʌmɪŋli] *adv.* not appropriately（不适当地；不得体地）。

her, in French.

"In what way has my behavior been unbecoming?" she said aloud, turning her head swiftly and looking him straight in the face, not with the bright expression that seemed covering something, but with a look of determination, under which she concealed with difficulty the dismay she was feeling.

"Be careful," he said, pointing to the open window opposite the coachman.

He got up and pulled up the window.

"What did you consider unbecoming?" she repeated.

"The despair you were unable to conceal at the accident to one of the riders."

He waited for her to retort, but she was silent, looking straight before her.

"I have already begged you so to conduct yourself in society that even malicious tongues can find nothing to say against you. There was a time when I spoke of your inward attitude, but I am not speaking of that now. Now I speak only of your external attitude. You have behaved improperly, and I would wish it not to occur again."

She did not hear half of what he was saying; she felt panic-stricken before him, and was thinking whether it was true that Vronsky was not killed. Was it of him they were speaking when they said the rider was unhurt, but that the back of the horse had been broken? She merely smiled with a forced smile when he finished, and made no reply, because she had not heard what he said. Alexei Alexandrovich had begun to speak boldly, but as he realized plainly what he was speaking of, the dismay she was feeling infected him too. He saw the smile, and a strange misapprehension came over him.

"She is smiling at my suspicions. Yes, she will tell me directly what she told me before; that there is no foundation for my suspicions, that the whole thing is absurd."

At that moment, when the revelation of everything was hanging over him, there was nothing he expected so much as that she would answer mockingly, as before, that his suspicions were absurd and utterly groundless. So terrible to him was what he knew that now he was ready to believe anything. But the expression of her face, scared and gloomy, did not now promise even deception.

"Possibly I was mistaken," said he. "If so, I beg your pardon."

"No, you were not mistaken," she said slowly, looking desperately into his frigid① face. "You were not mistaken. I was in despair, nor could I help being in despair. I am listening to you, but I am thinking of him. I love him, I am his mistress; I can't bear you; I'm afraid of you, and I hate you ... You can do what you like to me."

And dropping back into the corner of the carriage, she broke into sobs, hiding her face in her hands. Alexei Alexandrovich did not stir, and kept looking straight before him. But his whole face suddenly bore the solemn rigidity of the dead, and his expression did not change during the whole time of the drive home. On reaching the house he turned

---

① frigid [ˈfrɪdʒɪd] *adj.* extremely cold (寒冷的;酷寒的)。

his head to her, still with the same expression.

"Very well! But I expect a strict observance[①] of the external forms of propriety till such time." — his voice shook — "as I may take measures to secure my honor, and communicate them to you."

He got out first and helped her to get out. Before the servants he pressed her hand, took his seat in the carriage, and drove back to Petersburg.

Immediately afterward a footman came from Princess Betsy and brought Anna a note.

"I sent to Alexei to find out how he is, and he writes me he is quite well and unhurt, but in despair."

"So he will be here," she thought. "What a good thing I told him all."

She glanced at her watch. She had still three hours to wait, and the memories of their last meeting set her blood in flame.

"My God, how light it is! It's dreadful, but I do love to see his face, and I do love this fantastic light ... My husband! Oh! Yes ... Well, thank God! Everything's at an end with him."

Ⅵ. Anton Chekhov

Anton Chekhov (1860 ~ 1904), the famous Russian short-story writer and playwright, was born in the small seaport of Taganrog, southern Russia. He is considered to be one of the greatest short-story writers in the history of world literature.

Anton Chekhov graduated in 1884 from the Medical School of Moscow University. He practiced as a doctor throughout most of his literary career: "Medicine is my lawful wife," he once said, "and literature is my mistress. When I get fed up with one, I spend the night with the other. Though it is irregular, it is less boring this way, and besides, neither of them loses anything through my infidelity."

As a dramatist, Anton Chekhov produced four classics: *The Cherry Orchard*, *Uncle Vanya*, *The Three Sisters* and *The Seagull*. His best short stories are held in high esteem by writers and critics. In his literary works Anton Chekhov combined the dispassionate attitude of a scientist and doctor with the sensitivity and psychological understanding of an artist.

Vanka

Vanka Zhukov, a boy of nine, who had been for three months apprenticed to Alyahin the shoemaker, was sitting up on Christmas Eve. Waiting till his master and mistress and

---

① observance [əbˈzɜːvəns] *n.* the act of observing a law; custom (遵守;惯例)。

their workmen had gone to the midnight service, he took out of his master's cupboard a bottle of ink and a pen with a rusty nib, and, spreading out a crumpled sheet of paper in front of him, began writing. Before forming the first letter he several times looked round fearfully at the door and the windows, stole a glance at the dark ikon, on both sides of which stretched shelves full of lasts, and heaved a broken sigh. The paper lay on the bench while he knelt before it.

"Dear grandfather, Konstantin Makaritch," he wrote, "I am writing you a letter. I wish you a happy Christmas, and all blessings from God Almighty. I have neither father nor mother, you are the only one left for me."

Vanka raised his eyes to the dark ikon on which the light of his candle was reflected, and vividly recalled his grandfather, Konstantin Makaritch, who was night watchman to a family called Zhivarev. He was a thin but extraordinarily nimble① and lively little old man of sixty-five, with an everlastingly laughing face and drunken eyes. By day he slept in the servants' kitchen, or made jokes with the cooks; at night, wrapped in an ample sheepskin, he walked round the grounds and tapped with his little mallet②. Old Kashtanka and Eel③, so-called on account of his dark colour and his long body like a weasel's④, followed him with hanging heads. This Eel was exceptionally polite and affectionate, and looked with equal kindness on strangers and his own masters, but had not a very good reputation. Under his politeness and meekness was hidden the most Jesuitical cunning. No one knew better how to creep up on occasion and snap at one's legs, to slip into the store-room, or steal a hen from a peasant. His hind legs had been nearly pulled off more than once, twice he had been hanged, every week he was thrashed till he was half dead, but he always revived.

At this moment grandfather was, no doubt, standing at the gate, screwing up his eyes at the red windows of the church, stamping with his high felt boots, and joking with the servants. His little mallet was hanging on his belt. He was clasping his hands, shrugging with the cold, and, with an aged chuckle, pinching first the housemaid, then the cook.

"How about a pinch of snuff?" he was saying, offering the women his snuff-box.

The women would take a sniff and sneeze. Grandfather would be indescribably delighted, go off into a merry chuckle, and cry:

"Tear it off, it has frozen on!"

They give the dogs a sniff of snuff too. Kashtanka sneezes, wriggles her head, and walks away offended. Eel does not sneeze, from politeness, but wags his tail. And the

---

① nimble [ˈnɪmbl] *adj*. quick (敏捷的)。

② mallet [ˈmælɪt] *n*. a short-handled hammer (槌棒)。

③ Eel [iːl] *n*. 鳗鱼(此处是狗的名字)。

④ weasel [ˈwiːzl] *n*. 鼬鼠;黄鼠狼。

weather is glorious. The air is still, fresh, and transparent. The night is dark, but one can see the whole village with its white roofs and coils of smoke coming from the chimneys, the trees silvered with hoar frost, the snowdrifts. The whole sky spangled with gay twinkling stars, and the Milky Way is as distinct as though it had been washed and rubbed with snow for a holiday...

Vanka sighed, dipped his pen, and went on writing:

"And yesterday I had a wigging[①]. The master pulled me out into the yard by my hair, and whacked me with a boot-stretcher because I accidentally fell asleep while I was rocking their brat[②] in the cradle. And a week ago the mistress told me to clean a herring, and I began from the tail end, and she took the herring and thrust its head in my face. The workmen laugh at me and send me to the tavern for vodka, and tell me to steal the master's cucumbers for them, and the master beats me with anything that comes to hand. And there is nothing to eat. In the morning they give me bread, for dinner, porridge, and in the evening, bread again; but as for tea, or soup, the master and mistress gobble it all up themselves. And I am put to sleep in the passage, and when their wretched brat cries I get no sleep at all, but have to rock the cradle. Dear grandfather, show the divine mercy, take me away from here, home to the village. It's more than I can bear. I bow down to your feet, and will pray to God for you for ever, take me away from here or I shall die."

Vanka's mouth worked, he rubbed his eyes with his black fist, and gave a sob.

"I will powder your snuff for you," he went on. "I will pray for you, and if I do anything you can thrash me like Sidor's goat. And if you think I've no job, then I will beg the steward for Christ's sake to let me clean his boots, or I'll go for a shepherd-boy instead of Fedka. Dear grandfather, it is more than I can bear, it's simply no life at all. I wanted to run away to the village, but I have no boots, and I am afraid of the frost. When I grow up big I will take care of you for this, and not let anyone annoy you, and when you die I will pray for the rest of your soul, just as for my mammy's.

"Moscow is a big town. It's all gentlemen's houses, and there are lots of horses, but there are no sheep, and the dogs are not spiteful[③]. The lads here don't go out with the star[④], and they don't let anyone go into the choir, and once I saw in a shop window fishing-hooks for sale, fitted ready with the line and for all sorts of fish, awfully good ones, there was even one hook that would hold a forty-pound sheatfish[⑤]. And I have seen shops where there are guns of all sorts, after the pattern of the master's guns at home, so

---

① wigging [ˈwɪgɪŋ] *n.* a rebuke or reprimand (责备;叱责)。

② brat [bræt] *n.* a child, especially a spoiled or ill-mannered one (乳臭未干的娃娃;被宠坏的或举止粗鲁的小孩)。

③ spiteful [ˈspaɪtfl] *adj.* filled with spite; malicious (怀恨的;恶意的)。

④ 指基督教的习俗:圣诞节前夜,小孩子们举着用箔纸糊的星星走来走去。

⑤ sheatfish [ˈʃiːtfɪʃ] *n.* 鲇鱼。

that I shouldn't wonder if they are a hundred roubles each ... And in the butchers' shops there are grouse and woodcocks and fish and hares, but the shopmen don't say where they shoot them.

"Dear grandfather, when they have the Christmas tree at the big house, get me a gilt walnut, and put it away in the green trunk. Ask the young lady Olga Ignatyevna, say it's for Vanka."

Vanka gave a tremulous sigh, and again stared at the window. He remembered how his grandfather always went into the forest to get the Christmas tree for his master's family, and took his grandson with him. It was a merry time! Grandfather made a noise in his throat, the forest crackled with the frost, and looking at them Vanka chortled too. Before chopping down the Christmas tree, grandfather would smoke a pipe, slowly take a pinch of snuff, and laugh at frozen Vanka ... The young fir trees, covered with hoar frost, stood motionless, waiting to see which of them was to die. Wherever one looked, a hare flew like an arrow over the snowdrifts ... Grandfather could not refrain from shouting: "Hold him, hold him ... hold him! Ah, the bob-tailed devil!"

When he had cut down the Christmas tree, grandfather used to drag it to the big house, and there set to work to decorate it ... The young lady, who was Vanka's favourite, Olga Ignatyevna, was the busiest of all. When Vanka's mother Pelageya was alive, and a servant in the big house, Olga Ignatyevna used to give him goodies, and having nothing better to do, taught him to read and write, to count up to a hundred, and even to dance a quadrille. When Pelageya died, Vanka had been transferred to the servants' kitchen to be with his grandfather, and from the kitchen to the shoemaker's in Moscow.

"Do come, dear grandfather," Vanka went on with his letter. "For Christ's sake, I beg you, take me away. Have pity on an unhappy orphan like me; here everyone knocks me about, and I am fearfully hungry; I can't tell you what misery it is, I am always crying. And the other day the master hit me on the head with a last, so that I fell down. My life is wretched, worse than any dog's ... I send greetings to Alyona, one-eyed Yegorka, and the coachman, and don't give my concertina to anyone. I remain, your grandson, Ivan Zhukov. Dear grandfather, do come."

Vanka folded the sheet of writing-paper twice, and put it into an envelope he had bought the day before for a kopeck① ... After thinking a little, he dipped the pen and wrote the address:

To grandfather in the village.

Then he scratched his head, thought a little, and added: Konstantin Makaritch. Glad that he had not been prevented from writing, he put on his cap and, without putting on his little greatcoat, ran out into the street as he was in his shirt ...

---

① kopeck [ˈkəupek] *n.* 戈比(货币单位)。

The shopmen at the butcher's, whom he had questioned the day before, told him that letters were put in post-boxes, and from the boxes were carried about all over the earth in mailcarts with drunken drivers and ringing bells. Vanka ran to the nearest post-box, and thrust the precious letter in the slit ...

An hour later, lulled by sweet hopes, he was sound asleep ... He dreamed of the stove. On the stove was sitting his grandfather, swinging his bare legs, and reading the letter to the cooks ...

By the stove was Eel, wagging[①] his tail.

The Death of a Government Clerk[②]

One fine evening, a no less fine government clerk called Ivan Dmitritch Tchervyakov was sitting in the second row of the stalls, gazing through an opera glass at the *Cloches de Corneville*[③]. He gazed and felt at the acme of bliss. But suddenly ... In stories one so often meets with this "But suddenly." The authors are right: life is so full of surprises! But suddenly his face puckered up, his eyes disappeared, his breathing was arrested ... he took the opera glass from his eyes, bent over and ... "Aptchee!" he sneezed as you perceive. It is not reprehensible for anyone to sneeze anywhere. Peasants sneeze and so do police superintendents[④], and sometimes even privy councillors. All men sneeze. Tchervyakov was not in the least confused, he wiped his face with his handkerchief, and like a polite man, looked round to see whether he had disturbed any one by his sneezing. But then he was overcome with confusion. He saw that an old gentleman sitting in front of him in the first row of the stalls was carefully wiping his bald head and his neck with his glove and muttering something to himself. In the old gentleman, Tchervyakov recognised Brizzhalov, a civilian general serving in the Department of Transport.

"I have spattered him," thought Tchervyakov, "he is not the head of my department, but still it is awkward. I must apologise."

Tchervyakov gave a cough, bent his whole person forward, and whispered in the general's ear.

"Pardon, your Excellency, I spattered you accidentally ..."

"Never mind, never mind."

"For goodness sake excuse me, I ... I did not mean to."

"Oh, please, sit down! Let me listen!"

Tchervyakov was embarrassed, he smiled stupidly and fell to gazing at the stage. He

---

① wag [wæg] *vt.* to move briskly and repeatedly from side to side (摇摆;摇动)。

② 译文参见本书第 268 至 269 页。

③ *Cloches de Corneville*:《科尔涅维利的钟声》(法国作曲家普朗盖特所作的轻歌剧)。

④ superintendent [ˌsjuːpərɪnˈtendənt] *n.* a person who has the authority to supervise or direct (主管;负责人)。

gazed at it but was no longer feeling bliss. He began to be troubled by uneasiness. In the interval, he went up to Brizzhalov, walked beside him, and overcoming his shyness, muttered:

"I spattered you, your Excellency, forgive me ... you see ... I didn't do it to ..."

"Oh, that's enough ... I'd forgotten it, and you keep on about it!" said the general, moving his lower lip impatiently.

"He has forgotten, but there is a fiendish light in his eye," thought Tchervyakov, looking suspiciously at the general. "And he doesn't want to talk. I ought to explain to him ... that I really didn't intend ... that it is the law of nature or else he will think I meant to spit on him. He doesn't think so now, but he will think so later!"

On getting home, Tchervyakov told his wife of his breach of good manners. It struck him that his wife took too frivolous a view of the incident; she was a little frightened, but when she learned that Brizzhalov was in a different department, she was reassured.

"Still, you had better go and apologise," she said, "or he will think you don't know how to behave in public."

"That's just it! I did apologise, but he took it somehow queerly ... he didn't say a word of sense. There wasn't time to talk properly."

Next day Tchervyakov put on a new uniform, had his hair cut and went to Brizzhalov's to explain; going into the general's reception room he saw there a number of petitioners[①] and among them the general himself, who was beginning to interview them. After questioning several petitioners the general raised his eyes and looked at Tchervyakov.

"Yesterday at the 'Arcadia', if you recollect, your Excellency," the latter began, "I sneezed and ... accidentally spattered ... Exc ..."

"What nonsense ... It's beyond anything! What can I do for you," said the general addressing the next petitioner.

"He won't speak," thought Tchervyakov, turning pale; "that means that he is angry ... No, it can't be left like this ... I will explain to him."

When the general had finished his conversation with the last of the petitioners and was turning towards his inner apartments, Tchervyakov took a step towards him and muttered:

"Your Excellency! If I venture to trouble your Excellency, it is simply from a feeling I may say of regret! ... It was not intentional if you will graciously believe me."

The general made a lachrymose[②] face, and waved his hand.

"Why, you are simply making fun of me, sir," he said as he closed the door behind him.

"Where's the making fun in it?" thought Tchervyakov, "there is nothing of the sort! He is a general, but he can't understand. If that is how it is I am not going to apologise to

---

① petitioner [pɪ'tɪʃənə] *n.* a person who presents a petition (请求者)。

② lachrymose ['lækrɪməʊs] *adj.* weeping or inclined to weep; tearful (爱哭的)。

that fanfaron[①] any more! The devil take him. I'll write a letter to him, but I won't go. By Jove, I won't."

So thought Tchervyakov as he walked home; he did not write a letter to the general, he pondered and pondered and could not make up that letter. He had to go next day to explain in person.

"I ventured to disturb your Excellency yesterday," he muttered, when the general lifted enquiring eyes upon him, "not to make fun as you were pleased to say. I was apologising for having spattered you in sneezing ... And I did not dream of making fun of you. Should I dare to make fun of you, if we should take to making fun, then there would be no respect for persons, there would be ..."

"Be off!" yelled the general, turning suddenly purple, and shaking all over.

"What?" asked Tchervyakov, in a whisper turning numb with horror.

"Be off!" repeated the general, stamping.

Something seemed to give way in Tchervyakov's stomach. Seeing nothing and hearing nothing he reeled to the door, went out into the street, and went staggering along ... Reaching home mechanically, without taking off his uniform, he lay down on the sofa and died.

---

① fanfaron ['fænfərɔn] *n.* a swaggerer; an empty boaster (吹牛者;大言不惭的人)。

Chapter Eight 19th-Century Literature (Ⅱ)

Ⅰ. Introduction

Realistic literature flourished during the 19th century not only in European countries but also in America. Having discussed the literary achievements in France and Russia, we probe into English and American realistic writings of the 19th century in this chapter.

English Realistic Literature

English literature after the Romantic period can be called English literature of the Victorian Age, which roughly coincides with Queen Victoria's reign (1837～1901).

The victorian period was a time of rapid economic development and serious social problems. The reform of 1832 gave the middle class the political power it needed to consolidate the economic position it had already achieved. While the affluence of the middle class increased, the lower classes, thrown off their land and into the cities to form the great urban working class, lived ever more wretchedly.

English literature of the Victorian Age is closely connected with the social and political issues of the time, and is famous for its novelists as Charles Dickens, William Thackeray, Charlotte Brontë, Thomas Hardy and many others. The writers had to deal in some way with the upheavals of the age, and criticized the obvious inequities in the society. The novels of Charles Dickens, with an endless variety of vivid characters and plot complications, set up a large scale criticism of the nineteenth century England. Thomas Hardy's profound pessimistic novels are set in the harsh midland county called Wessex. The famous novels of this time also include *Vanity Fair* by William Thackeray, *Jane Eyre* by Charlotte Brontë, *Wuthering Heights* by Emily Brontë, and *The Mill on the Floss* by George Eliot.

American Realistic Literature

Conventionally speaking, American realism as a historical phase of literature began in 1865 with the end of the civil War and ended in 1914, the year before World War I.

The Civil War (1861～1865) between the industrial North and the agricultural, slave-owning South was a watershed in American history. The innocent optimism of the young democratic nation gave way, after the war, to a period of exhaustion. This period is characterized with changes, in relation to every aspect of American life, politically, economically and culturally. First, America had transformed itself from an agrarian country into an industrialized and commercialized society. American idealism remained but was rechanneled. Before the war, idealists championed human rights, especially the abolition of slavery; after the war, Americans increasingly idealized progress and the self-made man. However, the industrialization was accompanied by the incessant laboring and unbearable poverty of the masses.

Because of the social situations mentioned above, realistic literature, emerged in America. Under the influence of European writers, American realists believed that literature imitated reality and claimed "the faithful representation of reality". So they paid more emphases on "objectivity". But they had their own typical characteristics. American realists were philosophically allied with pragmatism.

The great writers of American realistic literature include Mark Twain, Henry James, Jack London, O. Henry, Theodore Dreiser and many others. Their fictions accurately represent and explore American lives in various ways.

Ⅱ. Charles Dickens

Charles Dickens (1812～1870) is considered to be one of the greatest English novelists of the Victorian period. He was born in Landport, Hampshire. His father, John Dickens, was a clerk in the navy pay office, who was well paid but ended up in financial troubles. His debts had become so severe that all the household goods were sold. Still unable to satisfy his creditors, John Dickens was arrested and sent to prison.

At this time, Charles Dickens was only twelve years old, but he had to find work at a sweatshop, where he was paid six shillings a week wrapping shoe-black bottles.

Six months after being sent to prison, one of John Dickens's relatives died. He was left enough money in the will to pay off his debts and to leave prison. Some of the inheritance was used to educate Charles at a nearby private school, Wellington House Academy. Charles was only a moderate student and at the age of fifteen he left school and found work as an office boy in a firm of solicitors. Charles disliked the work but he did enjoy walking the streets in the evening observing the people of London.

Charles Dickens worked very hard and his career as a novelist started in 1833 when his short stories and essays appeared in periodicals. His *Sketches by Boz* and *The Pickwick Papers* were published in 1836. From then on, Dickens continued to write until his death in 1870, leaving his last novel *The Mystery of Edwin Drood* unfinished.

Dickens's important novels include *Oliver Twist* (1837～39), *Nicholas Nickelby* (1838～39), *The Old Curiosity Shop* (1840～41), *A Tale of Two Cities* (1859) and *Great Expectations* (1860～61).

In his novel *A Tale of Two Cities*, Dickens successfully integrated fiction and history, and he tried to draw attention to the social and political problems in England by using the French Revolution as the setting.

A Tale of Two Cities[①]

(Excerpt)

From the time of our alighting at the outer gate (which we found locked, and which one of the brothers had opened to admit us, and had relocked), I had heard cries proceeding from an upper chamber. I was conducted to this chamber straight, the cries growing louder as we ascended the stairs, and I found a patient in a high fever of the brain, lying on a bed.

The patient was a woman of great beauty, and young; assuredly not much past twenty. Her hair was torn and ragged, and her arms were bound to her sides with sashes[②] and handkerchiefs. I noticed that these bonds were all portions of a gentleman's dress. On one of them, which was a fringed[③] scarf for a dress of ceremony, I saw the armorial bearings of a Noble, and the letter E.

I saw this, within the first minute of my contemplation of the patient; for, in her restless strivings she had turned over on her face on the edge of the bed, had drawn the end of the scarf into her mouth, and was in danger of suffocation[④]. My first act was to put out my hand to relieve her breathing; and in moving the scarf aside, the embroidery in the corner caught my sight.

I turned her gently over, placed my hands upon her breast to calm her and keep her down, and looked into her face. Her eyes were dilated[⑤] and wild, and she constantly uttered piercing shrieks, and repeated the words, "My husband, my father, and my brother!" and then counted up to twelve, and said, "Hush!" For an instant, and no more, she would pause to listen, and then the piercing shrieks would begin again, and she would repeat the cry, "My husband, my father, and my brother!" and would count up to twelve, and say "Hush!" There was no variation in the order, or the manner. There was no cessation, but the regular moment's pause, in the utterance of these sounds.

"How long," I asked, "has this lasted?"

To distinguish the brothers, I will call them the elder and the younger; by the elder, I mean him who exercised the most authority. It was the elder who replied, "Since about this hour last night."

---

① 译文参见本书第 269 至 272 页。

② sash [sæʃ] *n.* a band or ribbon worn about the waist (腰带;带子)。

③ fringed [frɪndʒd] *adj.* having a decorative edging (绣有花边的)。

④ suffocation [ˈsʌfəˈkeɪʃən] *n.* the condition of being deprived of oxygen (窒息)。

⑤ dilated [daɪˈleɪtɪd] *adj.* expanded; having been widened (扩大的;瞪着的)。

"She has a husband, a father, and a brother?"

"A brother."

"I do not address her brother?"

He answered with great contempt, "No."

"She has some recent association with the number twelve?"

The younger brother impatiently rejoined, "With twelve o'clock."

"See, gentlemen," said I, still keeping my hands upon her breast, "how useless I am, as you have brought me! If I had known what I was coming to see, I could have come provided. As it is, time must be lost. There are no medicines to be obtained in this lonely place."

The elder brother looked to the younger, who said haughtily①, "There is a case of medicines here;" and brought it from a closet, and put it on the table.

I opened some of the bottles, smelt them, and put the stoppers to my lips. If I had wanted to use anything save narcotic② medicines that were poisons in themselves, I would not have administered any of those.

"Do you doubt them?" asked the younger brother.

"You see, monsieur, I am going to use them," I replied, and said no more.

I made the patient swallow, with great difficulty, and after many efforts, the dose that I desired to give. As I intended to repeat it after a while, and as it was necessary to watch its influence, I then sat down by the side of the bed. There was a timid and suppressed woman in attendance (wife of the man down-stairs), who had retreated into a corner. The house was damp and decayed, indifferently furnished — evidently, recently occupied and temporarily used. Some thick old hangings had been nailed up before the windows, to deaden the sound of the shrieks. They continued to be uttered in their regular succession, with the cry, "My husband, my father, and my brother!" the counting up to twelve, and "Hush!" The frenzy was so violent, that I had not unfastened the bandages restraining the arms, but, I had looked to them, to see that they were not painful. The only spark of encouragement in the case, was, that my hand upon the sufferer's breast had this much soothing influence, that for minutes at a time it tranquillised the figure. It had no effect upon the cries: no pendulum③ could be more regular.

For the reason that my hand had this effect (I assume), I had sat by the side of the bed for half an hour, with the two brothers looking on, before the elder said:

"There is another patient."

---

① haughtily [ˈhɔːtɪli] *adv.* scornfully; proudly (傲慢地;骄傲地)。

② narcotic [nɑːˈkɔtɪk] *n./adj.* an addictive drug; inducing sleep or stupor; causing narcosis (麻醉药;镇静剂;麻醉的;催眠的)。

③ pendulum [ˈpendjələm] *n.* a body suspended from a fixed support so that it swings freely back and forth under the influence of gravity (钟摆;摇锤)。

I was startled and asked, "Is it a pressing case?"

"You had better see," he carelessly answered; and took up a light.

The other patient lay in a back room across a second staircase, which was a species of loft over a stable. There was a low plastered[①] ceiling to a part of it; the rest was open, to the ridge of the tiled roof, and there were beams across. Hay and straw were stored in that portion of the place, fagots for firing, and a heap of apples in sand. I had to pass through that part, to get at the other. My memory is circumstantial and unshaken. I try it with these details, and I see them all, in this my cell in the Bastille, near the close of the tenth year of my captivity, as I saw them all that night.

On some hay on the ground, with a cushion thrown under his head, lay a handsome peasant-boy — a boy of not more than seventeen at the most. He lay on his back, with his teeth set, his right hand clenched on his breast, and his glaring eyes looking straight upward. I could not see where his wound was, as I kneeled on one knee over him; but, I could see that he was dying of a wound from a sharp point.

"I am a doctor, my poor fellow," said I. "Let me examine it."

"I do not want it examined," he answered; "let it be."

It was under his hand, and I soothed him to let me move his hand away. The wound was a sword-thrust, received from twenty to twenty-four hours before, but no skill could have saved him if it had been looked to without delay. He was then dying fast. As I turned my eyes to the elder brother, I saw him looking down at this handsome boy whose life was ebbing[②] out, as if he were a wounded bird, or hare, or rabbit; not at all as if he were a fellow-creature.

"How has this been done, monsieur?" said I.

"A crazed young common dog! A serf! Forced my brother to draw upon him, and has fallen by my brother's sword — like a gentleman."

There was no touch of pity, sorrow, or kindred humanity, in this answer. The speaker seemed to acknowledge that it was inconvenient to have that different order of creature dying there, and that it would have been better if he had died in the usual obscure routine of his vermin[③] kind. He was quite incapable of any compassionate feeling about the boy, or about his fate.

The boy's eyes had slowly moved to him as he had spoken, and they now slowly moved to me.

"Doctor, they are very proud, these Nobles; but we common dogs are proud too, sometimes. They plunder us, outrage us, beat us, kill us; but we have a little pride left, sometimes. She — have you seen her, Doctor?"

---

① plastered [ˈplɑːstəd] *adj.* covered with a mixture of lime or gypsum (涂了灰泥的)。

② ebb [eb] *vi.* to fall away; to decline (衰退;消逝)。

③ vermin [ˈvɜːmɪn] *n.* various small animals or insects (虫子)。

The shrieks and the cries were audible there, though subdued by the distance. He referred to them, as if she were lying in our presence.

I said, "I have seen her."

"She is my sister, Doctor. They have had their shameful rights, these Nobles, in the modesty and virtue of our sisters, many years, but we have had good girls among us. I know it, and have heard my father say so. She was a good girl. She was betrothed① to a good young man, too: a tenant② of his. We are all tenants of his — that man's who stands there. The other is his brother, the worst of a bad race."

It was with the greatest difficulty that the boy gathered bodily force to speak; but, his spirit spoke with a dreadful emphasis.

"We were so robbed by that man who stands there, as all we common dogs are by those superior Beings — taxed by him without mercy, obliged to work for him without pay, obliged to grind our corn at his mill, obliged to feed scores of his tame birds on our wretched crops, and forbidden for our lives to keep a single tame bird of our own, pillaged and plundered to that degree that when we chanced to have a bit of meat, we ate it in fear, with the door barred and the shutters closed, that his people should not see it and take it from us — I say, we were so robbed, and hunted, and were made so poor, that our father told us it was a dreadful thing to bring a child into the world, and that what we should most pray for, was, that our women might be barren and our miserable race die out!"

I had never before seen the sense of being oppressed, bursting forth like a fire. I had supposed that it must be latent in the people somewhere; but, I had never seen it break out, until I saw it in the dying boy.

"Nevertheless, Doctor, my sister married. He was ailing at that time, poor fellow, and she married her lover, that she might tend and comfort him in our cottage — our dog-hut, as that man would call it. She had not been married many weeks, when that man's brother saw her and admired her, and asked that man to lend her to him — for what are husbands among us! He was willing enough, but my sister was good and virtuous, and hated his brother with a hatred as strong as mine. What did the two then, to persuade her husband to use his influence with her, to make her willing?"

The boy's eyes, which had been fixed on mine, slowly turned to the looker-on, and I saw in the two faces that all he said was true. The two opposing kinds of pride confronting one another, I can see, even in this Bastille; the gentleman's, all negligent indifference; the peasant's, all trodden-down sentiment, and passionate revenge.

"You know, Doctor, that it is among the Rights of these Nobles to harness us common dogs to carts, and drive us. They so harnessed him and drove him. You know that it is among their Rights to keep us in their grounds all night, quieting the frogs, in

① betrothed [bɪˈtrəʊðd] *adj.* engaged to be married (订婚了的)。

② tenant [ˈtenənt] *n.* one that pays rent to use or occupy land or a building (承租者;佃户)。

order that their noble sleep may not be disturbed. They kept him out in the unwholesome mists at night, and ordered him back into his harness in the day. But he was not persuaded. No! Taken out of harness one day at noon, to feed — if he could find food — he sobbed twelve times, once for every stroke of the bell, and died on her bosom."

Nothing human could have held life in the boy but his determination to tell all his wrong. He forced back the gathering shadows of death, as he forced his clenched right hand to remain clenched, and to cover his wound.

"Then, with that man's permission and even with his aid, his brother took her away; in spite of what I know she must have told his brother — and what that is, will not be long unknown to you, Doctor, if it is now — his brother took her away — for his pleasure and diversion[①], for a little while. I saw her pass me on the road. When I took the tidings home, our father's heart burst; he never spoke one of the words that filled it. I took my young sister (for I have another) to a place beyond the reach of this man, and where, at least, she will never be *his* vassal. Then, I tracked the brother here, and last night climbed in — a common dog, but sword in hand. — Where is the loft window? It was somewhere here?"

The room was darkening to his sight; the world was narrowing around him. I glanced about me, and saw that the hay and straw were trampled over the floor, as if there had been a struggle.

"She heard me, and ran in. I told her not to come near us till he was dead. He came in and first tossed me some pieces of money; then struck at me with a whip. But I, though a common dog, so struck at him as to make him draw. Let him break into as many pieces as he will, the sword that he stained with my common blood; he drew to defend himself — thrust at me with all his skill for his life."

My glance had fallen, but a few moments before, on the fragments of a broken sword, lying among the hay. That weapon was a gentleman's. In another place, lay an old sword that seemed to have been a soldier's.

"Now, lift me up, Doctor; lift me up. Where is he?"

"He is not here," I said, supporting the boy, and thinking that he referred to the brother.

"He! Proud as these nobles are, he is afraid to see me. Where is the man who was here? Turn my face to him."

I did so, raising the boy's head against my knee. But, invested for the moment with extraordinary power, he raised himself completely: obliging me to rise too, or I could not have still supported him.

"Marquis," said the boy, turned to him with his eyes opened wide, and his right hand raised, "in the days when all these things are to be answered for, I summon you and

---

① diversion [daɪˈvɜːʃən] *n.* something that distracts the mind or entertains (消遣)。

yours, to the last of your bad race, to answer for them. I mark this cross of blood upon you, as a sign that I do it. In the days when all these things are to be answered for, I summon your brother, the worst of the bad race, to answer for them separately. I mark this cross of blood upon him, as a sign that I do it."

Twice, he put his hand to the wound in his breast, and with forefinger drew a cross in the air. He stood for an instant with the finger yet raised, and, as it dropped, he dropped with it, and I laid him down dead.

When I returned to the bedside of the young woman, I found her raving in precisely the same order and continuity. I knew that this might last for many hours, and that it would probably end in the silence of the grave.

I repeated the medicines I had given her, and I sat at the side of the bed until the night was far advanced. She never abated the piercing quality of her shrieks, never stumbled in the distinctness or the order of her words. They were always "My husband, my father, and my brother! One, two, three, four, five, six, seven, eight, nine, ten, eleven, twelve! Hush!"

This lasted twenty-six hours from the time when I first saw her. I had come and gone twice, and was again sitting by her, when she began to falter. I did what little could be done to assist that opportunity, and by-and-by she sank into a lethargy①, and lay like the dead.

It was as if the wind and rain had lulled at last, after a long and fearful storm. I released her arms, and called the woman to assist me to compose her figure and the dress she had torn. It was then that I knew her condition to be that of one in whom the first expectations of being a mother have arisen; and it was then that I lost the little hope I had had of her.

Ⅲ. Thomas Hardy

Thomas Hardy (1840～1928) was a great English novelist of the 19th century and a lyrical poet of the 20th century. He was born in Higher Bockhampton, Dorsetshire, and educated in local schools. His father, a stonemason, apprenticed him early to a local architect engaged in restoring old churches.

From 1862 to 1867 Hardy worked for an architect in London and later continued to practice architecture, despite ill health, in Dorset. Meanwhile, he was writing poetry with little success. He then turned to novels as more salable, and by 1874 he was able to support himself by writing. This is also the year that Hardy married his first wife, Emma Gifford. Their marriage lasted until her death in 1912, which prompted Hardy to write his

---

① lethargy [ˈleθədʒi] *n.* a state of sluggishness; inactivity (无生气)。

collection of poems called *Veteris Vestigiae Flammae* (Vestiges of an Old Flame). These poems are some of Hardy's finest and describe their meeting and his subsequent loss. In 1914 Florence Dugdale became Hardy's second wife and she wrote his biography after he died.

As a 19th-century novelist, Thomas Hardy published 14 novels, including such masterpieces as *The Return of the Native* (1878), *The Mayor of Casterbridge* (1886), *Tess of the d'Urbervilles* (1891), and *Jude the Obscure* (1895).

As a 20th-century poet, Thomas Hardy published 8 volumes of lyrical poems and he is considered by some critics as the "father of modern poetry".

The novel *Tess of the d'Urbervilles* is Thomas Hardy's representative work, and it is considered as a great classic of English literature. The following selection is the Chapter 35 of the novel. In this selection, from Angel Clare's attitude towards Tess after her confession at their night as a newly married couple, we can see clearly that Angel Clare is equally a dogmatic and obstinate character.

Tess of the D'Urbervilles①

(Excerpt)

Her narrative ended; even its re-assertions and secondary explanations were done. Tess's voice throughout had hardly risen higher than its opening tone; there had been no exculpatory② phrase of any kind, and she had not wept.

But the complexion even of external things seemed to suffer transmutation as her announcement progressed. The fire in the grate③ looked impish — demoniacally funny, as if it did not care in the least about her strait. The fender grinned idly, as if it too did not care. The light from the water-bottle was merely engaged in a chromatic problem. All material objects around announced their irresponsibility with terrible iteration. And yet nothing had changed since the moments when he had been kissing her; or rather, nothing in the substance of things. But the essence of things had changed.

When she ceased, the auricular impressions from their previous endearments④ seemed to hustle away into the corners of their brains, repeating themselves as echoes from a time of supremely purblind foolishness.

Clare performed the irrelevant act of stirring the fire; the intelligence had not even yet got to the bottom of him. After stirring the embers⑤ he rose to his feet; all the force of

---

① 译文参见本书第 272 至 273 页。

② exculpatory [ɪk'skʌlpətəri] *adj.* acting or tending to exculpate (辩解的;辩明无罪的)。

③ grate [greɪt] *n.* a fireplace (壁炉;炉子)。

④ endearment [ɪn'diəmənt] *n.* the act of endearing (亲爱;钟爱)。

⑤ ember ['embə] *n.* a small, glowing piece of coal or wood (灰烬;余烬)。

her disclosure had imparted itself now. His face had withered. In the strenuousness[①] of his concentration he treadled fitfully on the floor. He could not, by any contrivance, think closely enough; that was the meaning of his vague movement. When he spoke it was in the most inadequate, commonplace voice of the many varied tones she had heard from him.

"Tess!"

"Yes, dearest."

"Am I to believe this? From your manner I am to take it as true. O you cannot be out of your mind! You ought to be! Yet you are not ... My wife, my Tess — nothing in you warrants such a supposition as that?"

"I am not out of my mind," she said.

"And yet —" He looked vacantly at her, to resume with dazed senses: "Why didn't you tell me before? Ah, yes, you would have told me, in a way — but I hindered you, I remember!"

These and other of his words were nothing but the perfunctory babble of the surface while the depths remained paralyzed. He turned away, and bent over a chair. Tess followed him to the middle of the room where he was, and stood there staring at him with eyes that did not weep. Presently she slid down upon her knees beside his foot, and from this position she crouched in a heap.

"In the name of our love, forgive me!" she whispered with a dry mouth. "I have forgiven you for the same!"

And, as he did not answer, she said again —

"Forgive me as you are forgiven! I forgive *you*, Angel."

"You — yes, you do."

"But you do not forgive me?"

"O Tess, forgiveness does not apply to the case! You were one person; now you are another. My God — how can forgiveness meet such a grotesque[②]— prestidigitation[③] as that!"

He paused, contemplating this definition; then suddenly broke into horrible laughter — as unnatural and ghastly as a laugh in hell.

"Don't — don't! It kills me quite, that!" she shrieked. "O have mercy upon me-have mercy!"

He did not answer; and, sickly white, she jumped up.

"Angel, Angel! what do you mean by that laugh?" she cried out. "Do you know what this is to me?"

---

① strenuousness [ˈstrenjuəsnɪs] *n.* vigorousness; activeness (使劲;紧张;热烈)。

② grotesque [grəʊˈtesk] *n.* ludicrous distortion, as of appearance or manner (奇异;怪诞)。

③ prestidigitation [ˈprestɪˌdɪdʒɪˈteɪʃən] *n.* manual skill and dexterity in the execution of tricks; sleight of hand (变戏法;魔术)。

He shook his head.

"I have been hoping, longing, praying, to make you happy! I have thought what joy it will be to do it, what an unworthy wife I shall be if I do not! That's what I have felt, Angel!"

"I know that."

"I thought, Angel, that you loved me — me, my very self! If it is I you do love, O how can it be that you look and speak so? It frightens me! Having begun to love you, I love you for ever — in all changes, in all disgraces, because you are yourself. I ask no more. Then how can you, O my own husband, stop loving me?"

"I repeat, the woman I have been loving is not you."

"But who?"

"Another woman in your shape."

She perceived in his words the realization of her own apprehensive foreboding① in former times. He looked upon her as a species of impostor; a guilty woman in the guise of an innocent one. Terror was upon her white face as she saw it; her cheek was flaccid, and her mouth had almost the aspect of a round little hole. The horrible sense of his view of her so deadened her that she staggered; and he stepped forward, thinking she was going to fall.

"Sit down, sit down," he said gently. "You are ill; and it is natural that you should be."

She did sit down, without knowing where she was, that strained look still upon her face, and her eyes such as to make his flesh creep.

"I don't belong to you any more, then; do I, Angel?" she asked helplessly. "It is not me, but another woman like me that he loved, he says."

The image raised caused her to take pity upon herself as one who was ill-used. Her eyes filled as she regarded her position further; she turned round and burst into a flood of self-sympathetic tears.

The Darkling Thrush②

I leant upon a coppice③ gate
    When Frost was spectre-gray,
And Winter's dregs made desolate
    The weakening eye of day.
The tangled bine-stems scored the sky

① foreboding [fɔːˈbəudɪŋ] *n.* a sense of impending evil; an evil omen (预感;预兆)。

② 译文参见本书第273至274页。

③ coppice [ˈkɔpɪs] *n.* a thicket or grove of small trees or shrubs (矮林)。

Like strings of broken lyres,
And all mankind that haunted nigh[1]
Had sought their household fires.

The land's sharp features seemed to be
The Century's corpse outleant,
His crypt[2] the cloudy canopy,
The wind his death-lament.
The ancient pulse of germ and birth
Was shrunken hard and dry,
And every spirit upon earth
Seemed fevourless as I.

At once a voice arose among
The bleak twigs overhead
In a full-hearted evensong
Of joy illimited;
An aged thrush, frail, gaunt[3], and small,
In blast-beruffled plume,
Had chosen thus to fling his soul
Upon the growing gloom.

So little cause for carolings
Of such ecstatic sound
Was written on terrestrial things
Afar or nigh around,
That I could think there trembled through
His happy good-night air
Some blessed Hope, whereof he knew
And I was unaware.

Ⅳ. O. Henry

O. Henry was the pen name of American writer William Sydney Porter (1862～

① nigh [naɪ] *adj./adv.* near; nearly (在附近的;在附近)。
② crypt [krɪpt] *n.* an underground vault or chamber (土窖;地穴)。
③ gaunt [gɔːnt] *adj.* emaciated and haggard (憔悴的)。

1910). He was a prolific American short-story writer, who wrote about the life of ordinary people in New York City. His short stories are well known for their wit, wordplay, warm characterization and surprising ending.

His best collections of short stories include *Cabbages and King*s (1904), *The Four Million* (1906) and *The Trimmed Lamp* (1907).

The Gift of the Magi is one of his famous short stories. It is about a young couple who are short of money but desperately wants to buy each other Christmas gifts. Unbeknownst to Jim, Della sells her most valuable possession, her beautiful hair, in order to buy a platinum fob chain for Jim's watch; while unbeknownst to Della, Jim sells his own most valuable possession, his watch, to buy jeweled combs for Della's hair. In this story, O. Henry uses a folksy narrator to tell the story of Jim and Della and to express their selfless love.

The Gift of the Magi①

One dollar and eighty-seven cents. That was all. And sixty cents of it was in pennies. Pennies saved one and two at a time by bulldozing② the grocer and the vegetable man and the butcher until one's cheeks burned with the silent imputation of parsimony③ that such close dealing implied. Three times Della counted it. One dollar and eighty-seven cents. And the next day would be Christmas.

There was clearly nothing to do but flop down on the shabby little couch and howl. So Della did it. Which instigates the moral reflection that life is made up of sobs, sniffles④, and smiles, with sniffles predominating.

While the mistress of the home is gradually subsiding from the first stage to the second, take a look at the home. A furnished flat at $8 per week. It did not exactly beggar description, but it certainly had that word on the lookout for the mendicancy squad⑤.

In the vestibule below was a letter-box into which no letter would go, and an electric button from which no mortal finger could coax⑥ a ring. Also appertaining thereunto was a card bearing the name "Mr. James Dillingham Young."

The "Dillingham" had been flung to the breeze during a former period of prosperity when its possessor was being paid $30 per week. Now, when the income was shrunk to

① 译文参见本书第274至276页。

② bulldoze [ˈbuldəuz] *v.* to treat in an abusive manner; to bully (威吓;欺负;强迫)。

③ parsimony [ˈpɑːsɪməni] *n.* unusual or excessive frugality; extreme economy or stinginess (过度节俭;吝啬)。

④ sniffle [ˈsnɪfl] *v.* n. to breathe audibly through a runny nose; whimper (抽鼻涕;抽噎)。

⑤ mendicancy squad: 乞丐帮。mendicancy [ˈmendɪkənsi] *n.* 乞丐;squad [skwɔd] *n.* 班;小组。

⑥ coax [kəuks] *vt.* to persuade or try to persuade by pleading or flattery; cajole (劝诱;哄骗)。

$20, the letters of "Dillingham" looked blurred, as though they were thinking seriously of contracting to a modest and unassuming D. But whenever Mr. James Dillingham Young came home and reached his flat above he was called "Jim" and greatly hugged by Mrs. James Dillingham Young, already introduced to you as Della. Which is all very good.

Della finished her cry and attended to her cheeks with the powder rag. She stood by the window and looked out dully at a gray cat walking a gray fence in a gray backyard. Tomorrow would be Christmas Day, and she had only $1.87 with which to buy Jim a present. She had been saving every penny she could for months, with this result. Twenty dollars a week doesn't go far. Expenses had been greater than she had calculated. They always are. Only $1.87 to buy a present for Jim. Her Jim. Many a happy hour she had spent planning for something nice for him. Something fine and rare and sterling — something just a little bit near to being worthy of the honor of being owned by Jim.

There was a pier-glass between the windows of the room. Perhaps you have seen a pier-glass in an $8 flat. A very thin and very agile person may, by observing his reflection in a rapid sequence of longitudinal strips, obtain a fairly accurate conception of his looks. Della, being slender, had mastered the art.

Suddenly she whirled from the window and stood before the glass. Her eyes were shining brilliantly, but her face had lost its color within twenty seconds. Rapidly she pulled down her hair and let it fall to its full length.

Now, there were two possessions of the James Dillingham Youngs in which they both took a mighty pride. One was Jim's gold watch that had been his father's and his grandfather's. The other was Della's hair. Had the queen of Sheba lived in the flat across the airshaft, Della would have let her hair hang out the window some day to dry just to depreciate Her Majesty's jewels and gifts. Had King Solomon been the janitor, with all his treasures piled up in the basement, Jim would have pulled out his watch every time he passed, just to see him pluck at his beard from envy.

So now Della's beautiful hair fell about her, rippling and shining like a cascade① of brown waters. It reached below her knee and made itself almost a garment for her. And then she did it up again nervously and quickly. Once she faltered for a minute and stood still while a tear or two splashed on the worn red carpet.

On went her old brown jacket; on went her old brown hat. With a whirl of skirts and with the brilliant sparkle still in her eyes, she fluttered out the door and down the stairs to the street.

Where she stopped the sign read: "Mme. Sofronie. Hair Goods of All Kinds." One flight up Della ran, and collected herself, panting. Madame, large, too white, chilly, hardly looked the "Sofronie."

"Will you buy my hair?" asked Della.

---

① cascade [kæsˈkeɪd] *n.* a waterfall or a series of small waterfalls over steep rocks (小瀑布;喷流)。

"I buy hair," said Madame. "Take yer hat off and let's have a sight at the looks of it."

Down rippled the brown cascade.

"Twenty dollars," said Madame, lifting the mass with a practised hand.

"Give it to me quick," said Della.

Oh, and the next two hours tripped by on rosy wings. Forget the hashed metaphor. She was ransacking① the stores for Jim's present.

She found it at last. It surely had been made for Jim and no one else. There was no other like it in any of the stores, and she had turned all of them inside out. It was a platinum② fob③ chain simple and chaste in design, properly proclaiming its value by substance alone and not by meretricious ornamentation④— as all good things should do. It was even worthy of The Watch. As soon as she saw it she knew that it must be Jim's. It was like him. Quietness and value — the description applied to both. Twenty-one dollars they took from her for it, and she hurried home with the 87 cents. With that chain on his watch Jim might be properly anxious about the time in any company. Grand as the watch was, he sometimes looked at it on the sly on account of the old leather strap that he used in place of a chain.

When Della reached home her intoxication⑤ gave way a little to prudence and reason. She got out her curling irons and lighted the gas and went to work repairing the ravages made by generosity added to love. Which is always a tremendous task, dear friends — a mammoth⑥ task.

Within forty minutes her head was covered with tiny, close-lying curls that made her look wonderfully like a truant schoolboy. She looked at her reflection in the mirror long, carefully, and critically.

"If Jim doesn't kill me," she said to herself, "before he takes a second look at me, he'll say I look like a Coney Island chorus girl. But what could I do — oh! what could I do with a dollar and eighty-seven cents?"

At 7 o'clock the coffee was made and the frying-pan was on the back of the stove hot and ready to cook the chops.

Jim was never late. Della doubled the fob chain in her hand and sat on the corner of the table near the door that he always entered. Then she heard his step on the stair away

---

① ransack [ˈrænsæk] *vt.* to search or examine thoroughly; to pillage (到处搜索;洗劫)。

② platinum [ˈplætɪnəm] *n.* 白金;铂。

③ fob [fɔb] *n.* a short chain or ribbon attached to a pocket watch (短表链)。

④ ornamentation [ˌɔːnəmenˈteɪʃən] *n.* the act or process of decorating, adorning, or embellishing (装饰)。

⑤ intoxication [ɪnˌtɔksɪˈkeɪʃən] *n.* exhilaration, excitement, or euphoria (陶醉)。

⑥ mammoth [ˈmæməθ] *n.* a large, hairy, extinct elephant; something of great size (长毛象;庞然大物); *adj.* enormous; huge (长毛象似的,巨大的)。

down on the first flight, and she turned white for just a moment. She had a habit for saying little silent prayer about the simplest everyday things, and now she whispered: "Please God, make him think I am still pretty."

The door opened and Jim stepped in and closed it. He looked thin and very serious. Poor fellow, he was only twenty-two — and to be burdened with a family! He needed a new overcoat and he was without gloves.

Jim stopped inside the door, as immovable as a setter at the scent of quail①. His eyes were fixed upon Della, and there was an expression in them that she could not read, and it terrified her. It was not anger, nor surprise, nor disapproval, nor horror, nor any of the sentiments that she had been prepared for. He simply stared at her fixedly with that peculiar expression on his face.

Della wriggled off the table and went for him.

"Jim, darling," she cried, "don't look at me that way. I had my hair cut off and sold because I couldn't have lived through Christmas without giving you a present. It'll grow out again — you won't mind, will you? I just had to do it. My hair grows awfully fast. Say 'Merry Christmas!' Jim, and let's be happy. You don't know what a nice — what a beautiful, nice gift I've got for you."

"You've cut off your hair?" asked Jim, laboriously, as if he had not arrived at that patent fact yet even after the hardest mental labor.

"Cut it off and sold it," said Della. "Don't you like me just as well, anyhow? I'm me without my hair, ain't I?"

Jim looked about the room curiously.

"You say your hair is gone?" he said, with an air almost of idiocy.

"You needn't look for it," said Della. "It's sold, I tell you — sold and gone, too. It's Christmas Eve, boy. Be good to me, for it went for you. Maybe the hairs of my head were numbered," she went on with sudden serious sweetness, "but nobody could ever count my love for you. Shall I put the chops② on, Jim?"

Out of his trance③ Jim seemed quickly to wake. He enfolded his Della. For ten seconds let us regard with discreet scrutiny④ some inconsequential⑤ object in the other direction. Eight dollars a week or a million a year — what is the difference? A mathematician or a wit would give you the wrong answer. The magi brought valuable gifts, but that was not among them. This dark assertion⑥ will be illuminated later on.

---

① quail [kweɪl] *n.* 鹌鹑。

② chop [tʃɔp] *n.* a piece that has been chopped off, especially a cut of meat, usually taken from the rib (排骨)。

③ trance [trɑːns] *n.* a hypnotic, cataleptic, or ecstatic state (恍惚;出神)。

④ scrutiny [ˈskruːtɪni] *n.* a close, careful examination (详细审查)。

⑤ inconsequential [ɪnˌkɔnsɪˈkwenʃəl] *adj.* lacking importance; illogical (无关紧要的;不合逻辑的)。

⑥ assertion [əˈsɜːʃən] *n.* the act of asserting (断言;命题)。

Jim drew a package from his overcoat pocket and threw it upon the table.

"Don't make any mistake, Dell," he said, "about me. I don't think there's anything in the way of a haircut or a shave or a shampoo that could make me like my girl any less. But if you'll unwrap that package you may see why you had me going a while at first."

White fingers and nimble tore at the string and paper. And then an ecstatic scream of joy; and then, alas! a quick feminine change to hysterical tears and wails, necessitating the immediate employment of all the comforting powers of the lord of the flat.

For there lay The Combs — the set of combs, side and back, that Della had worshipped long in a Broadway window. Beautiful combs, pure tortoise shell, with jewelled rims — just the shade to wear in the beautiful vanished hair. They were expensive combs, she knew, and her heart had simply craved and yearned over them without the least hope of possession. And now, they were hers, but the tresses that should have adorned the coveted[①] adornments were gone.

But she hugged them to her bosom, and at length she was able to look up with dim eyes and a smile and say: "My hair grows so fast, Jim!"

And then Della leaped up like a little singed cat and cried, "Oh, oh!"

Jim had not yet seen his beautiful present. She held it out to him eagerly upon her open palm. The dull precious metal seemed to flash with a reflection of her bright and ardent spirit.

"Isn't it a dandy, Jim? I hunted all over town to find it. You'll have to look at the time a hundred times a day now. Give me your watch. I want to see how it looks on it."

Instead of obeying, Jim tumbled down on the couch and put his hands under the back of his head and smiled.

"Dell," said he, "let's put our Christmas presents away and keep 'em a while. They're too nice to use just at present. I sold the watch to get the money to buy your combs. And now suppose you put the chops on."

The magi, as you know, were wise men — wonderfully wise men — who brought gifts to the Babe in the manger[②]. They invented the art of giving Christmas presents. Being wise, their gifts were no doubt wise ones, possibly bearing the privilege of exchange in case of duplication. And here I have lamely related to you the uneventful chronicle of two foolish children in a flat who most unwisely sacrificed for each other the greatest treasures of their house. But in a last word to the wise of these days let it be said that of all who give gifts these two were the wisest. Of all who give and receive gifts, such as they are wisest. Everywhere they are wisest. They are the magi.

---

① coveted [ˈkʌvɪtɪd] *adj.* envious (垂涎的)。

② Babe in the manger：马槽里的圣婴。

Ⅴ. Henrik Ibsen

Henrik Ibsen (1828～1906) was born to a relatively well-to-do merchant family, in the small port town of Skien, Norway,

Ibsen was a major 19th-century Norwegian playwright. He is often referred to as the "father of modern drama" and often ranked as one of the truly great playwrights in the European tradition, alongside such other notable playwrights as Sophocles, William Shakespeare, and Molière.

Ibsen's plays examined realities that lay behind many facades. It utilized a critical eye and free inquiry into the conditions of life and issues of morality. He had his reputation for the series of masterpieces *The Pillars of Society* (1877), *A Doll's House* (1879), *Ghosts* (1881) and *An Enemy of the People* (1882).

A Doll's House is Henrik Ibsen's representative work. It criticizes the traditional roles of men and women in 19th-century marriage and it is often called the first true feminist play in the history of Norwegian literature.

In the selected Act Ⅲ of the play, Nora has realized that her husband is not the man she thought he was, and her fantasy of love is just a fantasy. She has been treated like a plaything, first by her father and then by her husband. She decides that she must leave to find out who she is and what to make of her life.

A Doll's House

(Excerpt)

Nora (shaking her head). You have never loved me. You have only thought it pleasant to be in love with me.

Helmer. Nora, what do I hear you saying?

Nora. It is perfectly true, Torvald. When I was at home with papa, he told me his opinion about everything, and so I had the same opinions; and if I differed from him I concealed the fact, because he would not have liked it. He called me his doll-child, and he played with me just as I used to play with my dolls. And when I came to live with you —

Helmer. What sort of an expression is that to use about our marriage?

Nora (undisturbed). I mean that I was simply transferred from papa's hands into yours. You arranged everything according to your own taste, and so I got the same tastes as you — or else I pretended to, I am really not quite sure which — I think sometimes the one and sometimes the other. When I look back on it, it seems to me as if I had been living here like a poor woman — just from hand to mouth. I have existed merely to perform tricks for you, Torvald. But you would have it so. You and papa have committed a great sin against me. It is your fault that I have made nothing of my life.

Helmer. How unreasonable and how ungrateful you are, Nora! Have you not been happy here?

Nora. No, I have never been happy. I thought I was, but it has never really been so.

Helmer. Not — not happy!

Nora. No, only merry. And you have always been so kind to me. But our home has been nothing but a playroom. I have been your doll-wife, just as at home I was papa's doll-child; and here the children have been my dolls. I thought it great fun when you played with me, just as they thought it great fun when I played with them. That is what our marriage has been, Torvald.

Helmer. There is some truth in what you say — exaggerated and strained as your view of it is. But for the future it shall be different. Playtime shall be over, and lesson-time shall begin.

Nora. Whose lessons? Mine, or the children's?

Helmer. Both yours and the children's, my darling Nora.

Nora. Alas, Torvald, you are not the man to educate me into being a proper wife for you.

Helmer. And you can say that!

Nora. And I — how am I fitted to bring up the children?

Helmer. Nora!

Nora. Didn't you say so yourself a little while ago — that you dare not trust me to bring them up?

Helmer. In a moment of anger! Why do you pay any heed to that?

Nora. Indeed, you were perfectly right. I am not fit for the task. There is another task I must undertake first. I must try and educate myself — you are not the man to help me in that. I must do that for myself. And that is why I am going to leave you now.

Helmer (springing up). What do you say?

Nora. I must stand quite alone, if I am to understand myself and everything about me. It is for that reason that I cannot remain with you any longer.

Helmer. Nora, Nora!

Nora. I am going away from here now, at once. I am sure Christine will take me in for the night —

Helmer. You are out of your mind! I won't allow it! I forbid you!

Nora. It is no use forbidding me anything any longer. I will take with me what belongs to myself. I will take nothing from you, either now or later.

Helmer. What sort of madness is this!

Nora. Tomorrow I shall go home — I mean, to my old home. It will be easiest for me to find something to do there.

Helmer. You blind, foolish woman!

Nora. I must try and get some sense, Torvald.

Helmer. To desert[①] your home, your husband and your children! And you don't consider what people will say!

Nora. I cannot consider that at all. I only know that it is necessary for me.

Helmer. It's shocking. This is how you would neglect your most sacred duties.

Nora. What do you consider my most sacred duties?

Helmer. Do I need to tell you that? Are they not your duties to your husband and your children?

Nora. I have other duties just as sacred.

Helmer. That you have not. What duties could those be?

Nora. Duties to myself.

Helmer. Before all else, you are a wife and a mother.

Nora. I don't believe that any longer. I believe that before all else I am a reasonable human being, just as you are — or, at all events, that I must try and become one. I know quite well, Torvald, that most people would think you right, and that views of that kind are to be found in books; but I can no longer content myself with what most people say, or with what is found in books. I must think over things for myself and get to understand them.

Helmer. Can you not understand your place in your own home? Have you not a reliable guide in such matters as that? — have you no religion?

Nora. I am afraid, Torvald, I do not exactly know what religion is.

Helmer. What are you saying?

Nora. I know nothing but what the clergyman said, when I went to be confirmed. He told us that religion was this, and that, and the other. When I am away from all this, and am alone, I will look into that matter too. I will see if what the clergyman said is true, or at all events if it is true for me.

Helmer. This is unheard of in a girl of your age! But if religion cannot lead you aright, let me try and awaken your conscience. I suppose you have some moral sense? Or — answer me — am I to think you have none?

Nora. I assure you, Torvald, that is not an easy question to answer. I really don't know. The thing perplexes[②] me altogether. I only know that you and I look at it in quite a different light. I am learning, too, that the law is quite another thing from what I supposed; but I find it impossible to convince myself that the law is right. According to it a woman has no right to spare her old dying father, or to save her husband's life. I can't believe that.

Helmer. You talk like a child. You don't understand the conditions of the world in which

---

① desert [dɪˈzɜːt] *vt.* to leave alone; to abandon (放弃;遗弃)。

② perplex [pəˈpleks] *v.* to confuse or trouble with uncertainty or doubt; to puzzle (困惑)。

you live.

Nora. No, I don't. But now I am going to try. I am going to see if I can make out who is right, the world or I.

Helmer. You are ill, Nora; you are delirious[①]; I almost think you are out of your mind.

Nora. I have never felt my mind so clear and certain as tonight.

Helmer. And is it with a clear and certain mind that you forsake your husband and your children?

Nora. Yes, it is.

Helmer. Then there is only one possible explanation.

Nora. What is that?

Helmer. You do not love me anymore.

Nora. No, that is just it.

Helmer. Nora! — and you can say that?

Nora. It gives me great pain, Torvald, for you have always been so kind to me, but I cannot help it. I do not love you any more.

Helmer (regaining his composure[②]). Is that a clear and certain conviction too?

Nora. Yes, absolutely clear and certain. That is the reason why I will not stay here any longer.

Helmer. And can you tell me what I have done to forfeit[③] your love?

Nora. Yes, indeed I can. It was tonight, when the wonderful thing did not happen; then I saw you were not the man I had thought you were.

Helmer. Explain yourself better. I don't understand you.

Nora. I have waited so patiently for eight years; for, goodness knows, I knew very well that wonderful things don't happen every day. Then this horrible misfortune came upon me; and then I felt quite certain that the wonderful thing was going to happen at last. When Krogstad's letter was lying out there, never for a moment did I imagine that you would consent to accept this man's conditions. I was so absolutely certain that you would say to him: Publish the thing to the whole world. And when that was done —

Helmer. Yes, what then? — when I had exposed my wife to shame and disgrace?

Nora. When that was done, I was so absolutely certain, you would come forward and take everything upon yourself, and say: I am the guilty one.

Helmer. Nora —!

Nora. You mean that I would never have accepted such a sacrifice on your part? No, of

---

① delirious [dɪ'lɪriəs] *adj.* characteristic of delirium; marked by uncontrolled excitement (神志昏迷的;发狂的)。

② composure [kəm'pəʊʒə] *n.* a calm or tranquil state of mind (镇静;沉着)。

③ forfeit ['fɔːfɪt] *vt.* to subject to seizure (没收;丧失)。

course not. But what would my assurances have been worth against yours? That was the wonderful thing which I hoped for and feared; and it was to prevent that, that I wanted to kill myself.

Helmer. I would gladly work night and day for you, Nora — bear sorrow and want for your sake. But no man would sacrifice his honour for the one he loves.

Nora. It is a thing hundreds of thousands of women have done.

Helmer. Oh, you think and talk like a heedless[①] child.

Nora. Maybe. But you neither think nor talk like the man I could bind myself to. As soon as your fear was over — and it was not fear for what threatened me, but for what might happen to you — when the whole thing was past, as far as you were concerned it was exactly as if nothing at all had happened. Exactly as before, I was your little skylark, your doll, which you would in future treat with doubly gentle care, because it was so brittle[②] and fragile. (Getting up.) Torvald — it was then it dawned upon me that for eight years I had been living here with a strange man, and had borne him three children —. Oh, I can't bear to think of it! I could tear myself into little bits!

Helmer (sadly). I see, I see. An abyss[③] has opened between us — there is no denying it. But, Nora, would it not be possible to fill it up?

Nora. As I am now, I am no wife for you.

Helmer. I have it in me to become a different man.

Nora. Perhaps — if your doll is taken away from you.

Helmer. But to part! — to part from you! No, no, Nora, I can't understand that idea.

Nora (going out to the right). That makes it all the more certain that it must be done. (She comes back with her cloak and hat and a small bag which she puts on a chair by the table.)

Helmer. Nora, Nora, not now! Wait until tomorrow.

Nora (putting on her cloak). I cannot spend the night in a strange man's room.

Helmer. But can't we live here like brother and sister —?

Nora (putting on her hat). You know very well that would not last long. (Puts the shawl round her.) Goodbye, Torvald. I won't see the little ones. I know they are in better hands than mine. As I am now, I can be of no use to them.

Helmer. But some day, Nora — some day?

Nora. How can I tell? I have no idea what is going to become of me.

Helmer. But you are my wife, whatever becomes of you.

Nora. Listen, Torvald. I have heard that when a wife deserts her husband's house, as I

---

① heedless [ˈhiːdlɪs] *adj.* marked by or paying little heed; unmindful or thoughtless (不留心的;心不在焉的)。

② brittle [ˈbrɪtl] *adj.* likely to break (易碎的;脆弱的)。

③ abyss [əˈbɪs] *n.* an unfathomable chasm (深渊)。

am doing now, he is legally freed from all obligations towards her. In any case, I set you free from all your obligations. You are not to feel yourself bound in the slightest way, any more than I shall. There must be perfect freedom on both sides. See, here is your ring back. Give me mine.

Helmer. That too?

Nora. That too.

Helmer. Here it is.

Nora. That's right. Now it is all over. I have put the keys here. The maids know all about everything in the house — better than I do. Tomorrow, after I have left her, Christine will come here and pack up my own things that I brought with me from home. I will have them sent after me.

Helmer. All over! All over! — Nora, shall you never think of me again?

Nora. I know I shall often think of you, the children, and this house.

Helmer. May I write to you, Nora?

Nora. No — never. You must not do that.

Helmer. But at least let me send you —

Nora. Nothing — nothing —

Helmer. Let me help you if you are in want.

Nora. No. I can receive nothing from a stranger.

Helmer. Nora — can I never be anything more than a stranger to you?

Nora (taking her bag). Ah, Torvald, the most wonderful thing of all would have to happen.

Helmer. Tell me what that would be!

Nora. Both you and I would have to be so changed that —. Oh, Torvald, I don't believe any longer in wonderful things happening.

Helmer. But I will believe in it. Tell me! So changed that —?

Nora. That our life together would be a real wedlock. Goodbye. (She goes out through the hall.)

Helmer (sinks down on a chair at the door and buries his face in his hands). Nora! Nora! (Looks round, and rises.) Empty. She is gone. (A hope flashes across his mind.) The most wonderful thing of all —?

(The sound of a door shutting is heard from below.)

Tr. by Otto Reinert

Chapter Nine Modern Poetry

Ⅰ. Introduction

Generally speaking, modern poetry consists of traditional poetry, modernist poetry and post-modernist poetry.

Traditional poetry has a great store of principles. For instance, poetry is language organized for aesthetic purposes. In the 20th century, the important poets like Thomas Hardy, Robert Frost and some others are regarded as traditional poets. Although they inherited the traditional styles, sometimes they also used some modern techniques in their poems.

The modernist poetry was represented by such poetical movements as symbolism and imagism.

Symbolism in literature was largely a reaction against realism by employing symbols and evocative suggestion in place of direct statement in order to transcend the humble and the ordinary.

Symbol is something in the world of the senses, including an action, which manifests or signifies something abstract, otherworldly, or numinous. Samuel Johnson termed it as a type, which comprehends in its figure a representation of something else.

Writers use symbols normally when they believe in a transcendental reality. If a metaphor is symbolic, one of its pair of elements must manifest or reveal yet something else transcendental. Cleanth Brooks and Robert Penn Warren in *Understanding Poetry* asserted, "The symbol may be regarded as a metaphor from which the first term has been omitted."

Symbolist poetry has the following fundamental features:

1. The symbolists attached importance to the symbolized image. Like the Romantic poets, the symbolists paid attention to the sensibility of experience of human souls. The difference is that the Romantic poets liked to express their powerful feelings frankly. And the symbolists tried to capture sensations and states of minds that lay beyond normal consciousness by disordering their senses, indulging in decadence, occultism, and opposition to sober bourgeois values and to express their ideals circuitously through a series of symbolized images to arouse the association and imagination of the readers.

2. Symbolist poetry has deep mysticism and philosophic implication. The symbolist poets adored the instinct, opposed the reason, and because they thought that there existed a more real and mystic world beyond the perceptible objective world, so, to realize and transmit this mystic and unaware world was considered as the highest mission.

3. The symbolist poets paid great attention to the musicality in the poetry. They insisted that there was an ideal and inherent conjunction between music and poetry. Russian symbolist poet Andrei Bely theoretically increased the musicality in the poetry to the highest degree, and French symbolist poet Verlaine in his *Art of Poetry* even declared, "Music is the principle factor in poetry among all things."

The symbolist movement, originated in France and heralded by Charles Baudelaire, has exerted a great influence on all the European poetry ever since. Mallarme, Verlaine, and Rimbaud were representatives of French symbolist poetry.

In the English-speaking world, the closest counterpart to symbolism was aestheticism; and the Pre-Raphaelites, also, were contemporaries of the earlier symbolists, and have much in common with them. Symbolism had a significant influence on modernism and its traces can be seen in a number of modernist artists, including T. S. Eliot. And the major representatives of symbolist poetry in English-speaking world included Arthur Symons, William Butler Yeats and others.

And the Russian symbolism also has its roots in French symbolism. But it is a lopsided view when some critics deny the national cultural originalities of Russian symbolist poetry. The trends and ideas applied in the atmosphere of the times in the Western Europe, the philosophical ideas of A. Schopenhauer, F. Nietzsche, A. Bergson, and the literary ideas of Baudelaire and other French symbolists, had a significant influence on the philosophical and aesthetic concepts of Russian symbolist movement. And at the same time, deep inside the symbolist groups there existed doubtlessly an underlying succession of Russian traditional philosophical and cultural principles, and the Russian symbolists had their own national characteristics of culture and poetics. The Russian symbolists not only inherited the technique of the French symbolism, but also succeeded and developed the Russian traditional culture. So, the Russian symbolist poetry is the refraction of the tone and the emotion of the special period in Russian history, and it has its unique cultural characteristics and cognitive value.

Imagism has been described as the grammar school of modern poetry, the instruction and drill in basic principles.

The name "Imagism" is given to a movement in poetry, originating in 1912 and represented by Ezra Pound, Amy Lowell, and others, aiming at clarity of expression through the use of precise visual images.

This group of American and English poets whose poetic program was formulated about 1912 by Ezra Pound — in conjunction with fellow poets Hilda Doolittle (H. D.), Richard Aldington, and F. S. Flint — and was inspired by the critical views of T. E.

Hulme, in revolt against the careless thinking and Romantic optimism he saw prevailing.

In the spring or early summer of 1912, Ezra Pound, H. D., and Richard Aldington decided that they were agreed upon the following three principles:

1. Direct treatment of the "thing" whether subjective or objective.
2. To use absolutely no word that does not contribute to the presentation.
3. As regarding rhythm: to compose in the sequence of the musical phrase, not in sequence of a metronome.

This succinct statement can be regarded as the three general artistic charateristics of the Imagist poetry.

Post-modernism began in the sixties with pop-art, the beat generation, the magic realism of Latin American novelists, and the post-structuralist theories of Barthes, Derrida and others. For post-modernists the world exists only through our understanding of it, and the prime medium of that understanding is ordinary language.

Ⅱ. Paul Verlaine

Paul Verlaine (1844～1896) was one of the leaders of the French symbolist movement in poetry.

Born in Metz, he was educated in Paris. He began writing poetry at an early age of 14, and was initially influenced by Parnassianism. And after graduation he worked as a clerk in an insurance agency and later in the Paris City Hall. But at night, he devoted himself to poetry.

Verlaine was one of the first poets to focus on the pure musicality and rhythm of French language without concern for classical form. Though his innovations in rhythm laid a foundation for free verse, Verlaine himself always thought rhyme was a necessity for French poetry. His influence is so pervasive that a modern reader may not notice the innovations he developed. His rhythms, imagery and way of depicting his themes are now so common in modern poetic language. Verlaine's true talent did not lie in the depth of his subject matter but in the sound images in his poems.

There Is a Weeping in My Heart[①]

There is weeping in my heart
Like the rain falling on the town.
What is this languor[②]

---

① 译文参见本书第 276 页。

② languor [ˈlæŋgə] *n.* lack of physical or mental energy (衰弱无力)。

That pervades my heart?

Oh the soft patter of the rain
On the ground and the roofs!
For a heart growing weary
Oh the song of the rain!

There is weeping without cause
In this disheartened heart.
What! No betrayal?
There's no reason for this grief.

Truly the worst pain
Is not knowing why,
Without love or hatred,
My heart feels so much pain.

Tr. by Peter Low

Moonlight[1]

Your soul is as a moonlit landscape fair,
Peopled with maskers[2] delicate and dim,
That play on lutes and dance and have an air
Of being sad in their fantastic trim.

The while they celebrate in minor strain
Triumphant love, effective enterprise,
They have an air of knowing all is vain, —
And through the quiet moonlight their songs rise,

The melancholy moonlight, sweet and lone,
That makes to dream the birds upon the tree,
And in their polished basins of white stone

---

① 译文参见本书第 276 页。
② masker [ˈmɑːskə] *n.* one who wears a mask (戴面具者)。

The fountains tall to sob with ecstasy.

Tr. by Gertrude Hall

Ⅲ. William Butler Yeats

William Butler Yeats (1865～1939) was an Irish poet and dramatist, and Nobel laureate. He was a leader of the Irish Renaissance that aimed at reviving ancient Irish folklore, legends and traditions in new literary works. He was also one of the forerunners modernism in the 20th century.

William Butler Yeats was born in Dublin, Ireland, in 1865, the son of a well-known Irish painter, John Butler Yeats. His childhood was largely spent in County Sligo and London. He returned to Dublin at the age of fifteen to continue his education and to study painting, but quickly he discovered he preferred poetry. Born into the Anglo-Irish landowning class, Yeats became involved with the Celtic Revival, a movement against the cultural influences of English rule in Ireland during the Victorian period, which sought to promote the spirit of Ireland's native heritage. Though Yeats never learned Gaelic himself, his writing at the turn of the century drew extensively from sources in Irish mythology and folklore. Also a potent influence on his poetry was the Irish revolutionary Maud Gonne, whom he met in 1889, a woman equally famous for her passionate nationalist politics and her beauty. Though she married another man in 1903 and grew apart from Yeats (and Yeats himself was eventually married to another woman, Georgie Hyde Lees), she remained the most important figure in his poetry.

Yeats was deeply involved in politics in Ireland, and in the twenties, despite Irish independence from England, his verse reflected pessimism about the political situation in his country and the rest of Europe, paralleling the increasing conservatism of his American counterparts in London, T. S. Eliot and Ezra Pound. His poetry after 1910 was strongly influenced by Pound, which can be considered as a modernist one owing to its concision and imagery, but Yeats never abandoned his strict adherence to traditional verse forms. He had a life-long interest in mysticism, which was off-putting to some readers, but helpful in advancing his idiosyncratic philosophy. His poetry grew more profound as he grew older. Appointed a senator of the Irish Free State in 1922, he is remembered as an important cultural leader, as a major playwright (he was one of the founders of the famous Abbey Theatre in Dublin), and as one of the greatest poets — in any language — of the century. W. B. Yeats was awarded the Nobel Prize in 1923. He died in 1939 at the age of 73.

When You Are Old[①]

When you are old and gray and full of sleep
And nodding by the fire, take down this book,
And slowly read, and dream of the soft look
Your eyes had once, and of their shadows deep;

How many loved your moments of glad grace,
And loved your beauty with love false or true;
But one man loved the pilgrim soul in you,
And loved the sorrows of your changing face.

And bending down beside the glowing bars,
Murmur, a little sadly, how love fled
And paced upon the mountains overhead,
And hid his face amid a crowd of stars.

Leda and the Swan[②]

A sudden blow: the great wings beating still
Above the staggering girl, her thighs caressed
By the dark webs, her nape caught in his bill,
He holds her helpless breast upon his breast.

How can those terrified vague fingers push
The feathered glory from her loosening thighs?
And how can body, laid in that white rush,
But feel the strange heart beating where it lies?

A shudder in the loins engenders there
The broken wall, the burning roof and tower
And Agamemnon[③] dead.
                    Being so caught up,
So mastered by the brute blood of the air,

---

① 译文参见本书第 276 至 277 页。

② 译文参见本书第 277 页。

③ Agamemnon [ˌæɡəˈmemnən] *n.* the king of Mycenae and leader of the Greeks in the Trojan War, who was the son of Atreus and the father of Orestes, Electra, and Iphigenia (阿伽门农)。

Did she put on his knowledge with his power
Before the indifferent beak could let her drop?

Ⅳ. Ezra Pound

Ezra Pound (1885～1972) is generally considered the poet most responsible for defining and promoting a modernist aesthetic in poetry. In the early teens, he opened an exchange of work and ideas between British and American writers, and was famous for the influence he exerted to his contemporaries as W. B. Yeats, Robert Frost, William Carlos Williams, Marianne Moore, H. D., James Joyce, Ernest Hemingway, and especially T. S. Eliot. His own significant contributions to poetry begin with his promulgation of Imagism, a movement in poetry which derived its technique from classical Chinese and Japanese poetry — stressing clarity, precision, and economy of language, and foregoing traditional rhyme and meter in order to, in Pound's words, "compose in the sequence of the musical phrase, not in the sequence of the metronome." His later work, focused on the encyclopedic epic poem he entitled *The Cantos*.

Ezra Pound was born in Hailey, Idaho Territory, in 1885. He completed two years of college at the University of Pennsylvania, but after studying there for two years transferred to Hamilton College, where he earned a degree in 1905. After teaching at Wabash College for two years, he travelled abroad to Spain, Italy and London, where, as the literary executor of the scholar Ernest Fenellosa, he became interested in Japanese and Chinese poetry. He married Dorothy Shakespear in 1914 and became London editor of the *Little Review* in 1917. In 1924, he moved to Italy; during this period of voluntary exile, Pound became involved in Fascist politics, and did not return to the United States until 1945, when he was arrested on charges of treason for broadcasting Fascist propaganda by radio to the United States during the Second World War. In 1946, he was acquitted, but declared mentally ill and committed to St. Elizabeths Hospital in Washington, D. C. During his confinement, the jury of the Bollingen-Library of Congress Award (which included a number of the most eminent writers of the time) decided to overlook Pound's political career in the interest of recognizing his poetic achievements, and awarded him the prize for the *Pisan Cantos* (1948). After continuous appeals from writers won his release from the hospital in 1958, Pound returned to Italy and settled in Venice, where he died, a semi-recluse, in 1972.

Ezra Pound's "In the Station of the Metro" is characteristic for the features of Chinese poetry. The Features of Chinese poetry of this poem include two aspects. One is parallelism because it has the contrasting imagery of the two lines. Actually, it is not two sentences, but two phrases, consisting of two images: they are the faces and the petals.

The other is the intervention of the concept of the Chinese "word" or Chinese characters. Ezra Pound used the "juxtaposition of images" instead of 17 syllables of Haiku. The basic unit of this poem is not the English syllable, but the Chinese word, there are four content words in each of the two lines, and the others are only the function words.

In a Station of the Metro①

The apparition② of these faces in the crowd;
Petals on a wet, black bough.

A Girl③

The tree has entered my hands,
The sap has ascended my arms,
The tree has grown in my breast —
Downward,
The branches grow out of me, like arms.

Tree you are,
Moss you are,
You are violets with wind above them.
A child — so high — you are,
And all this is folly to the world.

Ⅴ. William Carlos Williams

William Carlos Williams (1883～1963) was born in Rutherford, New Jersey. He began experimenting with poetry when he was a student at Horace Mann High School. Although his parents were both admirers of literature and art, they encouraged Williams to pursue a career in medicine. Ultimately, Williams decided to become both a writer and a doctor: he enrolled in the University of Pennsylvania's medical program while continuing to write poetry in his free time. And he received his M. D. from this university. It was at the University of Pennsylvania that Williams befriended Ezra Pound, whose "Imagism" was to have a great influence on Williams's early work. Through Pound, Williams met several other poets, including H. D. (Hilda Doolittle).

---

① 译文参见本书第 277 页。

② apparition [ˌæpəˈrɪʃən] *n.* a sudden or unusual sight; a specter.（离奇出现的东西;幻影）。

③ 译文参见本书第 277 页。

Following Pound, he was one of the principal poets of the Imagist movement. His major works include *Kora in Hell* (1920), *Spring and All* (1923), *Pictures from Brueghel and Other Poems* (1962), the five-volume epic *Paterson* (1963), and *Imaginations*(1970). Williams's health began to decline after a heart attack in 1948 and a series of strokes, but he continued writing up until his death in New Jersey on March 4, 1963, two months later posthumously winning his first and only Pulitzer Prize for his last book of poems.

The Red Wheelbarrow①

so much depends
upon

a red wheel
barrow

glazed with rain
water

beside the white
chickens.

Ⅵ. T. S. Eliot

T. S. Eliot (1888～1965) was born in St. Louis, Missouri, and was once educated at Milton Academy (a private boarding school outside of Boston, Massachusetts) and at Harvard University, where he earned his undergraduate degree, after three years of study, in 1909. He then continued at Harvard, studying philosophy under George Santayana. Eliot received his M. A. degree in philosophy in 1910, after which he studied literature and languages at the Sorbonne in Paris, France; at the University of Marburg in Germany; and at the University of Oxford in England.

Eliot's earliest masterpiece, *The Love Song of J. Alfred Prufrock*, was published in *Poetry* magazine in 1915. This poem deals with spiritually exhausted people who exist in the impersonal modern city. Prufrock is a representative character who cannot reconcile his thoughts and understanding with his feelings and will. Written in the form of a dramatic monologue, the poem is an examination of the soul of a timid man paralyzed by

---

① 译文参见本书第 277 页。

indecision and worry about his appearance to others, particularly women.

T. S. Eliot is regarded as one of the greatest poets of the 20th century. His best-known poem, *The Waste Land* (1922), stands as one of the most original and influential poems of the twentieth century. Eliot also wrote drama and literary criticism. In his plays, which use unrhymed verse, he attempted to revive poetic drama for the contemporary audience. His most influential criticism looked at the way the poet should approach the act of writing. Eliot won the Nobel Prize for literature in 1948.

Morning at the Window①

They are rattling breakfast plates in basement kitchens,
And along the trampled edges of the street
I am aware of the damp souls of housemaids
Sprouting despondently at area gates.

The brown waves of fog toss up to me
Twisted faces from the bottom of the street,
And tear from a passer-by with muddy skirts
An aimless smile that hovers in the air
And vanishes along the level of the roofs.

Ⅷ. Sergei Yesenin

Sergei Yesenin (1895～1925) was a famous Russian lyrical poet, whose poetry is distinguished by deep sincerity and an intense emotionalism.

Yesenin was born in a peasant's family. He began to write verse at the age of 9 and graduated from a school in his native village when he was 16. He obtained the rest of his education by his own efforts.

In 1912 Yesenin moved to Moscow, and two years later he relocated to St. Petersburg, where he became acquainted with some of the Russian symbolists, including Aleksandr Blok. Yesenin's first book of poetry was published in 1916. From 1919 to 1921 he led the literary group called the Imagists, and in the early 1920s he made several trips to Western Europe and to the United States.

His several failed marriages (including to the American dancer Isadora Duncan, 1922, and to Sophia, the granddaughter of the great Russian novelist Leo Tolstoy, 1925) and alcoholism contributed to his suicide in St. Petersburg (then called Leningrad) in

---

① 译文参见本书第 277 页。

December 1925.

I've Quit My Father's Home[①]

I've quit my father's home
And left blue Russ. With three
Bright stars the birch-tree grove
Consoles[②] my mother's grief.

The moon has, like a frog,
Upon the pond appeared.
Like apple blossom, locks
Of grey fleck father's beard.

I shall not soon come back!
Long shall snow blow in the yard.
Our one-legged maple shall
Over blue Russ stand guard.

To kiss its raining leaves
Is joy, and none so fine —
The head of the maple-tree
So closely resembles mine.

Tr. by Peter Tempest

Ⅷ. Robert Frost

Robert Frost (1874～1963) was born in San Francisco in 1874. He moved to New England at the age of eleven and became interested in reading and writing poetry during his high school years in Lawrence, Massachusetts. He was enrolled at Dartmouth College in 1892, and later at Harvard, but never earned a formal degree.

In 1895, Frost married Elinor Miriam White, who became a major inspiration in his poetry until her death in 1938. The couple moved to England in 1912, and it was abroad that Frost met and was influenced by such contemporary British poets as Edward Thomas, Rupert Brooke, and Robert Graves. While in England, Frost also established a friendship

① 译文参见本书第 278 页。
② console [kən'səʊl] *vt.* to comfort; to allay the sorrow or grief (安慰；慰藉)。

with the poet Ezra Pound, who helped to promote and publish his work. By the time Frost returned to the United States in 1915, he had published two full-length collections, *A Boy's Will* and *North of Boston*, and his reputation was established. By the 1920s, he was the most celebrated poet in America.

His work is principally associated with the life and landscape of New England, and he was a poet of traditional verse forms and metrics who remained steadfastly aloof from the poetic movements and fashions of his time.

Robert Frost once said: "A poem begins in delight, and ends in wisdom." This statement can be his principle of writing. Many of his poems, for example, "Stopping by Woods on a Snowy Evening" and "The Road Not Taken", begin with the natural scene of New England, and move along the rhythm of spoken language to the end of each catchphrase.

Stopping by Woods on a Snowy Evening①

Whose woods these are I think I know.
His house is in the village, though;
He will not see me stopping here
To watch his woods fill up with snow.

My little horse must think it queer
To stop without a farmhouse near
Between the woods and frozen lake
The darkest evening of the year.

He gives his harness② bells a shake
To ask if there is some mistake.
The only other sound's the sweep
Of easy wind and downy flake.

The woods are lovely, dark and deep,
But I have promises to keep,
And miles to go before I sleep,
And miles to go before I sleep.

---

① 译文参见本书第 278 页。

② harness [ˈhɑːnɪs] *n.* the gear or tackle, other than a yoke, with which a draft animal pulls a vehicle or an implement.（马具;系在身上的绳子）。

The Road Not Taken[①]

Two roads diverged in a yellow wood,
And sorry I could not travel both
And be one traveller, long I stood
And looked down one as far as I could
To where it bent in the undergrowth[②];

Then took the other, as just as fair,
And having perhaps the better claim,
Because it was grassy and wanted wear;
Though as for that the passing there
Had worn them really about the same,

And both that morning equally lay
In leaves no step had trodden black.
Oh, I kept the first for another day!
Yet knowing how way leads on to way,
I doubted if I should ever come back.
I shall be telling this with a sigh
Somewhere ages and ages hence:
Two roads diverged in a wood, and I —
I took the one less traveled by,
And that has made all the difference.

Ⅸ. Rabindranath Tagore

Rabindranath Tagore (1861～1941), the greatest writer in modern Indian literature and Nobel Prize winner for literature (1913), was born in Calcutta, India into a wealthy and prominent Brahmin family.

Tagore wrote more then fifty volumes of poetry in Bengali. His most acclaimed book is the collection of prose poems *Gitanjali*, which is about divine and human love and it was translated into English by the author himself. Tagore's poetical works not only established

---

① 译文参见本书第 278 页。

② undergrowth [ˈʌndəgrəʊθ] *n.* low-growing plants, saplings, and shrubs beneath trees in a forest (下层灌丛)。

his reputation as the founder of modern Indian poetry, but also stood for the great achievements of Eastern countries in the world literature, and his influence over the modern world literature was enormous.

Gitanjali

XLI

Where dost thou stand behind them all, my lover, hiding thyself in the shadows? They push thee and pass thee by on the dusty road, taking thee for naught. I wait here weary hours spreading my offerings for thee, while passers-by come and take my flowers, one by one, and my basket is nearly empty.

The morning time is past, and the noon. In the shade of evening my eyes are drowsy with sleep. Men going home glance at me and smile and fill me with shame. I sit like a beggar maid, drawing my skirt over my face, and when they ask me, what it is I want, I drop my eyes and answer them not.

Oh, how, indeed, could I tell them that for thee I wait, and that thou hast promised to come. How could I utter for shame that I keep for my dowry this poverty. Ah, I hug this pride in the secret of my heart.

I sit on the grass and gaze upon the sky and dream of the sudden splendour of thy coming — all the lights ablaze①, golden pennons② flying over thy car, and they at the roadside standing agape, when they see thee come down from thy seat to raise me from the dust, and set at thy side this ragged beggar girl a-tremble with shame and pride, like a creeper in a summer breeze.

But time glides on and still no sound of the wheels of thy chariot. Many a procession passes by with noise and shouts and glamour of glory. Is it only thou who wouldst stand in the shadow silent and behind them all? And only I who would wait and weep and wear out my heart in vain longing?

LXIX

The same stream of life that runs through my veins night and day runs through the world and dances in rhythmic③ measures.

It is the same life that shoots in joy through the dust of the earth in numberless blades of grass and breaks into tumultuous waves of leaves and flowers.

It is the same life that is rocked in the ocean-cradle of birth and of death, in ebb④ and

---

① ablaze [əˈbleɪz] *adj.* being on fire; radiant with bright color (着火的;闪耀的)。

② pennon [ˈpenən] *n.* a long, narrow banner or streamer borne upon a lance (狭长三角旗;旗帜)。

③ rhythmic [ˈrɪðmɪk] *adj.* having rhythm; recurring with measured regularity (有节奏的)。

④ ebb [eb] *n.* a period of decline or diminution (退潮)。

in flow.

I feel my limbs are made glorious by the touch of this world of life. And my pride is from the life-throb of ages dancing in my blood this moment.

Chapter Ten Modern Fictions

Ⅰ. Introduction

Like poetical works, the achievements of fictions in modern literature are tremendous. Modern literature is an ongoing study of the 20th and 21st century literature which focuses on the modernist shift in style and subject matter as well as a writer's background, biography, contemporaries, and current criticism.

Generally speaking, modern Western literature consists of three periods; which are periods of traditional literature, modernist literature and post-modernist literature. Traditional fiction writers inherited the traditional themes and styles, but sometimes they also used the modern techniques in their works. The important fiction writers of the 20th century include such novelists as Mikhail Sholokhov from Russia, D. H. Lawrence and Theodore Dreiser from English-speaking countries, Thomas Mann from Germany and Romain Rolland from France. The so-called "socialist realism" in Soviet Russian literature can also regarded as traditional literature, because the writers were regarded as "engineers of the soul" and the literary creation defined in the statutes as "demanding of the artist the truthful, historically concrete representation of reality in its revolutionary development"[①].

Modernism was a complex and diverse concept, based on different social realities and influenced by different ideas and thoughts. In general, Modernism is characterized by a conscious rejection of established rules and traditions both in content and in form. Modernist literature was profoundly influenced by new philosophical ideas and the persons it was indebted most, among which the most influential were Sigmund Freud (1856～1939), Friedrich Nietzsche (1844～1900) and Menri Bergson (1859～1941). Sigmund Freud was the originator of psychoanalysis, and in his theory, the unconscious is emphasized and human sexuality is given prime importance in analyzing human behavior. His theory had an enormous influence upon the modernist literature, especially the fictions of "stream of consciousness". Friedrich Nietzsche's key idea — the Dionysian spirit — and Menri Bergson's methord of intuition also had a profound influence upon literature.

① Caryl Emerson. *The Cambridge Introduction to Russian Literature*, Cambridge University Press, 2008, p. 199.

Important modernist novelists include Mikhail Bulgakov from Russia, Marcel Proust from France, Stefan Zweig and Franz Kafka from German speaking countries, James Joyce, William Faulkner, Ernest Hemingway and Virginia Woolf from English speaking countries.

Post-modernism began in the sixties with pop-art, the beat generation, the magic realism of Latin American literature, and the post-structuralist theories of Rolan Barthes (1915～1980), Jacques Derrida (1930～2004) and others. For post-modernists the world exists only through our understanding of it, and the prime medium of that understanding is everyday language. Rejecting modernist nostalgia for an organic wholeness and feeling that life's quandary not resolvable, the post-modernists attempt to generate meaning in the face of chaos and absurdity.

The masterpieces of the 20th-century fiction works also include the works by such Nobel laureates as Boris Pasternak, Solzhenitsyn, Ernest Hemingway, Saul Bellow, García Márquez, Yasunari Kawabata and many others. Over the years, the Nobel Prize in the field of literature has distinguished the works of authors from many different languages and cultural backgrounds.

Ⅱ. Virginia Woolf

Virginia Woolf (1882～1941), an English novelist and writer of short stories, is regarded as one of the foremost modernist literary figures of the twentieth century. She was born Adeline Virginia Stephen in London, and her father was the Victorian man of letters Leslie Stephen. When she was young, she was educated by her parents in their literate and well-connected household. Virginia Woolf began writing professionally in 1905. Her first novel, *The Voyage Out*, was published in 1915. Her important works include *Mrs Dalloway* (1925), *To the Lighthouse* (1927), *Orlando* (1928) and *A Room of One's Own* (1929).

Virginia Woolf's great contribution to world literature is the use of the technique of "stream of consciousness".

The phrase "stream of consciousness" was first used by American psychologist William James in his book *Principles of Psychology*. He believed that human mind was a continuous stream that could not be cut off. Originated from this idea, "stream of consciousness" was widely used in modern literature as a manner of writing. The writers of this manner avoided artificial omniscience and let their characters reveal themselves through their minds without the intervention of the author.

So, in her famous short story *The Mark on the Wall*, the important thing is not the objective fact — what is the mark on the wall, but the subjective narrative — the individual's inner world.

The Mark on the Wall[①]

Perhaps it was the middle of January in the present year that I first looked up and saw the mark on the wall. In order to fix a date it is necessary to remember what one saw. So now I think of the fire; the steady film of yellow light upon the page of my book; the three chrysanthemums[②] in the round glass bowl on the mantelpiece. Yes, it must have been the winter time, and we had just finished our tea, for I remember that I was smoking a cigarette when I looked up and saw the mark on the wall for the first time. I looked up through the smoke of my cigarette and my eye lodged for a moment upon the burning coals, and that old fancy of the crimson flag flapping from the castle tower came into my mind, and I thought of the cavalcade[③] of red knights riding up the side of the black rock. Rather to my relief the sight of the mark interrupted the fancy, for it is an old fancy, an automatic fancy, made as a child perhaps. The mark was a small round mark, black upon the white wall, about six or seven inches above the mantelpiece.

How readily our thoughts swarm upon a new object, lifting it a little way, as ants carry a blade of straw so feverishly, and then leave it ... if that mark was made by a nail, it can't have been for a picture, it must have been for a miniature[④]— the miniature of a lady with white powdered curls, powder-dusted cheeks, and lips like red carnations[⑤]. A fraud of course, for the people who had this house before us would have chosen pictures in that way — an old picture for an old room. That is the sort of people they were — very interesting people, and I think of them so often, in such queer places, because one will never see them again, never know what happened next. They wanted to leave this house because they wanted to change their style of furniture, so he said, and he was in process of saying that in his opinion art should have ideas behind it when we were torn asunder, as one is torn from the old lady about to pour out tea and the young man about to hit the tennis ball in the back garden of the suburban villa as one rushes past in the train.

But as for that mark, I'm not sure about it; I don't believe it was made by a nail after all; it's too big, too round, for that. I might get up, but if I got up and looked at it, ten to one[⑥] I shouldn't be able to say for certain; because once a thing's done, no one ever knows how it happened. Oh! dear me, the mystery of life! The inaccuracy of thought!

---

① 译文参见本书第 278 至 282 页。

② chrysanthemum [krɪ'sænθəməm] *n.* 菊花。

③ cavalcade [ˌkævəl'keɪd] *n.* a procession of riders（队伍）。

④ miniature ['mɪnjjətʃə] *n.* a copy or model that represents something in a greatly reduced size（小画像；缩影）。

⑤ carnation [kɑː'neɪʃən] *n.* 荷兰石竹；康乃馨。

⑥ ten to one：十之八九；很可能。ten to one I shouldn't be able to say for certain：it is very likely that I'm not sure what it is.

The ignorance of humanity! To show how very little control of our possessions we have — what an accidental affair this living is after all our civilisation — let me just count over a few of the things lost in our lifetime, beginning, for that seems always the most mysterious of losses — what cat would gnaw[①], what rat would nibble[②]— three pale blue canisters of book-binding tools? Then there were the bird cages, the iron hoops, the steel skates, the Queen Anne coal-scuttle[③], the bagatelle board, the hand organ — all gone, and jewels too. Opals[④] and emeralds[⑤], they lie about the roots of turnips. What a scraping paring affair it is to be sure![⑥] The wonder is that I've any clothes on my back, that I sit surrounded by solid furniture at this moment. Why, if one wants to compare life to anything, one must liken it to being blown through the Tube[⑦] at fifty miles an hour — landing at the other end without a single hairpin in one's hair! Shot out at the feet of God entirely naked! Tumbling head over heels in the asphodel[⑧] meadows like brown paper parcels pitched down a shoot in the post office! With one's hair flying back like the tail of a racehorse. Yes, that seems to express the rapidity of life, the perpetual waste and repair; all so casual, all so haphazard ...

But after life. The slow pulling down of thick green stalks so that the cup of the flower, as it turns over, deluges one with purple and red light. Why, after all, should one not be born there as one is born here, helpless, speechless, unable to focus one's eyesight, groping at the roots of the grass, at the toes of the Giants? As for saying which are trees, and which are men and women, or whether there are such things, that one won't be in a condition to do for fifty years or so. There will be nothing but spaces of light and dark, intersected by thick stalks, and rather higher up perhaps, rose-shaped blots of an indistinct colour — dim pinks and blues — which will, as time goes on, become more definite, become — I don't know what ...

And yet the mark on the wall is not a hole at all. It may even be caused by some round black substance, such as a small rose leaf, left over from the summer, and I, not being a very vigilant housekeeper — look at the dust on the mantelpiece, for example, the dust which, so they say, buried Troy three times over, only fragments of pots utterly refusing annihilation[⑨], as one can believe.

The tree outside the window taps very gently on the pane ... I want to think quietly,

---

① gnaw [nɔː] *v.* to bite, chew on, or erode with the teeth (咬;咬断)。

② nibble [ˈnɪbl] *n.* to eat with small, quick bites or in small morsels (细咬;啃)。

③ scuttle [ˈskʌtl] *n.* 天窗;煤桶。the Queen Anne coal-scuttle:安妮女皇时代的煤斗子。

④ opal [ˈəupəl] *n.* 蛋白石;猫眼石。

⑤ emerald [ˈemərəld] *n.* 祖母绿;翡翠;绿宝石。

⑥ What a scraping paring affair it is to be sure: It takes a lot of time and money to gather them.

⑦ tube [tjuːb] *n.* metro (地铁)。

⑧ asphodel [ˈæsfədəl] *n.* 日光兰;常春花;水仙。

⑨ annihilation [əˌnaɪəˈleɪʃən] *n.* utter destruction (歼灭;灭绝)。

calmly, spaciously, never to be interrupted, never to have to rise from my chair, to slip easily from one thing to another, without any sense of hostility, or obstacle. I want to sink deeper and deeper, away from the surface, with its hard separate facts. To steady myself, let me catch hold of the first idea that passes ... Shakespeare ... Well, he will do as well as another. A man who sat himself solidly in an arm-chair, and looked into the fire, so — A shower of ideas fell perpetually from some very high Heaven down through his mind. He leant his forehead on his hand, and people, looking in through the open door — for this scene is supposed to take place on a summer's evening-But how dull this is, this historical fiction! It doesn't interest me at all. I wish I could hit upon a pleasant track of thought, a track indirectly reflecting credit upon myself, for those are the pleasantest thoughts, and very frequent even in the minds of modest mouse-coloured people, who believe genuinely that they dislike to hear their own praises. They are not thoughts directly praising oneself; that is the beauty of them; they are thoughts like this:

"And then I came into the room. They were discussing botany. I said how I'd seen a flower growing on a dust heap on the site of an old house in Kingsway①. The seed, I said, must have been sown in the reign of Charles the First. What flowers grew in the reign of Charles the First?" I asked — (but I don't remember the answer). Tall flowers with purple tassels to them perhaps. And so it goes on. All the time I'm dressing up the figure of myself in my own mind, lovingly, stealthily, not openly adoring it, for if I did that, I should catch myself out, and stretch my hand at once for a book in self-protection. Indeed, it is curious how instinctively one protects the image of oneself from idolatry or any other handling that could make it ridiculous, or too unlike the original to be believed in any longer. Or is it not so very curious after all? It is a matter of great importance. Suppose the looking-glass smashes, the image disappears, and the romantic figure with the green of forest depths all about it is there no longer, but only that shell of a person which is seen by other people — what an airless, shallow, bald, prominent world it becomes! A world not to be lived in. As we face each other in omnibuses and underground railways we are looking into the mirror; that accounts for the vagueness, the gleam of glassiness, in our eyes. And the novelists in future will realise more and more the importance of these reflections, for of course there is not one reflection but an almost infinite number; those are the depths they will explore, those the phantoms they will pursue, leaving the description of reality more and more out of their stories, taking a knowledge of it for granted, as the Greeks did and Shakespeare perhaps — but these generalisations are very worthless. The military sound of the word is enough. It recalls leading articles, cabinet ministers — a whole class of things indeed which as a child one thought the thing itself, the standard thing, the real thing, from which one could not depart save at the risk of nameless damnation. Generalisations bring back somehow

---

① Kingsway: a street in London.

Sunday in London, Sunday afternoon walks, Sunday luncheons, and also ways of speaking of the dead, clothes, and habits — like the habit of sitting all together in one room until a certain hour, although nobody liked it. There was a rule for everything. The rule for tablecloths at that particular period was that they should be made of tapestry with little yellow compartments marked upon them, such as you may see in photographs of the carpets in the corridors of the royal palaces. Tablecloths of a different kind were not real tablecloths. How shocking, and yet how wonderful it was to discover that these real things, Sunday luncheons, Sunday walks, country houses, and tablecloths were not entirely real, were indeed half phantoms, and the damnation which visited the disbeliever in them was only a sense of illegitimate freedom. What now takes the place of those things I wonder, those real standard things? Men perhaps, should you be a woman; the masculine point of view which governs our lives, which sets the standard, which establishes Whitaker's Table of Precedency①, which has become, I suppose, since the war half a phantom to many men and women, which soon, one may hope, will be laughed into the dustbin where the phantoms go, the mahogany sideboards and the Landseer② prints, Gods and Devils, Hell and so forth, leaving us all with an intoxicating sense of illegitimate freedom — if freedom exists ...

In certain lights that mark on the wall seems actually to project from the wall. Nor is it entirely circular. I cannot be sure, but it seems to cast a perceptible③ shadow, suggesting that if I ran my finger down that strip of the wall it would, at a certain point, mount and descend a small tumulus④, a smooth tumulus like those barrows on the South Downs which are, they say, either tombs or camps. Of the two I should prefer them to be tombs, desiring melancholy like most English people, and finding it natural at the end of a walk to think of the bones stretched beneath the turf ... There must be some book about it. Some antiquary must have dug up those bones and given them a name ... What sort of a man is an antiquary, I wonder? Retired Colonels for the most part, I dare say, leading parties of aged labourers to the top here, examining clods of earth and stone, and getting into correspondence with the neighbouring clergy, which, being opened at breakfast time, gives them a feeling of importance, and the comparison of arrowheads necessitates cross-country journeys to the county towns, an agreeable necessity both to them and to their elderly wives, who wish to make plum jam or to clean out the study, and have every reason for keeping that great question of the camp or the tomb in perpetual suspension,

---

① Whitaker's Table of Precedency: a book which laid out the ranking of the aristocracy in England. Whitaker (1820～1895), a famous British publisher.

② Landseer: Edwin Henry Landseer (19 世纪动物画家)。

③ perceptible [pəˈseptəbl] *adj.* capable of being perceived by the senses or the mind (显而易见的；可以感觉得到的)。

④ tumulus [ˈtjuːmjʊləs] *n.* an ancient grave mound; a barrow (坟墓；古墓)。

while the Colonel himself feels agreeably philosophic in accumulating evidence on both sides of the question. It is true that he does finally incline to believe in the camp; and, being opposed, indites[①] a pamphlet which he is about to read at the quarterly meeting of the local society when a stroke lays him low, and his last conscious thoughts are not of wife or child, but of the camp and that arrowhead there, which is now in the case at the local museum, together with the foot of a Chinese murderess, a handful of Elizabethan nails, a great many Tudor clay pipes, a piece of Roman pottery, and the wine-glass that Nelson drank out of — proving I really don't know what.

No, no, nothing is proved, nothing is known. And if I were to get up at this very moment and ascertain that the mark on the wall is really — what shall I say? — the head of a gigantic old nail, driven in two hundred years ago, which has now, owing to the patient attrition of many generations of housemaids, revealed its head above the coat of paint, and is taking its first view of modern life in the sight of a white-walled fire-lit room, what should I gain? Knowledge? Matter for further speculation? I can think sitting still as well as standing up. And what is knowledge? What are our learned men save the descendants of witches and hermits who crouched in caves and in woods brewing herbs, interrogating shrew-mice and writing down the language of the stars? And the less we honour them as our superstitions dwindle and our respect for beauty and health of mind increases ... Yes, one could imagine a very pleasant world. A quiet spacious world, with the flowers so red and blue in the open fields. A world without professors or specialists or house-keepers with the profiles of policemen, a world which one could slice with one's thought as a fish slices the water with his fin, grazing the stems of the water-lilies, hanging suspended over nests of white sea eggs ... How peaceful it is down here, rooted in the centre of the world and gazing up through the grey waters, with their sudden gleams of light, and their reflections — if it were not for Whitaker's Almanack — if it were not for the Table of Precedency!

I must jump up and see for myself what that mark on the wall really is — a nail, a rose-leaf, a crack[②] in the wood?

Here is Nature once more at her old game of self-preservation. This train of thought, she perceives, is threatening mere waste of energy, even some collision[③] with reality, for who will ever be able to lift a finger against Whitaker's Table of Precedency? The Archbishop of Canterbury is followed by the Lord High Chancellor; the Lord High Chancellor is followed by the Archbishop of York. Everybody follows somebody, such is the philosophy of Whitaker; and the great thing is to know who follows whom. Whitaker knows, and let that, so Nature counsels, comfort you, instead of enraging you; and if you

---

① indite [ɪn'daɪt] *vt.* to write; compose.(写;创作)。

② crack [kræk] *n.* a slight, narrow space (裂缝)。

③ collision [kə'lɪʒən] *n.* the act or process of colliding; a crash or conflict (碰撞;冲突)。

can't be comforted, if you must shatter this hour of peace, think of the mark on the wall.

I understand Nature's game — her prompting to take action as a way of ending any thought that threatens to excite or to pain. Hence, I suppose, comes our slight contempt for men of action — men, we assume, who don't think. Still, there's no harm in putting a full stop to one's disagreeable thoughts by looking at a mark on the wall.

Indeed, now that I have fixed my eyes upon it, I feel that I have grasped a plank① in the sea; I feel a satisfying sense of reality which at once turns the two Archbishops and the Lord High Chancellor to the shadows of shades. Here is something definite, something real. Thus, waking from a midnight dream of horror, one hastily turns on the light and lies quiescent②, worshipping the chest of drawers, worshipping solidity, worshipping reality, worshipping the impersonal world which is proof of some existence other than ours. That is what one wants to be sure of ... Wood is a pleasant thing to think about. It comes from a tree; and trees grow, and we don't know how they grow. For years and years they grow, without paying any attention to us, in meadows, in forests, and by the side of rivers — all things one likes to think about. The cows swish their tails beneath them on hot afternoons; they paint rivers so green that when a moor hen dives one expects to see its feathers all green when it comes up again. I like to think of the fish balanced against the stream like flags blown out; and of water-beetles slowly raising domes of mud upon the bed of the river. I like to think of the tree itself: first the close dry sensation of being wood; then the grinding of the storm; then the slow, delicious ooze③ of sap. I like to think of it, too, on winter's nights standing in the empty field with all leaves close-furled, nothing tender exposed to the iron bullets of the moon, a naked mast upon an earth that goes tumbling, tumbling all night long. The song of birds must sound very loud and strange in June; and how cold the feet of insects must feel upon it, as they make laborious progresses up the creases of the bark, or sun themselves upon the thin green awning of the leaves, and look straight in front of them with diamond-cut red eyes .... One by one the fibres snap beneath the immense cold pressure of the earth, then the last storm comes and, falling, the highest branches drive deep into the ground again. Even so, life isn't done with; there are a million patient, watchful lives still for a tree, all over the world, in bedrooms, in ships, on the pavement, lining rooms, where men and women sit after tea, smoking cigarettes. It is full of peaceful thoughts, happy thoughts, this tree. I should like to take each one separately — but something is getting in the way ... Where was I? What has it all been about? A tree? A river? The Downs? Whitaker's Almanack? The fields of asphodel? I can't remember a thing. Everything's moving, falling, slipping, vanishing ...

---

① plank [plæŋk] *n.* a piece of lumber cut thicker than a board; a support (厚木板;支架)。

② quiescent [kwaɪ'esənt] *adj.* being quiet or at rest (静止的)。

③ ooze [uːz] *n.* to flow or leak out slowly, as through small openings (渗漏;分泌)。ooze of sap: 树液慢慢渗出。

There is a vast upheaval[①] of matter. Someone is standing over me and saying —

"I'm going out to buy a newspaper."

"Yes?"

"Though it's no good buying newspapers ... Nothing ever happens. Curse this war; God damn this war! ... All the same, I don't see why we should have a snail on our wall."

Ah, the mark on the wall! It was a snail.

Ⅲ. Ernest Hemingway

Ernest Hemingway (1899～1961), one of the best-known American writer and the Nobel Prize winner for literature in 1954, came from the Midwest of America. He is famous to modern readers for his styles in writing, his permanent interest in sports and his four marriages.

Hemingway's first novel *The Sun Also Rises* was an autobiographical novel that epitomized the post-war expatriate generation for future generations. His other important prose works include *A Farewell to Arms*, *For Whom the Bell Tolls* and *The Old Man and the Sea*.

Hemingway's distinctive writing style is characterized by simplicity and understatement. He liked to use nouns and verbs and rarely use adjectives. In sentence structure, he liked to use coordinated clauses to avoid subordinated ones. His aesthetic theory states that omitting the right thing from a story could actually strengthen it. He equated this theory with the structure of an iceberg where only one-eighth of it could be seen above water while the remaining seven-eighths of it under the surface provided the iceberg's dignity of motion and contributed to its momentum.

Hemingway's famous short story *Hills Like White Elephants* was first published in the 1927 collection *Men Without Women*. He used the simple straightforward style to tell a single-line story that takes place in one place on a single day. It is about a young couple and their polemic issue of abortion. The story takes place at a train station in the Ebro River valley of Spain and ends with the couple expecting their train's arrival. There is no resolution in the story and there is no decision stated regarding the abortion, but it is doubtlessly understood through Hemingway's powerful use of literary elements such as setting and symbolism.

---

① upheaval [ʌpˈhiːvəl] *n.* a sudden, violent disruption or upset (剧变；动荡)。

Hills Like White Elephants[①]

The hills across the valley of the Ebro[②] were long and white. On this side there was no shade and no trees and the station was between two lines of rails in the sun. Close against the side of the station there was the warm shadow of the building and a curtain, made of strings of bamboo beads, hung across the open door into the bar, to keep out flies. The American and the girl with him sat at a table in the shade, outside the building. It was very hot and the express from Barcelona[③] would come in forty minutes. It stopped at this junction for two minutes and went to Madrid.

"What should we drink?" the girl asked. She had taken off her hat and put it on the table.

"It's pretty hot," the man said.

"Let's drink beer."

"Dos cervezas,"[④] the man said into the curtain.

"Big ones?" a woman asked from the doorway.

"Yes. Two big ones."

The woman brought two glasses of beer and two felt pads. She put the felt pads and the beer glass on the table and looked at the man and the girl. The girl was looking off at the line of hills. They were white in the sun and the country was brown and dry.

"They look like white elephants," she said.

"I've never seen one," the man drank his beer.

"No, you wouldn't have."

"I might have," the man said. "Just because you say I wouldn't have doesn't prove anything."

The girl looked at the bead curtain. "They've painted something on it," she said. "What does it say?"

"Anis del Toro.[⑤] It's a drink."

"Could we try it?"

The man called "Listen" through the curtain. The woman came out from the bar.

"Four reales[⑥]."

"We want two Anis del Toro."

"With water?"

---

① 译文参见本书第 282 至 284 页。

② Ebro [ˈeɪbrəʊ] *n.* a river in the north of Spain（位于西班牙北部的埃布罗河）。

③ Barcelona [ˌbɑːsɪˈləʊnə] *n.* 巴塞罗那（西班牙东北部港市）。

④ Dos cervezas：（西班牙语）来两杯啤酒。

⑤ Anis del Toro：（西班牙语）茴香酒。

⑥ reale：里亚尔（西班牙昔时硬币）。

"Do you want it with water?"

"I don't know," the girl said. "Is it good with water?"

"It's all right."

"You want them with water?" asked the woman.

"Yes, with water."

"It tastes like liquorice[①]," the girl said and put the glass down.

"That's the way with everything."

"Yes," said the girl. "Everything tastes of liquorice. Especially all the things you've waited so long for, like absinthe."

"Oh, cut it out."

"You started it," the girl said. "I was being amused. I was having a fine time."

"Well, let's try and have a fine time."

"All right. I was trying. I said the mountains looked like white elephants. Wasn't that bright?"

"That was bright."

"I wanted to try this new drink. That's all we do, isn't it — look at things and try new drinks?"

"I guess so."

The girl looked across at the hills.

"They're lovely hills," she said, "They don't really look like white elephants. I just meant the colouring of their skin through the trees."

"Should we have another drink?"

"All right."

The warm wind blew the bead curtain against the table.

"The beer's nice and cool," the man said.

"It's lovely," the girl said.

"It's really an awfully simple operation, Jig," the man said. "It's not really an operation at all."

The girl looked at the ground the table legs rested on.

"I know you wouldn't mind it, Jig. It's really not anything. It's just to let the air in."

The girl did not say anything.

"I'll go with you and I'll stay with you all the time. They just let the air in and then it's all perfectly natural."

"Then what will we do afterwards?"

"We'll be fine afterwards. Just like we were before."

"What makes you think so?"

"That's the only thing that bothers us. It's the only thing that's made us unhappy."

---

① liquorice [ˈlɪkərɪs] *n.* 甘草。

The girl looked at the bead curtain, put her hand out and took hold of two of the strings of beads.

"And you think then we'll be all right and be happy."

"I know we will. Yon don't have to be afraid. I've known lots of people that have done it."

"So have I," said the girl. "And afterwards they were all so happy."

"Well," the man said, "if you don't want to you don't have to. I wouldn't have you do it if you didn't want to. But I know it's perfectly simple."

"And you really want to?"

"I think it's the best thing to do. But I don't want you to do it if you don't really want to."

"And if I do it you'll be happy and things will be like they were and you'll love me?"

"I love you now. You know I love you."

"I know. But if I do it, then it will be nice again if I say things are like white elephants, and you'll like it?"

"I'll love it. I love it now but I just can't think about it. You know how I get when I worry."

"If I do it you won't ever worry?"

"I won't worry about that because it's perfectly simple."

"Then I'll do it. Because I don't care about me."

"What do you mean?"

"I don't care about me."

"Well, I care about you."

"Oh, yes. But I don't care about me. And I'll do it and then everything will be fine."

"I don't want you to do it if you feel that way."

The girl stood up and walked to the end of the station. Across, on the other side, were fields of grain and trees along the banks of the Ebro. Far away, beyond the river, were mountains. The shadow of a cloud moved across the field of grain and she saw the river through the trees.

"And we could have all this," she said. "And we could have everything and every day we make it more impossible."

"What did you say?"

"I said we could have everything."

"No, we can't."

"We can have the whole world."

"No, we can't."

"We can go everywhere."

"No, we can't. It isn't ours any more."

"It's ours."

"No, it isn't. And once they take it away, you never get it back."

"But they haven't taken it away."

"We'll wait and see."

"Come on back in the shade," he said. "You mustn't feel that way."

"I don't feel any way," the girl said. "I just know things."

"I don't want you to do anything that you don't want to do —"

"Nor that isn't good for me," she said. "I know. Could we have another beer?"

"All right. But you've got to realize — "

"I realize," the girl said. "Can't we maybe stop talking?"

They sat down at the table and the girl looked across at the hills on the dry side of the valley and the man looked at her and at the table.

"You've got to realize," he said, "that I don't want you to do it if you don't want to. I'm perfectly willing to go through with it if it means anything to you."

"Doesn't it mean anything to you? We could get along."

"Of course it does. But I don't want anybody but you. I don't want anyone else. And I know it's perfectly simple."

"Yes, you know it's perfectly simple."

"It's all right for you to say that, but I do know it."

"Would you do something for me now?"

"I'd do anything for you."

"Would you please please please please please please please stop talking?"

He did not say anything but looked at the bags against the wall of the station. There were labels on them from all the hotels where they had spent nights.

"But I don't want you to," he said, "I don't care anything about it."

"I'll scream," the girl said.

The woman came out through the curtains with two glasses of beer and put them down on the damp felt pads. "The train comes in five minutes," she said.

"What did she say?" asked the girl.

"That the train is coming in five minutes."

The girl smiled brightly at the woman, to thank her.

"I'd better take the bags over to the other side of the station," the man said. She smiled at him.

"All right. Then come back and we'll finish the beer."

He picked up the two heavy bags and carried them around the station to the other tracks. He looked up the tracks but could not see the train. Coming back, he walked through the bar-room, where people waiting for the train were drinking. He drank an Anis at the bar and looked at the people. They were all waiting reasonably for the train. He went out through the bead curtain. She was sitting at the table and smiled at him.

"Do you feel better?" he asked.

"I feel fine," she said, "There's nothing wrong with me. I feel fine."

Ⅳ. William Faulkner

William Faulkner (1897～1962), a famous American writer and the Nobel Prize winner, was born in New Albany, Mississippi. His family settled in Oxford in north-central Mississippi when he was a child. He lived most of his life in the town. About the age of 13, he began to write poetry. When he studied at the Oxford High School, he played quarterback on football team and suffered a broken nose. After the war he studied literature at the University of Mississippi, but he left the university without taking a degree.

In 1929 Faulkner wrote *Sartoris*, the first of fifteen novels set in Yoknapatawpha County, a fictional region of Mississippi. His other important novels include *Light in August* (1932), *As I Lay Dying* (1930) and *The Sound and the Fury* (1929). His representative novel *The Sound and the Fury* is a sad story about the Compson family. The Compsons are shown degenerating, fallen from their former gentility, leading a doomed life. The story is told through the stream of consciousness of three family members. They are Benjy the idiot, the sensitive Quentin and the twisted, mean Jason.

Faulkner's famous short story *A Rose for Emily*, told in five sections, is about Miss Emily Grierson's life, the remaining emblem of a dying world of Southern aristocracy. No one knows the Emily that exists beyond what they can see, and her true self is visible to them only after she dies and her secrets are revealed.

A Rose for Emily[①]

I

When Miss Emily Grierson died, our whole town went to her funeral: the men through a sort of respectful affection for a fallen monument[②], the women mostly out of curiosity to see the inside of her house, which no one save an old man-servant — a combined gardener and cook — had seen in at least ten years.

It was a big, squarish[③] frame house that had once been white, decorated with cupolas[④] and spires[⑤] and scrolled balconies in the heavily lightsome style of the seventies,

① 译文参见本书第 284 至 288 页。
② a fallen monument：一块倒下的纪念碑。
③ squarish [ˈskweərɪʃ] *adj.* somewhat or almost square (有点方的)。
④ cupola [ˈkjuːpələ] *n.* a small rounded and domed structure, as for observation (炮塔；尖塔)。
⑤ spire [ˈspaɪə] *n.* a top part or point that tapers upward; a pinnacle (尖顶)。

set on what had once been our most select street. But garages and cotton gins had encroached and obliterated even the august names of that neighborhood; only Miss Emily's house was left, lifting its stubborn and coquettish decay above the cotton wagons and the gasoline pumps — an eyesore[①] among eyesores. And now Miss Emily had gone to join the representatives of those august names where they lay in the cedar-bemused cemetery among the ranked and anonymous graves of Union and Confederate soldiers who fell at the battle of Jefferson.

Alive, Miss Emily had been a tradition, a duty, and a care; a sort of hereditary obligation upon the town, dating from that day in 1894 when Colonel Sartoris, the mayor — he who fathered the edict that no Negro woman should appear on the streets without an apron — remitted her taxes, the dispensation dating from the death of her father on into perpetuity. Not that Miss Emily would have accepted charity. Colonel Sartoris invented an involved tale to the effect that Miss Emily's father had loaned money to the town, which the town, as a matter of business, preferred this way of repaying. Only a man of Colonel Sartoris' generation and thought could have invented it, and only a woman could have believed it.

When the next generation, with its more modern ideas, became mayors and aldermen[②], this arrangement created some little dissatisfaction. On the first of the year they mailed her a tax notice. February came, and there was no reply. They wrote her a formal letter, asking her to call at the sheriff's office[③] at her convenience. A week later the mayor wrote her himself, offering to call or to send his car for her, and received in reply a note on paper of an archaic[④] shape, in a thin, flowing calligraphy[⑤] in faded ink, to the effect that she no longer went out at all. The tax notice was also enclosed, without comment.

They called a special meeting of the Board of Aldermen. A deputation waited upon her, knocked at the door through which no visitor had passed since she ceased giving china-painting lessons eight or ten years earlier. They were admitted by the old Negro into a dim hall from which a stairway mounted into still more shadow. It smelled of dust and disuse — a close, dank[⑥] smell. The Negro led them into the parlor. It was furnished in heavy, leather-covered furniture. When the Negro opened the blinds of one window, they could see that the leather was cracked; and when they sat down, a faint dust rose sluggishly about their thighs, spinning with slow motes in the single sun-ray. On a

---

① eyesore [ˈaɪsɔː(r)] *n.* something that is unpleasant to view (丑的东西;眼中钉)。eyesore among eyesores: 丑中之丑。

② alderman [ˈɔːlدəmən] *n.* a member of the municipal legislative body in a city (市府参事;市议员)。

③ sheriff's office: 司法长官办公室。sheriff [ˈʃerɪf] *n.* 行政司法长官。

④ archaic [ɑːˈkeɪɪk] *adj.* antiquated; no longer current or applicable (古老的;古体的)。

⑤ calligraphy [kəˈlɪgrəfi] *n.* fine handwriting (书法)。

⑥ dank [dæŋk] *adj.* damp; wet (潮湿的;阴湿寒冷的)。

tarnished gilt easel[①] before the fireplace stood a crayon portrait of Miss Emily's father.

They rose when she entered — a small, fat woman in black, with a thin gold chain descending to her waist and vanishing into her belt, leaning on an ebony[②] cane with a tarnished gold head. Her skeleton was small and spare; perhaps that was why what would have been merely plumpness in another was obesity[③] in her. She looked bloated, like a body long submerged in motionless water, and of that pallid hue. Her eyes, lost in the fatty ridges of her face, looked like two small pieces of coal pressed into a lump of dough as they moved from one face to another while the visitors stated their errand.

She did not ask them to sit. She just stood in the door and listened quietly until the spokesman came to a stumbling halt. Then they could hear the invisible watch ticking at the end of the gold chain.

Her voice was dry and cold. "I have no taxes in Jefferson. Colonel Sartoris explained it to me. Perhaps one of you can gain access to the city records and satisfy yourselves."

"But we have. We are the city authorities, Miss Emily. Didn't you get a notice from the sheriff, signed by him?"

"I received a paper, yes," Miss Emily said. "Perhaps he considers himself the sheriff ... I have no taxes in Jefferson."

"But there is nothing on the books to show that, you see. We must go by the —"

"See Colonel Sartoris. I have no taxes in Jefferson."

"But, Miss Emily —"

"See Colonel Sartoris." (Colonel Sartoris had been dead almost ten years.) "I have no taxes in Jefferson. Tobe!" The Negro appeared. "Show these gentlemen out."

II

So she vanquished[④] them, horse and foot, just as she had vanquished their fathers thirty years before about the smell. That was two years after her father's death and a short time after her sweetheart — the one we believed would marry her — had deserted her. After her father's death she went out very little; after her sweetheart went away, people hardly saw her at all. A few of the ladies had the temerity to call, but were not received, and the only sign of life about the place was the Negro man — a young man then—going in and out with a market basket.

"Just as if a man — any man — could keep a kitchen properly," the ladies said; so they were not surprised when the smell developed. It was another link between the gross,

① easel [ˈi:zl] *n.* an upright frame for displaying or supporting something, such as an artist's canvas (画架)。

② ebony [ˈebəni] *adj.* 黑檀木的。ebony cane：黑檀木拐杖。

③ obesity [əʊˈbɪsɪti] *n.* the condition of being obese (肥胖；肥大)。

④ vanquish [ˈvæŋkwɪʃ] *vt.* to defeat or conquer (征服)。

teeming world and the high and mighty Griersons.

A neighbor, a woman, complained to the mayor, Judge Stevens, eighty years old.

"But what will you have me do about it, madam?" he said.

"Why, send her word to stop it," the woman said. "Isn't there a law?"

"I'm sure that won't be necessary," Judge Stevens said. "It's probably just a snake or a rat that nigger of hers killed in the yard. I'll speak to him about it."

The next day he received two more complaints, one from a man who came in diffident deprecation. "We really must do something about it, Judge. I'd be the last one in the world to bother Miss Emily, but we've got to do something." That night the Board of Aldermen met — three graybeards and one younger man, a member of the rising generation.

"It's simple enough," he said. "Send her word to have her place cleaned up. Give her a certain time to do it in, and if she don't ..."

"Dammit, sir," Judge Stevens said, "will you accuse a lady to her face of smelling bad?"

So the next night, after midnight, four men crossed Miss Emily's lawn and slunk about the house like burglars, sniffing along the base of the brickwork and at the cellar openings while one of them performed a regular sowing motion with his hand out of a sack slung from his shoulder. They broke open the cellar door and sprinkled lime there, and in all the outbuildings. As they recrossed the lawn, a window that had been dark was lighted and Miss Emily sat in it, the light behind her, and her upright torso motionless as that of an idol. They crept quietly across the lawn and into the shadow of the locusts① that lined the street. After a week or two the smell went away.

That was when people had begun to feel really sorry for her. People in our town, remembering how old lady Wyatt, her great-aunt, had gone completely crazy at last, believed that the Griersons held themselves a little too high for what they really were. None of the young men were quite good enough for Miss Emily and such. We had long thought of them as a tableau②, Miss Emily a slender figure in white in the background, her father a spraddled③ silhouette④ in the foreground, his back to her and clutching a horsewhip, the two of them framed by the back-flung front door. So when she got to be thirty and was still single, we were not pleased exactly, but vindicated⑤; even with insanity⑥ in the family she wouldn't have turned down all of her chances if they had really materialized.

---

① locust [ˈləukəst] *n.* 洋槐。

② tableau [ˈtæbləu] *n.* a vivid or graphic description (生动画面;戏剧性局面)。

③ spraddled [ˈsprædld] *adj.* 两腿叉开的。

④ silhouette [ˌsiluˈet] *n.* a drawing consisting of the outline of something, especially a human profile (侧面影像;轮廓)。

⑤ vindicate [ˈvɪndɪkeɪt] *vt.* to provide justification or to support for (证明……正确)。

⑥ insanity [ɪnˈsænɪti] *n.* mental disorder or derangement (疯癫)。

When her father died, it got about that the house was all that was left to her; and in a way, people were glad. At last they could pity Miss Emily. Being left alone, and a pauper, she had become humanized. Now she too would know the old thrill and the old despair of a penny more or less.

The day after his death all the ladies prepared to call at the house and offer condolence① and aid, as is our custom Miss Emily met them at the door, dressed as usual and with no trace of grief on her face. She told them that her father was not dead. She did that for three days, with the ministers calling on her, and the doctors, trying to persuade her to let them dispose of the body. Just as they were about to resort to law and force, she broke down, and they buried her father quickly.

We did not say she was crazy then. We believed she had to do that. We remembered all the young men her father had driven away, and we knew that with nothing left, she would have to cling to that which had robbed her, as people will.

Ⅲ

She was sick for a long time. When we saw her again, her hair was cut short, making her look like a girl, with a vague resemblance to those angels in colored church windows — sort of tragic and serene.

The town had just let the contracts for paving the sidewalks, and in the summer after her father's death they began the work. The construction company came with niggers and mules and machinery, and a foreman② named Homer Barron, a Yankee — a big, dark, ready man, with a big voice and eyes lighter than his face. The little boys would follow in groups to hear him cuss the niggers, and the niggers singing in time to the rise and fall of picks. Pretty soon he knew everybody in town. Whenever you heard a lot of laughing anywhere about the square, Homer Barron would be in the center of the group. Presently we began to see him and Miss Emily on Sunday afternoons driving in the yellow-wheeled buggy③ and the matched team of bays from the livery stable.

At first we were glad that Miss Emily would have an interest, because the ladies all said, "Of course a Grierson would not think seriously of a Northerner, a day laborer." But there were still others, older people, who said that even grief could not cause a real lady to

---

① condolence [kən'dəuləns] *n.* sympathy with a person who has experienced grief or misfortune (哀悼)。

② foreman ['fɔːmən] *n.* a man who serves as the leader of a work crew (领班;工头)。

③ buggy ['bʌgi] *n.* a small, light, one-horse carriage (轻便马车)。

forget noblesse oblige[①]— without calling it noblesse oblige. They just said, "Poor Emily. Her kinsfolk should come to her." She had some kin in Alabama; but years ago her father had fallen out with them over the estate of old lady Wyatt, the crazy woman, and there was no communication between the two families. They had not even been represented at the funeral.

And as soon as the old people said, "Poor Emily," the whispering began. "Do you suppose it's really so?" they said to one another. "Of course it is. What else could ..." This behind their hands; rustling of craned silk and satin behind jalousies closed upon the sun of Sunday afternoon as the thin, swift clop-clop-clop of the matched team passed: "Poor Emily."

She carried her head high enough — even when we believed that she was fallen. It was as if she demanded more than ever the recognition of her dignity as the last Grierson; as if it had wanted that touch of earthiness to reaffirm her imperviousness. Like when she bought the rat poison, the arsenic[②]. That was over a year after they had begun to say "Poor Emily," and while the two female cousins were visiting her.

"I want some poison," she said to the druggist. She was over thirty then, still a slight woman, though thinner than usual, with cold, haughty black eyes in a face the flesh of which was strained across the temples and about the eye sockets as you imagine a lighthouse-keeper's face ought to look. "I want some poison," she said.

"Yes, Miss Emily. What kind? For rats and such? I'd recom — "

"I want the best you have. I don't care what kind."

The druggist named several. "They'll kill anything up to an elephant. But what you want is —"

"Arsenic," Miss Emily said. "Is that a good one?"

"Is ... arsenic? Yes, ma'am. But what you want —"

"I want arsenic."

The druggist looked down at her. She looked back at him, erect, her face like a strained flag. "Why, of course," the druggist said. "If that's what you want. But the law requires you to tell what you are going to use it for."

Miss Emily just stared at him, her head tilted back in order to look him eye for eye, until he looked away and went and got the arsenic and wrapped it up. The Negro delivery boy brought her the package; the druggist didn't come back. When she opened the

---

① noblesse [nəʊˈbles] *n.* noble birth or condition（贵族阶层）。noblesse oblige：贵族举止。The literal translation from French of "Noblesse oblige" is "nobility obliges". The *Oxford English Dictionary* says that the term "suggests noble ancestry constrains to honourable behavior; privilege entails to responsibility". Being a noble meant that one had responsibilities to lead, manage and so on. One was not to simply spend one's time in idle pursuits.

② arsenic [ˈɑːsənɪk] *n.* 砒霜。

package at home there was written on the box, under the skull and bones: "For rats."

Ⅳ

So the next day we all said, "She will kill herself"; and we said it would be the best thing. When she had first begun to be seen with Homer Barron, we had said, "She will marry him." Then we said, "She will persuade him yet," because Homer himself had remarked — he liked men, and it was known that he drank with the younger men in the Elks' Club① — that he was not a marrying man. Later we said, "Poor Emily" behind the jalousies as they passed on Sunday afternoon in the glittering buggy, Miss Emily with her head high and Homer Barron with his hat cocked and a cigar in his teeth, reins and whip in a yellow glove.

Then some of the ladies began to say that it was a disgrace to the town and a bad example to the young people. The men did not want to interfere, but at last the ladies forced the Baptist minister② — Miss Emily's people were Episcopal③ — to call upon her. He would never divulge④ what happened during that interview, but he refused to go back again. The next Sunday they again drove about the streets, and the following day the minister's wife wrote to Miss Emily's relations in Alabama.

So she had blood-kin⑤ under her roof again and we sat back to watch developments. At first nothing happened. Then we were sure that they were to be married. We learned that Miss Emily had been to the jeweler's and ordered a man's toilet set in silver, with the letters H. B. on each piece. Two days later we learned that she had bought a complete outfit of men's clothing, including a nightshirt, and we said, "They are married." We were really glad. We were glad because the two female cousins were even more Grierson than Miss Emily had ever been.

So we were not surprised when Homer Barron — the streets had been finished some time since — was gone. We were a little disappointed that there was not a public blowing-off, but we believed that he had gone on to prepare for Miss Emily's coming, or to give her a chance to get rid of the cousins. (By that time it was a cabal, and we were all Miss Emily's allies to help circumvent the cousins.) Sure enough, after another week they departed. And, as we had expected all along, within three days Homer Barron was back in town. A neighbor saw the Negro man admit him at the kitchen door at dusk one evening.

And that was the last we saw of Homer Barron. And of Miss Emily for some time. The Negro man went in and out with the market basket, but the front door remained

---

① Elks' Club：麋鹿俱乐部。elk [elk] *n.* 麋鹿。
② Baptist [ˈbæptɪst] *n.* 浸礼会。Baptist minister：浸礼会牧师。
③ Episcopal [ɪˈpɪskəpəl] *adj.* /*n.* 圣公会的；圣公会。
④ divulge [daɪˈvʌldʒ] *vt.* to reveal（泄露；暴露）。
⑤ blood-kin *n.* close relative（近亲）。

closed. Now and then we would see her at a window for a moment, as the men did that night when they sprinkled the lime, but for almost six months she did not appear on the streets. Then we knew that this was to be expected too; as if that quality of her father which had thwarted her woman's life so many times had been too virulent and too furious to die.

When we next saw Miss Emily, she had grown fat and her hair was turning gray. During the next few years it grew grayer and grayer until it attained an even pepper-and-salt[①] iron-gray, when it ceased turning. Up to the day of her death at seventy-four it was still that vigorous iron-gray, like the hair of an active man.

From that time on her front door remained closed, save for a period of six or seven years, when she was about forty, during which she gave lessons in china-painting. She fitted up a studio in one of the downstairs rooms, where the daughters and granddaughters of Colonel Sartoris' contemporaries were sent to her with the same regularity and in the same spirit that they were sent to church on Sundays with a twenty-five-cent piece for the collection plate. Meanwhile her taxes had been remitted.[②]

Then the newer generation became the backbone and the spirit of the town, and the painting pupils grew up and fell away and did not send their children to her with boxes of color and tedious brushes and pictures cut from the ladies' magazines. The front door closed upon the last one and remained closed for good. When the town got free postal delivery, Miss Emily alone refused to let them fasten the metal numbers above her door and attach a mailbox to it. She would not listen to them.

Daily, monthly, yearly we watched the Negro grow grayer and more stooped, going in and out with the market basket. Each December we sent her a tax notice, which would be returned by the post office a week later, unclaimed. Now and then we would see her in one of the downstairs windows — she had evidently shut up the top floor of the house — like the carven torso of an idol in a niche, looking or not looking at us, we could never tell which. Thus she passed from generation to generation — dear, inescapable, impervious[③], tranquil, and perverse.

And so she died. Fell ill in the house filled with dust and shadows, with only a doddering Negro man to wait on her. We did not even know she was sick; we had long since given up trying to get any information from the Negro. He talked to no one, probably not even to her, for his voice had grown harsh and rusty, as if from disuse.

She died in one of the downstairs rooms, in a heavy walnut bed with a curtain, her

---

① pepper-and-salt: having a close mixture of black and white (黑白相间精细地交织成的;椒盐色的)。

② remit [rɪˈmɪt] *vt.* to pardon; to forgive (赦免;免除)。

③ impervious [ɪmˈpɜːvjəs] *adj.* incapable of being penetrated (不让渗入的;密封的)。

gray head propped on a pillow yellow and moldy[①] with age and lack of sunlight.

V

The Negro met the first of the ladies at the front door and let them in, with their hushed, sibilant[②] voices and their quick, curious glances, and then he disappeared. He walked right through the house and out the back and was not seen again.

The two female cousins came at once. They held the funeral on the second day, with the town coming to look at Miss Emily beneath a mass of bought flowers, with the crayon face of her father musing profoundly above the bier and the ladies sibilant and macabre[③]; and the very old men — some in their brushed Confederate uniforms — on the porch and the lawn, talking of Miss Emily as if she had been a contemporary of theirs, believing that they had danced with her and courted her perhaps, confusing time with its mathematical progression, as the old do, to whom all the past is not a diminishing road but, instead, a huge meadow which no winter ever quite touches, divided from them now by the narrow bottle-neck of the most recent decade of years.

Already we knew that there was one room in that region above stairs which no one had seen in forty years, and which would have to be forced. They waited until Miss Emily was decently in the ground before they opened it.

The violence of breaking down the door seemed to fill this room with pervading dust. A thin, acrid pall as of the tomb seemed to lie everywhere upon this room decked and furnished as for a bridal: upon the valance curtains of faded rose color, upon the rose-shaded lights, upon the dressing table, upon the delicate array of crystal and the man's toilet things backed with tarnished silver, silver so tarnished that the monogram[④] was obscured. Among them lay a collar and tie, as if they had just been removed, which, lifted, left upon the surface a pale crescent in the dust. Upon a chair hung the suit, carefully folded; beneath it the two mute shoes and the discarded socks.

The man himself lay in the bed.

For a long while we just stood there, looking down at the profound and fleshless grin. The body had apparently once lain in the attitude of an embrace, but now the long sleep that outlasts love, that conquers even the grimace[⑤] of love, had cuckolded him. What was left of him, rotted beneath what was left of the nightshirt, had become inextricable[⑥] from

---

① moldy [ˈməuldi] *adj.* covered with or containing mold (发霉的)。

② sibilant [ˈsɪbɪənt] *adj.* producing a hissing sound like that of (s) or (sh) (咝咝作声的)。

③ macabre [məˈkɑːbrə] *adj.* suggesting the horror of death and decay; gruesome (恐怖的;令人毛骨悚然的)。

④ monogram [ˈmɔnəugræm] *n.* a design composed of one or more letters (字母组合)。

⑤ grimace [grɪˈmeɪs] *n.* a sharp contortion of the face expressive of pain or disgust (面部的歪扭;痛苦的表情)。

⑥ inextricable [ɪnˈekstrɪkəbl] *adj.* impossible to disentangle or untie (无法解脱的;解不开的)。

the bed in which he lay; and upon him and upon the pillow beside him lay that even coating of the patient and biding dust.

Then we noticed that in the second pillow was the indentation of a head. One of us lifted something from it, and leaning forward, that faint and invisible dust dry and acrid in the nostrils, we saw a long strand of iron-gray hair.

Ⅴ. Yasunari Kawabata

Yasunari Kawabata (1899～1972) was born in Osaka and was orphaned when he was four, after which he lived with his grandparents.

While still a university student, he re-established the Tokyo University literary magazine *New Tide of Thought* and began to write short stories. He graduated from Tokyo Imperial University in 1924 and wrote his graduation thesis entitled as *A Short History of Japanese Novels*. Shortly after graduation, his short stories began to attract attention.

Kawabata is famous for his short story *The Dancing Girl of Izu* (1926) and his three novels *Snow Country* (1948), *Thousand Cranes* (1952), and *The Old Capital* (1962).

In 1968 Kawabata became the first Japanese to receive the Nobel Prize for Literature "for his narrative mastery, which with great sensibility expresses the essence of the Japanese mind".

The novel *Snow Country* is a stark tale of a love affair in a remote hot-spring town somewhere in the mountainous regions between a Tokyo dilettante and a provincial geisha Komako who gives herself to him without illusions or regrets. It established Kawabata as one of Japan's foremost authors.

What we selected here is from the beginning part of the novel. It tells a chance meeting of Shimamura with Yoko in the train to the remote hot-spring town. While the hero is thinking of his Komako, he is drawn to the image of Yoko, a strange, intense girl, bearing a close resemblance to Komako, who glows like a light off in the mountain darkness.

The typical manner Kawabata used here can be called as the haiku manner. It presents a great challenge to the novelist. The manner is notable for its terseness and austerity, so that his novel must rather be like a series of brief flashes in a void.

Snow Country①

(Excerpt)

The train came out of the long tunnel into the snow country. The earth lay white

---

① 译文参见本书第 288 至 290 页。

under the night sky. The train pulled up at a signal stop.

A girl who had been sitting on the other side of the car came over and opened the window in front of Shimamura. The snow cold poured in. Leaning far out the window, the girl called to the station master as though he were a great distance away.

The station master walked slowly over the snow, a lantern in his hand. His face was buried to the nose in a muffler①, and the flaps② of his cap were turned down over his ears.

It's that cold, is it, thought Shimamura. Low, barrack-like buildings that might have been railway dormitories were scattered here and there up the frozen slope of the mountain. The white of the snow fell away into the darkness some distance before it reached them.

"How are you?" the girl called out. "It's Yoko."

"Yoko, is it. On your way back? It's gotten cold again."

"I understand my brother has come to work here. Thank you for all you've done."

"It will be lonely, though. This is no place for a young boy."

"He's really no more than a child. You'll teach him what he needs to know, won't you?"

"Oh, but he's doing very well. We'll be busier from now on, with the snow and all. Last year we had so much that the trains were always being stopped by avalanches③, and the whole town was kept busy cooking for them."

"But look at the warm clothes, would you? My brother said in his letter that he wasn't even wearing a sweater yet."

"I'm not warm unless I have on four layers, myself. The young ones start drinking when it gets cold, and the first thing you know they're over there in bed with colds."

He waved his lantern toward the dormitories.

"Does my brother drink?"

"Not that I know of."

"You're on your way home now, are you?"

"I had a little accident. I've been going to the doctor."

"You must be more careful."

The station master, who had an overcoat on over his kimono④, turned as if to cut the freezing conversation short. "Take care of yourself," he called over his shoulder.

"Is my brother here now?" Yoko looked out over the snow-covered platform. "See that he behaves himself."

It was such a beautiful voice that it struck one as sad. In all its high resonance it

---

① muffler [ˈmʌflə] *n.* a heavy scarf; a device that absorbs noise (围巾；消声器)。

② flap [flæp] *n.* (帽子的)耳。

③ avalanche [ˈævəˌlɑːnʃ] *n.* a fall of a large mass of snow down a mountainside (雪崩)。

④ kimono [kɪˈməʊnəʊ] *n.* a long, wide-sleeved Japanese robelike dress (和服)。

seemed to come echoing back across the snowy night.

The girl was still leaning out the window when the train pulled away from the station. "Tell my brother to come home when he has a holiday," she called out to the station master, who was walking along the tracks.

"I'll tell him," the man called back.

Yoko closed the window and pressed her hands to her red cheeks.

Three snowplows[①] were waiting for the heavy snow here on the Border Range. There was an electric avalanche-warning system at the north and south entrances to the tunnel. Five thousand workers were ready to clear away the snow, and two thousand young men from the volunteer fire-departments could be mobilized if they were needed.

Yoko's brother would be working at this signal stop, so soon to be buried under the snow — somehow that fact made the girl more interesting to Shimamura.

"The girl!" — something in her manner suggested the unmarried girl. Shimamura of course had no way of being sure what her relationship was to the man with her. They acted rather like a married couple. The man was clearly ill, however, and illness shortens the distance between a man and a woman. The more earnest the ministrations[②], the more the two come to seem like husband and wife. A girl taking care of a man far older than she, for all the world like a young mother, can from a distance be taken for his wife.

But Shimamura in his mind had cut the girl off from the man with her and decided from her general appearance and manner that she was unmarried. And then, because he had been looking at her from a strange angle for so long, emotions peculiarly his own had perhaps colored his judgment.

It had been three hours earlier. In his boredom, Shimamura stared at his left hand as the forefinger bent and unbent. Only this hand seemed to have a vital and immediate memory of the woman he was going to see. The more he tried to call up a clear picture of her, the more his memory failed him, the farther she faded away, leaving him nothing to catch and hold. In the midst of this uncertainty only the one hand, and in particular the forefinger, even now seemed damp from her touch, seemed to be pulling him back to her from afar. Taken with the strangeness of it, he brought the hand to his face, then quickly drew a line across the misted-over window. A woman's eye floated up before him. He almost called out in his astonishment. But he had been dreaming, and when he came to himself he saw that it was only the reflection in the window of the girl opposite. Outside it was growing dark, and the lights had been turned on in the train, transforming the window into a mirror. The mirror had been clouded over with steam until he drew that line across it.

The one eye by itself was strangely beautiful, but, feigning a traveler's weariness and

---

① snowplow [ˈsnəʊplaʊ] *n.* a vehicle used to remove snow (雪犁;扫雪车)。

② ministration [ˌmɪnɪsˈtreɪʃən] *n.* the act of serving or aiding (服侍)。

putting his face to the window as if to look at the scenery outside, he cleared the steam from the rest of the glass.

...

In the depths of the mirror the evening landscape moved by, the mirror and the reflected figures like motion pictures superimposed① one on the other. The figures and the background were unrelated, and yet the figures, transparent and intangible②, and the background, dim in the gathering darkness, melted together into a sort of symbolic world not of this world. Particular when a light out in the mountains shone in the center of the girl's face, Shimamura felt his chest rise at the inexpressible beauty of it.

The mountain sky still carried traces of evening red. Individual shapes were clear far into the distance, but the monotonous mountain landscape, undistinguished for mile after mile, seemed all the more undistinguished for having lost its last traces of color. There was nothing in it to catch the eye, and it seemed to flow along in a wide, unformed emotion. That was of course because the girl's face was floating over it. Cut off by the face, the evening landscape moved steadily by around its outline. The face too seemed transparent — but was it really transparent? Shimamura had the illusion that the evening landscape was actually passing over the face, and the flow did not stop to let him be sure it was not.

The light inside the train was not particularly strong, and the reflection was not as clear as it would have been in a mirror. Since there was no glare③, Shimamula came to forget that it was a mirror he was looking at. The girl's face seemed to be out in the flow of the evening mountains.

It was then that a light shone in the face. The reflection in the mirror was not strong enough to blot out the light outside, nor was the light strong enough to dim the reflection. The light moved across the face, though not to light it up. It was a distant, cold light. As it sent its small rays through the pupil of the girl's eye, as the eye and the light were superimposed one on the other, the eye became a weirdly④ beautiful bit of phosphorescence on the sea of evening mountains.

Tr. by Edward G. Seidensticker

Ⅵ. Gabriel García Márquez

Gabriel García Márquez (1928～), the great Latin-American writer and the Nobel

① superimpose [ˈsjuːpərɪmˈpəuz] *vt.* to lay something on something else (重叠;叠合)。

② intangible [ɪnˈtændʒəbl] *adj.* incapable of being realized or defined (不可捉摸的;模糊的)。

③ glare [gleə] *n.* an intense, blinding light (炫目的反光)。

④ weirdly [wiədli] *adv.* uncannily (古怪地)。

Prize Laureate, was born in Aracataca, a small town in Northern Colombia, where he was raised by his maternal grandparents. The imaginary town of Macondo in his works is believed to be his birth place.

Márquez went to a Jesuit college and began to study law, but his studies were soon broken off for his work as a journalist. His first book was published in 1947 and in 1955 he published his important work *Leaf Storm*. He became an established novelist. Besides his large output of fiction he has written screenplays and has continued to work as a journalist.

In 1982, he received the Nobel Prize in literature "for his novels and short stories, in which the fantastic and the realistic are combined in a richly composed world of imagination, reflecting a continent's life and conflicts".

Gabriel García Márquez is a central figure in the so-called Magic Realism movement. His representative work is the novel entitled as *One Hundred Years of Solitude* which was published in 1967 and was translated into over two dozen languages. Critics often consider it as exemplary of magical realism, a style of writing in which the supernatural is presented as mundane, and the mundane as supernatural or extraordinary. This novel is not only the Buendía family saga covering 100 years, but also a sort of history of South America as seen through the experiences and imagination of the family and the isolated community.

The following two passages are respectively from Chapter Six and Chapter Seven of the novel.

One Hundred Years of Solitude①

(Excerpt)

Colonel Aureliano Buendía organized thirty-two armed uprisings and he lost them all. He had seventeen male children by seventeen different women and they were exterminated one after the other on a single night before the oldest one had reached the age of thirty-five. He survived fourteen attempts on his life, seventy-three ambushes, and a firing squad. He lived through a dose of strychnine② in his coffee that was enough to kill a horse. He refused the Order of Merit③, which the President of the Republic awarded him. He rose to be Commander in Chief of the revolutionary forces, with jurisdiction④ and command from one border to the other, and the man most feared by the government, but he never let himself be photographed. He declined the lifetime pension offered him after the war and until old age he made his living from the little gold fishes that he manufactured

---

① 译文参见本书第 290 至 291 页。

② strychnine [ˈstrɪkniːn] *n.* 士的宁(一种毒药)。

③ Order of Merit：荣誉勋章。

④ jurisdiction [ˌdʒuərɪsˈdɪkʃən] *n.* the extent of authority or control（权限）。

in his workshop in Macondo[①]. Although he always fought at the head of his men, the only wound that he received was the one he gave himself after signing the Treaty of Neerlandia, which put an end to almost twenty years of civil war. He shot himself in the chest with a pistol and the bullet came out through his back without damaging any vital organ. The only thing left of all that was a street that bore his name in Macondo. And yet, as he declared a few years before he died of old age, he had not expected any of that on the dawn he left with his twenty-one men to join the forces of General Victorio Medina.

Not all the news was good. A year after the flight of Colonel Aureliano Buendía, José Arcadio and Rebeca went to live in the house Arcadio had built. No one knew about his intervention to halt the execution. In the new house, located on the best corner of the square, in the shade of an almond tree that was honored by three nests of redbreasts[②], with a large door for visitors and four windows for light, they set up a hospitable home. Rebeca's old friends, among them four of the Moscote sisters who were still single, once more took up the sessions of embroidery that had been interrupted years before on the porch with the begonias[③]. José Arcadio continued to profit from the usurped lands, the title to which was recognized by the Conservative government. Every afternoon he could be seen returning on horseback, with his hunting dogs and his double-barreled shotgun[④] and a string of rabbits hanging from his saddle. One September afternoon, with the threat of a storm, he returned home earlier than usual. He greeted Rebeca in the dining room, tied the dogs up in the courtyard, hung the rabbits up in the kitchen to be salted later, and went to the bedroom to change his clothes. Rebeca later declared that when her husband went into the bedroom she was locked in the bathroom and did not hear anything. It was a difficult version to believe, but there was no other more plausible[⑤], and no one could think of any motive for Rebeca to murder the man who had made her happy. That was perhaps the only mystery that was never cleared up in Macondo. As soon as José Arcadio closed the bedroom door the sound of a pistol shot echoed through the house. A trickle[⑥] of blood came out under the door, crossed the living room, went out into the street, continued on in a straight line across the uneven terraces, went down steps and climbed over curbs[⑦], passed along the Street of the Turks, turned a corner to the right and another to the left, made a right angle at the Buendía house, went in under the closed door, crossed through the parlor, hugging the walls so as not to stain the rugs, went on to the other living room, made a wide curve to avoid the dining-room table, went along the

---

① Macondo：马孔多。
② redbreast [ˈredbrest] *n.* 知更鸟。
③ begonia [bɪˈgəuniə] *n.* 秋海棠。
④ double-barreled shotgun：双管枪。
⑤ plausible [ˈplɔːzəbl] *adj.* seemingly valid or acceptable（似乎可能的）。
⑥ trickle [ˈtrɪkl] *n.* a flow or fall in drops（细流；滴）。
⑦ curb [kɜːb] *n.* the edge of a road or a street（路边；街边）。

porch with the begonias, and passed without being seen under Amaranta's chair as she gave an arithmetic lesson to Aureliano José, and went through the pantry and came out in the kitchen, where Ursula was getting ready to crack thirty-six eggs to make bread.

"Holy Mother of God!" Ursula shouted.

She followed the thread of blood back along its course, and in search of its origin she went through the pantry, along the begonia porch where Aureliano José was chanting that three plus three is six and six plus three is nine, and she crossed the dining room and the living rooms and followed straight down the street, and she turned first to the right and then to the left to the Street of the Turks, forgetting that she was still wearing her baking apron and her house slippers, and she came out onto the square and went into the door of a house where she had never been, and she pushed open the bedroom door and was almost suffocated① by the smell of burned gunpowder, and she found José Arcadio lying face down on the ground on top of the leggings he had just taken off, and she saw the starting point of the thread of blood that had already stopped flowing out of his right ear. They found no wound on his body nor could they locate the weapon. Nor was it possible to remove the smell of powder from the corpse. First they washed him three times with soap and a scrubbing brush, and they rubbed him with salt and vinegar, then with ashes and lemon, and finally they put him in a barrel of lye② and let him stay for six hours. They scrubbed him so much that the arabesques③ of his tattooing④ began to fade. When they thought of the desperate measure of seasoning him with pepper, cumin⑤ seeds, and laurel leaves and boiling him for a whole day over a slow fire, he had already begun to decompose⑥ and they had to bury him hastily. They sealed him hermetically⑦ in a special coffin seven and a half feet long and four feet wide, reinforced inside with iron plates and fastened together with steel bolts, and even then the smell could be perceived on the streets through which the funeral procession passed. Father Nicanor, with his liver enlarged and tight as a drum, gave him his blessing from bed. Although in the months that followed they reinforced the grave with walls about it, between which they threw compressed ash, sawdust⑧, and quicklime⑨, the cemetery still smelled of powder for many years after, until the engineers from the banana company covered the grave over

---

① suffocate [ˈsʌfəkeɪt] *vt.* to kill or destroy by preventing access of air (使窒息;噎住)。

② lye [laɪ] *n.* 碱液。

③ arabesque [ˌærəˈbesk] *n.* 阿拉伯式图饰;蔓藤花纹。

④ tattooing [tæˈtuːiŋ] *n.* 刺字;文身。

⑤ cumin [ˈkʌmɪn] *n.* 孜然芹;小茴香。

⑥ decompose [ˌdiːkəmˈpəʊz] *v.* to separate into components; to cause to rot (分解;腐烂)。

⑦ hermetically [həːˈmetɪkəli] *adv.* in an airtight manner (密封地)。

⑧ sawdust [ˈsɔːdʌst] *n.* the small particles of wood that fall from an object being sawed (锯屑)。

⑨ quicklime [ˈkwIklaIm] *n.* another name for calcium oxide (生石灰)。

with a shell of concrete[①]. As soon as they took the body out, Rebeca closed the doors of her house and buried herself alive, covered with a thick crust[②] of disdain that no earthly temptation was ever able to break. She went out into the street on one occasion, when she was very old, with shoes the color of old silver and a hat made of tiny flowers, during the time that the Wandering Jew passed through town and brought on a heat wave that was so intense that birds broke through window screens to come to die in the bedrooms. The last time anyone saw her alive was when with one shot she killed a thief who was trying to force the door of her house. Except for Argénida, her servant and confidante[③], no one ever had any more contact with her after that. At one time it was discovered that she was writing letters to the Bishop, whom she claimed as a first cousin, but it was never said whether she received any reply. The town forgot about her.

---

① concrete [ˌkɔnkriːt] *n.* a strong construction material consisting of sand, broken stone and cement (混凝土)。

② crust [krʌst] *n.* a hard, crisp covering or surface (硬壳;甲壳)。

③ confidante [ˌkɔnfɪˈdænt] *n.* a woman to whom secrets or private matters are disclosed (知己的女友)。

Appendix Ⅰ. Some Chinese Translations for Reference

Chapter One Ancient Literature

伊利亚特(节选)

荷　马

雅典娜为着她的目的借用得伊福玻斯的相貌和不倦的声音,从他身边走到赫克托耳那儿去向他打招呼。"我的亲爱的兄弟,"她对赫克托耳说道,"那捷足的阿喀琉斯那么快地绕着城圈子追赶你,一定把你累乏了。咱们站下来,就在这儿一起跟他对敌吧。"

"得伊福玻斯,"那头盔闪亮的伟大的赫克托耳说道,"在赫卡柏和普里阿摩斯给我的所有兄弟们当中,我一径都是最最爱你的。可是从今以后我要更加觉得你好了,因为其余的人都躲在城里不出来,只有你见我有难敢从城里出来帮助我。"

"亲爱的兄弟,"闪眼的雅典娜说道,"我可以老实告诉你,咱们的父王和母后曾经轮流着劝告我,哀求我,要我待在城里不出来。我的部下也在那里,也这样的劝告我——他们大家都怕阿喀琉斯怕得那个样儿的。可是我替你急坏了呢。现在咱们放开胆去向他攻击,咱们枪下不可以容情。咱们马上就可以见分晓,到底是阿喀琉斯杀了咱们两个人,带着咱们的血污铠甲回楼船去呢,还是他自己被你的枪所征服。"

雅典娜的巧计成功了,她就引导他走上前去。赫克托耳和阿喀琉斯彼此遭遇了。那个头盔闪亮的伟大的赫克托耳第一个说话:"我的阿喀琉斯爷,我已经绕着这普里阿摩斯的伟大城市被你追了三匝了,没敢停下来让你近身。可是现在我不再逃跑了。我已经下了决心跟你个对个的打,或是杀了你,或是被你杀。可是咱们先来谈一谈条件,你叫你的神作证,我叫我的神作证——没有哪一种契约能有比这再好的担保人。如果宙斯让我活下去,我把你杀了,那我保证决不在你的身体上头施行习惯所不批准的暴行。我所要做的,阿喀琉斯,就只从你身上把你那套辉煌的铠甲剥下来。然后我就把你的尸体交给阿开亚人去。你对于我也愿意这样做吗?"

那捷足的阿喀琉斯恶狠狠地对他看了一眼回答道:"赫克托耳,你一定是发疯了,还要来跟我订条约呢。狮子不跟人来讲条件,狼也不跟绵羊分庭抗礼的——他们始终是仇敌。你和我也是这样。友谊在我们之间是不可能的,而且不到我们倒下一个来,拿他的血去让那顽强的战神吃个饱,也决不会有任何方式的休战。所以,鼓起你所能够有的任何勇气来吧。这是你显出你的枪法和胆量的时候了。现在帕拉斯·雅典娜正在等着拿我的枪来打倒你,任何东西都救不得你了。你曾经用你的矛子折了我的那些个朋友,使我伤了那么大的心,这一刻儿你要把这些债一总偿清了。"

阿喀琉斯说完话,就拿稳了他的长杆枪投了出去。但那显赫的赫克托耳是留神着的,居然被他躲开了。他眼睛看着那支枪,往下面一蹲,那支枪就飞过他的头顶插进地里去。可是帕拉斯·雅典娜马上去把它捡起,交还给阿喀琉斯。那大头领赫克托耳并没有看见这个行动,就向那天下无双的珀琉斯之子叫道:"神样的阿喀琉斯也失错了呢,似乎是宙斯给你报错我的死期了!你把事情拿得未免太稳些。可是你的嘴能讲,你的舌头巧,竟想吓唬我,把我的力气吓干净。你可吓不跑我的,也不能够向我的背后投枪。你得先躲开我这一枪。上天保佑这支枪上的铜全部陷进你的肉里去!只要你这个头号的瘟神死掉了,这场战争对于特洛亚人就容易办了。”

说完，他就舞起他的长杆枪来投出去。一点没有错，他是投中阿喀琉斯的盾牌中心的，可是他那支枪给蹦回来了。赫克托耳看见这么好的一枪竟投了个空，不觉心中大怒，可是他只得站在那里发愣，因为他没有第二支枪了。他大声喊叫那个带白盾牌的得伊福玻斯，问他要一支长枪。可是得伊福玻斯并不在他的身边。赫克托耳这才知道是怎么回事，就嚷道：“啊呀！那么是神们招我来就死的了！我还以为那好心的得伊福玻斯在我的身边，谁知他还在城里，是雅典娜愚弄我的。死已经离我不远了；他正对我的脸上瞠视着，我是无法躲避他的了。宙斯和他那个当射手的儿子虽然那么好意地对待我，那么的帮助我，可是他们一定早就决心要这样的了。所以现在我要遭遇我的死亡了。让我至少把我这条命卖得贵些，不要去走上一个不光荣的结局，也好传些赫赫的声威到未来世代人的耳朵里。”

当时赫克托耳身边挂着一把锋利的、又长又重的剑。他就把它抽出来，振作起精神，一个回旋扫上去，仿佛一只飞得高高的老鹰从黑云里向地面上来扑一头稚嫩的绵羊或是一只蹲着的兔子一般。那赫克托耳也就像这样地舞着他的利剑向前冲上去。阿喀琉斯也燃起了一股烈火一般的蛮劲跳上去迎他。他拿他那有装饰的盾牌掩护着前面；他的脑袋动一动，那顶装着四片铜牌的闪亮头盔也跟着摇摆起来，并且使得赫淮斯托斯不惜黄金给他装上去的那一部辉煌的盔饰绕着盔顶上跳舞；同时，他右手里平提着那一支枪。一心要杀赫克托耳，正在找他身上最可能有肉的地方，那尖锐的枪头闪闪地发出光芒，亮得如同天空那颗最最可爱的宝石，那在夜晚时分跟其余的星一同出现的太白星一样。

阿喀琉斯看见赫克托耳的身体全部由他杀死伟大的帕特洛克罗斯之后从他身上脱去的那套精铜的铠甲掩护着，就只那咽喉上，就是锁骨从肩膀上连到脖颈上去的地方，也就是最容易杀死一个人的所在，留着一个孔隙。阿喀琉斯王子趁赫克托耳向他冲上来的当口儿，就拿他的矛子向那一点戳进去，矛尖笔正插进赫克托耳颈上的嫩肉，只是那沉重的铜头并没有把他的气管戳穿，所以他还能够对他的征服者说话。当时赫克托耳倒在尘埃里，伟大的阿喀琉斯就对他夸耀胜利。“赫克托耳，”他说道，“无疑的，当你剥那帕特洛克罗斯身上的时候，你总以为自己是万无一失的了。你始终都没有想到我，因为我跟你离开太远。你是一个傻子。一直在那楼船的旁边，还有一个比帕特洛克罗斯强得多的人储备在那里，这一个人已经把你打倒了。现在狗和食肉鸟就要来毁伤你，扯碎你，我们亚该亚人可要去给帕特洛克罗斯举行葬礼了。”

（傅东华 译）

我觉得，谁能坐在你面前

萨　福

我觉得，谁能坐在你面前，
幸福真不亚于任何神仙，
他静静听着你的软语呢喃，
声音那么甜。

啊，你的笑容真叫人爱煞。
每次我看见你，只消一刹那，
心房就在胸口里狂跳不已，
我说不出话。

我舌头好像断了，奇异的火
突然在我皮肉里流动、烧灼，
我因炫目而失明，一片嗡嗡
充塞了耳朵。

冷汗淋漓，把我的全身浇湿，
我颤抖着，苍白得赛过草叶，
只觉得我似乎马上要死去，
马上要昏厥。

永生的阿芙洛狄忒

萨　福

永生的阿芙洛狄忒，宝座上的女神
宙斯的善用心计的女儿，求求你，
女神啊，别再用痛苦和忧愁
折磨我的心！

求你像从前一样，只要远远
听到我的声音在求告在呼唤，
你就翩然降临，离开你父亲的
金色的宫殿，

为你驾车的是一群金翅之雀，
它们迅捷地飞向黑暗的下界，
扑着无数翅膀下降而穿越
天空的皎洁，

转眼就飞到此地，女神啊，于是你
永远年轻的脸上浮着笑意，
会叫我说出一切烦恼的缘由，
我为何唤你。

我狂热的心在把什么追逐。
你会问："你希望蓓脱女神把谁说服
而领入你的情网？告诉我，是谁
委屈了萨福？

要知道逃避者不久会来追逐你
拒收礼物者自己会来送礼，
那位冷淡者不久就会爱的，
不由她不愿意。"

求你再度降临，亲爱的女神，
求你解救我于万般痛苦之中，
保佑我的一切心愿能够实现，——
请和我结盟！

饮 酒 歌

阿那克里翁

饮我的杯吧，爱人！活我的生命，
因我的青春而年轻！共有一颗心，
同戴一个花冠，共享一片爱情，
和我一同疯狂，和我一起聪明。

（以上飞白 译）

向酒神祈求

阿那克里翁

主啊，那征服人心的爱情，
那些深蓝色眼睛的山林女神，
那肤色红润的美神
在你遨游这高峻的山岭时，
都伴着你一同游玩，
我跪下求你，请你
对我发慈悲，垂听我
请求你开恩的祈祷：
请你劝克勒布罗斯
把我对他的一番爱情，
酒神啊，接受下来。

（水建馥 译）

俄狄浦斯王（节选）

索福克勒斯

〔伊俄卡斯忒自宫中上。

伊俄卡斯忒 我邦的长老们啊，我想起了拿着这缠羊毛的树枝和香料到神的庙上，因为俄狄浦斯由于各种忧虑，心里很紧张，他不像一个清醒的人，不会凭旧事推断到新事；只要有人说出恐怖的话，他就随他摆布。我既然劝不了他，只好带着这些象征祈求的礼物来求你，吕刻俄斯·阿波罗啊——因为你离我最近——请给我们一个避免污染的方法。我们看见他受惊，像乘客看见船上舵工受惊一样，大家都害怕。

〔报信人自观众左方上。

报信人 啊，客人们，我可以向你们打听俄狄浦斯王的宫殿在哪里吗？最好告诉我他本人在哪里，要是你们知道的话。

歌队 啊，客人，这就是他的家，他本人在里面；这位夫人是他儿女的母亲。

报信人 愿他在幸福的家里永远幸福，既然她是他的全福的妻子！

伊俄卡斯忒 啊，客人，愿你也幸福；你说了吉祥话，应当受我回敬。请你告诉我，你来求什么，或者有什么消息见告。

报信人 夫人，对你家和你丈夫是好消息。

伊俄卡斯忒 什么消息？你是从什么人那里来的？

报信人 从科任托斯来的。你听了我要报告的消息一定高兴，怎么会不高兴呢？但也许还会发愁呢。

伊俄卡斯忒 到底是什么消息？怎么会使我高兴又使我发愁？

报信人 人民要立俄狄浦斯为伊斯特摩斯地方的王，那里是这样说的。

伊俄卡斯忒 怎么？老波吕波斯不是还在掌权吗？

报信人 不掌权了，因为死神已把他关进坟墓了。

伊俄卡斯忒　你说什么？老人家，波吕玻斯死了吗？

报信人　倘若我撒谎，我愿意死。

伊俄卡斯忒　侍女呀，还不快去告诉主人！（侍女进宫。）

啊，天神的预言，你成了什么东西了？俄狄浦斯多年来所害怕、所要躲避的正是这人，他害怕把他杀了；现在他已寿终而死，不是死在俄狄浦斯手中的。

〔俄狄浦斯偕众侍从自宫中上。

俄狄浦斯　啊，伊俄卡斯忒，最亲爱的夫人，为什么把我从屋里叫来？

伊俄卡斯：请听这人说话，你一边听，一边想天神的可怕的预言成了什么东西了。

俄狄浦斯　他是谁？有什么消息见告？

伊俄卡斯忒　他是从科任托斯来的，来讣告你父亲波吕玻斯不在了，去世了。

俄狄浦斯　你说什么，客人？亲自告诉我吧。

报信人　如果我得先把事情讲明白，我就让你知道，他死了，去世了。

俄狄浦斯　他是死于阴谋，还是死于疾病？

报信人　天平稍微倾斜，一个老年人便长眠不醒。

俄狄浦斯　那不幸的人好像是害病死的。

报信人　并且因为他年高寿尽了。

俄狄浦斯　啊！夫人呀，我们为什么要重视皮托的颁布预言的庙宇，或空中啼叫的鸟儿呢？它们曾指出过我命中注定要杀我父亲。但是他已经死了，埋进了泥土；我却还在这里，没有动过刀枪。除非说他是因为思念我而死的，那么倒是我害死了他。这似灵不灵的神示已被波吕玻斯随身带着，和他一起躺在冥府里，不值半文钱了。

伊俄卡斯忒　我不是早就这样告诉了你吗？

俄狄浦斯　你倒是这样说过，可是，我因为害怕，迷失了方向。

伊俄卡斯忒　现在别再把这件事放在心上了。

俄狄浦斯　难道我不该害怕玷污我母亲的床榻吗？

伊俄卡斯忒　偶然控制着我们，未来的事又看不清楚，我们为什么惧怕呢？最好尽可能随随便便的生活。别害怕你会玷污你母亲的婚姻；许多人曾在梦中娶过母亲；但是那些不以为意的人却安乐的生活。

俄狄浦斯　要不是我母亲还活着，你这话倒也对；可是她既然健在，即使你说得对，我也应当害怕啊！

伊俄卡斯忒　可是你父亲的死总是个很大的安慰。

俄狄浦斯　我知道是个很大的安慰，可是我害怕那活着的妇人。

报信人　你害怕的妇人是谁呀？

俄狄浦斯　老人家，是波吕玻斯的妻子墨洛珀。

报信人　她哪一点使你害怕？

俄狄浦斯　啊，客人，是因为神送来的可怕的预言。

报信人　说得说不得？是不是不可以让人知道？

俄狄浦斯　当然可以。罗克西阿斯曾说我命中注定要娶自己的母亲，亲手杀死自己的父亲。因此多年来我远离着科任托斯。我在此虽然幸福，可是看见父母的容颜是件很大的乐事啊。

报信人　你真的因为害怕这件事，离开了那里？

俄狄浦斯　啊，老人家，还因为我不想成为杀父的凶手。

报信人　主上啊，我怀着好意前来，怎么不能解除你的恐惧呢？

俄狄浦斯　你依然可以从我手里得到很大的应得的报酬。

报信人　我是特地为此而来的，等你回去的时候，我可以得到一些好处呢。

俄狄浦斯　但是我决不肯回到父母家里。

报信人　年轻人！显然你不知道你在做什么。

俄狄浦斯　怎么不知道呢，老人家？看在天神面上，告诉我吧。

报信人　如果你是为了这个缘故不敢回家。

俄狄浦斯　我害怕福玻斯的预言在我身上应验。

报信人　是不是害怕因为杀父娶母而犯罪？

俄狄浦斯　是的，老人家，这件事一直在吓唬我。

报信人　你知道你没有理由害怕么？

俄狄浦斯　怎么没有呢，如果我是他们的儿子？

报信人　因为你和波吕玻斯没有血统关系。

俄狄浦斯　你说什么？难道波吕玻斯不是我的父亲？

报信人　正像我不是你的父亲，他也同样不是。

俄狄浦斯　我的父亲怎能和你这个同我没关系的人同样不是？

报信人　你不是他生的，也不是我生的。

俄狄浦斯　那么他为什么称呼我作他的儿子呢？

报信人　告诉你吧，是因为他从我手中把你当一件礼物接受了下来。

俄狄浦斯　但是他为什么十分爱别人送的孩子呢？

报信人　他从前没有儿子，所以才这样爱你。

俄狄浦斯　是你把我买来，还是把我捡来送给他的？

报信人　是我从喀泰戎峡谷里把你捡来送给他的。

俄狄浦斯　你为什么到那一带去呢？

报信人　我在那里放牧山上的羊。

俄狄浦斯　你是个牧人，还是个到处漂泊的佣工？

报信人　年轻人，那时候我是你的救命恩人。

俄狄浦斯　你把我抱在怀里的时候，我有没有什么痛苦？

报信人　你的脚跟可以证实你的痛苦。

俄狄浦斯　哎呀，你为什么提起这个老毛病？

报信人　那时候你的左右脚跟是钉在一起的，我给你解开了。

俄狄浦斯　那是我襁褓时期遭受的莫大的耻辱。

报信人　是呀，你是由这不幸而得到你现在的名字的。

俄狄浦斯　看在天神面上，告诉我，这件事是我父亲还是我母亲做的？你说。

报信人　我不知道；那把你送给我的人比我知道得清楚！

俄狄浦斯　怎么？你是从别人那里把我接过来的，不是自己捡来的吗？

报信人　不是自己捡来的，是另一个牧人把你送给我的。

俄狄浦斯　他是谁？你指得出来吗？

报信人　他被称为拉伊俄斯的仆人。

俄狄浦斯　是这地方从前的国王的仆人吗？

报信人　是的，是国王的牧人。

俄狄浦斯　他还活着吗？我可以看见他吗？

报信人　（向歌队）你们这些本地人应当知道得最清楚。

俄狄浦斯　你们这些站在我面前的人里面，有谁在乡下或城里见过他所说的牧人，认识他？赶快说吧！这是水落石出的时机。

歌队长：我认为他所说的不是别人，正是你刚才要找的乡下人；这件事伊俄卡斯忒最能够说明。

俄狄浦斯　夫人，你还记得我们刚才想召见的人吗？这人所说的是不是他？

伊俄卡斯忒　为什么问他所说的是谁？不必理会这事。不要记住他的话。

俄狄浦斯　我得到了这样的线索，还不能发现我的血缘，这可不行。

伊俄卡斯忒　看在天神面上，如果你关心自己的性命，就不要再追问了；我自己的苦闷已经够了。

俄狄浦斯　你放心，即使我发现我母亲三世为奴，我有三重奴隶身份，你出身也不卑贱。

伊俄卡斯忒　我求你听我的话，不要这样。

俄狄浦斯　我不听你的话，我要把事情弄清楚。

伊俄卡斯忒　我愿你好，好心好意劝你。

俄狄浦斯　你这片好心好意一直在使我苦恼。

伊俄卡斯忒　啊，不幸的人，愿你不知道你的身世。

俄狄浦斯　谁去把牧人带来？让这个女人去赏玩她的高贵门第吧！

伊俄卡斯忒　哎呀，哎呀，不幸的人呀！我只有这句话对你说，从此再没有别的话可说了！

〔伊俄卡斯忒冲进宫。

歌队长：俄狄浦斯，王后为什么在这样忧伤的心情下冲了进去？我害怕她这样闭着嘴，会有祸事发生。

俄狄浦斯　要发生就发生吧！即使我的出身卑贱，我也要弄清楚。那女人——女人总是很高傲的——她也许因为我出身卑贱感觉羞耻。但是我认为我是仁慈的幸运的宠儿，不至于受辱。幸运的是我的母亲；十二个月份是我的弟兄，他们能划出我什么时候渺小，什么时候伟大。这就是我的身世，我决不会被证明是另一个人；因此我一定要追问我的血统。

（罗念生　译）

小雀呀，我的情人的宠物

卡图鲁斯

小雀呀，我的情人的宠物
她常与你玩耍，在她膝上，
或者把指尖儿给你啄食，
还逗你啄得狠些，狠些，
因为她呀——光彩照人的
我的情人，想要借此自娱，
想从痛感中得到些许安慰，
同时爱情的剧痛就会消减。
但愿我也能如此同你玩耍
而减轻压在我心头的相思！

（飞白　译）

“生活吧，我的蕾丝比亚……”

卡图鲁斯

生活吧，我的蕾丝比亚，爱吧，
那些古板凳指责一文不值，
对那些闲话我们一笑置之。
太阳一次次沉没又复升起，
而我们短促的光明一旦熄灭，
就将沉入永恒的漫漫长夜！
给我一千个吻吧，再给一百，
然后再添上一千，再添一百，
然后再接着一千，再接一百。
让我们把它凑个千千万万，
就连我们自己也算不清楚，
免得胸怀狭窄的奸邪之徒
知道了吻的数目而心生嫉妒。

（飞白　译）

圣经·创世纪（节选）

起初神创造天地。地是空虚混沌。渊面黑暗。神的灵运行在水面上。神说，要有光，就有了光。神看光是好的，就把光暗分开了。神称光为昼，称暗为夜。有晚上，有早晨，这是头一日。

神说，诸水之间要有空气，将水分为上下。神就造出空气，将空气以下的水和空气以上的水分开了。事就这样成了。神称空气为天。有晚上，有早晨，是第二日。

神说，天下的水要聚在一处，使旱地露出来。事就这样成了。神称旱地为地，称水的聚处为海。神看着是好的。神说，地要发生青草，和结种子的菜蔬，并结果子的树木，各从其类，果子都包着核。事就这样成了。于是地发生了青草，和结种子的菜蔬，各从其类，并结果子的树木，各从其类，果子都包着核。神看着是好的。有晚上，有早晨，是第三日。

神说，天上要有光体，可以分昼夜，作记号，定节令，日子，年岁。并要发光在天空，普照在地上。事就这样成了。于是神造了两个大光，大的管昼，小的管夜。又造众星。就把这些光摆列在天空，普照在地上。管理昼夜，分别明暗。神看着是好的。有晚上，有早晨，是第四日。

神说，水要多多滋生有生命的物，要有雀鸟飞在地面以上，天空之中。神就造出大鱼和水中所滋生各样有生命的动物，各从其类。又造出各样飞鸟，各从其类。神看着是好的。神就赐福给这一切，说，滋生繁多，充满海中的水。雀鸟也要多生在地上。有晚上，有早晨，是第五日。

神说，地要生出活物来，各从其类。牲畜，昆虫，野兽，各从其类。事就这样成了。于是神造出野兽，各从其类。牲畜，各从其类。地上一切昆虫，各从其类。神看着是好的。神说，我们要照着我们的形象，按着我们的样式造人，使他们管理海里的鱼，空中的鸟，地上的牲畜，和全地，并地上所爬的一切昆虫。神就照着自己的形象造人，乃是照着他的形象造男造女。神就赐福给他们，又对他们说，要生养众多，遍满地面，治理这地。也要管理海里的鱼，空中的鸟，和地上各样行动的活物。神说，看哪，我将遍地上一切结种子的菜蔬和一切树上所结有核的果子，全赐给你们做食物。至于地上的走兽和空中的飞鸟，并各样爬在地上有生命的物，我将青草赐给它们做食物。事就这样成了。神看着一切所造的都甚好。有晚上，有早晨，是第六日。

天地万物都造齐了。到第七日，神造物的工已经完毕，就在第七日歇了他一切的工，安息了。神赐福给第七日，定为圣日，因为在这日神歇了他一切创造的工，就安息了。创造天地的来历，在耶和华神造天地的日子，乃是这样。

野地还没有草木，田间的菜蔬还没有长起来，因为耶和华神还没有降雨在地上，也没有人耕地。但有雾气从地上腾，滋润遍地。耶和华神用地上的尘土造人，将生气吹在他鼻孔里，他就成了有灵的活人。

（简体中文和合本）

圣经·箴言（节选）

我在父亲面前为孝子，在母亲眼中为独一的娇儿。父亲教训我说，“你心要存记我的言语，遵守我的命令，便得存活。

“要得智慧，要得聪明。不可忘记，也不可偏离我口中的言语。

“不可离弃智慧，智慧就护卫你。要爱他，他就保护你。

“智慧为首。所以要得智慧。在你一切所得之内，必得聪明（或用你一切所得的去换聪明）。

“高举智慧，他就使你高升。怀抱智慧，他就使你尊荣。

“他必将华冠加在你头上，把荣冕交给你。

“我儿，你要听受我的言语，就必延年益寿。

“我已指教你走智慧的道，引导你行正直的路。

“你行走，脚步必不致狭窄。你奔跑，也不致跌倒。

“要持定训诲，不可放松。必当谨守，因为他是你的生命。

“不可行恶人的路。不要走坏人的道。

“要躲避，不可经过。要转身而去。”

（简体中文和合本）

圣经·雅歌(节选)

男：
你是多么美丽，我的爱！
你的眼睛在面纱里流露爱的光辉。
你的秀发飞舞，如一群山羊
跳跃着奔下基列的山冈。
你的牙洁白如同绵羊
　刚剪过毛，刚洗干净。
整群羊一只也不少；
　只只都无比匀称。
你的嘴唇像朱红缎带，
　当你启齿时更加秀美。
你的面颊在面纱后燃烧。
　你的颈像大卫王的塔
　那样又圆又润，
一串项链像一千面盾牌挂在周围。
你的双乳像一对羚羊，
一对双生的小羊在百合花间吃草
我要在没药山上留下，
　在乳香山上留下，
　直到晨风吹拂，
　直到黑暗消散。
你是多么美丽，我的爱，
　你是多么完美无瑕！
跟我来吧，我的新娘，从黎巴嫩，
　从黎巴嫩的群山。
从亚玛拿山顶下来，
　从狮子和豹子住的
　示尼珥山和黑门山来。
我的爱人我的新娘，
　你的眼神、你戴的项链
偷走了我的心，
你的爱使我欢喜，
　我的爱侣我的新娘，
你的爱胜过美酒，
　任何香料都比不上你芬芳。
你的唇上有蜜的甜味，我亲爱的；
你的舌头对于我就是奶与蜜。
你的衣服啊，有整个黎巴嫩的芳香。

我爱侣我新娘是一座秘密的园，
　高墙围住的花园，隐秘的泉；
　里面有花草繁茂。
仿佛是一座石榴园
　结出了最美好的果实。
这里有的是指甲花、甘松香，
　番红花、菖蒲、玉桂。
　还有百冬种乳香木。
这里长着没药和沉香，
　又有各种最迷人的香料。
泉水滋润着这座花园，
　活水潺潺流动，
　溪水喷涌，流下黎巴嫩的群山。

女：
醒来吧！北风啊。
南风啊，吹拂我的花园；
　使空气充满香气。
让我的爱人来到属于他的园里
　享用最好的果实。

（飞白 译）

Chapter Two Medieval Literature

“我女郎的眸子里……”

但　丁

我女郎的眸子里荡漾着爱情，
流盼时使一切都显得高洁温文，

她经过时，男士们无不凝眸出神，
她向谁致意，谁的心就跳个不停。
以致他低垂着脸，心神不宁，
并为自己的种种缺陷叹息不已，
在她面前，骄傲愤恨无藏身之地，
帮助我同声把她赞美，女士们。

凡是听见她说话的人，心里
就充满温情，且显得很谦虚，
谁见她一面，谁真幸福无比；
她嫣然一笑，真是千娇百媚，
无法形容，也难以记在心头，
为人们展现新的动人的奇迹。

（钱鸿嘉 译）

我的恋人如此娴雅

但 丁

我的恋人如此娴雅如此端庄，
当她向人行礼问候的时刻，
总使人因舌头发颤而沉默，
双眼也不敢正对她的目光。

她走过，在一片赞美的中央，
但她全身却透着谦逊温和，
她似乎不是凡女，而来自天国，
只为显示神迹才降临世上。

她的可爱，使人眼睛一眨不眨，
一股甜蜜通过眼睛流进心里，
你绝不能体会，若不曾尝过它：
从她樱唇间，似乎在微微散发
一种饱含爱情的柔和的灵气，
它叩着你的心扉命令道："叹息吧！"

（飞白 译）

破 晓 歌

贝特朗·德·阿拉玛农

一名骑士睡在他心仪的女人身边，
在亲吻间发出询问，情意绵绵：
亲人啊，我该怎么办呢，亲人？
黑夜即将终结，白昼就要降临。
我听到巡夜人在高喊"离开"，
破晓之后，白昼便接踵而来。

亲爱的，倘若白昼和破晓
不再迫使情侣分道扬镳，
那么最好的祝福就是真挚的骑士
躺在他最动心的女人的怀里。
我听到巡夜人在高喊"离开"，
破晓之后，白昼便接踵而来。

亲爱的，世界上的任何痛苦和悲戚，
都比不上情侣之间的别离；
我自己能够根据短暂的残夜
来计算我们遭受的痛苦何等剧烈。
我听到巡夜人在高喊"离开"，
破晓之后，白昼便接踵而来。

亲爱的，我得走了，可你必须记住：
我属于你，无论我走到何处；
请把我永远铭刻在你的心头，
因为我虽然离去，心却在此处存留。
我听到巡夜人在高喊"离开"，
破晓之后，白昼便接踵而来。

亲爱的，没有你，死神就会将我追寻，
是爱情让我忘记了我的全部生命。
我一定会回来的，尽一切力量，
因为没有你，我如同死了一样。
我听到巡夜人在高喊"离开"，
破晓之后，白昼便接踵而来。

（吴笛 译）

起来，给我出去把门闩上

故事大概发生在圣马丁节，
这是一个欢乐的时光，
女主人正在收拾着布丁，
然后放进铁锅煮得滚烫。

刺骨的寒风自南北方向吹来，
穿过大门刮进了住房；
男主人急忙朝他的老婆喊道：
"赶快，去把大门闩上！"

"老伴，我可正忙得够呛！
难道你脑袋上没长眼睛？
那扇破门压根儿就没闩过，
这会儿也不用我来费神。"

于是，他俩立下一项协定，
制订得周密而严谨：
谁要是先开口说了话，
谁就得起身出去闩门。

不久，两位乡绅来到这里，
可他们辨不清房屋和厅堂，
因为现在已是深更半夜，
他们也看不见炉火和烛光。

"这到底是富人家的豪宅，
还是穷鬼搭的破草房？"
夫妻俩听了不发一言，
因为谁都不愿输给对方。

两个家伙开始狼吞虎咽，
吃了白布丁又把黑的品尝，
女主人心里着实难熬，
但她强忍着一句话也不讲。

这时一个乡绅对另一个说：
"拿着，伙计，拿着这把刀；
趁我去和他女人亲个火热，
你快把那老东西的胡子剃掉！"

"黑灯瞎火的上哪儿找水，
没有水又怎能把他的胡须剃光？"
"锅里不是还有布丁汤吗，
难道不能端来派上用场？"

男主人一听惊愕万分，
只见他顿时怒气冲天：
"你们真要当面亲我的女人，
还要拿布丁汤烫我的脸？"

谁知女主人赶紧跳下床来，
一蹦三跳喜气洋洋：
"当家的，是你最先开口说话，
起来，给我出去把门闩上！"

（樊维娜 译）

两只乌鸦

当我在路上踽踽独行，
　　听见两只乌鸦在低吟；
这一只在问另一只，
　　"今天咱们上哪儿觅食？"

"在你背后有堵长满荒草的旧河坝，
　　躺着个骑士刚被人谋杀。
此事至今仍无人知情，
　　除了他的猎鹰、猎犬和漂亮的夫人。
"他的猎犬已行猎在山林，

　　他的猎鹰已出去捕捉野禽，
他的夫人另找了意中人，
　　咱俩正好飞下去美餐一顿。"

"你飞去停息在他的脖颈，
　　让我啄掉他那双美丽眼睛；
再取一束他那金黄色的头发，
　　咱们好用它来筑窝安家。

"许多人在为他伤心痛哭，
　　但无人知道他今在何方，
尸体上的肉一旦啄食殆尽，
　　骷髅上唯有风呼啸作响。"

（陈才宇 译）

鲁拜集（节选）

海亚姆

12

只要在树荫下有一卷诗章，
一壶葡萄酒和面包一方，
还有你，在荒野里伴我歌吟，
荒野呀就是完美的天堂！

20

我俩枕着绿草覆盖的河唇，

苏生的春草啊柔美如茵，——
轻轻地枕吧，有谁知道
它在哪位美人唇边萌生！

24

啊，尽情利用所余的时日，
趁我们尚未沉沦成泥，——
土归于土，长眠上下，
无酒浆，无歌声，且永无尽期！

29

我像流水不由自主地来到宇宙，
不知何来，也不知何由；
像荒漠之风不由自主地飘去，
不知何往，也不能停留。

35

我把唇俯向这可怜的陶樽，
想把我生命的奥秘探询；
樽口对我低语道："生时饮吧！
一旦死去你将永无回程。"

36

我想这隐约答话的陶樽
一定曾经活过，曾经畅饮；
而我吻着的无生命的樽唇
曾接受和给予过多少热吻！

37

因为我记起曾在路上遇见
陶匠在捶捣黏土一团；
黏土在用湮没了的语言抱怨：
"轻点吧，兄弟，求你轻点！"

38

岂不闻自古有故事流传，
世世代代一直传到今天，
说是造物主当年造人
用的就是这样的湿泥一团？

（飞白 译）

Chapter Three Renaissance Literature

爱的忠诚

彼特拉克

不论我在南方冒着赤日炎炎，
或在阳光无力融化冰雪之处，
或在阳光和煦的温暖国土，
不论与狂人为伍或在哲人之间；

不论我身份是高贵或是低贱，
不论是长夜漫漫或白昼短促，
不论是晴空如洗或乌云密布，
不论是年华正茂或双鬓斑斑；

不论我在人间、地狱或天堂，
在滔滔洪水中，或在高山深谷，
不论患病或健康，快乐或忧伤，
不论住在何处，自由或为奴，
我永属于她；哪怕我的希望
永成泡影，这念头已令我满足。

（飞白 译）

爱的矛盾

彼特拉克

我结束了战争，却找不到和平，
我发烧又发冷，希望混着恐怖，
我乘风飞翔，又离不开泥土，
我占有整个世界，却两手空空；

我并无绳索缠身枷锁套颈，
我却仍是个无法脱逃的囚徒，
我既无生之路，也无死之途，
即便我自寻，也仍求死不能；

我不用眼而看，不用舌头而抱怨，
我愿灭亡，但我仍要求康健，
我爱一个人，却又把自己怨恨；

我在悲哀中食，我在痛苦中笑，
不论生和死都一样叫我苦恼，
我的欢乐啊，正是愁苦的原因。

（飞白 译）

十日谈（节选）

卜伽丘

萨莱诺的亲王唐克莱本是一位仁慈宽大的王爷，可是到了晚年，他的双手却沾染了一对情侣的鲜血。他的膝下并无三男两女，只有一个独养的郡主，亲王对她真是百般疼爱，自古以来，父亲爱女儿也不过是这样罢了；谁想到，要是不养这个女儿，他的晚境或许倒会快乐些呢。那亲王既然这么疼爱郡主，所以也不管耽误了女儿的青春，竟一直舍不得让她出嫁；直到后来，再也藏不住了。这才把她嫁给了卡普亚公爵的儿子。不幸婚后不久，丈夫去世，她成了一个寡妇，重又回到她父亲那儿。

她正当青春年华，天性活泼，身段容貌，都长得十分俏丽，而且才思敏捷。只可惜做了一个女人。她住在父亲的宫里，养尊处优，过着豪华的生活；后来看见父亲这么爱她，根本不想把她再嫁，自己又不好意思开口，就私下打算找一个中意的男子做他的情人。

出入她父亲的宫廷里的，上中下三等人都有，她留意观察了许多男人的举止行为，看见父亲跟前有一个年轻的侍从，名叫纪斯卡多，虽说出身微贱，但是人品高尚，气宇轩昂，确是比众人高出一等。她非常中意，竟暗中爱上了他，而且朝夕相见，越看越爱。那小伙子并非傻瓜，不久也就觉察了她的心意，也不由得动了情，整天只想念着她，把什么都抛在脑后了。

两人这样眉目传情，已非一日，郡主只想找个机会和他幽会，可又不敢把心事托付别人，结果她想出一个极好的主意。她写了封短简，叫他第二天怎样来和她相会。又把这信藏在一根空心的竹竿里面，交给纪斯卡多，还开玩笑地说道："把这个拿去当个风箱吧，那么你的女仆今儿晚上可以用这个生火了。"

纪斯卡多接过竹竿，觉得郡主决不会无缘无故给他这样东西，而且说出这样的话来。他回到自己房里，检查竹竿，看见中间有一条裂缝，劈开一看，原来里面藏着一封信。他急忙展读，明白了其中的究竟，这时候他真是成了世上最快乐的人儿；于是他就依着信里的话，做好准备，去和郡主幽会。

在亲王的宫室附近有一座山，山上有一个许多年前开凿的石室，在山腰里，当时又另外凿了一条隧道，透着微光，直通那洞府。那石室久经废弃，所以那隧道的出口处，也荆棘杂草丛生，几乎把洞口都掩蔽了。在那石室里，有一道秘密的石级，直通宫室，石级和宫室之间，隔着一扇沉重的门，把门打开，就是郡主楼下的一间屋子。

因为山洞久已废弃不用，大家早把这道石级忘了。可是什么也逃不过情人的眼睛，所以居然给那位多情的郡主记了起来。

她不愿让任何人知道她的秘密，便找了几样工具，亲自动手来打开这道门，经过好几天的努力，终于把门打开了。她就登上石级，直找到那山洞的出口处，她把隧道的地形、洞口离地大约多高等都写在信上，叫纪斯卡多设法从这隧道潜入她宫里来。

纪斯卡多立即预备了一条绳子，中间打了许多结，绕了许多圈，以便攀上爬下。第二天晚上，他穿了一件皮衣，免得叫荆棘刺伤，就独个儿偷偷来到山脚边，找到了那个洞口，把绳子的一端在一株坚固的树桩上系牢，自己就顺着绳索，降落到洞底，在那里静候郡主。

第二天，郡主假说要午睡，把侍女都打发出去，独自关在房里。于是她打开那扇暗门，沿着石级，走下山洞，果然找到了纪斯卡多，彼此都喜不自胜。郡主就把他领进自己的卧室，两人在房里逗留了大半天，真像神仙般快乐。

分别时，两人约定，一切都要谨慎行事，不能让别人得知他们的私情。于是纪斯卡多回到山洞，郡主锁上暗门，去找她的侍女。等到天黑之后，纪斯卡多攀着绳子上升，从进来的洞口出去，回到自己的住所。自从发现了这条捷径以后，这对情人就时常幽会。

谁知命运之神却不甘心让这对情人长久浸沉在幸福里，竟借着一件意外的事故，把这一对情人满怀的欢乐化作断肠的悲痛。这厄运是这样降临的：

原来唐克莱常常独自一人来到女儿房中，跟她聊一会儿天，然后离去。

有一天，他吃过早饭，又到他女儿绮思梦达的寝宫里去，看见女儿正带着她那许多宫女在花园里玩儿，他不愿打断她的兴致，就悄悄走进她的卧室，不曾让人看到或是听见。来到房中，他看见窗户紧闭、帐帷低垂，就在床脚边的一张软凳上坐了下来，头靠在床边，拉过帐子来遮掩了自己，好像有意要躲藏起来似的，不觉就这么睡熟了。

也是合该有事，绮思梦达偏偏约好纪斯卡多在这天里幽会，所以她在花园里玩了一会，就让那些宫女继续玩去，自己悄悄溜到房中，把门关上了，却不知道房里还有别人，走去开了那扇暗门，把在隧道里等候着的纪斯卡多放进来。他们俩像平常一样，一同登上了床，寻欢作乐，正在得意忘形的当儿，不想唐克莱醒了。他听到声响，惊醒过来，看见女儿和纪斯卡多两个正在干着好事，气得他直想咆哮起来，可是再一转念，他自有办法对付他们，还是暂且隐忍一时，免得家丑外扬。

那一对情人像往常一样，温存了半天，直到不得不分手的时候，这才走下床来，全不知道唐克莱正躲在他们身边。纪斯卡多从洞里出去，她自己也走出了卧房。

唐克莱也不顾自己年事已高，却从一个窗口跳到花园里去，趁着没有人看见，赶回宫去，几乎气得要死。

当天晚上，到了睡觉时分，纪斯卡多从洞底里爬上来，不想早有两个大汉，奉了唐克莱的命令守候在那里，将他一把抓住；他身上还裹着皮衣，就这么给悄悄押到唐克莱跟前。亲王一看见他，差一点儿掉下泪来，说道：

"纪斯卡多，我平时待你不薄，不想今日里却让我亲眼看见你色胆包天，竟敢败坏我女儿的名节！"

纪斯卡多一句话都没有，只是这样回答他："爱情的力量不是你我所管束得了的。"

唐克莱下令把他严密看押起来，他当即给禁锢在宫中的一间幽室里。唐克莱左思右想，该怎样发落他的女儿，吃过饭后，就像平日一样，来到女儿房中，把她叫了来。绮思梦达怎么也没想到已经出了岔子，唐克莱把门关上，单剩自己和女儿在房中，老泪纵横，对她说道：

"绮思梦达，我一向以为你端庄稳重，想不到竟会干出这种事来。要不是我亲眼看见，而是听别人告诉我，那么就是你跟你丈夫以外的男人发生关系，就是说你存了这种欲念，我也绝对不会相信的。我已经到了风烛残年，再没有几年可活了，不想碰到这种丑事，叫我从此以后一想起来，就觉得心痛！

"即使你要做出这种无耻的事来，天哪，那也得挑一个身份相称的男人才好！多少王孙公子出入我的宫廷，你却偏偏看中了纪斯卡多——这是一个下贱的奴仆，可以说，从小就靠我们行好，把他收留在宫中。你这种行为真叫我心烦意乱，不知该把你怎样发落才好。

"至于纪斯卡多，昨天晚上他一爬出山洞，我就把他捉住、关了起来，我自有处置他的办法。对于你，天知道，我却一点主意都拿不定。

"一方面，我对你狠不起心来。天下做父亲的爱女儿，总没有像我那样爱你爱得深。另一方面，我想到你这么轻薄，又怎能不怒火直冒？如果看在父女的份上，那我只好饶了你；如果以事论事，我就顾不得骨肉之情，非要重重惩罚你不可。不过，在我还没拿定主意以前，我且先听听你自己有什么好说的。"

说到这里，他低下头去，号啕大哭起来，竟像一个挨了打的孩子一般。

绮思梦达听了父亲的话，知道不但他们的私情已经败露，而且纪斯卡多也已经给关了起来，她心里感到一阵说不出的悲痛，好几次都险些儿要像一般女人那样大哭大叫起来。她知道她的纪斯卡多必死无疑，可是崇高的爱情战胜了那脆弱的感情，她凭着惊人的意志力，强自镇定，并且打定主意，宁可一死也绝不说半句求饶的话。

因此，她在父亲面前并不像一个因为犯了过错、受了责备而哭泣的女人，却是无所畏惧，眼无泪痕，面无愁容，坦坦荡荡地回答她父亲说：

"唐克莱，我不准备否认这回事，也不想向你讨饶；因为第一件事对我不会有半点好处，第二件事就是有好处我也不愿意干。我也不想请你看着父女的情分来开脱我，不，我只要把事情的真相讲出来，用充分的理由来为我的名誉辩护，接着就用行动来坚决响应我灵魂的伟大的号召。

"不错，我确是爱上了纪斯卡多，只要我还活着——只怕是活不长久了——我就始终如一地爱他。假使人死后还会爱，那我死了之后还要继续爱他。我堕入情网，与其说是由于女人的意志脆弱，倒不如说，由于你不想再给我找一个丈夫，同时也为了他本人可敬可爱。

"唐克莱，你既然自己是血肉之躯，你应该知道你养出来的女儿，她的心也是血肉做成的，并非铁石心肠。你现在年老力衰了，但是应该还记得那青春的规律，以及它对青年人具有多大的支配力量。虽说你的青春多半是消磨在战场上，你也总该知道饱暖安逸的生活对于一个老头儿会有什么影响，别说对于一个青年人了。

“我是你生养的，是个血肉之躯，在这世界上又没度过多少年头，还很年轻，那么怎怪得我春情荡漾呢？况且我已结过婚，尝到过其中的滋味，这种欲念就格外迫切了。

“我按捺不住这片青春烈火，我年轻，又是个女人，我情不自禁，私下爱上了一个男人。我凭着热情冲动，做出这事来，但是我也曾费尽心机，免得你我蒙受耻辱。

“多情的爱神和好心的命运，指点了我一条外人不知道的秘密的通路，好让我如愿以偿。这回事，不管是你自己发现的也罢，还是别人报告你的也罢，我决不否认。

“有些女人只要随便找到一个男人，就满足了，我可不是那样；我是经过了一番观察和考虑，才在许多男人中间选中了纪斯卡多，有心去挑逗他的，而我们俩凭着小心行事，确实享受了不少欢乐。

“你方才把我痛骂了一顿，听你的口气，我缔结了一段私情，罪过还轻；只是千不该万不该去跟一个低三下四的男人发生关系，倒好像我要是找一个王孙公子来做情夫，那你就不会生我的气了。这完全是没有道理的世俗成见。你不该责备我，要埋怨，只能去埋怨那命运之神，为什么他老是让那些庸俗无能之辈窃据着显赫尊荣的高位，把那些人间英杰反而埋没在草莽里。

“可是我们暂且不提这些，先来谈一谈一个根本的道理。你应该知道，我们人类的血肉之躯都是用同样的物质造成的，我们的灵魂都是天主赐给的，具备着同等的机能，同样的效用，同样的德性。

“我们人类本是天生一律平等的，只有品德才是区分人类的标准，那发挥大才大德的才当得起一个‘贵’，否则就只能算是‘贱’。这条最基本的法律虽然被世俗的谬见所掩蔽了，可并不是就此给抹杀掉，它还是在人们的天性和举止中间显露出来，所以凡是有品德的人就证明了自己的高贵。如果这样的人被人说是卑贱，那么这不是他的错，而是这样看待他的人的错。

“请你看看满朝的贵人，打量一下他们的品德、他们的举止、他们的行为吧；然后再看看纪斯卡多又是怎么样。只要你不存偏见，下一个判断，那么你准会承认，最高贵的是他，而你那班朝贵都只是些鄙夫而已。说到他的品德、他的才能，我不信任别人的判断，只信任你的话和我自己的眼光。

“谁曾像你那样几次三番赞美他，把他当做一个英才？真的，你这许多赞美不是没有理由的。要是我没有看错人，我敢说：你赞美他的话他句句都当之无愧，你以为把他赞美够了，可是他比你所赞美的还要胜三分呢。要是我把他看错了，那么我是上了你的当。

“现在你还要说我结识了一个低三下四的人吗？如果你这么说，那就是违心之论。

“你不妨说，他是个穷人，可是这种话只会给你自己带来羞耻，因为你有了人才不知道提拔，把他埋没在仆人的队伍里。贫穷不会磨灭一个人的高贵的品质，不，反而是富贵叫人丧失了志气。多少帝王，多少公侯将相，都是白手起家的，而现在有许多村夫牧人，从前都是豪富巨族呢。

“那么，你要怎样处置我，用不到再这样踌躇不决了。如果你决心要下毒手——要在你风烛残年干出你年轻的时候从来没干过的事，那么你尽管用残酷的手段对付我吧，我绝不向你乞怜求饶，因为如果这算得是罪恶，那我就是罪魁祸首。我还要告诉你，如果你怎样处置了纪斯卡多，或者准备怎样处置他，却不肯用同样的方法来处置我，那我也会自己动手来处置我自己的。

“现在，你可以去了，跟那些娘们儿一块儿去哭吧。哭够之后，就狠起心肠一刀子把我们俩一起杀了吧——要是你认为我们非死不可的话。”

亲王这才知道他的女儿有一颗伟大的灵魂，不过还是不相信她的意志真会像她的言词那样坚决。他走出了郡主的寝宫，决定不用暴力对待她，却打算惩罚她的情人来打击她的热情，叫她死了那颗心。当天晚上，他命令看守纪斯卡多的那两个禁卫，私下把他绞死，挖出心脏，拿来给他。那两个禁卫果然按照他的命令执行了。

第二天，亲王叫人拿出一只精致的大金杯，把纪斯卡多的心脏盛在里面，又吩咐自己的心腹仆人把金杯送给郡主，同时叫他传言道：“你的父王因为你用他最心爱的东西来安慰他，所以现在他也把你最心爱的东西送来慰问你。”

再说绮思梦达，等父亲走后，矢志不移，便叫人去采了那恶草毒根，煎成毒汁，准备一旦她的疑虑成为事实，就随时要用到它。

那侍从送来了亲王的礼物，还把亲王的话传述了一遍。她面不改色，接过金杯，揭开一看，里面盛着一颗心脏，就懂得了亲王为什么要说这一番话，同时也明白了这必然是纪斯卡多的心脏无疑；于是她回过头来对那仆人说：

“只有拿黄金做坟墓，才算不委屈了这颗心脏，我父亲这件事做得真得体！”

说着，她举起金杯，凑向唇边，吻着那颗心脏，说着：“我父亲对我的慈爱，一向无微不至，如今在我生命的最后一刻里，对我越发慈爱了。为了这么尊贵的礼物，我要最后一次向他表示感谢！”

于是她紧拿着金杯，低下头去，注视着那心脏，说道：“唉，你是我的安乐窝，我一切的幸福全都栖息在你身上。最可诅咒的是那个人的狠心的行为——是他叫我现在用这双肉眼注视着你！只要我能够用我那精神上的眼睛时时刻刻注视你，我就满足了。

“你已经走完了你的路程，已经尽了命运指派给你的任务，你已经到了每个人迟早都要来到的终点。你已经解脱了尘世的劳役和苦恼，你的仇敌把你葬在一个跟你身份相称的金杯里。

“你的葬礼，除了还缺少你生前所爱的人儿的眼泪外，可说什么都齐全了。现在，你连这也不会欠缺了，天空感化了我那狠毒的父亲，指使他把你送给我。我本来准备面不改色，从容死去，不掉一滴泪，现在我要为你痛哭一场，哭过之后，我的灵魂立即就要飞去跟你曾经守护的灵魂结合在一起。

“只有你的灵魂使我乐于跟从、倾心追随，一同到那不可知的冥域里去。我相信你的灵魂还在这里徘徊，凭吊着我们从前的乐园；那么，我相信依然爱着我的灵魂呀，为我深深地爱着的灵魂呀，你等一下我吧！”

说完，她就低下头去，凑在金杯上，泪如雨下，可绝不像娘们儿那样哭哭啼啼，她一面眼泪流个不停，一面只顾跟那颗心脏亲吻，也不知亲了多少回，吻了多少遍，总是没完没结，真把旁边的人看得呆住了。

侍候她的女伴不知道这是谁的心脏，又不明白她说这些话是什么意思，可是都被她深深感动了，陪她伤心掉泪，再三问她伤心的原因，可是任凭怎样问，怎样慰劝，她总是不肯说，她们只得极力安慰她一番。

后来郡主觉得哀悼够了，就抬起头来，揩干了眼泪，说道：“最可爱的心儿呀，我对你已经尽了我的本分，现在只剩下最后的一步了，那就是：让我的灵魂来和你的灵魂结个伴儿吧！”

说完，她叫人取出那昨日备下的盛毒液的瓶子来，只见她拿起瓶子就往金杯里倒去，把毒液全倾注在那颗给泪水洗刷过的心脏上；于是她毫无畏惧地举起金杯，送到嘴边，把毒汁一饮而尽。饮罢，她手里依然拿着金杯，登上绣榻，睡得十分端正安详，把情人的心脏按在自己的心上，一言不发，静待死神的降临。

侍候她的女伴，这时虽然还不知道她已经服毒，但是听她的说话、看她的行为有些反常，就急忙派人去把种种情形向唐克莱报告。他恐怕发生什么变故，急匆匆地赶到女儿房中，正好这时候她在床上睡了下来。他想用好话来安慰她，可是已经迟了，这时候她已经命在顷刻了，他不觉失声痛哭起来。谁知郡主却向他说道：

“唐克莱，我看你何必浪费这许多眼泪呢，等碰到比我更糟心的事，再哭不迟呀；我用不到你来哭，因为我不需要你的眼泪。除了你，有谁达到了目的反而哭泣的呢。如果你从前对我的那一片慈爱，还没完全泯灭，请你给我最后的一个恩典——那就是说，虽然你反对我跟纪斯卡多做一时不体面的夫妻，但是请你把我和他的遗体（不管你把他的遗体扔在什么地方）公开合葬在一处吧。”

亲王听得她这么说，心如刀割，一时竟不能作答。年轻的郡主觉得她的大限已到，紧握着那心脏、贴在自己的心头，说道：“天主保佑你，我要去了。”说罢，她闭上眼睛，随即完全失去知觉，摆脱了这苦恼的人生。

这就是纪斯卡多和绮思梦达这一对苦命的情人的结局。唐克莱哭也无用，悔也太迟，于是把他们两人很隆重地合葬在一处，全萨莱诺的人民听到他们的事迹，无不感到悲恸。

（方平、王科一 译）

堂吉诃德（节选）

塞万提斯

这时候，他们远远望见郊野里有三四十架风车。堂吉诃德一见，就对他的侍从说：

“命运的安排，比咱们要求的还好。你瞧，桑丘·潘沙朋友，那边出现了三十多个大得出奇的巨人。我打算去跟他们交手，把他们一个个杀死，咱们得了胜利品，可以发财。这是正义的战争，消灭地球上这种坏东西是为上帝立大功。”

桑丘·潘沙道：“什么巨人呀？”

他主人说：“那些长胳膊的，你没看见吗？有些巨人的胳膊差不多好几里长呢。”

桑丘说：“您仔细瞧瞧，那不是巨人，是风车；上面胳膊似的东西是风车的翅膀，给风吹动了就能推转石磨。”

堂吉诃德道：“你真是外行，不懂冒险。他们确是货真价实的巨人。你要是害怕，就走开些，做你的祷告去，我一人单干，跟他们大伙儿拼命好了。”

他一面说，一面踢着坐骑冲去。侍从桑丘大喊：“那明明是风车，不是巨人。”他满不理会，认准了那是巨人，既没听见桑丘叫喊，跑近了也没看清是什么东西，只顾往前冲，嘴里嚷道：“你们这伙儿没胆量的下流东西！不要跑！来跟你们厮杀的只是个单枪匹马的骑士！”这时微微刮起一阵风，转动了那些庞大的翅翼。

堂吉诃德见了说：“即使你们挥舞的胳膊比巨人布利亚瑞欧的还多，我也要和你们见个高低！”

说罢，他虔诚地向他那位杜尔西内娅小姐祷告一番，求她在这个紧要关头保佑自己，然后把盾牌遮稳身体，横托着长枪飞马向第一架风车冲杀上去。他一枪刺中了风车的翅膀，翅膀在风里转得正猛，把长枪迸作几段，一股劲儿把堂吉诃德连人带马直扫出去；堂吉诃德滚翻在地，狼狈不堪。桑丘·潘沙赶紧骑驴来救。跑近一看，他已经不能动弹，驽骍难得把他摔得太厉害了。

桑丘说：“天哪！我不是跟您说了吗，仔细着点儿，那不过是风车。除非自己的头脑给风车转糊涂了，谁还不知道这是风车呢？”

堂吉诃德答道：“甭说了，桑丘朋友，打仗的胜败最拿不稳，看来把我的书连带书房一起抢走的弗瑞斯冬法师对我冤仇很深，一定是他把巨人变成风车，来剥夺我胜利的光荣。可是到头来，他的邪法毕竟敌不过我这把剑的锋芒。”

桑丘说：“这就要瞧老天爷怎么安排了。”桑丘扶起堂吉诃德。他重又骑上几乎跌歪了肩膀的驽骍难得。他们谈论着方才的险遇，顺着往拉比塞峡口的大道前去，因为据堂吉诃德说，那地方来往人多，必定会碰到许多形形色色的奇事。可是他折断了长枪心上老大不痛快，和他的侍从计议说：

“我记得在书上读到一位西班牙骑士名叫狄艾果·贝瑞斯·台·巴尔咖斯，他一次打仗把剑斫断了，就从橡树上劈下一根粗壮的树枝，凭那根树枝，那一天干下许多了不起的事，打闷不知多少摩尔人，因此得到个绰号，叫做‘大棍子’。后来他本人和子孙都称为‘大棍子’巴尔咖斯。我跟你讲这番话有个计较：我一路上见到橡树，料想他那根树枝有多粗多壮，照样也折它一枝。我要凭这根树枝大显身手，你亲眼看见了种种说来也不可信的奇事，才会知道跟了我多么运气。”

桑丘说：“这都听凭老天爷安排吧。您说的话我全相信；可是您把身子挪正中些，您好像闪到一边去了，准是摔得身上疼呢。”

堂吉诃德说：“是啊，我吃了痛没做声，因为游侠骑士受了伤，尽管肠子从伤口掉出也不得哼痛。”

桑丘说：“要那样的话，我就没什么说的了。不过天晓得，我宁愿您有痛就哼。我自己呢，说老实话，我要有一丁点儿疼就得哼哼，除非游侠骑士的侍从也得遵守这个规矩，不许哼痛。”

堂吉诃德瞧他侍从这么傻，忍不住笑了。他声明说：不论桑丘喜欢怎么哼、或什么时候哼，不论他是忍不住要哼、或不哼也可，反正他尽管哼好了，因为他还没读到什么游侠骑士的规则不准侍从哼痛。

桑丘提醒主人说，该是吃饭的时候了。他东家说这会子还不想吃，桑丘什么时候想吃就可以吃。桑丘得了这个准许，就在驴背上尽量坐舒服了，把褡裢袋里的东西取出来，慢慢儿跟在主人后面一边走一边吃，还频频抱起酒袋来喝酒，喝得津津有味，玛拉咖最享口福的酒馆主人见了都会羡慕。他这样喝着酒一路走去，早把东家许他的愿抛在九霄云外，觉得四处冒险尽管担惊受怕，也不是什么苦差，倒是很舒坦的。

长话短说，他们当夜在树林里过了一宿。堂吉诃德折了一根可充枪柄的枯枝，换去断柄把枪头挪上。他曾经读到骑士们在穷林荒野里过夜，想念自己的意中人，好几夜都不睡觉。他要学样，当晚彻夜没睡，只顾想念他的意中人杜尔西内娅。

桑丘·潘沙却另是一样。他肚子填得满满的，又没喝什么提神醒睡的饮料，倒头一觉，直睡到大天亮。阳光照射到他脸上，鸟声嘈杂，欢迎又一天来临，他都不理会，要不是东家叫唤，他还沉睡不醒呢。

（杨绛 译）

十四行诗集

莎士比亚

十四行诗·十八

我怎么能够把你来比作夏天?
你不独比它可爱也比它温婉:
狂风把五月宠爱的嫩蕊作践,
夏天出赁的期限又未免太短:
天上的眼睛有时照得太酷烈,
它那炳耀的金颜又常遭掩蔽:
被机缘或无常的天道所摧折,
没有芳艳不终于凋残或销毁。
但是你的长夏永远不会凋落,
也不会损失你这皎洁的红芳,
或死神夸口你在他影里漂泊,
当你在不朽的诗里与时同长。
只要一天有人类,或人有眼睛,
这诗将长存,并且赐给你生命。

十四行诗·六十六

厌了这一切,我向安息的死疾呼,
比方,眼见天才注定做叫化子,
无聊的草包打扮得衣冠楚楚,
纯洁的信义不幸而被人背弃,
金冠可耻地戴在行尸的头上,
处女的贞操遭受暴徒的玷辱,
严肃的正义被人非法地诟让,
壮士被当权的跛子弄成残缺,
愚蠢摆起博士架子驾驭才能,
艺术被官府统治得结舌箝口,
淳朴的真诚被人瞎称为愚笨,
囚徒"善"不得不把统帅"恶"伺候:
厌了这一切,我要离开人寰,
但,我一死,我的爱人便孤单。

十四行诗·七十三

在我身上你或许会看见秋天,
当黄叶,或尽脱,或只三三两两
挂在瑟缩的枯枝上索索抖颤——
荒废的歌坛,那里百鸟曾合唱。
在我身上你或许会看见暮霭,
它在日落后向西方徐徐消退:
黑夜,死的化身,渐渐把它赶开,
严静的安息笼住纷纭的万类。
在我身上你或许会看见余烬,
它在青春的寒灰里奄奄一息,
在惨淡灵床上早晚总要断魂,
给那滋养过它的烈焰所销毁。
看见了这些,你的爱就会加强,
因为他转瞬要辞你溘然长往。

十四行诗·一一六

我绝不承认两颗真心的结合
会有任何障碍;爱算不得真爱,
若是一看见人家改变便转舵,
或者一看见人家转弯便离开。
哦,决不!爱是亘古长明的塔灯,
它定睛望着风暴却兀不为动;
爱又是指引迷舟的一颗恒星,
你可量它多高,它所值却无穷。
爱不受时光的播弄,尽管红颜
和皓齿难免遭受时光的毒手;
爱并不因瞬息的改变而改变,
它巍然矗立直到末日的尽头。
我这话若说错,并被证明不确,
就算我没写诗,也没人真爱过。

十四行诗·一三〇

我情妇的眼睛一点不像太阳;
珊瑚比她的嘴唇还要红得多:
雪若算白,她的胸就暗褐无光,
发若是铁丝,她头上铁丝婆娑。
我见过红白的玫瑰,轻纱一般;
她颊上却找不到这样的玫瑰;
有许多芳香非常逗引人喜欢,
我情妇的呼吸并没有这香味。
我爱听她谈话,可是我很清楚
音乐的悦耳远胜于她的嗓子;
我承认从没有见过女神走路,
我情妇走路时候却脚踏实地:
可是,我敢指天发誓,我的爱侣
胜似任何被捧作天仙的美女。

(以上梁宗岱译)

哈姆莱特（节选）

莎士比亚

〔国王、王后、波洛涅斯、奥菲利娅、罗森格兰兹及吉尔登斯恩上。

国王　你们不能用迂回婉转的方法，探出他为什么这样神魂颠倒，让紊乱而危险的疯狂困扰他的安静的生活吗？

罗森格兰兹　他承认他自己有些神经迷惘，可是绝口不肯说为了什么缘故。

吉尔登斯恩　他也不肯虚心接受我们的探问；当我们想要引导他吐露他自己的一些真相的时候，他总是用假作痴呆的神气故意回避。

王后　他对待你们还客气吗？

罗森格兰兹　很有礼貌。

吉尔登斯恩　可是不大自然。

罗森格兰兹　他很吝惜自己的话，可是我们问他话的时候，他回答起来却是毫无拘束。

王后　你们有没有劝诱他找些什么消遣？

罗森格兰兹　娘娘，我们来的时候，刚巧有一班戏子也要到这儿来，给我们追上了；我们把这消息告诉了他，他听了好像很高兴。现在他们已经到了宫里，我想他已经吩咐他们今晚为他演出了。

波洛涅斯　一点不错；他还叫我来请两位陛下同去看看他们演得怎样哩。

国王　那好极了；我非常高兴听见他在这方面感到兴趣。请你们两位还要更进一步鼓起他的兴味，把他的心思移转到这种娱乐上面。

罗森格兰兹　是，陛下。（罗森格兰兹、吉尔登斯恩同下。）

国王　亲爱的乔特鲁德，你也暂时离开我们；因为我们已经暗中差人去唤哈姆莱特到这儿来，让他和奥菲利娅见见面，就像他们偶然相遇一般。她的父亲跟我两人将要权充一下密探，躲在可以看见他们，却不能被他们看见的地方，注意他们会面的情形，从他的行为上判断他的疯病究竟是不是因为恋爱上的苦闷。

王后　我愿意服从您的意旨。奥菲利娅，但愿你的美貌果然是哈姆莱特疯狂的原因；更愿你的美德能够帮助他恢复原状，使你们两人都能安享尊荣。

奥菲利娅　娘娘，但愿如此。（王后下。）

波洛涅斯　奥菲利娅，你在这儿走走。陛下，我们就去躲起来吧。（向奥菲利娅）你拿这本书去读，他看见你这样用功，就不会疑心你为什么一个人在这儿了。人们往往用至诚的外表和虔敬的行动，掩饰一颗魔鬼般的内心，这样的例子是太多了。

国王　（旁白）　啊，这句话是太真实了！它在我的良心上抽了多么重的一鞭！涂脂抹粉的娼妇的脸，还不及掩藏在虚伪的言辞后面的我的行为更丑恶。难堪的重负啊！

波洛涅斯　我听见他来了；我们退下去吧，陛下。（国王及波洛涅斯下。）

〔哈姆莱特上。

哈姆莱特　生存还是毁灭，这是一个值得考虑的问题；默然忍受命运的暴虐的毒箭，或是挺身反抗人世的无涯的苦难，通过斗争把它们扫清，这两种行为，哪一种更高贵？死了；睡着了；什么都完了；要是在这一种睡眠之中，我们心头的创痛，以及其他无数血肉之躯所不能避免的打击，都可以从此消失，那正是我们求之不得的结局。死了；睡着了；睡着了也许还会做梦；嗯，阻碍就在这儿：因为当我们摆脱了这一具朽腐的皮囊以后，在那死的睡眠里，究竟将要做些什么梦，那不能不使我们踌躇顾虑。人们甘心久困于患难之中，也就是为了这个缘故；谁愿意忍受人世的鞭挞和讥嘲、压迫者的凌辱、傲慢者的冷眼、被轻蔑的爱情的惨痛、法律的迁延、官吏的横暴和费尽辛勤所换来的小人的鄙视，要是他只要用一柄小小的刀子，就可以清算他自己的一生？谁愿意负着这样的重担，在烦劳的生命的压迫下呻吟流汗，倘不是因为惧怕不可知的死后，惧怕那从来不曾有一个旅人回来过的神秘之国，是它迷惑了我们的意志，使我们宁愿忍受目前的折磨，不敢向我们所不知道的痛苦飞去？这样，重重的顾虑使我们全变成了懦夫，决心的赤热的光彩，被审慎的思维盖上了一层灰色，伟大的事业在这一种考虑之下，也会逆流而退，失去了行动的意义。且慢！美丽的奥菲利娅！——女神，在你的祈祷之中，不要忘记替我忏悔我的罪孽。

奥菲利娅　我的好殿下，您这许多天来贵体安好吗？

哈姆莱特　谢谢你，很好，很好，很好。

奥菲利娅　殿下，我有几件您送给我的纪念品，我早就想把它们还给您；请您现在收回去吧。

哈姆莱特　不，我不要；我从来没有给你什么东西。

奥菲利娅　殿下，我记得很清楚您把它们送给了我，那时候您还向我说了许多甜言蜜语，使这些东西格外显得贵重；现在它们的芳香已经消散，请您拿回去吧，因为在有骨气的人看来，送礼的人要是变了心，礼物虽贵，也会失去了价值。拿去吧，殿下。

哈姆莱特　哈哈！你贞洁吗？

奥菲利娅　殿下！

哈姆莱特　你美丽吗？

奥菲利娅　殿下是什么意思？

哈姆莱特　要是你既贞洁又美丽，那么你的贞洁应该断绝跟你的美丽来往。

奥菲利娅　殿下，难道美丽除了贞洁以外，还有什么更好的伴侣吗？

哈姆莱特　嗯，真的；因为美丽可以使贞洁变成淫荡，贞洁却未必能使美丽受它自己的感化；这句话从前像是怪诞之谈，可是现在时间已经把它证实了。我的确曾经爱过你。

奥菲利娅　真的，殿下，您曾经使我相信您爱我。

哈姆莱特　你当初就不应该相信我，因为美德不能熏陶我们罪恶的本性；我没有爱过你。

奥菲利娅　那么我真是受了骗了。

哈姆莱特　进尼姑庵去吧；为什么你要生一群罪人出来呢？我自己还不算是一个顶坏的人；可是我可以指出我的许多过失，一个人有了那些过失，他的母亲还是不要生下他来的好。我很骄傲，有仇必报，富于野心，我的罪恶是那么多，连我的思想也容纳不下，我的想象也不能给它们形象，甚至于我都没有充分的时间可以把它们实行出来。像我这样的家伙，匍匐于天地之间，有什么用处呢？我们都是些十足的坏人；一个也不要相信我们。进尼姑庵去吧。你的父亲呢？

奥菲利娅　在家里，殿下。

哈姆莱特　把他关起来，让他只好在家里发发傻劲。再会！

奥菲利娅　哎哟，天哪！救救他！

哈姆莱特　要是你一定要嫁人，我就把这一个咒诅送给你做嫁奁：尽管你像冰一样坚贞，像雪一样纯洁，你还是逃不过谗人的诽谤。进尼姑庵去吧，去；再会！或者要是你必须嫁人的话，就嫁给一个傻瓜吧；因为聪明人都明白你们会叫他们变成怎样的怪物。进尼姑庵去吧，去；越快越好。再会！

奥菲利娅　天上的神明啊，让他清醒过来吧！

哈姆莱特　我也知道你们会怎样涂脂抹粉；上帝给了你们一张脸，你们又替自己另外造了一张。你们烟视媚行，淫声浪气，替上帝造下的生物乱取名字，卖弄你们不懂事的风骚。算了吧，我再也不敢领教了；它已经使我发了狂。我说，我们以后再不要结什么婚了；已经结过婚的，除了一个人以外，都可以让他们活下去；没有结婚的不准再结婚，进尼姑庵去吧，去。（下。）

奥菲利娅　啊，一颗多么高贵的心是这样陨落了！朝臣的眼睛、学者的辩舌、军人的利剑、国家所瞩望的一朵娇花；时流的明镜、人伦的雅范、举世瞩目的中心，这样无可挽回地陨落了！我是一切妇女中间最伤心而不幸的，我曾经从他音乐一般的盟誓中吮吸芬芳的甘蜜，现在却眼看着他的高贵无上的理智，像一串美妙的银铃失去了谐和的音调，无比的青春美貌，在疯狂中凋谢！啊！我好苦，谁料过去的繁华，变作今朝的泥土！

〔国王及波洛涅斯重上。

国王　恋爱！他的精神错乱不像是为了恋爱；他说的话虽然有些颠倒，也不像是疯狂。他有些什么心事盘踞在他的灵魂里，我怕它也许会产生危险的结果。为了防止万一，我已经当机立断，决定了一个办法：他必须立刻到英国去，向他们追索延宕未纳的贡物；也许他到海外各国游历一趟以后，时时变换的环境，可以替他排解去这一桩使他神思恍惚的心事。你看怎么样？

波洛涅斯　那很好；可是我相信他的烦闷的根本原因，还是为了恋爱上的失意。啊，奥菲利娅！你不用告诉我们哈姆莱特殿下说些什么话；我们全都听见了。陛下，照您的意思办吧；可是您要是认为可以的话，不妨在戏剧终场以后，让他的母后独自一人跟他在一起，恳求他向她吐露他的心事；她必须很坦白地跟他谈谈，我就找一个所在听他们说些什么。要是她也探听不出他的秘密来，您就叫他到英国去，或者凭着您的高见,把他关禁在一个适当的地方。

国王　就这样吧;大人物的疯狂是不能听其自然的。(同下。)

(朱生豪 译)

Chapter Four
17th-Century Literature

早　安
多　恩

我真不明白;你我相爱之前
在干什么?莫非我们还没断奶,
只知吮吸田园之乐像孩子一般,
或是在七个睡眠者的洞中打鼾?
确实如此,但一切欢乐都是虚拟,
如果我见过,追求并获得过美,
那全都是——且仅仅是——梦见的你。

现在向我们苏醒的灵魂道声早安,
两个灵魂互相信赖,毋须警戒;
因为爱控制了对其他景色的爱,
把小小的房间点化成大千世界。
让航海发现家向新世界远游,
让无数世界的舆图把别人引诱
我们却自成世界,又互相拥有。

我映在你眼里,你映在我眼里,
两张脸上现出真诚坦荡的心地。
哪儿能找到两个更好的半球啊,
没有严酷的北,没有下沉的西?
凡是死亡,都属调和失当所致,
如果我俩的爱合二为一,或是
爱得如此一致,那就谁也不会死。

(飞白 译)

别离辞:节哀
多　恩

正如德高人逝世很安然,
对灵魂轻轻地说一声走,
悲伤的朋友们聚在旁边,
有的说断气了,有的说没有。

让我们化了,一声也不做,
泪浪也不翻,叹风也不兴;
那是亵渎我们的欢乐——
要是对俗人讲我们的爱情。

地动会带来灾害和惊恐,
人们估计它干什么,要怎样
可是那些天体的震动,
虽然大得多,什么也不伤。

世俗的男女彼此的相好,
(他们的灵魂是官能)就最忌
别离,因为那就会取消
组成爱恋的那一套东西。

我们被爱情提炼得纯净,
自己都不知道存什么念头
互相在心灵上得到了保证,
再不愁碰不到眼睛、嘴和手。

两个灵魂打成了一片,
虽说我得走,却并不变成
破裂,而只是向外伸延,
像金子打到薄薄的一层。

就还算两个吧,两个却这样
和一副两脚规情况相同;
你的灵魂是定脚,并不像
移动,另一脚一移,它也动。

虽然它一直是坐在中心,
可是另一个去天涯海角,
它就侧了身,倾听八垠;
那一个一回家,它马上挺腰。

你对我就会这样子,我一生
像另外那一脚,得侧身打转;
你坚定,我的圆圈才会准,
我才会终结在开始的地点。

(卞之琳 译)

给羞怯的情人

马韦尔

只要我们的世界大，时间多，
小姐，羞怯就算不了罪过，
我们就坐下来，想想上哪边
去散步，过我们长长的情爱天。
你就跑到印度的恒河旁
去觅红宝石；我守着潮浪
对洪泊湾兴叹。我会在
洪水前十年就开始把你爱，
如果你拒绝，不答应也好，
直到犹太人改信了宗教。
我的植物性爱情的滋长
比许多帝国还要慢，还要广：
一百年我都用来赞美
你的眼，用来凝视你的眉；
两百年崇仰每一个乳房，
三万年才遍及其余的地方；
每一个部分至少要一世代，
最后一世代你的心才登台：
小姐，你应有这等身价，
我用情也不愿草草上马。

可是我背后总听到声音：
时间的飞轮急促的逼近；
而摆在我们前头的一切
就是永恒的无边荒野。
你的美决不会重新找到，
你的大理石坟窖里也短少
我的歌声；蛆虫会成阵
来品尝那一瓶久藏的童贞，
你的娇情化成了尘土
我的欲情白白的烧枯：
坟墓是好地方，没有人打扰，
可是也没有人在那里拥抱。

因此，现在就趁你的嫩皮肤
还色泽新鲜，俨然像朝露，
趁你情愿的灵魂直冒烟，
旺盛而透出每一个皮肤眼，
我们能玩就玩一个尽兴；
我们像一对发情的飞鹰
宁可把我们的时光一口吞，
不在它慢嚼的嘴里委顿。
让我们把全部力量，再加满
全部蜜糖，揉成了一团，
攻破人生的铁门，一举
而夺得我们应得的欢喜：
这样子，虽不能叫太阳停止，
就叫它跑个七伤八死。

（高东山 译）

爱的定义

马韦尔

我的爱是罕见地珍贵，
它追求着崇高与奇异；
绝望与否定的交配
孕育出这一个孩子。

宽宏大度的绝望
向我展示非凡的东西，
虚弱的希望无法飞翔，
只会扑腾华丽的羽翼。

尽管，我很快就会进抵
我扩张的灵魂定居的所在；
然而命运插进了铁楔，
总是站在中间百般阻碍。

命运睁开好嫉妒的眼睛，
决不愿看见完美的爱之接触；
我俩的结合是她末日的来临，
她娇横的权威将被废黜。

因此，她发布铁的命令，
将我们流放到遥远的两极，
（虽然爱的世界仍围绕我们运行）
这两极呀，无法拥抱亲昵；

除非旋转的天庭崩坍，
地球在痉挛之中破裂；
世界被挤压成一个平面，
我俩才可能得以团聚。

虚伪的爱恰似那条斜线，
总能从各个角度致意问好，
而我们的爱却是平行线，
永远延伸，却绝不相交。

因此，将我俩拴在一起的爱，
遇上了命运在从中作梗，
只能是精神的相互交缠，
恍如两颗遥遥相对的星星。

（汪剑钊 译）

“我仿佛看见……”

弥尔顿

我仿佛看见我圣洁的新妇
　苍白而昏晕，从死神手中回归，
　恰似被宙斯的伟大儿子夺回——
　阿尔克提斯来见快乐的丈夫。
我的新妇正如按照古法救赎，
　由洁净祭礼洗去了产褥的污秽，
　正如我深信我必将再有机会
　在天上看见她，清楚而无拘束，
她披着白袍来到，纯洁如她的心灵。
　她带着面纱，但我幻想的视觉
　看见她发出爱、甜而善的光明，
再没有别人脸上会有更大的欢悦。
　但当她想拥抱我的一瞬，我已醒，
　她消失，白昼又把我带回黑夜。

（飞白 译）

伪君子（节选）

莫里哀

〔出场人：柏奈尔夫人和她的女仆爱尔卜特，欧米尔，玛丽亚娜，桃丽娜，达米斯，克雷央特。

柏奈尔夫人　咱们走吧，爱尔卜特，咱们走吧！让我躲开他们吧！

欧米尔　您这么个走法，我们简直跟不上您了。

柏奈尔夫人　站住吧，我的少奶奶，站住吧，别远送啦。这对我都是用不着的客套。

欧米尔　这是我们对您应该有的礼节呀。不过，我的娘，您为什么这么快就出来了呢？

柏奈尔夫人　皆因我看不惯这里的派头儿，你们一点也不想讨我的喜欢。是的，我原是很不痛快才走出你们的大门的。我教训的话，你们一句也没听，这儿的人什么顾忌也没有，每个人都大声嚷嚷，不折不扣这是一个叫花子窝。

桃丽娜　如果……

柏奈尔夫人　朋友，你是一个侍女，有点儿太爱说话，并且一点儿规矩也不懂：不管什么事你都要插进去表示你的意见。

达米斯　不过……

柏奈尔夫人　你啊，我的孩子，你是三个字的考语：糊涂虫；是我，你的祖母对你说的这句话；我早对我的儿子，你的父亲说过一百遍了，说你完全是一副坏小子的神气，照这样子下去，他就尽等着受罪吧。

玛丽亚娜　我以为……

柏奈尔夫人　天啊，你是他的妹妹，你假装不爱多说多道，好像多么温柔，多么老实，可是人说得好，坏不过不流的死水，你背后做的那些事儿真叫我恨得牙痒痒。

欧米尔　可是我的娘啊……

柏奈尔夫人　我的少奶奶，不怕你见怪的话，你的一切行为也不见得十分高明：你本应该在他们眼前树立起一个好榜样，他们已故的母亲在这点上就比你强得多。你太好花钱，你的穿着打扮简直跟一位公主一样，这种生活方式真叫我看了难过。仅仅为讨丈夫的喜欢，我的少奶奶，是用不着这么样装饰打扮的。

克雷央特　不过，夫人，仔细想来……

柏奈尔夫人　提起了你，好舅爷的话，我很看重你，也爱你，也敬你；不过如果我是我儿子的话，我一定要求你别再登我们的门。你不停地宣讲一些关于生活的格言，但那些格言是正人君子根本不应该遵循的。我对你，说话未免太直率了一点；不过我的脾气就是这样，我心里想的事，我就得说出来。

达米斯　您那位答尔丢夫先生当然很高明……

柏奈尔夫人　他是一位道德君子，大家都应该听他的话；像你这样一个疯子也想来跟他捣乱，这是我不能容忍的，这不能不叫我气得发狂。

达米斯　什么！我难道就任凭这个一味说短道长的教会假虔徒在我们这里擅作威福吗？不得到此公的允许，我们便任何消遣也不能有了？

桃丽娜　倘使定要听从他的话，信从他的格言，那么我们无论做什么事，都成了罪恶了；因为这位热心的批评家，他是样样都要检查的。

柏奈尔夫人　凡是经他检查过的事都检查得很好。他希望引导你们走向天堂的大路；我的儿子原应该设法让你们喜爱他。

达米斯　不，祖母；父亲也罢，别人也罢，无论谁都不能强迫我叫我跟他和好；我若说出两样的话来，便是口不应心，他的一举一动我都看着生气；我早预料到一个结局，就是我非和这个坏蛋大闹一场不可。

桃丽娜　当然这是一桩叫人看了气愤不平的事，一个素昧平生的人竟顿时做起主人来；一个穷光蛋，来的时候连双鞋子都没有，全身的衣裳顶多值到六十个铜子，现在居然忘了本来面目，居然对什么都要阻挠一下，居然以主人自居起来！

柏奈尔夫人　喂，求求上帝吧！倘使凡事都按着他的虔诚的意志来办理，那么一切就好得多了。

桃丽娜　那么叫您看起来，他简直是一位圣徒了：其实，请您相信我的话，他的行为、他的性情只是一味地假仁假义。

柏奈尔夫人　你看，又血口喷人了不是！

桃丽娜　没有一个妥当的保证人出来替他担保，他和他那个劳朗，我瞧着都一样地不能放心。

柏奈尔夫人　他的仆人究竟是怎样的人，我不知道，不过我担保主人是个道德君子。你们之所以恨他讨厌他，无非是因为他将你们的真情实况都给照直说了出来。其实他心里愤恨的是你们所造的罪孽，他所关心的只是上天的利益。

桃丽娜　好吧，不过为什么，尤其是这些日子，他简直不许任何人和我们来往了呢？正正经经的朋友前来拜访，有什么得罪上天的地方，何至于大吵大闹，让我们大家都头痛呢？趁现在没有外人，要不要我仔细说个清楚？……（指欧米尔）我想，真的，他是爱上太太了。

柏奈尔夫人　住口吧！未说话之前你先要仔细想一想。讨厌这些拜访的不只是他一个人：与你们来往的那些人实在吵得太凶，一辆辆的马车接二连三地都停在大门口，还有那么多的仆从乱糟糟地聚集在一起，实在吵得四邻都不安宁。我很愿意相信骨子里是任何事也没有；不过到底是有人说了闲话，这可是要不得的。

克雷央特　喂！老太太，您想阻挡别人说闲话吗？倘使因为旁人议论我们的那些蠢话，我们就和我们最好的朋友们断绝来往，那可真是人生中一桩太不幸的事了。并且纵使我们这样做了，您以为就能让大家都不说话了吗？蜚言诽语就是城墙也挡不住的。我们不必留意那些愚蠢的毁谤，我们只须努力过我们的纯洁生活，闲话让他们尽量去说好了。

桃丽娜　我们的邻居达甫奈和她的年轻的丈夫，这两位莫非就是说我们坏话的人？自己的行为最惹人耻笑的人却永远是头一个先说别人坏话的人。别人的恋爱还不过是刚刚露出一点苗头，他们总是立刻一把抓住再不放松，赶紧喜洋洋地将这新闻传布开去，并且还要按着他们的意思来改头换面，硬叫人相信根本就是那样经过的。他们拿了自己的彩色硬涂在别人的行为上，然后希望仗着这套把戏，使自己的行为在社会里不再遭到别人的反对。他们妄想仗着自己的行为与别人的好行为有一点相似之处，便会使自己的阴险龌龊变成了纯洁无瑕，或者把自己受了公众指摘所感到的精神痛苦分出一些让别人去接受。

柏奈尔夫人　你这番议论与本题毫不相干。大家都知道达甫奈过的是一种模范生活：她的全部精神都贯注在上帝身上；并且有人告诉过我，她也很不赞成这里有这么多的客人来来往往。

桃丽娜　这个榜样可真值得赞扬，这位太太可真算是个大好人！不错的，她过的是一种严肃的生活；但是她对上帝的那种虔诚是她那个岁数逼出来的，大家知道她所以这样安分守己并不是出于本心，当她还能够吸引男人来献殷勤的时节，她也曾尽量享受能享受的种种好处；但是眼看着她那双眼睛的光彩日渐暗淡下来，她才想起摆脱繁华世界，繁华世界也正想摆脱她。她那时才想到蒙上一层灿烂的高尚道德之幕来掩饰她花容凋谢的弱点。这些都是过了景的美人们的狡猾伎俩；眼看着情人们渐渐散去，在她们原是很难受的事。在这样人人见弃的情形下，她们凄凉惶惑的心，除了安分守己做上帝的信女以外，委实也想不出别的更美好的法子。

…………

（赵少候　译）

趁你的金发灿烂光辉

贡戈拉

趁你的金发灿烂光辉，
连太阳光也不敢竞争，
趁你的额素雅白净，
最美的百合花也要自愧；

趁你的唇有众目追随，
赛过早熟的康乃馨，
趁你线条优雅的颈
蔑视水晶的光莹优美；

享受你的秀发和樱唇吧，
莫等你黄金时代的财富——
你的黄金、百合、康乃馨

不但化为白银和折断的花，
而且将和你在烟尘、泥土、
黑夜、虚无中同归于尽。

（飞白 译）

啊，液体元素

贡戈拉

啊，液体元素的清澄的光荣，
奔流之银的甜蜜的小溪！
你的水蜿蜒着流经草地，
以缓缓的脚步轻柔地淙淙！
由于她——她叫我发烧又发冷，
在你安静温柔的流动里
照她的影，而爱神的画笔
描绘出她雪白艳红的芳容，
你就走你的路吧，别松辔，
用透明的马勒、波动的缰绳
驾驭好你的水流的轻快，
因为，可不该把这么多美
带给海中三叉戟的主人，
藏进他深而暧昧的胸怀。

（飞白 译）

古　池

松尾芭蕉

悠悠古池畔
寂寞蛙儿跳下岸
水声轻如幻。

（王树藩 译）

Chapter Five
18th-Century Literature

一朵红红的玫瑰

彭　斯

啊，我爱人像一朵红红的玫瑰，
它在六月里初开；
啊，我爱人像一支乐曲，
它美妙地演奏起来。

你是那么漂亮，美丽的姑娘，
我爱你是那么深切；
我会一直爱你，亲爱的，
一直到四海枯竭。

一直到四海枯竭，亲爱的，
到太阳把岩石烧化；
我会一直爱你，亲爱的，
只要生命之流不绝。

再见吧，我唯一的爱人，
让我和你小别片刻；
我会回来的，亲爱的，
即使我们万里相隔。

（袁可嘉 译）

我的心呀在高原

彭　斯

我的心呀在高原，我的心不在这儿，
我的心呀在高原，追逐着鹿儿。
追逐着鹿儿，跟踪着獐儿，
我的心呀在高原，不管我上哪儿。
别了啊高原，别了啊北国，
英雄的家乡，可敬的故国；
不管我上哪儿飘荡，上哪儿遨游，

我永远爱着高原上的山丘。

别了啊，高耸着积雪的山岳，
别了啊，山下的溪壑和翠谷，
别了啊，森林和枝丫纵横的丛林，
别了啊，急川和洪流的轰鸣。
我的心呀在高原，我的心不在这儿，
我的心呀在高原，追逐着鹿儿。
追逐着鹿儿，跟踪着獐儿，
我的心呀在高原，不管我上哪儿。

（袁可嘉 译）

老　虎

布莱克

老虎！老虎！黑夜的森林中
燃烧着的煌煌的火光，
是怎样的神手或天眼
造出了你这样的威武堂堂？

你炯炯的两眼中的火
燃烧在多远的天空或深渊？
他乘着怎样的翅膀搏击？
用怎样的手夺来火焰？

又是怎样的膂力，怎样的技巧，
把你的心脏的筋肉捏成？
当你的心脏开始搏动时，
使用怎样猛的手腕和脚胫？

是怎样的槌？怎样的链子？
在怎样的熔炉中炼成你的脑筋？
是怎样的铁砧？怎样的铁臂
敢于捉着这可怖的凶神？

群星投下了他们的投枪，
用它们的眼泪润湿了穹苍，
他是否微笑着欣赏他的作品？
他创造了你，也创造了羔羊？

老虎！老虎！黑夜的森林中
燃烧着的煌煌的火光，
是怎样的神手或天眼
造出了你这样的威武堂堂？

（郭沫若 译）

毒　树

布莱克

我对我的朋友发怒，
我和盘说出，怒气消除；
我对我的仇敌发怒，
我一声不响，怒气渐长。

我怀着疑惧，早早晚晚
用我的泪水把它浇灌；
我又带着诡诈的微笑，
用虚假的阳光把它照耀。

于是它日夜不停地生长，
结了个苹果发红光，
我的仇敌见它那么红，
认出这苹果是我所种。

于是他趁着夜幕遮天，
悄悄地潜入我的花园。
天亮时我看了心中欢喜；
树下倒毙了我的仇敌。

（飞白 译）

鲁滨孙漂流记（节选）

笛　福

最后，我想到，能否像热带地区的土人那样做一只独木舟呢，尽管我没有工具，没有人手。所谓独木舟，就是用一棵大树的树干做成的。我觉得这不但可能，而且很容易做到。做独木舟的想法，使我非常高兴。而且，我还认为，与黑人或印第安人相比，我还有不少有利条件。但我却完全没有想到，比起印第安人来，我还有许多特别不利的条件，那就是，独木舟一旦做成后，没有人手可以帮我让独木舟下水。是的，印第安人有印第安人的困难，他们没有工具，但是，我缺少人手的困难更难克服。如果我能在树林里找到一棵大树，费了很大的劲把树砍倒，再用我的工具把树的外部砍成小舟形状，然后把里面烧空或凿空，做成一只小船；假如这些工作全部完成后，小船仍不得不留在原地而无法下水，那对我又有什么用处呢？

人们也许会想到，我在做这小船时，不可能一点也不想到我所处的环境，我应该立即想到小舟下海的问题。可是，我当时一心一意只想乘小舟去航行，从不考虑怎样使小舟离开陆地的问题。而实际上，对我来说，驾舟在海上航行四十五英里，比在陆地上使它移动四十五寻后让它下水要容易得多。

任何有头脑的人都不会像我这样傻就着手去造船。我对自己的计划十分得意，根本不去仔细想想计划的可行性。虽然我也想到船建成后下水可能是一大难题，但对于自己的疑惑，我总是愚蠢地认为："把船造好了再说。到时总会想出办法的。"

这是最荒谬的办法。我真是思船心切，立即着手工作。我砍倒了一棵大柏树。我相信，连所罗门造耶路撒冷的圣殿时也没有用过这样大的木料。靠近树根的直径达五英尺十英寸，在二十二英尺处直径也达四英尺十一英寸，然后才渐渐细下去，并开始长出枝杈。我费尽辛苦才把树砍倒：用二十二天时间砍断根部，又花了十四天时间使用大斧小斧砍掉树枝和向四周张开的巨大的树顶。这种劳动之艰辛真是一言难尽。然后，又花了一个多月的时间又砍又削，最后刮出了船底的形状，使其下水后能浮在水上。这时，树干已砍削得初具船的形状了。接着又花了将近三个月的时间把中间挖空，做得完全像只小船。在挖空树干时，我不用火烧，而是用槌子和凿子一点一点地凿空，最后确实成了一只像模像样的独木舟，大得可乘二十六个人。这样，不仅我自己可以乘上船，而且可以把我所有的东西都装进去。

这项工程完成后，我心里高兴极了。这艘小船比我以前看到过的任何独木舟都大。当然，做成这只大型独木舟我是费尽心血的。现在，剩下的就是下水问题了。要是我的独木舟真的下水了，我肯定会进行一次有史以来最为疯狂、最不可思议的航行了。

尽管我想尽办法，费尽力气，可就是无法使船移动一步。小船所在的位置离水仅一百码，决不会再多。第一个难处是，从小船所在的位置到河边，正好是一个向上的斜坡。为此，我决定把地面掘平，掘出一个向下的斜坡。于是，我立即动手进行这项工程，并且也历尽艰辛。当想到有可能逃生的机会，谁还会顾得上艰难困苦呢？不料完成了这项工程，克服了这一障碍后，我还是一筹莫展。我根本无力移动这只独木舟一步，就像我无法移动搁浅在沙滩上的那只小艇一样。

既然我无法使独木舟下水，就只得另想办法。我把现场的距离丈量了一下，决定开个船坞或开条运河，把水引到船底下来。于是我又着手这项大工程。一开始，我就进行了一些估算：看看运河要挖多深多宽，怎样把挖出来的土运走。结果发现，若我一个人进行这项工程，至少要花十至十二年。因为河岸很高，达二十英尺。最后，我不得不放弃这个计划，尽管心里很不愿意。

这件事使我非常伤心。到这时我才明白——虽然为时已晚——做任何事，若不预先计算一下所需的代价，不正确估计一下自己的力量，那是十分愚蠢的！

（郭建中 译）

狩猎者的夜歌

歌　德

无声地逡巡在荒野里，
我给猎枪填好了子弹，
蓦地，你那可爱而甜蜜的
倩影，又在眼前浮现。

你也许正漫步田野和
幽谷，心境宁静、悠闲
我这转瞬即逝的身影，唉，
可曾再来到你的面前？

从东到西，从北到南，
心中充满忧愁和厌倦，
我在人世上漂泊，流浪，
因为必须离开你身畔。

可是只要我一想起你，
仿佛就看见天上的月亮，
我的心便安适而宁帖，
真不知为什么会这样。

（杨武能 译）

浪游者的夜歌

歌　德

群峰一片

沉寂，
树梢微风
敛迹。
林中栖鸟
缄默，
稍待你也
安息。

（钱春绮 译）

少年维特的烦恼（节选）

歌　德

五月十日

我整个灵魂都充满了奇妙的欢快，犹如我以整个心身欣赏的甜美的春晨。我独自一人，在这专为像我那样的人所创造的地方领受着生活的欢欣。我是多么幸福啊，我的挚友，我完全沉浸在宁静生活的感受之中，以至于把自己的艺术也搁置在一边。我现在无法作画，一笔也画不了，和以往相比，此刻我是位更伟大的画家。每当这可爱的山谷里的雾气在我周围蒸腾，太阳高悬在我那片幽暗的树林上空，只有几束阳光悄悄射进树林中的圣地时，我便卧躺在山涧那飞跌而下的溪水边的葳蕤的野草中，挨着地面观察千姿百态的小草；每当我感觉到我的心贴近草丛中麇集扰扰的小世界，贴近各种虫豸蚊蝇千差万别、不可胜数的形状时，我就感到那个照他自己的模样创造我们的全能的上帝的存在，感觉到那个飘逸地将我们带进永恒快乐之中的博爱天父的呼吸；我的朋友，每当后来我眼前暮色朦胧，我周围的世界以及天空像情人的倩影整个都憩息在我心灵中时，我往往便会生出憧憬，并思忖：啊，你要是能把这一切重现，要是能将你心中如此丰富、如此温馨的情景写在纸上，使之成为你心灵的镜子，犹如你的心灵是博大无垠的上帝的镜子一样，那该多好！——我的朋友——不过，我要是真是这样去做，就必将陨灭，在这些宏伟壮丽的景象的威力下，我定将魂销魄散。

七月十六日

每当我的手指无意间触着她的手指，我们的脚在桌底下相碰的时候，啊，热血便在我全身奔涌！我像碰了火似的立即缩回，但是一种隐蔽的力量又在拉我往前。——我所有的感官都晕乎乎的，像腾云驾雾一样。——哦，她纯洁无邪，她的灵魂毫不拘谨，全然感觉不到这些细小的亲密举动使我受到多大的折磨。当她谈话时把手搁在我的手上，为谈话方便起见，挪得挨我近些，她嘴里呼出的美妙绝伦的气息可以送到我的唇上，这时我就像挨了电击，身体都要往下塌了。——威廉呀，假如有朝一日我胆大包天，那么这天堂，这真心实意……你理解我。不，我的心并不如此堕落！软弱！够软弱的！——这难道不是堕落？——

在我心目中，她是神圣的。在她面前，一切欲念都沉寂了。在她身边的时候，我始终弄不明白自己是怎么回事，似乎我已经神魂颠倒了。她有一支曲子，这是她以天使之力在钢琴上弹奏出来的，那么淳朴，那么才气横溢！这是她心爱的歌，她只要奏出第一个音符，困扰我的一切痛苦、紊乱和郁闷就统统无影无踪了。

关于古老音乐具有魔力的说法，我觉得句句是真话。这首简单的歌令我多么感动！她弹奏这首歌的时机掌握得很好，往往在我恨不得一颗子弹射穿脑袋时，曲子响了！于是我灵魂中的迷误和阴暗情绪便随之烟消云散，我又可以更加自由地呼吸了。

八月二十一日

清晨，我从噩梦中醒来，向她伸出双臂，结果是竹篮子打水；夜里，一个幸福无邪的梦捉弄了我，仿佛我在草地上坐在她的身边，握着她的手，印上千百个吻，随后我在床上找她时，又是海底捞月。唉，我在半睡半醒中昏昏聩聩地向她摸索，摸了一阵就完全清醒了。——一股泪流从我压抑的心中迸涌而出，面对昏暗的前程，我绝望地哭了。

十一月二十一日

她看不出，她感觉不到，她正在酿造毒酒，我和她都将被毁掉；满怀狂喜，我将她递给我的这杯毁灭之酒一饮而尽。那亲切的目光，她那经常——经常？——不，不是经常，是有时凝视着我的目光，用意何在？她接受我下意识流露的感情时那喜形于色的样子，还有她额头上表露出来的对我所受痛苦的怜悯，用意又是何在？

昨天我离开的时候，她握着我的手说："再见，亲爱的维特!”——亲爱的维特！这是她第一次叫我“亲爱的”,我听了真是心花怒放,乐不可支。我把这句话反复说了上百次,昨天夜里正要上床的时候,我还自言自语叨叨了好一阵,有次竟脱口说:“晚安,亲爱的维特!”说过之后自己也禁不住笑自己了。

（韩耀成 译）

Chapter Six Romantic Literature

我孤独地漫游,像一朵云

华兹华斯

我孤独地漫游,像一朵云
在山丘和谷地上飘荡,
忽然间我看见一群
金色的水仙花迎春开放,
在树荫下,在湖水边,
迎着微风起舞翩翩。

连绵不绝,如繁星灿烂,
在银河里闪闪发光,
它们沿着湖湾的边缘
延伸成无穷无尽的一行;
我一眼看见了一万朵,
在欢舞之中起伏颠簸。

粼粼波光也在跳着舞,
水仙的欢欣却胜过水波;
与这样快活的伴侣为伍,
诗人怎能不满心欢乐!
我久久凝望,却想象不到
这奇景赋予我多少财宝,——

每当我躺在床上不眠,
或心神空茫,或默默沉思,
它们常在心灵中闪现,
那是孤独之中的福祉;
于是我的心便涨满幸福,
和水仙一同翩翩起舞。

（飞白 译）

我们是七个

华兹华斯

——天真的孩子,
呼吸得那样柔和!
只感到生命充沛在四肢,
对死亡,她知道什么?

我碰到一个乡下小姑娘,
她说,她今年八岁;
拳曲的头发盘绕在头上,
密密丛丛的一堆。

她一身山林乡野气息,
胡乱穿几件衣衫;
眼睛挺秀气,十分秀气,
那模样叫我喜欢。

“你兄弟姐妹一共几个?
说给我听听,小姑娘!”
“几个？一共是七个,”她说,
惊奇地向我张望。

“他们在哪儿？说给我听听。”
她说:“我们是七个;
两个当水手,在海上航行,
两个在康韦住着。

“还有两个躺进了坟地——
我姐姐和我哥哥;
靠近他们,教堂边,小屋里,
住着我妈妈和我。”

“你说有两个在康韦住着,
有两个到了海上,
却又说你们还有七个!
是怎么算的,好姑娘?”

这位小姑娘随口回答:
“我们七兄弟姐妹,
有两个睡在那棵树底下——

那儿是教堂的坟堆。”

“你到处跑来跑去，小姑娘，
你手脚多么活泼；
既然坟堆里睡下了一双，
那你们还剩五个。”

“坟堆看得见，青绿一片，”
这位小姑娘答道，
“离我家门口十二步左右，
两座坟相挨相靠。

“那儿，我常常织我的毛袜，
把手绢四边缝好；
我常常靠近坟头坐下，
给他们唱一支小调。

“先生，只要碰上了好天气，
太阳下山了，还不暗，
我便把我的小粥碗端起，
上那儿吃我的晚饭。

“我姐姐珍妮先走一步；
她躺着，哼哼叫叫，
上帝解除了她的痛苦，
她便悄悄地走掉。

“她被安顿在坟地里睡下；
等她的墓草一干，
我们便在她坟边玩耍——
我和我的哥哥约翰。

“等到下了雪，地下一片白，
我可以乱跑乱滑，
我哥哥约翰却又离开，
在姐姐身边躺下。”

“有两个进了天国，”我说，
“那你们还剩几个？”
小姑娘答得又快又利索：
“先生！我们是七个。”

“可他们死啦，那两个死啦！
他们的灵魂在天国！”
这些话我说了也是白搭，
小姑娘还是坚持回答：
“不！我们是七个！”

（杨德豫 译）

她走在美的光彩中

拜　伦

她走在美的光彩中，像夜晚
皎洁无云而且繁星漫天；
明与暗的最美妙的色泽
在她的仪容和秋波里呈现：
耀目的白天只嫌光太强，
它比那光亮柔和而幽暗。

增加或减少一分明与暗
就会损害这难言的美。
美波动在她乌黑的发上，
或者散布淡淡的光辉
在那脸庞，恬静的思绪
指明它的来处纯洁而珍贵。

呵，那额际，那鲜艳的面颊，
如此温和，平静，而又脉脉含情，
那迷人的微笑，那容颜的光彩，
都在说明一个善良的生命：
她的头脑安于世间的一切，
她的心充溢着真纯的爱情！

（查良铮 译）

致……

雪　莱

有一个字眼被人亵渎得太多，
我岂能再来辱没，
有一种情感被人贬低得太狠，
你岂能再添鄙薄；
有一种希望太像绝望，
无须谨小慎微，对它防备，
可是从你身上得来的怜悯，
也比别人的更加珍贵。

我不能奉献所谓的爱情，

只有崇拜升腾在心头，
就连上苍也不忍拒绝，
难道你不愿接受？
这是飞蛾对星辰的向往，
这是黑夜对黎明的企盼，
这是我们悲哀的星球
把一片赤诚倾注远方。

（吴笛 译）

西风颂

雪莱

一

剽悍的西风啊，你是暮秋的呼吸，
因你无形的存在，枯叶四处逃窜，
如同魔鬼见到了巫师，纷纷躲避；

那些枯叶，有黑有白，有红有黄，
像遭受了瘟疫的群体，哦，你呀，
西风，你让种子展开翱翔的翅膀，

飞落到黑暗的冬床，冰冷地躺下，
像一具具尸体深葬于坟墓，直到
你那蔚蓝色的阳春姐妹凯旋归家，

向睡梦中的大地吹响了她的号角，
催促蓓蕾，有如驱使吃草的群羊，
让漫山遍野注满生命的芳香色调；

剽悍的精灵，你的身影遍及四方，
哦，听吧，你既在毁坏，又在保藏！

二

在你的湍流中，在高空的骚动中，
纷乱的云块就像飘零飞坠的叶子，
你从天空和海洋相互交错的树丛

抖落出传送雷雨以及闪电的天使；
在你的气体波涛的蔚蓝色的表面，
恰似酒神女祭司的头上竖起缕缕

亮闪闪的青丝，从朦胧的地平线
一直到苍天的顶端，全都披散着
即将来临的一场暴风骤雨的发卷，

你就是唱给垂死岁月的一曲挽歌，
四合的夜幕，是巨大墓陵的拱顶，
它建构于由你所集聚而成的气魄，

可是从你坚固的气势中将会喷迸
黑雨、电火以及冰雹；哦，请听！

三

你啊，把蓝色的地中海从夏梦中
唤醒，它曾被清澈的水催送入眠，
就一直躺在那个地方，酣睡沉沉，

睡在拜伊海湾的一个石岛的旁边，
在睡梦中看到古老的宫殿和楼台
在烈日之下的海波中轻轻地震颤，

它们全都开满鲜花，又生满青苔，
散发而出的醉人的芳香难以描述！
见到你，大西洋的水波豁然裂开，

为你让出道路，而在海底的深处，
枝叶里面没有浆汁的淤泥的丛林
和无数的海花、珊瑚，一旦听出

你的声音，一个个顿时胆战心惊，
颤栗着，像遭了劫掠，哦，请听！

四

假如我是一片任你吹卷的枯叶，
假若我是一朵随你飘飞的云彩，
或是在你威力之下喘息的水波，

分享你强健的搏动，悠闲自在，
不羁的风啊，哪怕不及你自由，
或者，假若我能像童年的时代，

陪伴着你在那天国里任意遨游，
即使比你飞得更快也并非幻想——
那么我绝不向你这般苦苦哀求：

啊，卷起我吧！如同翻卷波浪、
或像横扫落叶、或像驱赶浮云！
我跃进人生的荆棘，鲜血直淌！

岁月的重负缚住了我这颗灵魂，
它太像你了：敏捷、高傲、不驯。

五

拿我当琴吧，就像那一片树林，
哪怕我周身的叶儿也同样飘落！
你以非凡谐调中的狂放的激情

让我和树林都奏出雄浑的秋乐，
悲凉而又甜美。狂暴的精灵哟，
但愿你我迅猛的灵魂能够契合！

把我僵死的思想撒向整个宇宙，
像枯叶被驱赶去催促新的生命！
而且，依凭我这首诗中的符咒，

把我的话语传给天下所有的人，
就像从未熄的炉中拨放出火花！
让那预言的号角通过我的嘴唇

向昏沉的大地吹奏！哦，风啊，
如果冬天来了，春天还会远吗？

（吴笛 译）

致 凯 恩

普希金

我记得那神奇的一瞬：
在我的眼前出现了你，
犹如瞬息即逝的幻影，
又像纯洁美丽的天使。

当我遭受难遣忧愁的煎熬，
当我在喧嚣世事中忙乱不堪，
你温柔的话语在我耳边萦绕，
你可爱的面容在我梦中显现。

岁月流逝。一阵阵暴风骤雨
驱散了我从前的美好的梦。
于是我忘记了你温柔的话语，
忘记了你的天仙般的面容。

囚禁于阴暗的穷乡僻壤，
我默默地挨过漫长的年岁。
没有灵感，没有崇拜的物件，
没有生活，也没有爱情和眼泪。

心灵复苏的时刻终于来临，
我的眼前再次出现了你，
犹如瞬息即逝的幻影，
又像纯洁美丽的天使。

于是心儿陶醉，跳得欢畅，
一切都为它而重新苏醒，
有了崇拜的物件，有了灵感，
有了生活，也有了眼泪和爱情。

（吴笛 译）

假如生活欺骗了你

普希金

假如生活欺骗了你，
不要忧郁，也不要愤慨！
不顺心时暂且克制自己，
相信吧，快乐之日就会到来。

我们的心儿憧憬着未来，
现今总是令人悲哀：
一切都是暂时的，转瞬即逝，
而那逝去的将变得可爱。

（乌兰汗 译）

驿 站 长

普希金

十四品的小小官儿，
驿站上的土皇帝。
——维雅齐姆斯基公爵

谁人不骂驿站长？哪个不跟他们吵架？有谁在大发雷霆的时候不索取那本要命的“功过册”，在那上头枉费笔墨控告他们盛气凌人、冥顽不灵和消极怠工呢？有谁不把他们当成不齿于人类的坏蛋，简直如同往日包揽讼狱的刀笔吏，或者，起码也酷似穆罗姆森林里剪径的土匪？不过，我们如果为人公道，设身处地为他们想一想，那么，我们评判他们的时候就会宽和得多了。驿站长是何许人？十四等官阶的背黑锅的角色，那官衔只够他抵挡拳打脚踢之用，而且并非每次都抵挡得住（我恳请读者凭良心）。维雅齐姆斯基公爵开玩笑称之为土皇帝的人的职务究竟如何呢？难道不是实实在在的苦役吗？日夜不得安宁。旅客把枯燥乏味的旅行中一路憋出来的满腔闷气一股脑儿都发泄到了驿站长身上。天气坏，行路难，车夫犟，马匹懒——全都怪他！一脚跨进他那寒酸的住房，过路客准得拿他当仇人一样怒目而视；倘若他能够很快打发掉一位不速之客，倒还好；不过，如果刚好没有马匹呢？……老天爷！会骂得他狗血淋头，恐吓之辞也跟着劈头盖脑！下雨或雨交雪的坏天气，他却被逼得挨家串户去奔波。暴风雪和主显节前后天寒地冻的时候，他却溜进穿堂里，暂时躲开发火的旅客的辱骂和冲撞，偷得一分钟的清闲。一位将军驾到，站长诚惶诚恐，拨给他最后两部三套马车，其中一部还是特快邮车。将军去了，连谢谢也不说一声。过了五分钟——又是一阵铃铛！……军机信使又到，把驿马使用证往桌上一扔！……我们只要把这一切好好体味一下，那么，我们心头的怒火便会自行熄灭，不由得对他怀抱真诚的同情心了。再多说几句：二十年来，我走遍了俄罗斯的东南西北。几乎所有的驿道我都熟悉，几代车夫我都认得，很少有驿站长我没打过交道，很少有驿站长我认不清其面孔。我旅途观察所积累的有趣的材料我打算在不久的将来整理出版。此刻我只指出一点：对驿站长这一类人的看法大都是不公正的。这些遭人唾骂的站长，一般说来大都为人平和，天性助人为乐，爱跟人交往，不求名，也不太逐利。听他们谈话（可惜过路君子对此毫不在意），真可以学到不少有趣和有益的东西。至于我本人，我得承认我宁愿听听他们聊天，不愿领教因公出差的某位六等文官高谈阔论。

不难猜到，在驿站长这些可敬的人物中间有我的朋友。实际上，对其中一个人的怀念我是珍惜的。情境曾经使得我跟他接近，下面我就打算跟我亲爱的读者谈谈这个人物。

1816年5月，我有事沿着现已废弃的某驿道经过某省。当时我官职卑微，只能乘坐到站换马的驿车，付两匹马的公费。因此站长们对我不讲客气，我得常常据理力争方能得到我自认为有权得到的东西。我年轻，火气大，一看到站长把为我准备的三匹马套到某位官老爷的轿车上，我便恼恨站长卑鄙，骂他没有骨头。同样，在省长的宴会上，精明势利的仆役按官阶次第上菜，走过我跟前而不予理睬，这种事，也令我长久耿耿于怀。上述两件事，现在我倒觉得是天经地义的了。倘若废弃通行的规矩“小官敬畏大官”，而改换另一个规矩“惺惺爱惜好汉”，那么，实际上我们将怎么办？那会争得打破头！仆役上菜从谁开始？闲话少说，再来说我的故事要紧。

那一日天气炎热。车子距离××站还有三俄里，开始下小雨了，不一会，大雨倾盆，淋得我浑身不剩一根干纱。到了站，我第一件事便是赶快换衣，第二件事便是要茶。

“喂！冬尼娅！”站长叫道，“茶炊拿来，再拿点奶油。”

他说了这话，从屏风后边走出一个约莫十四岁的女娃，跑进了前堂。她的美貌令我一惊。

“她是你的女儿？”我问站长。

“是女儿，大人！”他说，神态怡然自得。“她脑子聪明，手脚麻利，就像她过世的娘。”

于是他便动手登记我的驿马使用证。我闲着无事，便来观赏挂在他简陋而整洁的房间的墙上的一幅幅图画。这几幅画，画的是“浪子回头”的一套故事。第一幅，一个头戴便帽、身穿宽袍的可敬的老人送走一个心气浮躁的少年，他匆匆忙忙接受老人的祝福和一个钱袋。第二幅，集中尖锐地描绘了年轻人的堕落：他坐在桌边，一群酒肉朋友和厚脸皮的荡妇围绕着他。第三幅，荡光钱财的年轻人身穿粗布袍子，头戴三角帽，正在牧猪，跟一群猪同槽吃潲，他面带愁苦和悔恨之色。最后一幅，描绘他回到父亲身边：慈祥的老人穿戴同样的衣帽，迎接儿子跑出来，浪子跪下；远景画了厨子在屠宰一头肥牛，哥哥在探问仆人这天伦之乐的起因。每幅画下边，我都读到很贴切的诗句。这套画，还有栽在瓦盆里的凤仙花、挂了花幔子的床铺以及当时我周围的其他家什至今我还记忆犹新。此刻那主人的音容笑貌还历历在目，他五十来岁，气色很好，精力挺旺，穿一件深绿长制服，胸前挂着带子褪了色的三枚勋章。

我还没来得及给老车夫付清车钱，这时，冬尼娅捧着茶炊回来了。这小妖精瞅我第二眼便看出了她已经赢得了我的好印象,垂上蓝蓝的大眼睛。我找她谈话,她答话,全无半点忸怩之态,俨然像个见过世面的大姑娘了。我请她父亲喝杯果露酒,给冬尼娅倒了一杯茶。我们三人便开始聊天,好似我们早就是熟人了。

马匹已经准备停当,但我还是不愿离开驿站长和他的女儿。最后我只得向他们道别了。她父亲祝我一路平安,女儿一直送我上车。在门厅里,我停住,请求她允许我吻她,她同意了……

自从干了这件事情之后,我能掐指算计我有过多少次的接吻,但没有一次在我心坎里留下如许长久、如许甜蜜的回味。

过了几年,境遇又迫使我走上同一条驿道,我又到了先前的地方。我记起了老站长的女儿,一想起又将见到她,我的心就乐开了花。但是,我心里嘀咕,老站长或许调走了,冬尼娅或许已经嫁了人,甚至老人已死或冬尼娅已死的念头也曾在我脑子里一闪。我心头怀着不祥的预感驶向××站。

马匹在驿站前的小屋旁边停下。走进屋里,我立即认出了"浪子回头"的那几幅画。桌子和床铺仍然放在原地,但窗口已经没有了鲜花,周遭的一切显得零乱和衰败。站长睡下了,身上盖件大衣。我一进来就惊醒了他,他爬起来……他正是萨姆松·威林,老多了,当他正待动手登记我的驿马使用证的时候,我望着他一头白发,满脸皱纹,胡子拉碴好久没剃,背脊佝偻——三四年工夫竟能使一个身强力壮的汉子变成一个衰朽的老头儿,我怎能不惊讶呢?

"你认识我吗?"我问他,"我跟你是老相识了。"

"也许是,"他回答,神色阴沉,"这儿是一条大道,过路旅客很多。"

"你的冬尼娅还好吗?"我又问。

老头儿锁紧眉头。

"天晓得!"他回答。

"那么,她出嫁了?"我问。

老头儿假装没有听见我的话,继续小声念着我的驿马使用证,我不再问下去了,吩咐摆茶。好奇心使我不安了,我指望一杯果露酒会解放我的老相识的舌头。

我没看错,老头儿不嫌弃喝一杯。我看到,一杯甜酒下肚,他的阴沉的脸色便开朗了。第二杯倒下去,他的话就多了。他说他记起我了,或者装做记得。而我便从他嘴里听到了一段故事,当时使我感动不已。

"这么说,您认得我的冬尼娅啰?"他说起来,"有谁不知道她呢?唉!冬尼娅,冬尼娅!了不得的丫头!那时节,谁打从这儿路过,没有一个不夸她,没有一个说她的坏话。太太们送她东西,有的送头巾,有的送耳环。过路的老爷们借故停下不走,说是要吃顿午饭或者晚饭,其实嘛,不过是为了再多瞧她几眼。那时节,不论脾气多大的老爷,一见到她就老实了,跟我说话也变得和气了。先生!信不信由您:官差和军机信使跟她谈话,一口气就谈上半个钟头哩!她撑持着这个家:收拾屋子,张罗一切,这个家弄得顺顺当当。而我嘛,是个老傻瓜,真是看她看不厌,疼她疼不够哩!难道我不爱我的冬尼娅,不疼我的孩子吗?难道她的生活过得不好吗?可不是,祸从天降,在劫难逃呀!"

接着,他把他的痛苦详详细细告诉了我。

三年前,一个冬日的黄昏,驿站长正拿本新册子划格子,女儿在屏风后面缝衣,一驾三套马车到了。一个旅客头戴毛茸茸的冬帽,身穿军大衣,外罩披风,走将进来,开口就要马匹。而马匹全都出差去了。听了这话,旅客便提高嗓门,扬起马鞭。但是,见惯了这种场面的冬尼娅急忙从屏风后面跑出来,和颜悦色地问他:先生要不要吃点什么?冬尼娅一露面便产生了照例的效果。旅客怒火全消,他同意等待马匹并且要了一份晚餐。他摘去湿透了的毛茸茸的帽子,解开披风,脱掉大衣,此人却原来是个身材秀美、蓄了两撇黑胡须的年轻骠骑兵军官。他在站长身旁坐下,跟他和他的女儿愉快地聊天。晚餐端上来了。这时马匹已经回来,站长去吩咐,马不用喂了,给这位旅客的马车立即套上。他吩咐回来一看,年轻人已经晕倒在长凳上,几乎不省人事了:他感觉不妙,头痛头晕,走不得了……怎么办?站长把自己的床铺让给他,并且决定,病人如果还不见好,明晨便打发人到C城去请医生。

第二天病人更不得劲了。他的仆人骑马进城去请大夫。冬尼娅用浸了醋的手帕扎在他头上,坐在他床边做女红。站长在场,病人便哼哼唧唧,几乎不说一句话,不过嘛,他倒喝了两杯咖啡,一边哼哼,一边要吃午饭。冬尼娅一直守护他。他时不时喊口渴,冬尼娅便端给他一杯她亲手调制的柠檬水。病人只打湿一下嘴唇,趁每次递还杯子的机会,他照例伸出软绵绵的手捏一捏冬尼娅的小手儿，以示感激不尽。午饭前大夫来了，给病人按了脉，用德国话跟他谈了一阵子，然后用俄国话宣布，病人只需好好保养，再过两三天就可以上路了。骠骑兵给了他二十五个卢布的出诊费，并请他一道用膳。医生没有推辞。他两位胃口挺大，喝了一瓶酒，然后分手，双方得意。

再过一天，骠骑兵完全康复。他分外高兴，一个劲寻开心，要么找冬尼娅放刁，要么跟站长淘气，不然就自个儿吹吹口哨，跟过往客人闲聊天，帮助把他们的驿马使用证登记入册。如此这般，他便赢得了忠厚老实的站长的欢心，到第三天早晨，站长竟舍不得跟这个逗人怜爱的小伙子分手了。那天是礼拜日，冬尼娅打点去做祷告。骠骑兵的马车套好了。他跟站长告别，大大方方付了食宿费，再跟冬尼娅道别，自动提出要送他到村口教堂去，冬尼娅犹疑不定……

"你怕什么?"她父亲说，"大人又不是狼，不会把你吞掉。跟他坐车去教堂吧!"

冬尼娅上车坐在骠骑兵身旁，仆人跳上赶车台，车夫一声吆喝，马儿便起步了。

可怜的驿站长真糊涂，他怎么能允许他的冬尼娅跟骠骑兵一同坐车走呢？他怎么会那样懵懂，当时他的脑瓜干吗不顶用了？还没有过半个钟头，他心疼了，绞得痛，惶惶然失魂落魄，终于忍不住了，拔腿就去教堂。他到了那里一看，人都散了，不见冬尼娅，庭院里没有，教堂门口也没有。他急忙走进教堂，但见神甫从祭坛上走下来，执事在灭烛，两个老太婆还在角落里祈祷。冬尼娅还是不见！可怜的父亲搜罗浑身气力才打定主意去问教堂执事：她来做过祷告没有？执事回答：没来。站长往家走，已经半死不活了。只剩下一线希望了：冬尼娅由于少不更事而自作主张，也许滑溜到下一站，上她教母家做客去了。忧心忡忡，他坐等那驾三套马车回来(就是他允许她坐上去的那一辆呀!)黄昏时候车夫终于回来了，喝得烂醉，他带来一个致命的消息："冬尼娅从那一站又往前走了，跟骠骑兵一道。"

这一击，老头儿可受不住了。他颓然往床上一倒——就是年轻拐子手昨晚睡的那张床。此刻站长回想种种情景，猜透了那病是假装的。这可怜人生了一场厉害的热病。把他送到C城就医，调来了另一个人暂时代理他的职务。正是那个给骠骑兵按脉的医生现在给他治病。他向站长说，那年轻人根本没病，当时他早就猜出了此人居心不良，但他不敢做声，因为怕挨鞭子。不论这德国人说的是真话还是吹嘘他有先见之明，他的话反正一点也不能安慰可怜的病人。病刚刚好转，驿站长便向C城邮务局长告假两个月，对谁也不告知自己的打算，便徒步出门寻找女儿去了。他从驿马使用证上得知骑兵大尉明斯基是从斯摩棱斯克动身前往彼得堡去的。那个送走明斯基的车夫说，冬尼娅一路哭哭啼啼，不过，看起来，她倒心甘情愿。

"说不定，"站长暗自思量，"我会把我的迷途的羔羊领回家。"

心存一线希望，他到了彼得堡，住在伊兹曼诺夫斯基团的驻地，他的老同事，一个退伍军士家里，立即开始寻找女儿。不久他打听到骑兵大尉明斯基正在彼得堡，住在杰蒙特饭店。站长决定去找他。

一天清晨，他走进明斯基住宅的前厅，请求通报大人：有个老兵求见。那勤务兵一边擦着上了楦头的皮靴，一边说，老爷正在睡觉，十一点以前不会客。站长走了，到了指定的时刻他又回来。明斯基本人出来见他，身穿晨袍，头戴鲜红小帽。

"怎么，老兄？你要干吗?"他问站长。

老头子心里嘣嘣直跳，泪珠儿往上涌，嗓门发颤，仅仅挤出一句话来："大人！……请您做做好事吧！……"

明斯基眼风飞快地瞟了他一眼，脸红了，抓住他的手把他引进书房，随手倒闩门。

"大人!"站长接着说，"覆水难收，至少，请您把可怜的冬尼娅还给我吧！您把她已经玩够了，别毁了她!"

"我做过的事，你扳不转来了，"年轻人说，神色狼狈，"我在你面前有错，我乐意请你原谅。但是，要我离开冬尼娅，你甭想。她会幸福的，我向你发誓。你要她干吗？她爱我，她对从前的环境已经厌弃了。不论是你还是她——你们都不要忘记，事情已经发生过了。"

然后，他给站长袖口里塞了点儿东西，打开门，于是站长自己也搞不清不知怎地就到了街上。

他发呆，好久站住不动，后来他发觉袖口里塞了一团纸。他取出来展开一看，却原来是几张揉得皱巴巴的五卢布和十卢布的钞票。他眼眶里又涌出了泪水，这是愤怒的眼泪！他把钞票捏成一团，往地上一扔，用鞋跟使劲地踩，愤然而去……走了几步，停住脚，想了想……再回转身……但钞票已经没了。一个衣冠楚楚的后生，看到他，跳上马车，一屁股坐下，对车夫一声喊："走！"

站长不去追赶。他决定回到他的驿站去，但他想，动身前他跟可怜的冬尼娅至少总得再见一面。为了这事，两天以后他又去明斯基那里。但这一回勤务兵很严厉地对他说，老爷任何人也不接见；拿胸膛把他从前厅里顶出来，使劲砰地关门，门差点碰了他的鼻子。老头站着，站着——只得走！

就在这一天黄昏时候，他在救苦救难大教堂做了祷告，沿着翻砂街走过去。突然，一辆华丽的轿车急驰而过，站长认出了车上坐着明斯基。轿车停在一栋三层楼房的大门前，骠骑兵下车跑上了台阶。一个幸运的念头在站长脑子里一闪。他转过身，走到车夫跟前。

"这是谁家的马车，老弟？"他问，"不是明斯基的吗？"

"正是。"车夫回答，"你要干吗？"

"是这么回事，你家老爷吩咐我送张条子给他的冬尼娅。可我记不得他的冬尼娅住在什么地方。"

"就在这儿，第二层。不过，你的条子来迟了，老兄！现在，老爷本人已经在她那儿了。"

"不要紧，"站长说，心悸魄动，说不清什么滋味在心头，"谢谢你的指点，不过，我还有我的事情要办。"说了这话，他就走上楼梯。

门关着。他按了门铃，一颗心沉沉地等了几秒钟。钥匙响了，门对他打开。

"阿芙朵琪娅·萨姆松诺夫娜住这儿吗？"

"是这儿，"年轻的女仆回答，"你找她有什么事？"

站长不搭腔，走进客厅。

"不行！不行！"女仆在后面叫起来，"阿芙朵琪娅·萨姆松诺夫娜有客。"

但站长不听她，一直朝前走。头两间房里很暗，第三间房里有灯。他走到开着的门边，停住脚。房间陈设华丽，明斯基坐着在出神。冬尼娅周身珠光宝气，穿着时髦，侧身坐在明斯基靠椅的扶手上，模样活像个英国马鞍上的女骑士。她情意缠绵，注视着明斯基，撚一绺他那乌黑的鬈发缠绕在自己指环闪烁的纤指上。可怜的老站长啊！他从来没有见过女儿竟有这般美艳。他情不自禁从一旁欣赏着她。

"谁呀？"她问，没抬头。

他还是不吭声。冬尼娅没听到回答便抬起头……她大叫一声，跌倒在地毯上。明斯基吃了一惊，弯下身去把她抱起，突然，见到老站长站在门口，他便放下冬尼娅，向老人走过来，气势汹汹，浑身打战。

"你要干吗？"他对站长说，咬牙切齿，"你干吗老缠着我？你这土匪！或许，你要杀我吗？出去！滚！"一只有劲的手一把揪住老头的衣领，只一推，他便到了楼梯上。

老头回到自己的住处。他的那位朋友要他去告状。但是，老头想了想，摆摆手，决心忍气吞声算了。两天以后他从彼得堡回到自己的小站，重操旧业。

"眼看三年了，"最后他说，"我失去了冬尼娅，一个人过活，得不到她的一丝风声、半点消息。她活着，还是死了，天晓得！什么事都可能发生。这种姑娘，她不是头一个，也不是末一个，过路浪子拐了去，养一阵子然后扔掉了事。这种傻丫头彼得堡多的是，今日遍身罗绮，一眨眼，明日就跟穷光蛋一道去扫街了。我有时想，我的冬尼娅或许已经沦落了，想到这点，不由得把心一横，但愿她快点死掉……"

以上便是我的朋友老站长所说的故事。说这故事的时候，他几次喉口作梗，泣不成声。他操起上衣的下摆怆然擦掉泪水，就像是季米特里耶夫的叙事诗中的那个热心肠的杰连季奇一样。他掉泪，部分原因倒要怪果露酒，他灌下去足有五杯。不过，无论如何，这一滴滴泪珠儿强烈地感动了我，使我久久不能忘怀老站长，使我久久惦记着可怜的冬尼娅……

前不久我又路过××小地方。我记起了我的朋友。我打听到他管理的那个驿站已经撤销了。我问："老站长还在世吗？"没有谁能够肯定回答。我决定去寻访我那熟悉的老地方，便租了几匹马到了H村。

那是深秋时节。灰蒙蒙的云层布满天空。冷风从收割了的田野上扑面吹来，刮落枝头的黄叶和红叶飘飘乱舞。进村时太阳快落山了，我在驿站小屋旁边停车。门厅里（可怜的冬尼娅曾经在这儿吻过我）走出来一个胖婆娘，她对我的问题回答说：老站长过世快一年了，他原先的房子里住下了一个酿酒师傅，她便是那人的老婆。我感到白跑了一趟，并且惋惜白花掉的七个卢布。

“他怎么死的？”我问酿酒师傅娘子。

“喝酒醉死的，老爷！”

“他埋在哪里？”

“就在村子边上，挨着他老伴的坟。”

“带我到他坟上去看看行吗？”

“干吗不行？喂！万卡！你跟猫崽玩得也够了，来！领这位老爷上坟地去，把站长的坟指给他看。”

她说这话的时候，一个遍身褴褛的红头发独眼龙小孩跑到我面前，他马上带我去坟地。

“你认得过世的老站长吗？”路上我问他。

“怎么不认得？他教我削哨子。有的时候他从酒店走出来（祝他早进天国！）我们跟在他背后，口里叫：‘老爷爷！老爷爷！给几个核桃吧！’他就把核桃分给我们吃。他老是跟我们玩。”

“过路的旅客记得他吗？”

“如今旅客少了。陪审官有时也拐弯到这儿来，可他从不问死人。夏天里有个太太来过，她问起老站长，也上坟地来看过。”

“怎么样的太太呢？”我好奇地问。

“挺好看的一位太太，”小孩回答，“她坐六匹马拉的车来的，带了三个小少爷、一个奶妈、一只哈巴狗。人家告诉她，老站长死了，她就哭起来，对她的小崽子说：‘你们好生坐着，我到坟上去一下就来。’我走上前去愿意给她领路，可太太说：‘我自己认得路。’她还给了我一个五戈比的银币哩！——多好的一位太太呀！……”

我们到了坟地，那是一块光秃秃的地方，没有围栅，立了许多十字架，没有一棵树。我平生从没见过如此凄凉的墓地。

“这就是老站长的坟。”小孩对我说，他跳上一个沙堆，沙堆上埋了个黑黑的十字架，上头钉了个铜圣像。

“那位太太也来过这儿吗？”我问。

“来过，”万卡回答，“我远远地望着她。她倒下去躺了好久。后来她回到村子里，叫来神甫，给了他钱，坐车就走了。她还给了我一个五戈比的银币哩！——多好的一位太太呀！”

我也给了这小孩五戈比，不再后悔这次旅行了，花掉的七个卢布也不觉得可惜了。

（冯春 译）

帆

莱蒙托夫

在大海的蒙蒙青雾中
一叶孤帆闪着白光……
它在远方寻求什么？
它把什么遗弃在故乡？

风声急急，浪花涌起，
桅杆弯着腰声声喘息……
啊，——它既不是寻求幸福，
也不是在把幸福逃避！

帆下，水流比蓝天清亮，
帆上，一线金色的阳光……
而叛逆的帆呼唤着风暴，
仿佛唯有风暴中才有安详！

（飞白 译）

箭与歌

朗费罗

我把一支箭向空中射出，
它落下地来，不知在何处；
那么急，那么快，眼睛怎能
跟上它一去如飞的踪影？

我把一支歌向空中吐出，
它落下地来，不知在何处；
有谁的眼力这么尖，这么强，
竟能追上歌声的飞飏？

很久以后，我找到那支箭，
插在橡树上，还不曾折断；
也找到那支歌，首尾俱全，
一直藏在朋友的心间。

（杨德豫 译）

我自己的歌（节选）

惠特曼

一

我赞美我自己，歌唱我自己，

我承担的你也将承担，
因为属于我的每一个原子也同样属于你。

我闲步，还邀请了我的灵魂，
我俯身悠然观察着一片夏日的草叶。
我的舌，我血液的每个原子，是在这片土壤、这个空气里形成的，
是这里的父母生下的，父母的父母也是在这里生下的，他们的父母也一样，
我，现在三十七岁，一生下身体就十分健康，希望永远如此，直到死去。

信条和学派暂时不论，
且后退一步，明了它们当前的情况已足，但也决不是忘记，
不论我从善从恶，我允许随意发表意见，
顺乎自然，保持原始的活力。

二

屋里、室内充满了芳香，书架上也挤满了芳香，
我自己呼吸了香味，认识了它也喜欢它，
其精华也会使我陶醉，但我不容许这样。

大气层不是一种芳香，没有香料的味道，它是无气味的，
它永远供我口用，我热爱它，
我要去林畔的河岸那里，脱去伪装，赤条条地，
我狂热地要它和我接触。

我自己呼吸的云雾，回声，细浪，窃窃私语，爱根，丝线，枝丫和藤蔓，
我的呼和吸，我心脏的跳动，通过我肺部畅流的血液和空气，
嗅到绿叶和枯叶、海岸和黑色的海边岩石和谷仓里的干草，
我喉咙里迸出辞句的声音飘散在风的旋涡里，
几次轻吻，几次拥抱，伸出两臂想搂住什么，
树枝的柔条摆动时光和影在树上的游戏，
独居，在闹市或沿着田地和山坡一带的乐趣，
健康之感，正午时的颤音，我从床上起来迎接太阳时唱的歌。

你认为一千亩就很多了吗？你认为地球就很大了吗？
为了学会读书你练习了很久吗？
因为你想努力懂得诗歌的含意就感到十分自豪吗？

今天和今晚请和我在一起，你将明了所有诗歌的来源，
你将占有大地和太阳的好处（另外还有千百万个太阳），
你将不会再第二手、第三手起接受事物，
也不会借死人的眼睛观察，或从书本中的幽灵那里汲取营养，
你也不会借我的眼睛观察，不会通过我而接受事物，
你将听取各个方面，由你自己过滤一切。

五十二

那苍鹰从我身旁掠过而且责备我，他怪我饶舌，又怪我迟迟留着不走。

我也一样一点都不驯顺，我也一样不可翻译，
我在世界的屋脊上发出了粗野的喊叫声。

白天最后的日光为我停留，
它把我的影子抛在其他影子的后面而且和其他的一样，抛我在多黑影的旷野，
它劝诱我走向烟雾和黄昏。

我像空气一样走了，我对着那正在逃跑的太阳摇晃着我的绺绺白发，
我把我的肉体融化在旋涡中，让它漂浮在花边状的裂缝中。

我把自己交付给秽土，让它在我心爱的草丛中成长，
如果你又需要我，请在你的靴子底下寻找我。

你会不十分清楚我是谁，我的含义是什么，
但是我对你说来，仍将有益于你的健康，
还将滤净并充实你的血液。

如果你一时找不到我，请不要灰心丧气，
一处找不到再到别处去找，

我总在某个地方等候着你。

（赵萝蕤 译）

Chapter Seven 19th-Century Literature (Ⅰ)

红与黑（节选）

司汤达

一个钟头以后，仆人把一封信交给于连；这封信干脆就是爱情的表白。

“文笔还不太做作，”于连心想，他想用文字的评论控制喜悦，然而他的脸已经抽紧，禁不住笑了。

“终于，”他突然大声叫起来，激情太强烈，已经无法控制，“我，可怜的乡下人，我终于得到了一位贵妇人的爱情表白！”

“至于我，干得还不坏，”他想，尽可能压住心头的喜悦。“我知道如何保持我的性格的尊严。我从未说过我爱她。”他开始研究字体，德·拉莫尔小姐写得一手漂亮的英国式小字。他需要做点体力上的事，好从那快要使他发狂的喜悦中解脱出来。

“您要走了，我不能不说了……见不到您，我实在受不了……”

一个想法突然袭上他的心头，仿佛一大发现，打断了他对玛蒂尔德的信的研究，使他感到加倍的快乐。“我战胜了德·克鲁瓦泽努瓦侯爵，”他喊道，“我，一个只说些正经事的人！而他是那么漂亮！他留着小胡子，有迷人的军装；他总是能在合适的时候找到又聪明又巧妙的话来说。”

于连有了美妙的一刻，他在花园里信步来去，幸福得发狂。

稍后，他上楼来到自己的办公室，让人去通报德·拉莫尔侯爵，幸好他没有出门。他让侯爵看几份标明来自诺曼底的文件，很容易地证明了诺曼底的诉讼要处理，他不得不推迟到朗格多克的行期。

“您不走我很高兴，”侯爵谈完事务以后对他说，“我喜欢见到您。”于连退下，这句话使他感到别扭。

“而我呢，我却要去引诱他的女儿！而且可能还要使她和德·克鲁瓦泽努瓦侯爵的婚事告吹，这可是他的未来最迷人的一件事啊，如果他当不了公爵，至少他的女儿会有一个凳子。”于连打算不顾玛蒂尔德的信，也不顾已向侯爵做过的解释，动身去朗格多克。不过，这道德的光辉一闪即逝。

“我真善良，”他对自己说，“我，一介平民，居然可怜起一个这种地位的人家了！我，一个被肖纳公爵称为仆人的人！侯爵是如何增加他那巨大的家产的？他在宫里得知第二天可能会发生政变，立刻就把公债卖掉。可我呢，后娘般的苍天把我抛到社会的最底层，给了我一颗高贵的心，却没给我一千法郎的年金，也就是说没给我面包，不折不扣地没给我面包；而我却拒绝送上门来的快乐！我如此艰难地穿越这片充斥着平庸的灼热沙漠，却要拒绝能够解除我的干渴的一泓清泉！真的，别这么傻了。在人们称为生活的这片自私自利的沙漠里，人人为自己。”

他想起了德·拉莫尔夫人，特别是她的朋友，那些贵妇们向他投来的满含着轻蔑的目光。

战胜德·克鲁瓦泽努瓦侯爵的喜悦终于使这种道德的回忆败下阵来。

“我多么希望看见他发火！”于连说，“我现在多么有把握给他一剑啊。”他摆了个姿势，作二次进攻状。“在此之前，我是个学究，不光彩地自恃还有点儿勇气。这封信之后，我和他平等了。”

“是的，”他回想着信中的语句，怀着无限的欣喜对自己说，“侯爵和我，我们俩的价值已经衡量过了，汝拉山区的可怜木匠占了上风。”

“好，”他叫道，“我在回信上就这样落款，您别以为，德·拉莫尔小姐，我忘了自己的身份。我要让您明白并且清楚地感觉到，您是为了一个木匠的儿子而背弃了曾经跟随圣路易参加十字军东征的大名鼎鼎的居伊·德·克鲁瓦泽努瓦的一个后裔。”

于连喜不自胜。他不得不下楼到花园里去。他把自己锁在里面的那间屋子，他觉得太狭小，喘不过气来。

“我，汝拉山区的穷乡下人，”他不断地重复着，“我，注定一辈子穿这身惨兮兮的黑衣服！唉，早二十年，我会像他们一样穿军装，那时候一个像我这样的人，要么阵亡，要么三十六岁当上将军。”他紧紧握在手里的那封信，给了他一个英雄的个头儿和姿态。“现在，确实如此，穿上这身黑衣服，到了四十岁，也可以像博韦的主教先生那样有一万法郎的薪水和蓝绶带。”

“好吧！”他像靡非斯特那样笑着对自己说，“我比他们有更多的聪明才智，我知道怎么选择我这个时代的制服。”他觉得他的野心和对法衣的眷恋膨胀起来。“有多少红衣主教出身比我还低，而他们掌过大权！例如我的同乡朗倍维尔。”

（郭宏安 译）

高老头（节选）

巴尔扎克

“啊！原来是她的父亲，”大学生做了个不胜厌恶的姿势。

“可不是！这家伙有两个女儿，他都喜欢得要命，可是两个女儿差不多已经不认他了。”

“那小的一个，”子爵夫人望着特·朗日太太说，“不是嫁给一个姓名像德国人的银行家，叫做特·纽沁根男爵吗？她名字叫但斐纳，头发淡黄，在歌剧院有个侧面的包厢，也上喜剧院，常常高声大笑引人家注意，是不是？”

公爵夫人笑道：“哎，亲爱的，真佩服你。干嘛你对那些人这样留神呢？真要像特·雷斯多一样爱得发疯，才会跟阿娜斯大齐在面粉里打滚。嘿！他可没有学会生意经。他太太落在特·脱拉伊手里，早晚要倒霉的。”

“她们不认父亲！”欧也纳重复了一句。

“哎！是啊，”子爵夫人接着说，“不承认她们的亲爸爸，好爸爸。听说他给了每个女儿五六十万，让她们攀一门好亲事，舒舒服服的过日子。他自己只留下八千到一万法郎的进款，以为女儿永远是女儿，一朝嫁了人，他等于有了两个家，可以受到敬重，奉承。哪知不到两年，两个女婿把他赶出他们的圈子，当他是个要不得的下流东西……”

欧也纳冒出几颗眼泪。他最近还在家中体味到骨肉之爱，天伦之乐；他还没有失掉青年人的信仰，而且在巴黎文明的战场上还是第一天登台。真实的感情是极有感染力的：三个人都一声不出，愣了一会。

“唉！天哪，”特·朗日太太说，“这一类的事真是该死，可是我们天天看得到。……我完全明白那老面条商的遭遇，记得这个福里奥……”

“是高里奥，太太。”

“是啊，这莫里奥在大革命时代当过他本区的区长；那次有名的饥荒，他完全知道底细；当时面粉的售价比进价高出十倍，他从此发了财。那时他囤足面粉；光是我祖母的总管就卖给他一大批。当然，高里奥像所有那些人一样，是跟公安委员会分肥的。……他把大女儿高高地供在特·雷斯多家里，把老二接种接在特·纽沁根男爵身上，纽沁根是个加入保王党的有钱的银行家。……我相信，亲爱的，凡是真实的感情都有眼睛，都有聪明，所以那个大革命时代的可怜虫伤心死了。他看出女儿们觉得他丢了她们的脸；也看出要是她们爱丈夫，他却妨害了女婿，非牺牲不可。他便自己牺牲了，因为他是父亲，他自动退了出来。看到女儿因此高兴，他明白他做得很对……这个父亲把什么都给了。二十年间他给了他的心血，他的慈爱；又在一天之间给了他的财产。柠檬榨干了，那些女儿把剩下的皮扔在街上。”

“社会真卑鄙，”子爵夫人低着眼睛，拉着披肩上的经纬。特·朗日太太讲这个故事的时候，有些话刺了她的心。

“不是卑鄙！”公爵夫人回答，“社会就是那么一套。我这句话不过表示我看透了社会。实际我也跟你一般想法，”她紧紧握着子爵夫人的手，“社会是一个泥坑，我们得站在高地上。”

她起身亲了一下特·鲍赛昂太太的前额，说：

“亲爱的，你这一下真漂亮。气色好极了。”

然后她对欧也纳略微点点头，走了。

欧也纳想起那夜高老头扭绞镀金盘子的情形，说道：“高老头真伟大！”

特·鲍赛昂太太没有听见，她想得出神了。两人半天没有出声，可怜的大学生愣在那儿，既不敢走，又不敢留，也不敢开口。

“社会又卑鄙又残忍，”子爵夫人终于说，“只要我们碰到一桩灾难，总有一个朋友来告诉我们，拿把短刀掏我们的心窝，教我们欣赏刀柄。冷一句热一句，挖苦，奚落，一齐来了。啊！我可是要抵抗的。”

她抬起头来，那种庄严的姿势恰好显出她贵妇人的身份，高傲的眼睛射出闪电似的光芒。——“啊！”她一眼瞧见了欧也纳，“你在这里！”

“是的，还没有走，”他不胜惶恐地回答。

“哎，拉斯蒂涅先生，你得以牙还牙对付这个社会。你想成功吗？我帮你。你可以测量出来，女人堕落到什么田地，男人虚荣到什么田地。虽然人生这部书我已经读得烂熟，可是还有一些篇章不曾寓目。现在我全明白了。你越没有心肝，越高升得快。你得不留情地打击人家，叫人家怕你。只能把男男女女当做驿马，把它们骑得筋疲力尽，到了站上丢下来；这样你就能达到欲望的最高峰。不是吗，你要是没有一个女人关切，你在这儿便一文不值。这女人还得年轻，有钱，漂亮。倘使你有什么真情，必须像宝贝一样藏起，永远别给人家猜到，要不就完啦，你不但做不成刽子手，反过来要给人家开刀了。有朝一日你动了爱情，千万要守秘密！没有弄清楚对方的底细，决不能掏出你的心来。你现在还没有得到爱情；可是为保住将来的爱情，先得学会提防人家……”

（傅雷　译）

项　链

莫泊桑

世上有一些漂亮迷人的女子，仿佛是命运安排错了，生长在职员的家庭里；她便是其中的一个。她没有陪嫁费，希望渺茫，压根儿没法让一个既有钱又有地位的男子认识她，了解她，爱上她和娶了她；她只好听之任之，嫁给了教育部的一个小科员。

她打扮不起，只得穿着从简，但感到非常不幸，就像抱怨自己阶级地位下降的女子那样；因为女子原没有一定的阶层和种族，她们的美貌、娇艳和丰韵就作为她们的出身门第。天生的敏锐，高雅的本能，脑筋的灵活，只有这些才分出她们的等级，使平民的姑娘和最高贵的命运并驾齐驱。

她总觉得自己生来就配享受各种精美豪华的生活，因而感到连绵不绝的痛苦。住房寒伧，四壁空空，凳椅破旧，衣衫丑陋，都叫她苦不堪言。所有这些都折磨着她，使她气愤难平，而换了她那个阶层的另一个妇人的话，甚至会一无所感。看着那个替她料理家务的小个儿布列塔尼女人，她心中便抑郁不乐，想入非非。她幻想挂着东方料子的壁衣，被青铜高脚灯照亮了的寂静的前厅；幻想那两个穿着短裤的高大男仆，被暖气管发出的闷热催起睡意，在宽大的靠背椅里酣睡着。她幻想墙上罩着古老丝绸的大客厅，里面有陈设着奇珍古玩的精致家具；幻想香气扑鼻的、风雅的内客厅，那是专为下午五点娓娓清谈的地方，来客有最亲密的男友，还有知名之士，难得的稀客，那是所有妇女都欣羡不已，渴望得到他们青睐的。

每当她坐到那张铺着三天未洗的桌布的圆桌前吃饭，坐在对面的丈夫揭开盆盖，欣喜地说：“啊！多好的炖肉！世上哪有比这更好的东西……”那时候她便幻想那些精美的筵席，亮闪闪的银餐具，挂满四壁的壁毯，上面织着古代人物和仙境森林中的异鸟珍禽；她幻想盛在华美的盘碟里的美馔佳肴，幻想一边嚼着粉红的鲈鱼肉或者松鸡翅，一边带着深不可测的微笑倾听窃窃情话的景象。

她没有华丽衣装，没有珠宝首饰，统统没有。而她偏偏就爱这些；她觉得自己生来就应该享受这些东西。她多么希望讨人喜欢，惹人嫉羡，风流诱人，被人追求呀。

她有一个有钱的女友，那是教会学校的同学，现在她再也不愿去看她了，因为每次看望回来她感到非常痛苦。

可是有一天傍晚，她的丈夫回家时满脸得意洋洋，手里拿着一个大信封。

“嗨，”他说，“这玩意儿是给你的。”

她赶快撕开信封，从里面抽出一份请柬，上面印着这儿行字：

> 兹订于一月十八日（星期一）在本府举行晚会，敬请罗瓦赛尔夫妇莅临为荷。
>
> 教育部长乔治·朗波诺先生暨夫人谨上

她不但没有欢天喜地，像她丈夫所期待的那样，反而怨气冲天地把请柬往桌上一扔，嘟囔着说：

“你不想想，我要这个干吗？”

“可是，我亲爱的，我原以为你会很高兴的。你从来也不出个门儿，这可是一个机会，真是难得的机会！我费了多少周折才弄到这张请柬。人人都想要，很不易到手，给职员的不多。在那儿，大小官员你都可以看到。”

她瞪着他，眼都要冒出火来，按捺不住脱口而出：

“你可叫我穿什么上那儿去呢？”

这个，他却从未想到。他咕哝着说：

“你上剧场穿的那件袍子呢？照我看，那件好像够好的……”

他戛然而止，看见妻子哭起来了，他又是惊讶又是惶乱。两大滴眼泪从他妻子的眼角慢慢顺着嘴角流下来。他结结巴巴地问：

"你怎么啦？你怎么啦？"

她下了狠劲儿，把难言的苦衷压了下去，一面拭着沾湿的双颊，一面用镇静的嗓门回答：

"没有什么。只是我没有衣服，这次盛会我就去不成了。你有哪位同事，他的太太的衣衫总比我强的，你就把请柬送给他吧。"

他感到不是味儿。他于是开口说：

"玛蒂尔德，咱们来算一下。一套合适的衣服，你在别的场合还可以穿的，简简单单的，得花多少钱？"

她想了一想，算了一笔账，也考虑了一下数目，她可以提出来，而不会招致节俭的科员立即回绝和吓得叫起来。

末了，她犹犹豫豫地回答：

"我不知道准数，不过有四百法郎，我大概也就可以办妥了。"

他的脸色有点煞白，因为他正好备下这样一笔钱，要买一支枪，来年夏天好和几个朋友一道打猎作乐，星期日到南代尔平原去打云雀。

可是他还是说：

"好吧。我就给你四百法郎。不过得设法做一件漂亮的袍子。"

晚会那天临近了，而罗瓦赛尔太太却显得抑郁不安，忧虑重重。她的衣服可是已经做好了。她的丈夫有天晚上问她：

"你怎么啦？瞧你这三天，阴阳怪气的。"

她回答：

"我没有首饰，没有宝石，身上什么也戴不出来，真叫我心烦意乱。那样我就会显出一副十足的寒酸气。我简直宁愿不赴会了。"

他接口说：

"你可以戴几朵鲜花呀。眼下这个季节，这是很雅致的。花上十个法郎，你就有两三朵美丽鲜艳的玫瑰花了。"

她一点儿没有被说服。

"不行……在阔太太中显出一副穷酸相，没有什么比这更丢脸的了。"

她的丈夫嚷了起来：

"你真是糊涂！你去找你的朋友福莱斯蒂埃太太，问她借几件首饰嘛。你跟她交情够好的，准行。"

她高兴得叫了出来：

"这倒是真的。我竟一点儿也没想到。"

第二天她就上朋友家，给她诉说自己的苦恼。

福莱斯蒂埃太太起身走到镶镜大柜跟前，取出一个大首饰匣，拿到罗瓦赛尔太太面前打开，对她说：

"挑吧！亲爱的。"

她先看见几只手镯，再便是一串珠子项链，然后是一个威尼斯出品的十字架，镶嵌着黄金宝石，工巧精致。她戴上这些首饰，对着镜子试来试去，游移不决，舍不得摘下来放回去。她一个劲儿地问：

"你再没有别的了？"

"有啊。你自个儿找吧。我不知道你喜欢什么样儿的。"

突然，她在一个黑缎子的盒里发现一长串钻石项链，光彩夺目。一种过于强烈的欲望使她怦然心跳。她的手攥着它的时候直打哆嗦。她戴在脖子上，衬在袍子外面，对着镜子自我欣赏得出了神。

然后她欲言又止地、十分胆怯地问：

"你可以借给我这个吗？就借这一样。"

"当然可以啦。"

她扑过去搂住了朋友的脖子，激动地吻着她，随后带着宝贝一溜烟跑了。

晚会那天到了。罗瓦赛尔太太十分成功。她比所有女人都漂亮，又优雅又妩媚，笑容满面，快活得发狂。所有的男子都尽瞧着她，打听她的名字，设法能被介绍。办公厅的随员全都想跟她跳华尔兹舞。部长也注意到她。

她忘怀地、尽情地跳着，被乐趣陶醉了，什么也不想，沉浸在她的美丽的凯旋中，她的成功的荣光里，一片幸福的彩云中，那是所有这些献媚、赞美、挑起的欲望、妇女心中认为十全十美的胜利所组成的。

她在清晨将近四点时才离开。她的丈夫从半夜起就在一间空空落落的小客厅里睡着了；客厅里还躺着另外三位先生，他们的太太也在尽情欢乐。

他怕她出门受寒，把事先带来的衣服披在她的肩上，那是平日穿的普通便服，那种寒伧和舞装的雅致很不调和。她感觉到了，便想溜走，不让其他裹在锦裘里的太太们注意到。

罗瓦赛尔一把拉住她：

"等一等。到外边你要着凉的。我去叫一辆马车。"

可是她一点儿也不听他的，便迅速下了楼梯。等他们来到街上，却找不到马车。他们东寻西找，远远看见马车走过，就追着车夫呼喊。

他们走在通向塞纳河的下坡路上，垂头丧气，冻得发抖。临了，他们在岸边找到了一辆逛夜的旧马车，这种马车在巴黎只有夜里才看得见，仿佛白天它们会耻于外表的寒伧。

马车把他们一直送到殉教者街，他们的家门口。他们没精打采地上了楼，回到家里。对她说来，一切已经结束。而他呢，他在想着十点就该到部里去办公。

她脱下裹在肩上的衣服，站在镜前，想再一次看看自己满载光荣的情景。但她突然大叫一声。原来她颈上的项链不见了！

她的丈夫衣服已经脱了一半，他问：

"你怎么啦？"

她转身对着他，吓得发狂了似的：

"我……我……我把福莱斯蒂埃太太的项链丢了。"

他兀地站了起来，惊惶万分：

"什么！……怎么！……这不可能吧！"

于是他们在袍子的皱褶里，大衣的皱褶里，口袋里，到处都搜寻一遍。哪儿也找不到。

他问：

"你拿得稳离开舞会时，项链还戴在身上吗？"

"没错，在部里的衣帽室里，我还摸过它呢。"

"不过，要是丢在街上，我们会听见掉下来的声音的。准是掉在车里了。"

"对，这很可能。你注意过车号吗？"

"没注意。你呢，你也没有留意吧？"

"没有。"

他们相互对视，都变得痴呆了。末了，罗瓦赛尔又把衣服穿上，他说：

"刚才我们步行的那段路，我再去走一遍，看看是否能够找到。"

于是他出去了。她仍旧穿着晚会的服装，连上床去睡的气力都没有了，颓然倒在一张椅子上，既不生火，也毫无主意。

快七点时她丈夫回来了。他什么也没找到。

他又到警察厅和各报馆，请他们悬赏找寻，他还到租小马车的各个车行，总之凡是有一点希望的地方他都去了。

她整天都在等候着，面对这可怕的灾难，一直处在惶然若失的状态中。

罗瓦赛尔傍晚才回来，脸庞陷了进去，颜色苍白；他一无所获。他说：

"只好给你的朋友写封信，告诉她你把项链的搭扣弄断了，现在正让人修理。这样我们就可以有回旋的时间。"

在他口授下，她写了一封信。

一星期过去了，他们失去了一切希望。罗瓦赛尔仿佛老了五岁，他最后说：

"该考虑赔偿这件首饰了。"

第二天，他们拿着装项链的那只盒子，按照里面印着的字号，到了那家珠宝店。珠宝商查过账后说：

"太太，这串项链不是本店卖出的；只有盒子是本店给配的。"

于是他们从这家珠宝店跑到那家珠宝店，凭记忆要找一串一模一样的项链，两个人连愁带急眼看就要病倒。

他们在王宫附近一家店里找到一串钻石项链，看来跟他们寻找的完全一样。项链原价四万法郎。店里答应可以三万六千法郎让给他们。

他们请店商三天之内先不要卖出。他们还谈妥了，要是在二月底前找到原件，店里以三万四千法郎折价收回首饰。

罗瓦赛尔存有他父亲留给他的一万八千法郎。其余的便须去借了。

他向这个借一千法郎，向那个借五百，这儿借五个路易，那儿借三个。他签署借约，同意做足以败家的抵押，和高利贷者以及形形色色放债生利的人打交道。他整个晚年要大受影响，不管能不能偿还，他就冒险签押。对未来的忧患，即将压到身上的赤贫，瞻望到各种物质上的缺乏和种种精神上的折磨，就这样，他怀着惶惶不安，把三万六千法郎放到那个商人的柜台上，取来了那串新项链。

等罗瓦赛尔太太把首饰送还福莱斯蒂埃太太时，这位太太满脸不高兴地对她说：

"你本该早点儿还我，因为我说不定用得着呢。"

福莱斯蒂埃太太没有打开盒子，她的朋友害怕的正是这个。要是她发觉掉换了一件，她会怎么想？她会怎么说？不会把她看成偷窃吗？

罗瓦赛尔太太尝到了穷人那种可怕的生活。然而她勇气十足地横下了一条心。必须还清这笔骇人的债。她一定要还清。家里辞退了女仆，换了房子，租了一间屋顶下面的阁楼。

家庭里的粗活，厨下腻人的活计，她都尝遍了。碗碟锅盆都得自己洗刷，她粉红的指甲在油污的盆盆盖盖和锅子底儿上磕磕碰碰磨坏了。脏衣服、衬衫、抹布，也得自己搓洗，在绳上晾干；每天清早她把垃圾搬到楼下，送到街上，还要提水上楼，每一层都得停下来喘喘气。她穿着同下层妇女一样，挎着篮子上水果店、杂货店、猪肉店，讨价还价，挨骂受气，一个铜子一个铜子地保护她那一点儿可怜巴巴的钱。

每月都要偿付几笔债券，其余的则要续期，延长时间。

丈夫每天傍晚要替一个商人誊清账目，夜里常常干五个铜子一页的抄写活儿。

这样的生活过了十年。

十年之后，他们一切都还清了，不但高利贷的利息，连利滚利的利息也全都还清了。

罗瓦赛尔太太如今看来变得苍老了。她成了穷人家健壮有力的女人，又硬直，又粗犷。头发乱糟糟，裙子歪歪斜斜，两手通红，说话粗声大气，刷地板大冲大洗。不过有时候她丈夫还在办公，她坐到窗前，就想起从前那一次晚会，在舞会上她是那么美丽，真是出够了风头。

如果她没有丢失这串项链，那又会怎么样呢？谁知道？谁知道？生活是多么奇异，多么变化莫测啊！真是一丁点事儿就能断送你或者拯救你！

且说有一个星期天，她到香榭丽舍去溜溜，消除一星期干活的劳累。突然之间，她瞅见一个妇人带着一个孩子在散步。这是福莱斯蒂埃太太，她还是那么年轻、那么美丽、那么动人。

罗瓦赛尔太太感到很激动。要去跟她说话吗？当然要去。如今既已把债还清，她可以把一切都告诉她了。为什么不可以去说呢？

她走了过去。

“你好，让娜。”

那一个一点儿认不出她了，心里很诧异，这个小市民模样的女人怎么这样亲密地称呼她，她嘟嘟囔囔地说：

“可是……太太！……我不知道……您大概认错了人吧。”

“没有。我是玛蒂尔德·罗瓦赛尔。”

她的朋友喊了起来：

“哎呀！……我可怜的玛蒂尔德，你可是大变样啦！……”

“是呀，自从那一次和你见面之后，我过的日子可艰难啦；真是千辛万苦……而这都是因为你！……”

“因为我……那是怎么回事呀？”

“你还记得你借给我赴部里晚会去的那串钻石项链吧。”

“记得。那又怎样呢？”

“那又怎样！我把它丢了。”

“怎么会呢！你不是已经给我送回来了嘛。”

“我给你送回的是一模一样的另一串。这件首饰我们整整还了十年。你知道，对我们来说这可不是容易的事，我们是什么也没有呀……现在总算了结了，我是说不出的高兴。”

福莱斯蒂埃停住了脚步。

“你是说，你曾买了一串钻石项链来赔我那一串吗？”

“是的。你一直没有发觉吧，是不是？两串真是一式一样。”

她感到一种足以自豪的、发自本心的快乐，于是露出微笑来。

福莱斯蒂埃太太非常激动，抓住了她的两只手：

“哎呀！我可怜的玛蒂尔德！我那串可是假的呀。顶多也就值五百法郎！……”

（郑克鲁 译）

安娜·卡列尼娜（节选）

托尔斯泰

大家都大声地表示不满，大家都在重复不知谁说出来的一句话：“只差和狮子角斗哩。”而且大家都感到恐怖，因此当弗龙斯基翻下马来，安娜大声惊叫了一声的时候，并没有什么稀奇的地方。但是后来安娜的脸上起了一种实在有失体面的变化。她完全失去主宰了。她像一只笼中的鸟儿一样乱动起来，一会起身走开，一会又转向贝特西。

“我们走吧，我们走吧！”她说。

但是贝特西没有听见。她弯着身子，正跟走到她面前的一位将军说话。

阿列克谢·亚历山德罗维奇走到安娜面前，殷勤地把胳臂伸给她。

"我们走吧，假使你高兴的话，"他用法语说；但是安娜正在听将军说话，没有注意到她丈夫。

"听说他也摔断了腿，"将军说，"真是太糟糕了。"

安娜没有回答她丈夫，她举起望远镜，朝弗龙斯基堕马的地方眺望；但是离那地方那么远，而且那么多人拥挤在那里，她什么都看不见。她放下望远镜，正待起身走开，但是正在这时一个士官骑马跑来，向沙皇报告了什么消息。安娜向前探着身子倾听。

"斯季瓦！斯季瓦！"她叫她的哥哥。

但是她的哥哥没有听见。她又起身预备走。

"我再一次把胳臂伸给你，假使你要走的话，"阿列克谢·亚历山德罗维奇说，触了触她的手。

她厌恶地避开他，没有望着他的脸，回答说：

"不，不，不要管我，我要留在这里。"

她这时看到从弗龙斯基出事的地点一个士官正穿过赛马场朝着亭子跑来。贝特西向他挥着手帕。士官带来了骑者没有受伤，只是马折断了脊背的消息。

一听到这消息，安娜就连忙坐下，用扇子掩住脸。阿列克谢·亚历山德罗维奇看到她在哭泣，她不仅控制不住眼泪，连使她的胸膛起伏的呜咽也抑制不住了。阿列克谢·亚历山德罗维奇用身子遮住她，给她时间来恢复镇静。

"我第三次把胳臂伸给你，"他过了一会儿之后向她说。安娜望着他，不知道说什么好。贝特西公爵夫人来解围了。

"不，阿列克谢·亚历山德罗维奇，我邀安娜来的，我答应了送她回去，"贝特西插嘴说。

"对不起，公爵夫人，"他说，客气地微笑着，但是坚定地望着她的眼睛。"我看安娜身体不大舒服，我要她跟我一道回去。"

安娜吃惊地环顾了一下四周，顺从地站起身来，挽住她丈夫的胳臂。

"我派人到他那里去探问明白，就来通知你，"贝特西低声对她说。

当他们离开亭子的时候，阿列克谢·亚历山德罗维奇照常和他遇见的人们应酬，而安娜也要照常寒暄应酬；但是她完全身不由己了，像在梦中一样挽住她丈夫的胳臂走着。

"他跌死了没有呢？是真的吗？他会不会来呢？我今天要不要去看他？"她想着。

她默默地坐上她丈夫的马车，他们默默地从马车群里驶出去。阿列克谢·亚历山德罗维奇虽然看见了这一切，却还是不让自己考虑他妻子的实际处境。他只看见了外表的征候。他看见了她的举动有失检点，认为提醒她是自己的职责。不过单提这件事，不说别的，在他是非常困难的。他张开嘴，想要对她说她举动不检，但是不由自主地说了一句完全另外的话。

"说起来，我们大家多么爱好这些残酷的景象啊！"他说，"我看……"

"什么？我不明白，"安娜轻蔑地说。

他被激怒了，立刻说出他想要说的话。

"我不能不对你说，"他开口了。

"现在我们一切都要说穿了！"她想，感到恐惧。

"我不能不对你说今天你的举动是有失检点的。"他用法语对她说。

"我的举动什么地方有失检点？"她大声说，迅速地掉转头来，正视着他的眼睛，但已经不带着以前那种有所隐瞒的快活神色，而是带着一种坚定的神色，她很费力地想借此把她感到的恐怖隐藏起来。

"注意，"他指着马车夫背后开着的窗子说。

他起身把窗子关上。

"你觉得我什么地方有失检点？"她重复说。

"一个骑手出了事的时候，你没有能够掩盖住你的失望的神色。"

他等待她回答；但是她却沉默着，直视着前方。

"我曾要求你在社交场中一举一动都要做到连恶嘴毒舌的人也不能够诽谤你。有个时候我曾说过你内心的态度，但是现在我却不是说那个。现在我说的只是你外表的态度。你的举动有失检点，我希望这种事以后不再发生。"

他说的话她连一半都没有听进去，她在他面前感到恐惧，而心里却在想着弗龙斯基没有跌死是不是真的。他们说骑手没有受伤，只是马折断了脊骨，他们说的是他吗？当他说完的时候，她只带着假装的嘲弄神情微微一笑，并没有回答，因为她没有听见他说了什么。阿列克谢·亚历山德罗维奇开始大胆地说了，但是当他明白地意识到他所说的话的时候，她感到的恐怖也感染了他。他看见她的微笑，他心里产生了一种奇怪的错觉。

"她在嘲笑我疑心太重哩。是的，她马上就会对我说她以前对我说过的话：说我的猜疑是无根据的，是可笑的。”

在全部真相即将揭露的时刻，他最希望的是她还会像以前一样嘲笑地回答说他的猜疑是可笑的、毫无根据的。他所知道的事是这样可怕，以至他现在什么都愿意相信了。但是她脸上的惊惶而又忧郁的表情，现在看样子连欺骗也不会了。

“也许我错了，”他说。“假如是那样的话，就请你原谅我吧。”

“不，你没有错，”她从容地说，绝望地望着他的冷冷的面孔。“你没有错。我绝望了，我不能不绝望呢。我听着你说话，但是我心里却在想着他。我爱他，我是他的情妇，我忍受不了你，我害怕你，我憎恶你……随便你怎样处置我吧。”

她仰靠在马车角落里，突然呜咽起来，用两手掩着脸。阿列克谢·亚历山德罗维奇没有动，直视着前方。但是他的整个面孔突然显出死人一般庄严呆板的神色，而这神色直到他们到了别墅都没有变化。快到家的时候，他回过头转向她，还是带着同样的神色。

“很好！但是我要求你严格地遵守外表的体面直到这种时候，”他的声音发抖了，“直到我采取适当的措施来保全我的名誉，而且把那办法通知你为止。”

他先下车，然后扶她下了车。在仆人面前，他紧紧握了握她的手，又坐上马车，驶回彼得堡去。

他走后不一会，贝特西公爵夫人的仆人来了，给安娜送来一封短信。

“我差人到阿列克谢那里去探问他的健康情况，他回信说他很好，没有受伤，只是感到失望。”

“这样，他会来了，”她想。“我把一切都对他讲明了，这是多么好的一件事情啊。”

她看了看表。她还得等三个钟头，回忆起他们最后一次会面的详细情节使她的血沸腾起来。

“哎呀，多么光明啊！这是可怕的，但是我爱看他的脸，我爱这奇幻的光明……我的丈夫！啊！是的……哦，谢谢上帝！和他一切都完了。”

（周扬 译）

小公务员之死

契诃夫

一个美好的晚上，一位心情美好的庶务官伊凡·德米特里·切尔维亚科夫，坐在剧院第二排座椅上，正拿着望远镜观看轻歌剧《科尔涅维利的钟声》。他看着演出，感到无比幸福。但突然间……小说里经常出现这个“但突然间”。作家们是对的：生活中确实充满了种种意外事件。但突然间，他的脸皱起来，眼睛往上翻，呼吸停住了……他放下望远镜，低下头，便……阿嚏一声！！！他打了个喷嚏，你们瞧。无论何时何地，谁打喷嚏都是不能禁止的。庄稼汉打喷嚏，警长打喷嚏，有时连达官贵人也在所难免。人人都打喷嚏。切尔维亚科夫毫不慌张，掏出小手绢擦擦脸，而且像一位讲礼貌的人那样，举目看看四周：他的喷嚏是否溅着什么人了？但这时他不由得慌张起来。他看到，坐在他前面第一排座椅上的一个小老头，正用手套使劲擦他的秃头和脖子，嘴里还嘟哝着什么。切尔维亚科夫认出这人是三品文官布里扎洛夫将军，他在交通部门任职。

“我的喷嚏溅着他了！”切尔维亚科夫心想，“他虽说不是我的上司，是别的部门的，不过这总不妥当。应当向他赔个不是才对。”

切尔维亚科夫咳嗽一声，身子探向前去，凑着将军的耳朵小声说：

“务请大人原谅，我的唾沫星子溅着您了……我出于无心……”

“没什么，没什么……”

“看在上帝份上，请您原谅。要知道我……我不是有意的……”

“哎，请坐下吧！让人听嘛！”

切尔维亚科夫心慌意乱了，他傻笑一下，开始望着舞台。他看着演出，但已不再感到幸福。他开始惶惶不安起来。幕间休息时，他走到布里扎洛夫跟前，在他身边走来走去，终于克制住胆怯心情，嗫嚅道：

“我溅着您了，大人……务请宽恕……要知道我……我不是有意的……”

“哎，够了！……我已经忘了，您怎么老提它呢！”将军说完，不耐烦地撇了撇下嘴唇。

“他说忘了，可是他那眼神多凶！”切尔维亚科夫暗想，不时怀疑地瞧他一眼。“连话都不想说了。应当向他解释清楚，我完全是无意的……这是自然规律……否则他会认为我故意啐他。他现在不这么想，过后肯定会这么想的！……”

回家后，切尔维亚科夫把自己的失态告诉了妻子。他觉得妻子对发生的事过于轻率。她先是吓着了，但后来听说布里扎洛夫是“别的部门的”，也就放心了。

“不过你还是去一趟赔礼道歉的好，”她说，“他会认为你在公共场合举止不当！”

“说得对呀！刚才我道歉过了，可是他有点古怪……一句中听的话也没说。再者也没有时间细谈。”

第二天，切尔维亚科夫穿上新制服，刮了脸，去找布里扎洛夫解释……走进将军的接待室，他看到里面有许多请求接见的人。将军也在其中，他已经开始接见了。询问过几人后，将军抬眼望着切尔维亚科夫。

“昨天在‘阿尔卡吉亚’剧场，倘若大人还记得的话，”庶务官开始报告，“我打了一个喷嚏，无意中溅了……务请您原……”

“什么废话！……天知道怎么回事！”将军扭过脸，对下一名来访者说：“您有什么事？”

“他不想说！”切尔维亚科夫脸色煞白，心里想道，“看来他生气了……不行，这事不能这样放下……我要跟他解释清楚……”

当将军接见完最后一名来访首，正要返回内室时，切尔维亚科夫一步跟上去，又开始嗫嚅道：

“大人！倘若在下胆敢打搅大人的话，那么可以说，只是出于一种悔过的心情……我不是有意的，务请您谅解，大人！”

将军做出一副哭丧脸，挥一下手。

“您简直开玩笑，先生！”将军说完，进门不见了。

“这怎么是开玩笑？”切尔维亚科夫想，“根本不是开玩笑！身为将军，却不明事理！既然这样，我再也不向这个好摆架子的人赔不是了！去他的！我给他写封信，再也不来了！真的，再也不来了！”

切尔维亚科夫这么思量着回到家里。可是给将军的信却没有写成。想来想去，怎么也想不出这信该怎么写。只好次日又去向将军本人解释。

“我昨天来打搅了大人，”当将军向他抬起疑问的目光，他开始嗫嚅道，“我不是如您讲的来开玩笑的。我来是向您赔礼道歉，因为我打喷嚏时溅着您了，大人……说到开玩笑，我可从来没有想过。在下胆敢开玩笑吗？倘若我们真开玩笑，那样的话，就丝毫谈不上对大人的敬重了……谈不上……”

“滚出去！！”忽然间，脸色发青、浑身打颤的将军大喝一声。

“什么，大人？”切尔维亚科夫小声问道，他吓呆了。

“滚出去！！”将军顿着脚，又喊了一声。

切尔维亚科夫感到肚子里什么东西碎了。什么也看不见，什么也听不着，他一步一步退到门口。他来到街上，步履艰难地走着……他懵懵懂懂地回到家里，没脱制服，就倒在长沙发上，后来就……死了。

（汝龙 译）

Chapter Eight
19th-Century Literature (II)

双城记(节选)

狄更斯

住宅的门锁着。两兄弟之一开了门让我们进去，然后又反锁上了。从我们刚在院落大门下车时起我就听见楼上屋里有哭喊声。我被径直带进了那屋子。上楼时那叫声越来越大，我发现一个病人躺在床上，害了脑炎，发着高烧。

病人是个绝色美女，很年轻，无疑刚过二十。她头发蓬松披散，两臂用带子和手巾捆在身体两侧。我注意到这些捆绑用品都来自男人的服装。其中之一是穿礼服用的绣有花边的围巾。在那上面我看到一个贵族纹章和字母 E。

这一切是我在研究病人的第一分钟发现的，因为病人在不断挣扎时已翻过身子把脸转向了床边，让围巾的一角卷进了嘴里，有被窒息而死的危险。我的第一个动作是伸出手来解除她的危险；在拉开围巾时，巾角上的刺绣落入了我的眼里。

我把她轻轻翻过身来，双手放在她胸上，让她平静，也让她躺好，同时看看她的脸。她瞪大了眼睛，神志不清，不断发出尖锐的呼喊，反复地叫着：“我的丈夫，我的爸爸，我的弟弟！”接着便从一数到十二，然后说，“嘘！”说完之后，她会停下来，静听片刻。就一会儿工夫，她又开始尖叫起来，重复着“我的丈夫，我的爸爸，我的弟弟”的叫喊，又由一数到十二，再发出“嘘”的一声。像这样周而复始，次序不变，态度也不变。除了那固定的停顿之外一直没有住口。

"这种情况有多久了?"我问。

为了区别两个弟兄,我把他俩分别叫做哥哥和弟弟。我把那最权威的叫哥哥。哥哥回答道,"大约从昨天晚上这时候开始的。"

"她有丈夫、父亲和弟弟吗?"

"有一个弟弟。"

"我不是在跟她的弟弟说话吧?"

他非常轻蔑地回答道,"不是。"

"她近来有什么跟数字十二有关的事么?"

弟弟不耐烦地插嘴道,"十二点钟!"

"你们看,先生们,"我说,我的手仍在她胸口上,"你们像这样把我带了来,我是无能为力的!我若早知道是来看什么病,就可以带好应用的药品。像现在这样,只能是浪费时间。在这种偏远的地方哪儿有药呢。"

哥哥望了弟弟一眼,弟弟傲慢地说,"有个药品箱。"他便从一间小屋里把它取了出来,放在桌上。

我打开几个药瓶,嗅了嗅,用嘴唇碰了碰瓶塞,这里的药除了本身就是毒药的麻醉剂之外,并没有我要用的药。

"这些药你不放心么?"弟弟问。

"你看,先生,我会用的,"我回答,就再也没说话。

我费了很大的力气,想了许多办法把我要用的药给她喂了下去。因为过一会儿还得用药,现在也要观察疗效,我便在床边坐了下来。有一个很胆小的怯生生的妇女在服侍(她是楼下那人的妻子),此刻退到了一个角落里。那房子非常潮湿腐朽,家具也很平常——显然是最近才临时使用的。窗前钉了些陈旧的厚窗帘,想要挡住那尖叫声。尖叫继续有规律地发出,"我的丈夫,我的爸爸,我的弟弟!"数到十二,然后是"嘘!"病人很疯狂,我没敢解掉捆缚她双臂的带子,却也作了检查,设法不让她疼痛。病人溅出的唯一令我鼓舞的火星是我放在她胸前的手产生了抚慰的效果,有时能让那身躯平静一点,但是对尖叫却没有作用:没有钟摆比它更准时的。

因为自以为我的手有这种效果,我在床边坐了半个小时,弟兄俩在旁边看着。后来哥哥说:

"还有一个病人。"

我吃了一惊问,"是危重病么?"

"你还是自己去看吧,"他满不在乎地回答,说时拿起了一盏灯。

另一个病人在另一道楼梯后的一间房里。那房间在马厩的上方,也可算是一种阁楼。楼顶有低矮的天花板,一部分抹了石粉,剩下的部分却空着,露出瓦房顶的屋脊和横梁。那是堆放麦秸和干草的地方,也放木柴,还存放着一堆埋在沙里的苹果。我穿过那地方来到病号面前。我的记忆精确无误。我用这些细节来审查我的记忆力。在我被幽禁快满十年的此刻,在巴士底狱我的牢房里,那天晚上的景象全都历历如在我眼前。

一个英俊的农村少年躺在地上的干草里,头下枕着一个扔在地上的垫子。他最多只有十七岁。他右手捂着胸口躺在地上,咬紧牙关,圆睁着双眼望着头顶。我在他身边跪下一条腿,却看不见他的伤在哪里。我可以看出他因锐器刺伤,快要死去了。

"我是个医生,可怜的朋友,"我说,"让我检查一下吧。"

"我不要检查,"他回答,"随它去。"

伤口在他捂住的地方,我说服他拿开了手。是剑伤,受伤时间大约在二十至二十四小时以前。但是即使他当时立即得到治疗也已无术可治。他正在迅速死去。我转过眼去看那位哥哥,只见他低头望着这个英俊少年的生命在消逝,只如看着一只受了伤的鸟或兔,一点也不像看着跟他相同的人类。

"这是怎么回事,先生?"我问。

"一条小疯狗!一个农奴!逼着我弟弟拔剑决斗,把他刺倒了——倒像个贵族一样。"

那答话里没有一丝怜悯、痛苦,或是人类的同情。说话人似乎承认那个卑贱的生物死在这儿不太方便,认为他还是像虫子那样默默无闻地死去为好。对于那少年和他的命运,他根本不可能表示同情。

他说话时,那少年的眼睛慢慢转向了他,这时又慢慢转向了我。

"医生,这些贵族非常骄傲。可我们这些卑贱的狗有时也很骄傲。他们掠夺我们、侮辱我们、殴打我们、杀死我们,可我们有时也还剩下点自尊心。她——你见到她了么,医生?"

虽然距离很远,但那尖叫在这儿也还隐约可闻。他指的就是那尖叫,仿佛她就躺在我们身边。

我说,"我见到她了。"

"她是我姐姐,医生。多少年来这些贵族对我们的姐妹们的贞操和德行就拥有一种可耻的权利，可我们也有好姑娘。这我知道，也听我爸爸说过。我姐姐就是个好姑娘，而且跟一个好青年订了婚，我姐夫是他的佃户。我们都是他的佃户——站在那边那个家伙。那另一个是他的弟弟，是一个恶劣的家族里最恶劣的人。”

那少年是克服了最大的困难才集中了全身的力量说出话来的，但是他的神色却起着可怕的强调作用。

“我们这些卑贱的狗就要挨那些高贵的家伙的抢掠。站在那边的那个家伙，他抢夺我们，逼我们交苛捐杂税，逼我们给他们做事，不给报酬，逼我们到他的磨坊磨面。他的鸡鸭鹅大群大群地吃我们少得可怜的庄稼，却一只鸡鸭都不准我们喂养。他把我们抢得干干净净，我们若是有了一小片肉，只好闩上门，闭上窗，提心吊胆地吃，怕被他的人看见拿走——我说，我们给抢得、逼得、刮得太苦了，我爸爸对我们说，生孩子很可怕，我们最应当祈祷的就是让我们的妇女不要生育，让我们悲惨的种族灭绝！”

被压迫者的痛苦像烈火一样爆发燃烧的情况我还从来没看见过。我原以为它只能隐藏在人们心里的什么地方呢！可现在我却在这个快要死去的少年身上看见了。

“不过，我姐姐却结婚了。那时她的情人在生病，可怜的人，她却嫁给了他。她想在我们的农家屋里——这家伙叫它狗窝——照顾他，安慰他。她结婚才几个星期这家伙的弟弟就看见了她。他看中了她的漂亮，要求这家伙把我姐姐借给他使用——在我们这种人当中丈夫算得了什么！这家伙倒很愿意，但是我姐姐却又善良又贞洁，对这家伙的弟弟怀着跟我一样强烈的仇恨。为了逼迫我的姐夫对姐姐施加影响，让她同意，这一对弟兄干出了些什么样的事呀！”

那少年一双眼睛原先望着我，此时却慢慢转向了我身边那个人。我从这两张面孔上看出那少年的话全是真的。就是此刻在巴士底狱里我也还能看到两种针锋相对的骄傲彼此的对峙。一面是贵族的骄傲，轻蔑，冷淡；一面是农民的骄傲，被践踏的感情和强烈的复仇情绪。

“你知道，医生，按照贵族的权利，我们只是些卑贱的狗，他们可以把我们套在车辕上赶着走。他们便这样把我姐夫套上车辕赶着走了。你知道，他们有权让我们通夜在地里轰青蛙，不让它们干扰老爷们高贵的睡眠。他们夜里逼迫我姐夫在有害的雾气里干活，白天又命令他回来套车。可是我姐夫仍然不听他们的。不听！一天中午他被从车轭上放下来吃东西——若是他还找得到东西吃的话——他呜咽了十二次，每一次呜咽正好有一声钟声相伴，然后便死在我姐姐怀里。”

若不是有他倾诉冤情的决心支持，人世间是没有力量让他活下去的。他的右手仍然紧握着，捂住伤口，逼退了逐渐加重的死亡的阴影。

“然后，那弟弟得到了这家伙的同意，甚至帮助，把我姐姐弄来了，尽管她告诉了他一件事——我知道她一定会告诉他的，这事如果你现在还不知道，马上也会知道的。他的弟弟把我姐姐带走了。他拿她寻开心，消遣了几天。我在路上看见她路过，把消息带回家里，我爸爸便心碎而死。他满腹冤屈，却一个字也没说。我把我的小妹妹(我还有个妹妹)带到了一个这家伙找不到的地方，她在那儿至少可以不做他的奴仆。然后我便跟踪他的弟弟来到这里，昨天晚上溜进了院子——一条卑贱的狗，手里却有一柄剑。阁楼的窗户在哪儿？就在这旁边么？”

在他眼中全屋黑了下来，周围的世界越缩越小。我向四面望望，看到麦秸干草踩得乱成一片，似乎这里有过搏斗。

“我姐姐听见我的声音，跑了进来。我要她在我杀掉那家伙之前别靠近我。那家伙进来了，先是扔给我一些钱，然后便用鞭子抽我。可是我却用剑刺他，逼他跟我决斗——虽然我是条卑贱的狗。他拔出剑来保护自己，为了保住性命，他施展出了浑身解数。我使他把他那剑折成了几段，因为那上面染上了我卑贱的血。”

刚才我曾在干草堆里瞥见一把折成几段的剑。那是贵族的佩剑。在另一个地方，还有一把老式的剑，似乎是士兵用的。

“现在，扶我起来吧，医生，扶我起来。他在哪儿？”

“他不在这儿。”我扶起少年，估计他指的是那弟弟。

“他！这些贵族尽管骄傲，他却害怕见我。刚才还在这儿的那个人呢？把我的脸转向他。”

我照办了，抬起少年的头靠在我的膝盖上。但是少年此刻却具有了超乎寻常的力气，完全站直了身子,逼得我也站了起来,否则我便扶不住他。

“侯爵,”少年圆睁了双眼对他转过身去,举起右手,“等到清算这一笔笔血债的日子,我要你和你全家,直到你的种族的最后一个人对这一切承担责任。我对你画上这个血十字,记下我的要求。等到清算这一笔笔血债的日子,我要你的弟弟,你那卑劣种族中最卑劣的家伙,单独对此承担责任。我对他画上这个血十字,记下我的要求。”

他两次伸手到胸前的伤口上,然后用食指在空中画着十字。他举着手还站了一会儿,手落下时人也倒下了。我放下了他,他已经死了。

我回到那年轻妇女身边时,发现她仍按刚才的顺序一成不变地呓语尖叫。我知道那种情况还可能继续许多小时,十之八九要在坟墓的沉默里才能结束。

我又让她服下刚才用的药,然后在她身边直坐到深夜。她的呼喊仍然尖利,她的话语仍然清楚,顺序也从不改变。总是“我的丈夫,我的爸爸,我的弟弟!一,二,三,四,五,六,七,八,九,十,十一,十二。嘘!”

从我初见她时算起,她一直喊叫了二十六个小时。其间我曾离开过她两次。在我又一次坐到她身边时,她的声音开始变得虚弱。我竭尽全力帮助她,但愿能有几分希望,可是不久她便昏沉了,像死人一样躺着。

仿佛是一场可怕的漫长的风暴终于过去,风停了,雨止了。我解开了她的双臂,叫那个妇女来帮助我整理好她的容貌和撕开的衣衫。那时我才发觉她已经出现了最初的妊娠迹象,也是在那时我对她怀着的一点点希望终于破灭了。

(孙法理 译)

苔　丝(节选)

哈　代

苔丝的叙述结束了。就连反复申明和附加说明也都讲完了。她的嗓音自始至终都没有提高,和开口说的时候一样低沉。她既没有说出任何为自己开脱罪责的话语,也没有流下一滴眼泪。

但是,随着她的叙述,就连各种外部景物的面貌,也似乎经受了一番嬗变的过程。壁炉里的炭火变得鬼头鬼脑、怪模怪样的,仿佛对苔丝的窘迫完全无动于衷。炉栏懒洋洋地咧着嘴,好像一切都与自己毫不相干。盛水瓶子上发出来的光亮只是表明,它正在潜心研究有关色彩方面的问题。周围的一切物体,好像都在令人可怕地反复申明,逃脱责任。然而,自他吻她以来,什么也没改变,或者更确切地说,在外表上什么也没有发生变化,但是,事情的实质已经变了。

她说完之后,他们从前那卿卿我我、耳鬓厮磨的情韵,仿佛全都退缩到脑门后面,挤到那儿反复唠叨,觉得以前的行为完全是盲目和愚蠢的。

克莱尔做了一个离题的举动,把炉火拨弄了一下。她刚才那番话的真实意义还没有到达他的内心深处。拨弄了余火之后,他站了起来。这时,她那番话的全部力量才显示出来。他的脸变得憔悴苍老了。为了集中自己的思绪,他就用脚在地上乱踏乱踩。他不管用什么办法,都无法驱除杂念、集中心思,因此,只好做出茫然无措的举动。当他终于开口说话时,所发出的也不是那种她所听惯的富于变化的音调,而是极不恰当、极其呆板的声音。

“苔丝!”

“嗯,最亲爱的。”

“我该相信这番话吗?看你的样子,我该把这些话当成是真的。啊,你不可能是疯了吧!你要是疯了才好呐!可是你却没有疯……我的妻子,我的苔丝,你拿不出任何足以证明你已经发疯的东西,是吧?”

“我没有发疯。”她说。

“然而……”他神情茫然地看着她,又恍恍惚惚地说:“你以前为什么不告诉我呀?哦,对了,我想起来了,你本来是想告诉我的,可我没让你说出来!”

克莱尔说这说那只不过是表面上的敷衍塞责罢了,他的内心深处仍然如同瘫痪了似的。他转过身去,俯在一把椅子上。苔丝跟着他到了房间中央,用一双没有泪水的眼睛盯着他。接着,她在他的脚边跪了下来,又趴倒在地,蜷伏成一团。

“看在我们爱情的份上,请你饶恕我吧!”她舌敝唇焦,喃喃地说。“同样的事情,我可是宽恕你了呀!”

他没有回答,于是她又说:

“像我宽恕你一样宽恕我吧!安琪,我宽恕你!”

“你吗,是的,你宽恕我了。”

"可你就不宽恕我吗?"

"哦,苔丝,这不是什么宽恕不宽恕的问题! 你以前是一个人,你现在是另一个人了。天哪,宽恕两个字怎么对付得了这种荒诞无稽的戏法呢?"

他停了下来,思考着这一定义,然后突然可怕地狂笑起来,笑得像地狱里的笑声一样恐怖,一样不自然。

"别——别这样! 这笑声简直是要我的命!"她尖声叫着。"啊,你发发慈悲吧,你可怜可怜我吧!"

他没有回答。她脸色惨白,跳了起来。

"安琪,安琪! 你干吗这样狂笑?"她大声嚷叫着。"你知道这笑声对我意味着什么吗?"

他摇了摇头。

"我一直在期待着、盼望着、祈祷着,只想让你幸福! 我老是在想,我若是能够使你称心如意,那该是多么高兴的事啊,若是不能让你开心,那我该是一个多么不称职的妻子啊! 安琪,这就是我的想法呀!"

"这我知道。"

"安琪,我原以为你是爱我的——爱我这个人本身! 要是你爱的真是我,那么,你的神情怎么会变成这个样子? 你怎么会这样跟我说话? 真把我吓死了! 而我呢,我只要爱上了你,我就会永远爱你,不管遇到什么变故,遭到什么耻辱,我都永远爱你,因为你就是你呀。我不再另有所求。那么你,我的亲丈夫,你怎么能不再爱我了呢?"

"我再重复一遍,我一直爱着的女人并不是你。"

"是谁呢?"

"是长得跟你一模一样的另外一个女人。"

她从他这番话里觉察到,她自己以前的担忧,现在真的应验了。他把她看成一个骗子了,看成是假装纯洁的邪恶女人了。想到这一点,她那苍白的脸上掠过一阵恐惧,面颊上的肌肉松弛下垂了,嘴巴看起来几乎像是一个圆圆的小窟窿。意识到他对她的这种态度,她感到可怕极了,几乎失去知觉,几乎瘫倒在地。他以为她要栽倒,于是走上前去。

"坐下来,坐下来吧。"他轻轻地说,"你要晕倒了,这是很自然的。"

她倒是坐下来了,可是却不知道究竟坐在哪儿了,她脸上仍然是一副紧张的神情,她那眼光,叫人看了汗毛直竖。

"那么,安琪,我不再是你的人了,是吗?"她失望地问道。"他说他爱的不是我,而是长得跟我一模一样的另外一个女人。"

想到这里,她就像受了委屈的人一样,自己可怜起自己来了。当她进一步想了想自己的处境之后,眼眶里便噙满泪水,她急忙转过脸,自我怜悯的眼泪便像泉水一般涌了出来。

(吴笛 译)

黑暗中的鸫鸟

哈 代

我倚在以树丛作篱的门边,
寒霜像幽灵般发灰,
冬的沉渣使那白日之眼
在苍白中更添憔悴。
纠缠的藤蔓在天上划线,
宛如断了的琴弦,
而出没附近的一切人类
都已退到家中火边。

陆地轮廓分明,望去恰似
斜卧着世纪的尸体,
阴沉的天穹是他的墓室,
风在为他哀悼哭泣。
自古以来萌芽生长的冲动
已收缩得又干又硬,
大地上每个灵魂与我一同
似乎都已丧失热情。

突然间,头顶上有个声音
在细枝萧瑟间升起,
一曲黄昏之歌满腔热情
唱出了无限欣喜,——
这是一只鸫鸟,瘦弱、老衰,
羽毛被阵风吹乱,
却决心把它的心灵敞开,
倾泻向浓浓的黑暗。

远远近近,任你四处寻找,
在地面的万物上
值得欢唱的原因是那么少,
是什么使它欣喜若狂?
这使我觉得:它颤音的歌词,

它欢乐曲晚安曲调
含有某种幸福希望——为它所知
而不为我所晓。

（飞白 译）

麦琪的礼物

欧·亨利

一元八角七。全都在这儿了，其中六角是一分一分的铜板。这些分分钱是在杂货店老板、菜贩子和肉店老板那儿软硬兼施地一分两分地扣下来，直弄得自己羞愧难当，深感这种掂斤播两的交易实在丢人现眼。德拉反复数了三次，还是一元八角七，而第二天就是圣诞节了。

除了扑倒在那破旧的小睡椅上哭嚎之外，显然别无他途。

德拉这样做了，可精神上的感慨油然而生，生活就是哭泣、抽噎和微笑，尤以抽噎占统治地位。

当这位家庭主妇逐渐平静下来之际，让我们看看这个家吧。一套带家具的公寓房子，每周房租八美元。尽管难以用笔墨形容，可它真正够得上乞丐帮这个词儿。

楼下的门道里有个信箱，可从来没有装过信，还有一个电钮，也从没有人的手指按响过电铃。而且，那儿还有一张名片，上写着"詹姆斯·迪林厄姆·杨先生"。

"迪林厄姆"这个名号是主人先前春风得意之际，一时兴起加上去的，那时候他每星期挣三十美元。现在，他的收入缩减到二十美元，"迪林厄姆"的字母也显得模糊不清，似乎它们正严肃地思忖着是否缩写成谦逊而又讲求实际的字母D。不过，每当詹姆斯·迪林厄姆·杨回家，走进楼上的房间时，詹姆斯·迪林厄姆·杨太太，就是刚介绍给诸位的德拉，总是把他称作"吉姆"，而且热烈地拥抱他。那当然是再好不过的了。

德拉哭完之后，往面颊上抹了抹粉，她站在窗前，痴痴地瞅着灰濛濛的后院里一只灰白色的猫正行走在灰白色的篱笆上。明天就是圣诞节，她只有一元八角七给吉姆买一份礼物。她花去好几个月的时间，用了最大的努力一分一分地攒积下来，才得了这样一个结果。一周二十美元实在经不起花，支出大于预算，总是如此。只有一元八角七给吉姆买礼物，她的吉姆啊。她花费了多少幸福的时日筹划着要送他一件可心的礼物，一件精致、珍奇、贵重的礼物——至少应有点儿配得上吉姆所有的东西才成啊。

房间的两扇窗子之间有一面壁镜。也许你见过每周房租八美元的公寓壁镜吧。一个非常瘦小而灵巧的人，从观察自己在一连串的纵条影像中，可能会对自己的容貌得到一个大致精确的概念。德拉身材苗条，已精通了这门子艺术。

突然，她从窗口旋风般地转过身来，站在壁镜前面。她两眼晶莹透亮，但二十秒钟之内她的面色失去了光彩。她急速地拆散头发，使之完全披散开来。

现在，詹姆斯·迪林厄姆·杨夫妇俩各有一件特别引以自豪的东西。一件是吉姆的金表，是他祖父传给父亲，父亲又传给他的传家宝；另一件则是德拉的秀发。如果示巴女王也住在天井对面的公寓里，总有一天德拉会把头发披散下来，露出窗外晾干，使那女王的珍珠宝贝黯然失色；如果地下室堆满金银财宝、所罗门王又是守门人的话，每当吉姆路过那儿，准会摸出金表，好让那所罗门王嫉妒得吹胡子瞪眼睛。

此时此刻，德拉的秀发泼撒在她的周围，微波起伏，闪耀光芒，有如那褐色的瀑布。她的美发长及膝下，仿佛是她的一件长袍。接着，她又神经质地赶紧把头发梳好。踌躇了一分钟，一动不动地立在那儿，破旧的红地毯上溅落了一两滴眼泪。

她穿上那件褐色的旧外衣，戴上褐色的旧帽子，眼睛里残留着晶莹的泪花，裙子一摆，便飘出房门，下楼来到街上。

她走到一块招牌前停下来，上写着："索弗罗妮夫人——专营各式头发"。德拉奔上楼梯，气喘吁吁地定了定神。那位夫人身躯肥大，过于苍白，冷若冰霜，同"索弗罗妮"的雅号简直牛头不对马嘴。

"你要买我的头发吗？"德拉问。

"我买头发，"夫人说。"揭掉帽子，让我看看发样。"

那褐色的瀑布泼撒了下来。

"二十美元，"夫人一边说，一边内行似地抓起头发。

"快给我钱，"德拉说。

呵，接着而至的两个小时犹如长了翅膀，愉快地飞掠而过。请不用理会这胡诌的比喻。她正在彻底搜寻各家店铺，为吉姆买礼物。

她终于找到了，那准是专为吉姆特制的，决非为别人。她找遍了各家商店，哪儿也没有这样的东西，一条朴素的白金表链，镂刻着花纹。正如一切优质东西那样，它只以货色论长短，不以装潢来炫耀。而且它正配得上那只金表。她一见这条表链，就知道一定属于吉姆所有。它就像吉姆本人，文静而有价值——这一形容对两者都恰如其分。她花去二十一美元买下了，匆匆赶回家，只剩下八角七分钱。金表匹配这条链子，无论在任何场合，吉姆都可以毫无愧色地看时间了。

尽管这只表华丽珍贵，因为用的是旧皮带取代表链，他有时只偷偷地瞥上一眼。

德拉回家之后，她的狂喜有点儿变得审慎和理智了。她找出烫发铁钳，点燃煤气，着手修补因爱情加慷慨所造成的破坏，这永远是件极其艰巨的任务，亲爱的朋友们——简直是件了不起的任务呵。

不出四十分钟，她的头上布满了紧贴头皮的一绺绺小卷发，使她活像个逃学的小男孩。她在镜子里老盯着自己瞧，小心地、苛刻地照来照去。

“假如吉姆看我一眼不把我宰掉的话，”她自言自语，“他定会说我像个科尼岛上合唱队的卖唱姑娘。但是我能怎么办呢——唉，只有一元八角七，我能干什么呢?”

七点钟，她煮好了咖啡，把煎锅置于热炉上，随时都可做肉排。

吉姆一贯准时回家。德拉将表链对叠握在手心，坐在离他一贯进门最近的桌子角上。接着，她听见下面楼梯上响起了他的脚步声，她紧张得脸色失去了一会儿血色。她习惯于为了最简单的日常事物而默默祈祷，此刻，她悄声道:“求求上帝，让他觉得我还是漂亮的吧。”

门开了，吉姆步入，随手关上了门。他显得瘦削而又非常严肃。可怜的人儿，他才二十二岁，就挑起了家庭重担！他需要买件新大衣，连手套也没有呀。

吉姆站在屋里的门口边，纹丝不动地好像猎犬嗅到了鹌鹑的气味似的。他的两眼固定在德拉身上，其神情使她无法理解，令她毛骨悚然。既不是愤怒，也不是惊讶，又不是不满，更不是嫌恶，根本不是她所预料的任何一种神情。他仅仅是面带这种神情死死地盯着德拉。

德拉一扭腰，从桌上跳了下来，向他走过去。

“吉姆，亲爱的，”她喊道，“别那样盯着我。我把头发剪掉卖了，因为不送你一件礼物，我无法过圣诞节。头发会再长起来——你不会介意，是吗?我非这么做不可。我的头发长得快极了。说‘恭贺圣诞’吧！吉姆，让我们快快乐乐的。你肯定猜不着我给你买了一件多么好的——多么美丽精致的礼物啊!”

“你已经把头发剪掉了?”吉姆吃力地问道，似乎他绞尽脑汁也没弄明白这明摆着的事实。

“剪掉卖了，”德拉说。“不管怎么说，你不也同样喜欢我吗？没了长发，我还是我嘛，对吗?”

吉姆古怪地四下望望这房间。

“你说你的头发没有了吗?”他差不多是白痴似地问道。

“别找啦，”德拉说。“告诉你，我已经卖了——卖掉了，没有啦。这是圣诞前夜，好人儿。好好待我，这是为了你呀。也许我的头发数得清，”突然她特别温柔地接下去，“可谁也数不清我对你的恩爱啊。我做肉排了吗，吉姆?”

吉姆好像从恍惚之中醒来，把德拉紧紧地搂在怀里。现在，别着急，先让我们花个十秒钟从另一角度审慎地思索一下某些无关紧要的事。房租每周八美元，或者一百万美元——那有什么差别呢？数学家或才子会给你错误的答案。麦琪带来了宝贵的礼物，但就是缺少了那件东西。这句晦涩的话，下文将有所交代。

吉姆从大衣口袋里掏出一个小包，扔在桌上。

“别对我产生误会，德尔，”他说道，“无论剪发、修面，还是洗头，我以为世上没有什么东西能减低一点点对我妻子的爱情。不过，你只消打开那包东西，就会明白刚才为什么使我愣头愣脑了。”

白皙的手指灵巧地解开绳子，打开纸包。紧接着是欣喜若狂的尖叫，哎呀！突然变成了女性神经质的泪水和哭泣，急需男主人千方百计的慰藉。

还是因为摆在桌上的梳子——全套梳子，包括两鬓用的，后面的，样样俱全。那是很久以前德拉在百老汇的一个橱窗里见过并羡慕得要死的东西。这些美妙的发梳，纯玳瑁做的，边上镶着珠宝——其色彩正好同她失去的美发相匹配。她明白，这套梳子实在太昂贵，对此，她仅仅是羡慕渴望，但从未想到过据为已有。现在，这一切居然属于她了，可惜那有资格佩戴这垂涎已久的装饰品的美丽长发已无影无踪了。

不过，她依然把发梳搂在胸前，过了好一阵子才抬起泪水迷濛的双眼，微笑着说："我的头发长得飞快，吉姆！"

随后，德拉活像一只被烫伤的小猫跳了起来，叫道，"喔！喔！"

吉姆还没有瞧见他的美丽的礼物哩。她急不可耐地把手掌摊开，伸到他面前，那没有知觉的贵重金属似乎闪现着她的欢快和热忱。

"漂亮吗，吉姆？我搜遍了全城才找到了它。现在，你每天可以看一百次时间了。把表给我，我要看看它配在表上的样子。"

吉姆非但不按她的吩咐行事，反而倒在睡椅上，两手枕在头下，微微发笑。

"德尔，"他说，"让我们把圣诞礼物放在一边，保存一会儿吧。它们实在太好了，目前尚不宜用。我卖掉金表，换钱为你买了发梳。现在，你做肉排吧。"

正如诸位所知，麦琪是聪明人，聪明绝顶的人，他们把礼物带来送给出生在马槽里的耶稣。他们发明送圣诞礼物这玩意儿。由于他们是聪明人，毫无疑问，他们的礼物也是聪明的礼物，如果碰上两样东西完全一样，可能还具有交换的权利。在这儿，我已经笨拙地给你们介绍了住公寓套间的两个傻孩子不足为奇的平淡故事，他们极不明智地为了对方而牺牲了他们家最最宝贵的东西。不过，让我们对现今的聪明人说最后一句话，在一切馈赠礼品的人当中，那两个人是最聪明的。在一切馈赠又接收礼品的人当中，像他们两个这样的人也是最聪明的。无论在任何地方，他们都是最聪明的人。他们就是麦琪。

（潘明元 译）

Chapter Nine Modern Poetry

泪水流在我的心底

魏尔伦

泪水流在我的心底，
恰似那满城秋雨。
一股无名的愁绪
浸透到我的心底。

嘈杂而柔和的雨
在地上、在瓦上絮语！
啊，为一颗惆怅的心
而轻轻吟唱的雨！

泪水流得不合情理，
这颗心啊厌烦自己。
怎么？并没有人负心？
这悲哀说不出情理。

这是最沉重的痛苦，
当你不知它的缘故。
既没有爱，也没有恨，
我心中有这么多痛苦！

（飞白 译）

月　光

魏尔伦

你的心灵是一幅绝妙的风景画：
村野的假面舞令人陶醉忘情，
舞蹈者跳啊，唱啊，弹着琵琶，
奇幻的面具下透出一丝凄清。

当欢舞者用"小调"的音符，
歌唱爱的凯旋和生的吉祥，
他们似乎不相信自己的幸福，
当他们的歌声溶入了月光——

月光啊，忧伤、美丽、静寂，
照得小鸟在树丛中沉沉入梦，
照得那纤瘦的喷泉狂喜悲泣，
在大理石雕像之间腾向半空。

（飞白 译）

当你老了

叶　芝

当你老了，青丝成灰，昏倦欲睡，
在炉旁打着盹儿，且取下这卷诗文，
慢慢阅读，回想你昔日柔和的目光，
追忆你眼睛的浓重的黑晕；

有多少人爱你欢畅娇艳的时刻，
有多少人真真假假爱你的美丽，
但有个男人爱你圣洁的灵魂，
爱你衰老着的脸上的悲戚；

在灼亮的炉栅旁弯下身躯，
微微伤感地喃喃诉怨：
爱情怎会迅速溜到了山巅，
在群星中隐藏起自己的脸。

（吴笛 译）

丽达与天鹅

叶　芝

突然袭击：在踉跄的少女身上，
一双巨翅还在乱扑，一双黑蹼
抚弄她的大腿，鹅喙衔着她的颈项，
他的胸脯紧压她无计脱身的胸脯。

手指啊，被惊呆了，哪还有能力
从松开的腿间推开那白羽的荣耀？
身体呀，翻倒在雪白的灯心草里，
感到的唯有其中那奇异的心跳！

腰股内一阵颤栗，竟从中生出
断垣残壁、城楼上的浓烟烈焰
和阿伽门农之死。
当她被占有之时
当她如此被天空的野蛮热血制服
直到那冷漠的喙把她放开之前，
她是否获取了他的威力，他的知识？

（飞白 译）

在地铁车站

庞　德

这几张脸在人群中幻景般闪现；
湿漉漉的黑树枝上花瓣数点。

（飞白 译）

少　女

庞　德

树进入了我的双手，
树液升上我的双臂。
树生长在我的胸中——
往下长，
树枝从我身上长出，宛如臂膀。

你是树，
你是青苔，
你是风中紫罗兰。
你是个孩子——这么高——
而在世界看来这全是蠢话。

（飞白 译）

红色手推车

威廉・卡洛斯・威廉斯

很多事情
全靠

一辆红色
小车

被雨淋得
晶亮

傍着几只
白鸡

（飞白 译）

窗前的早晨

艾略特

她们在地下室厨房里弄得早餐盒子叮当响，
而沿着众人践踏的街边
我知道女仆们潮湿的心灵
正向着地下室的铁门沮丧地发芽。

棕色的雾的波浪把一张张扭曲的脸
从街底向我抛了上来，
从一个穿泥污裙子的过路人身上
撕下一个茫然的微笑在空中盘旋
然后消失于无数屋顶的平面。

（飞白 译）

我辞别了我出生的屋子

叶赛宁

我辞别了我出生的屋子，
离开了天蓝的俄罗斯。
白桦林像三颗星临照水池
温暖着老母亲的愁思。

月亮像一只金色的蛙
扁扁地趴在安静的水面。
恰似那流云般的苹果花——
老父的胡须已花白一片。

我的归来呀，遥遥无期，
风雪将久久地歌唱不止，
唯有老枫树单脚独立，
守护着天蓝色的俄罗斯。

凡是爱吻落叶之雨的人，
见到那棵树肯定喜欢，
就因为那棵老枫树啊——
它的容颜像我的容颜。

（顾蕴璞 译）

雪夜林边小立

弗罗斯特

我想我认识树林的主人，
他家住在林外的农村；
他不会看见我暂停此地，
欣赏他披上雪装的树林。

我的小马准抱着个疑团：
干吗停在这儿，不见人烟，
在一年中最黑的晚上，
停在树林和冰湖之间。

它摇了摇颈上的铃铎，
想问问主人有没有弄错。
除此以外唯一的声音
是风飘绒雪轻轻拂过。

树林真可爱，既深又黑，
但我有许多诺言不能违背，
还要赶多少路才能安睡，
还要赶多少路才能安睡。

（飞白 译）

没有走的路

弗罗斯特

金黄的林中有两条岔路，
可惜我作为一名过客，
不能两条都走，我久久踌躇，
极目遥望一条路的去处，
直到它在灌木丛中隐没。

我走了第二条，它也不坏，
而且说不定更加值得，
因为它草多，缺少人踩；
不过这点也难比较出来，
两条路踩的程度相差不多。

那天早晨两条路是一样的，
都撒满落叶，还没踩下足迹。
啊，我把第一条路留待来日！
尽管我明白：路是连着路的，
我怀疑是否还能重返旧地。

此后不论岁月流逝多少，
我提起此事总要伴一声叹息：
两条路在林中分了道，而我呢，
我选了较少人走的一条，
此后的一切都相差千里。

（飞白 译）

Chapter Ten Modern Fictions

墙上的斑点

伍尔夫

大约是在今年一月中旬，我抬起头来，第一次看见了墙上的那个斑点。为了要确定是在哪一天，就得回忆当时我看见了些什么。现在我记起了炉子里的火，一片黄色的火光一动不动地照射在我的书页上；壁炉上圆形玻璃缸里插着三朵菊花。对啦，一定是冬天，我们刚喝完茶，因为我记得当时我正在吸烟，我抬起头来，第一次看见了墙上那个斑点。我透过香烟的烟雾望过去，眼光在火红的炭块上停留了一下，过去关于在城堡塔楼上飘扬着一面鲜红的旗帜的幻觉又浮现在我脑际，我想到无数红色骑士潮水般地骑马跃上黑色岩壁的侧坡。这个斑点打断了我这个幻觉，使我觉得松了一口气，因为这是过去的幻觉，是一种无意识的幻觉，可能是在孩童时期产生的。墙上的斑点是一块圆形的小迹印，在雪白的墙壁上呈暗黑色，在壁炉上方大约六七英寸的地方。

我们的思绪是多么容易一哄而上，簇拥着一件新鲜事物，像一群蚂蚁狂热地抬一根稻草一样，抬了一会，又把它扔在那里……如果这个斑点是一只钉子留下的痕迹，那一定不是为了挂一幅油画，而是为了挂一幅小肖像画——一幅卷发上扑着白粉、脸上抹着脂粉、嘴唇像红石竹花的贵妇人肖像。它当然是一件赝品，这所房子以前的房客只会选那一类的画——老房子得有老式画像来配它。他们就是这种人家——很有意思的人家，我常常想到他们，都是在一些奇怪的地方，因为谁都不会再见到他们，也不会知道他们后来的遭遇了。据他说，那家人搬出这所房子是因为他们想换一套别种式样的家具，他正在说，按他的想法，艺术品背后应该包含着思想的时候，我们两人就一下子分了手，这种情形就像坐火车一样，我们在火车里看见路旁郊外别墅里有个老太太正准备倒茶，有个年轻人正举起球拍打网球，火车一晃而过，我们就和老太太以及年轻人分了手，把他们抛在火车后面。

但是，我还是弄不清那个斑点到底是什么；我又想，它不像是钉子留下的痕迹。它太大、太圆了。我本来可以站起来，但是，即使我站起身来瞧瞧它，十之八九我也说不出它到底是什么；因为一旦一件事发生以后，就没有人能知道它是怎么发生的了。唉！天哪，生命是多么神秘；思想是多么不准确！人类是多么无知！为了证明我们对自己的私有物品是多么无法加以控制——和我们的文明相比，人的生活带有多少偶然性啊——我只要列举少数几件我们一生中遗失的物件就够了。就从三只装着订书工具的浅蓝色罐子说起吧，这永远是遗失的东西当中丢失得最神秘的几件——哪只猫会去咬它们，哪只老鼠会去啃它们呢？再数下去，还有那几个鸟笼子、铁裙箍、钢滑冰鞋、安女王时代的煤斗子、弹子戏球台、手摇风琴——全都丢失了，还有一些珠宝，也遗失了。有乳白宝石、绿宝石，它们都散失在芜菁的根部旁边。它们是花了多少心血节衣缩食积蓄起来的啊！此刻我四周全是挺有分量的家具，身上还穿着几件衣服，简直是奇迹。要是拿什么来和生活相比的话，就只能比做一个人以一小时五十英里的速度被射出地下铁道，从地道口出来的时候头发上一根发针也不剩。光着身子被射到上帝脚下！头朝下脚朝天地摔倒在开满水仙花的草原上，就像一捆捆棕色纸袋被扔进邮局的输物管道一样！头发飞扬，就像一匹赛马会的跑马尾巴。对了，这些比拟可以表达生活的飞快速度，表达那永不休止的消耗和修理；一切都那么偶然，那么碰巧。

那么来世呢？粗大的绿色茎条慢慢地被拉得弯曲下来，杯盏形的花倾覆了，它那紫色和红色的光芒笼罩着人们。到底为什么人要投生在这里，而不投生到那里，不会行动、不会说话、无法集中目光，在青草脚下，在巨人的脚趾间摸索呢？至于什么是树，什么是男人和女人，或者是不是存在这样的东西，人们再过五十年也是无法说清楚的。别的什么都不会有，只有充塞着光亮和黑暗的空间，中间隔着一条条粗大的茎干，也许在更高处还有一些色彩不很清晰的——淡淡的粉红色或蓝色的——玫瑰花形状的斑块，随着时光的流逝，它会越来越清楚、越——我也不知道怎样……

可是墙上的斑点不是一个小孔。它很可能是什么暗黑色的圆形物体，比如说，一片夏天残留下来的玫瑰花瓣造成的，因为我不是一个警惕心很高的管家——只要瞧瞧壁炉上的尘土就知道了，据说就是这样的尘土把特洛伊城严严地埋了三层，只有一些罐子的碎片是它们没法毁灭的，这一点完全能叫人相信。

窗外树枝轻柔地敲打着玻璃…… 我希望能静静地、安稳地、从容不迫地思考，没有谁来打扰，一点也用不着从椅子里站起来，可以轻松地从这件事想到那件事，不感觉敌意，也不觉得有阻碍。我希望深深地、更深地沉下去，离开表面，离开表面上的生硬的个别事实。让我稳住自己，抓住第一个一瞬即逝的念头……莎士比亚……对啦，不管是他还是别人，都行。这个人稳稳地坐在扶手椅里，凝视着炉火，就这样——一阵骤雨似的念头源源不断地从某个非常高的天国倾泻而下，进入他的头脑。他把前额倚在自己的手上，于是人们站在敞开的大门外面向里张望——我们假设这个景象发生在夏天的傍晚——可是，所有这一切历史的虚构是多么沉闷啊！它丝毫引不起我的兴趣。我希望能碰上一条使人愉快的思路，同时这条思路也能间接地给我增添几分光彩，这样的想法是最令人愉快的了。连那些真诚地相信自己不爱听别人赞扬的谦虚而灰色的人们头脑里，也经常会产生这种想法。它们不是直接恭维自己，妙就妙在这里。这些想法是这样的："于是我走进屋子。他们在谈植物学。我说我曾经看见金斯威一座老房子地基上的尘土堆里开了一朵花。我说那粒花籽多半是查理一世在位的时候种下的。查理一世在位的时候人们种些什么花呢？"我问道——(但是我不记得回答是什么)也许是高大的、带着紫色花穗的花吧。于是就这样想下去。同时，我一直在头脑里把自己的形象打扮起来，是爱抚地，偷偷地，而不是公开地崇拜自己的形 象。因为，我如果当真公开地这么干了，就会马上被自己抓住，我就会马上伸出手去拿过一本书来掩盖自己。说来也真奇怪，人们总是本能地保护自己的形象，不让偶像崇拜或是什么别的处理方式使它显得可笑，或者使它变得和原型太不相像以至于人们不相信它。但是，这个事实也可能并不那么奇怪。这个问题极其重要。假定镜子打碎了，形象消失了，那个浪漫的形象和周围一片绿色的茂密森林也不复存在，只有其他的人看见的那个人的外壳——世界会变得多么闷人、多么浮浅、多么光秃、多么凸出啊！在这样的世界里是不能生活的。当我们面对面坐在公共汽车和地下铁道里的时候，我们就是在照镜子；这就说明为什么我们的眼神都那么呆滞而朦胧。未来的小说家们会越来越认识到这些想法的重要性，因为这不只是一个想法，而是无限多的想法；它们探索深处，追逐幻影，越来越把现实的描绘排除在他们的故事之外，认为这类知识是天生具有的，希腊人就是这样想的，或许莎士比亚也是这样想的——但是这种概括毫无价值。只要听听概括这个词的音调就够了。它使人想起社论，想起内阁大臣——想起一整套事物，人们在儿童时期就认为这些事物是正统，是标准的、真正的事物，人人都必须遵循，否则就得冒打入十八层地狱的危险。提起概括，不知怎么使人想起伦敦的星期日，星期日午后的散步，星期日的午餐，也使人想起已经去世的人的说话方式，衣着打扮、习惯——例如大家一起坐在一间屋子里直到某一个钟点的习惯，尽管谁都不喜欢这么做。每件事都有一定的规矩。在那个特定时期，桌布的规矩就是一定要用花毯做成，上面印着黄色的小方格子，就像你在照片里看见的皇宫走廊里铺的地毯那样。另外一种花样的桌布就不能算真正的桌布。当我们发现这些真实的事物、星期日的午餐、星期日的散步、庄园宅第和桌布等并不全是真实的，确实带着些幻影的味道，而不相信它们的人所得到的处罚只不过是一种非法的自由感时，事情是多么使人惊奇，又是多么奇妙啊！我奇怪现在到底是什么代替了它们，代替了那些真正的、标准的东西？也许是男人，如果你是个女人的话；男性的观点支配着我们的生活，是它制定了标准，订出惠特克的尊卑序列表；据我猜想，大战后它对于许多男人和女人已经带上幻影的味道，并且我们希望很快它就会像幻影、红木碗橱、兰西尔版画、上帝、魔鬼和地狱之类东西一样遭到讥笑，被送进垃圾箱，给我们大家留下一种令人陶醉的非法的自由感——如果真存在自由的话……

在某种光线下面看墙上那个斑点，它竟像是凸出在墙上的。它也不完全是圆形的。我不敢肯定，不过它似乎投下一点淡淡的影子，使我觉得如果我用手指顺着墙壁摸过去，在某一点上会摸着一个起伏的小小的古冢，一个平滑的古冢，就像南部丘陵草原地带的那些古冢，据说，它们要不是坟墓，就是宿营地。在两者之中，我倒宁愿它们是坟墓，我像多数英国人一样偏爱忧伤，并且认为在散步结束时想到草地下埋着白骨是很自然的事情……一定有一部书写到过它。一定有哪位古物收藏家把这些白骨发掘出来，给它们起了名字……我想知道古物收藏家会是什么样的人？多半是些退役的上校，领着一伙上了年纪的工人爬到这儿的顶上，检查泥块和石头，和附近的牧师互相通信。牧师在早餐的时候拆开信件来看，觉得自己颇为重要。为了比较不同的箭镞，还需要作多次乡间旅行，到本州的首府去，这种旅行对于牧师和他们的老伴都是一种愉快的职责，他们的老伴正想做樱桃酱，或者正想收拾一下书房。他们完全有理由希望那个关于营地或者坟墓的重大问题长期悬而不决。而上校本人对于就这个问题的两方面能否搜集到证据则感到愉快而达观。

的确，他最后终于倾向于营地说。由于受到反对，他便写了一篇文章，准备拿到当地会社的季度例会上宣读，恰好在这时他中风病倒，他的最后一个清醒的念头不是想到妻子和儿女，而是想到营地和箭镞，这个箭镞已经被收藏进当地博物馆的展柜，和一只中国女杀人犯的脚、一把伊丽莎白时代的铁钉、一大堆都铎王朝时代的土制烟斗、一件罗马时代的陶器，以及纳尔逊用来喝酒的酒杯放在一起——我真的不知道它到底证明了什么。

不，不，什么也没有证明，什么也没有发现。假如我在此时此刻站起身来，弄明白墙上的斑点果真是——我们怎么说不好呢？——一枚巨大的旧钉子的钉头，钉进墙里已经有两百年，直到现在，由于一代又一代女仆耐心的擦拭，钉子的顶端得以露出到油漆外面，正在一间墙壁雪白、炉火熊熊的房间里第一次看见现代的生活，我这样做又能得到些什么呢？知识吗？还是可供进一步思考的题材？不论是静坐着还是站起来我都一样能思考。

什么是知识？我们的学者除了是那些蹲在洞穴和森林里熬药草、盘问地老鼠、记载星辰的语言的巫婆和隐士们的后代，还能是什么呢？我们的迷信逐渐消失，我们对美和健康的思想越来越尊重，我们也就不那么崇敬他们了……是的，人们能够想象出一个十分可爱的世界。这个世界安宁而广阔，旷野里盛开着鲜红的和湛蓝的花朵。这个世界里没有教授，没有专家，没有警察面孔的管家，在这里人们可以像鱼儿用鳍翅划开水面一般，用自己的思想划开世界，轻轻地掠过荷花的梗条，在装满白色海鸟卵的鸟窠上空盘旋……在世界的中心扎下根，透过灰暗的海水和水里瞬间的闪光以及倒影向上看去，这里是多么宁静啊——假如没有惠特克年鉴——假如没有尊卑序列表！

我一定要跳起来亲眼看看墙上的斑点到底是什么——是一枚钉子？一片玫瑰花瓣？还是木块上的裂纹？

大自然又在这里玩弄她保存自己的老把戏了。她认为这条思路至多不过白白浪费一些精力，或许会和现实发生一点冲突，因为谁又能对惠特克的尊卑序列表妄加非议呢？排在坎特伯雷大主教后面的是大法官，而大法官后面又是约克大主教。每一个人都必须排在某人的后面，这是惠特克的哲学。最要紧的是知道谁该排在谁的后面。惠特克是知道的。大自然忠告你说，不要为此感到恼怒，而要从中得到安慰；假如你无法得到安慰，假如你一定要破坏这一小时的平静，那就去想想墙上的斑点吧。

我懂得大自然耍的是什么把戏——她在暗中怂恿我们采取行动以便结束那些容易令人兴奋或痛苦的思想。我想，正因如此，我们对实干家总不免稍有一点轻视——我们认为这类人不爱思索。不过，我们也不妨注视墙上的斑点，来打断那些不愉快的思想。真的，现在我越加仔细地看着它，就越发觉得好似在大海中抓住了一块木板。我体会到一种令人心满意足的现实感，把那两位大主教和那位大法官统统逐入了虚无的幻境。这里，是一件具体的东西，是一件真实的东西。我们半夜从一场噩梦中惊醒，也往往这样，急忙扭亮电灯，静静地躺一会儿，赞赏着衣柜，赞赏着实在的物体，赞赏着现实，赞赏着身外的世界，它证明除了我们自身以外还存在着其他的事物。我们想弄清楚的也就是这个问题。木头是一件值得加以思索的愉快的事物。它产生于一棵树，树木会生长，我们并不知道它们是怎样生长起来的。它们长在草地上、森林里、小河边——这些全是我们喜欢去想的事物——它们长着、长着，长了许多年，一点也没有注意到我们。

炎热的午后，母牛在树下挥动着尾巴；树木把小河点染得这样翠绿一片，让你觉得那只一头扎进水里去的雌红松鸡，应该带着绿色的羽毛冒出水面来。我喜欢去想那些像被风吹得鼓起来的旗帜一样逆流而上的鱼群；我还喜欢去想那些在河床上一点点地垒起一座座圆顶土堆的水甲虫。我喜欢想象那棵树本身的情景：首先是它自身木质的细密干燥的感觉，然后想象它感受到雷雨的摧残；接下去就感到树液缓慢地、舒畅地一滴滴流出来。我还喜欢去想这棵树怎样在冬天的夜晚独自屹立在空旷的田野上，树叶紧紧地合拢起来，对着月亮射出的铁弹，什么弱点也不暴露，像一根空荡荡的桅杆竖立在整夜不停地滚动着的大地上。

六月里鸟儿的鸣啭听起来一定很震耳，很不习惯；小昆虫在树皮的褶皱上吃力地爬过去，或者在树叶搭成的薄薄的绿色天篷上面晒太阳，它们红宝石般的眼睛直盯着前方，这时候它们的脚会感觉到多么寒冷啊……大地的寒气凛冽逼人，压得树木的纤维一根根地断裂开来。最后的一场暴风雨袭来，树倒了下去，树梢的枝条重新深深地陷进泥土。即使到了这种地步，生命也并没有结束。这棵树还有一百万条坚毅而清醒的生命分散在世界上。有的在卧室里，有的在船上，有的在人行道上，还有的变成了房间的护壁板，男人和女人们在喝过茶以后就坐在这间屋里抽烟。这棵树勾起了许许多多平静的、幸福的联想。我很愿意挨个儿去思索它们——可是遇到了阻碍……我想到什么地方啦？是怎么样想到这里的呢？一棵树？一条河？丘陵草原地带？惠特克年鉴？盛开水仙花的原野？我什么也记不起来啦。一切在转动、在下沉、在滑开去、在消失……事物陷进了大动荡之中。有人正在俯身对我说：

“我要出去买份报纸。”

“是吗？”

“不过买报纸也没有什么意思……什么新闻都没有。该死的战争，让这次战争见鬼去吧！……然而不论怎么说，我认为我们也不应该让一只蜗牛趴在墙壁上。”

哦，墙上的斑点！那是一只蜗牛。

（文美惠 译）

白象似的群山

海明威

埃布罗河河谷的那一边，白色的山冈起伏连绵。这一边，白地一片，没有树木，车站在阳光下两条铁路线中间。紧靠着车站的一边，是一幢笼罩在闷热的阴影中的房屋，一串串竹珠子编成的门帘挂在酒吧间敞开着的门口挡苍蝇。那个美国人和那个跟他一道的姑娘坐在那幢房屋外面阴凉处的一张桌子旁边。天气非常热，巴塞罗那来的快车还有四十分钟才能到站。列车在这个中转站停靠两分钟，然后继续行驶，开往马德里。

“咱们喝点什么呢？”姑娘问。她已经脱掉帽子，把它放在桌子上。

“天热得很。”男人说。

“咱们喝啤酒吧。”

“Dos cervezas，”（西班牙语：意为“来两杯啤酒”。）男人对着门帘里面说。

“大杯的？”一个女人在门口问。

“对。两大杯。”

那女人端来两大杯啤酒和两只毡杯垫。她把杯垫和啤酒杯一一放在桌子上，看看那男的，又看看那姑娘。姑娘正在眺望远处群山的轮廓。山在阳光下是白色的，而乡野则是灰褐色的干巴巴的一片。

“它们看上去像一群白象。”她说。

“我从来没有见过象。”男人把啤酒一饮而尽。

“你是不会见过的。”

“我也许见到过的，”男人说，“光凭你说我不会见过，并不说明什么问题。”

姑娘看看珠帘子。“他们在上面画了东西的，”她说，“那上面写的什么？”

“Anis del Toro（茴香酒）。是一种饮料。”

“咱们能尝尝吗？”

男人朝着珠帘子喊了一声“喂”。那女人从酒吧间走了出来。

“一共是四雷阿尔（银币）。”

“给我们再来两杯 Anis del Toro。”

“掺水吗？”

“你要掺水吗？”

“我不知道，”姑娘说，“掺了水好喝吗？”

“好喝。”

“你们要掺水吗？”女人问。

“好，掺水。”

“这酒甜丝丝的就像甘草。”姑娘说，一边放下酒杯。

“样样东西都是如此。”

“是的，”姑娘说，“样样东西都甜丝丝的像甘草。特别是一个人盼望了好久的那些东西，简直就像艾酒一样。”

“喔，别说了。”

“是你先说起来的，”姑娘说，“我刚才倒觉得挺有趣。我刚才挺开心。”

“好吧，咱们就想法开心开心吧。”

“行啊。我刚才就在想。我说这些山看上去像一群白象。这比喻难道不妙？”

“妙。”

“我还提出尝尝这种没喝过的饮料。咱们不就做了这么点儿事吗——看看风景，尝尝没喝过的饮料？”

“我想是的。”

姑娘又眺望远处的群山。

“这些山美极了，”她说，“看上去并不真像一群白象。我刚才只是说，透过树木看去，山表面的颜色是白的。”

“咱们要不要再喝一杯？”

“行。”

热风把珠帘吹得拂到了桌子。

“这啤酒凉丝丝的，味儿挺不错，”男人说。

“味道好极了，”姑娘说。

“那实在是一种非常简便的手术，吉格，”男人说，“甚至算不上一个手术。”

姑娘注视着桌腿下的地面。

“我知道你不会在乎的，吉格。真的没有什么大不了。只要用空气一吸就行了。”

姑娘没有做声。

“我陪你去，而且一直待在你身边。他们只要注入空气，然后就一切都正常了。”

“那以后咱们怎么办？”

“以后咱们就好了，就像从前那样。”

“你怎么会这么想呢？”

“因为使我们烦心的就只有眼下这一件事儿，使我们一直不开心的就只有这一件事儿。”

姑娘看着珠帘子，伸手抓起两串珠子。

“那你以为咱们今后就可以开开心心地再没有什么烦恼事了。”

“我知道咱们会幸福的。你不必害怕。我认识许多人，都做过这种手术。”

“我也认识许多人做过这种手术，”姑娘说，“手术以后他们都照样过得很开心。”

“好吧，”男人说，“如果你不想做，你不必勉强。如果你不想做的话，我不会勉强你。不过我知道这种手术是很便当的。”

“你真的希望我做吗？”

“我以为这是最妥善的办法。但如果你本人不是真心想做，我也绝不勉强。”

“如果我去做了，你会高兴、事情又会像从前那样、你会爱我——是吗？”

“我现在就爱着你。你也知道我爱你。”

“我知道。但是如果我去做了，那么倘使我说某某东西像一群白象，就又会和和顺顺的，你又会喜欢了？”

“我会非常喜欢的。其实我现在就喜欢听你这么说，只是心思集中不到那上面去。心烦的时候，我会变成什么样子，你是知道的。”

“如果我去做手术，你就再不会心烦了？”

“我不会为这事儿烦心的，因为手术非常便当。”

“那我就决定去做。因为我对自己毫不在乎。”

“你这话什么意思？”

“我对自己毫不在乎。”

“不过，我可在乎。”

“啊，是的。但我对自己却毫不在乎。我要去做手术，完了以后就会万事如意了。”

“如果你是这么想的，我可不愿让你去做手术。”

姑娘站起身来，走到车站的尽头。铁路对面，在那一边，埃布罗河两岸是农田和树木。远处，在河的那一边，便是起伏的山峦。一片云影掠过粮田；透过树木，她看到了大河。

“我们本来可以尽情欣赏这一切，”她说，“我们本来可以舒舒服服享受生活中的一切，但一天又一天过去，我们越来越不可能过上舒心的日子了。”

“你说什么？”

“我说我们本来可以舒舒服服享受生活中的一切。”

“我们能够做到这一点的。”

“不，我们不能。”

“我们可以拥有整个世界。”

“不，我们不能。”

“我们可以到处去逛逛。”

“不，我们不能。这世界已经不再是我们的了。”

“是我们的。”

“不，不是。一旦他们把它拿走，你便永远失去它了。”

“但他们还没有把它拿走呵。”

“咱们等着瞧吧。”

“回到阴凉处来吧，”他说，“你不应该有那种想法。”

“我什么想法也没有，”姑娘说，“我只知道事实。”

“我不希望你去做任何你不想做的事——”

“或者对我不利的事，”她说，“我知道。咱们再来杯啤酒好吗？”

“好的。但你必须明白——”

“我明白，”姑娘说，“咱们别再谈了好不好？”

他们在桌边坐下。姑娘望着对面干涸的河谷

和群山，男人则看着姑娘和桌子。

"你必须明白，"他说，"如果你不想做手术，我并不硬要你去做。我甘心情愿承受到底，如果这对你很重要的话。"

"难道这对你不重要吗？咱们总可以对付着过下去吧。"

"对我当然也重要。但我什么人都不要，只要你一个。随便什么别的人我都不要。再说，我知道手术是非常便当的。"

"你当然知道它是非常便当的。"

"随你怎么说好了，但我的的确确知道就是这么回事。"

"你现在能为我做点事儿么？"

"我可以为你做任何事情。"

"那就请你，请你，求你，求你，求求你，求求你，千万求求你，不要再讲了，好吗？"

他没吭声，只是望着车站那边靠墙堆着的旅行包。包上贴着他们曾过夜的所有旅馆的标签。

"但我并不希望你去做手术，"他说，"做不做对我完全一样。"

"你再说我可要尖声叫了。"

那女人端着两杯啤酒撩开珠帘走了出来，把酒放在湿漉漉的杯垫上。"火车五分钟之内到站，"她说。

"她说什么？"姑娘问。

"她说火车五分钟之内到站。"

姑娘对那女人愉快地一笑，表示感谢。

"我还是去把旅行包放到车站那边去吧。"男人说。姑娘对他笑笑。

"行。放好了马上回来，咱们一起把啤酒喝光。"

他拎起两只沉重的旅行包，绕过车站把它们送到另一条路轨处。他顺着铁轨朝火车开来的方向望去，但是看不见火车。他走回来的时候，穿过酒吧间，看见候车的人们都在喝酒。他在柜台上喝了一杯茴香酒，同时打量着周围的人。他们都在宁安毋躁地等候着列车到来。他撩开珠帘子走了出来。她正坐在桌子旁边，对他投来一个微笑。

"你觉得好些了吗？"他问。

"我觉得好极了，"她说，"我又没有什么毛病啰。我觉得好极了。"

（翟象俊 译）

献给艾米丽的玫瑰

福克纳

一

艾米丽·格里尔生小姐过世了，全镇的人都去送丧：男子们是出于敬慕之情，因为一个纪念碑倒下了；妇女们呢，则大多数出于好奇心，想看看她屋子的内部。除了一个花匠兼厨师的老仆人之外，至少已有十年光景谁也没进去看看这幢房子了。

那是一幢过去漆成白色的四方形大木屋，坐落在当年一条最考究的街道上，还装点着有十九世纪七十年代风味的圆形屋顶、尖塔和涡形花纹的阳台，带有浓厚的轻盈气息。可是汽车间和轧棉机之类的东西侵犯了这一带庄严的名字，把它们涂抹得一干二净。只有艾米丽小姐的屋子岿然独存，四周簇拥着棉花车和汽油泵。房子虽已破败，却还是执拗不驯，装模作样，真是丑中之丑。现在艾米丽小姐已经加入了那些名字庄严的代表人物的行列，他们沉睡在雪松环绕的墓园之中，那里尽是一排排在南北战争时期杰斐逊战役中阵亡的南方和北方的无名军人墓。

艾米丽小姐在世时，始终是一个传统的化身，是义务的象征，也是人们关注的对象。打一八九四年某日镇长沙多里斯上校——也就是他下了一道黑人妇女不系围裙不得上街的命令——豁免了她一切应纳的税款起，期限从她父亲去世之日开始，一直到她去世为止，这是全镇沿袭下来对她的一种义务。这也并非说艾米丽甘愿接受施舍，原来是沙多里斯上校编造了一大套无中生有的话，说是艾米丽的父亲曾经贷款给镇政府，因此，镇政府作为一种交易，宁愿以这种方式偿还。这一套话，只有沙多里斯一代的人以及像沙多里斯一样头脑的人才能编得出来，也只有妇道人家才会相信。

等到思想更为开明的第二代人当了镇长和参议员时，这项安排引起了一些小小的不满。那年元旦，他们便给她寄去了一张纳税通知单。二月份到了，还是杳无音信。他们发去一封公函，要她便中到司法长官办公处去一趟。一周之后，镇长亲自写信给艾米丽，表示愿意登门访问，或派车迎接她，而所得回信却是一张便条，写在古色古香的信笺上，书法流利，字迹细小，但墨水已不鲜艳，信的大意是说她已根本不外出。纳税通知附还,没有表示意见。

参议员们开了个特别会议,派出一个代表团对她进行了访问。他们敲敲门,自从八年或者十年前她停止开授瓷器彩绘课以来,谁也没有从这大门出入过。那个上了年纪的黑人男仆把他们接待进阴暗的门厅,从那里再由楼梯上去,光线就更暗了。一股尘封的气味扑鼻而来,空气阴湿而又不透气,这屋子长久没有人住了。黑人领他们到客厅里,里面摆设的笨重家具全都包着皮套子。黑人打开了一扇百叶窗,这时,便更可看出皮套子已经坼裂;等他们坐了下来,大腿两边就有一阵灰尘冉冉上升,尘粒在那一缕阳光中缓缓旋转。壁炉前已经失去金色光泽的画架上面放着艾米丽父亲的炭笔画像。

她一进屋,他们全都站了起来。一个小模小样、腰圆体胖的女人,穿了一身黑服,一条细细的金表链拖到腰部,落到腰带里去了,一根乌木拐杖支撑着她的身体,拐杖头的镶金已经失去光泽。她的身架矮小,也许正因为这个缘故,在别的女人身上显得不过是丰满,而她却给人以肥大的感觉。她看上去像长久泡在死水中的一具死尸,肿胀发白。当客人说明来意时,她那双凹陷在一脸隆起的肥肉之中,活像糅在一团生面中的两个小煤球似的眼睛不住地移动着,时而瞧瞧这张面孔,时而打量那张面孔。

她没有请他们坐下来。她只是站在门口,静静地听着,直到发言的代表结结巴巴地说完,他们这时才听到那块隐在金链子那一端的挂表嘀嗒作响。

她的声调冷酷无情。"我在杰斐逊无税可纳。沙多里斯上校早就向我交代过了。或许你们有谁可以去查一查镇政府档案,就可以把事情弄清楚。"

"我们已经查过档案,艾米丽小姐,我们就是政府当局。难道你没有收到过司法长官亲手签署的通知吗?"

"不错,我收到过一份通知,"艾米丽小姐说道,"也许他自封为司法长官……可是我在杰斐逊无税可交。"

"可是纳税册上并没有如此说明,你明白吧。我们应根据……"

"你们去找沙多里斯上校。我在杰斐逊无税可交。"

"可是,艾米丽小姐——"

"你们去找沙多里斯上校(沙多里斯上校死了将近十年了),我在杰斐逊无税可纳。托比!"黑人应声而来。"把这些先生们请出去。"

二

她就这样把他们"连人带马"地打败了,正如三十年前为了那股气味的事战胜了他们的父辈一样。那是她父亲死后两年,也就是在她的心上人——我们都相信一定会和她结婚的那个人——抛弃她不久的时候。父亲死后,她很少外出;心上人离去之后,人们简直就看不到她了。有少数几位妇女竟冒冒失失地去访问过她,但都吃了闭门羹。她居处周围唯一的生命迹象就是那个黑人男子拎着一个篮子出出进进,当年他还是个青年。

"好像只要是一个男子,随便什么样的男子,都可以把厨房收拾得井井有条似的。"妇女们都这样说。因此,那种气味越来越厉害时,她们也不感到惊异,那是芸芸众生的世界与高贵有势的格里尔生家之间的另一联系。

邻家一位妇女向年已八十的法官斯蒂芬斯镇长抱怨。

"可是太太,你叫我对这件事又有什么办法呢?"他说。

"哼,通知她把气味弄掉,"那位妇女说,"法律不是有明文规定吗?"

"我认为这倒不必要,"法官斯蒂芬斯说,"可能是她用的那个黑鬼在院子里打死了一条蛇或一只老鼠。我去跟他说说这件事。"

第二天,他又接到两起申诉,一起来自一个男的,用温和的语气提出意见。"法官,我们对这件事实在不能不过问了。我是最不愿意打扰艾米丽小姐的人,可是我们总得想个办法。"那天晚上全体参议员——三位老人和一位年纪较轻的新一代成员在一起开了个会。

"这件事很简单,"年轻人说,"通知她把屋子打扫干净,限期搞好,不然的话……"

"先生,这怎么行?"法官斯蒂芬斯说,"你能当着一位贵妇人的面说她那里有难闻的气味吗?"

于是,第二天午夜之后,有四个人穿过了艾米丽小姐家的草坪,像夜盗一样绕着屋子潜行,沿着墙角一带以及在地窖通风处拼命闻嗅,而其中一个人则用手从挎在肩上的袋子中掏出什么东西,不断做着播种的动作。他们打开了地窖门,在那里和所有的外屋里都撒上了石灰。等到他们回头又穿过草坪时，原来暗黑的一扇窗户亮起了灯：艾米丽小姐坐在那里，灯在她身后，她那挺直的身躯一动不动像是一尊偶像一样。他们蹑手蹑脚地走过草坪，进入街道两旁洋槐树树荫之中。一两个星期之后，气味就闻不到了。

而这时人们才开始真正为她感到难过。镇上的人想起艾米丽小姐的姑奶奶韦亚特老太太终于变成了十足疯子的事，都相信格里尔生一家人自视过高，不了解自己所处的地位。艾米丽小姐和像她一类的女子对什么年轻男子都看不上眼。长久以来，我们把这家人一直看做一幅画中的人物：身段苗条、穿着白衣的艾米丽小姐立在背后，她父亲叉开双脚的侧影在前面，背对艾米丽，手执一根马鞭，一扇向后开的前门恰好嵌住了他们俩的身影。因此当她年近三十，尚未婚配时，我们实在没有喜悦的心理，只是觉得先前的看法得到了证实。即令她家有着疯癫的血液吧，如果真有一切机会摆在她面前，她也不至于断然放过。

父亲死后，传说留给她的全部财产就是那座房子；人们倒也感到有点高兴。到头来，他们可以对艾米丽表示怜悯之情了。单身独处，贫苦无告，她变得懂人情了。如今她也体会到多一便士就激动喜悦、少一便士便痛苦失望的那种人皆有之的心情了。

她父亲死后的第二天，所有的妇女们都准备到她家拜望，表示哀悼和愿意接济的心意，这是我们的习俗。艾米丽小姐在家门口接待她们，衣着和平日一样，脸上没有一丝哀愁。她告诉她们，她的父亲并未死。一连三天她都是这样，不论是教会牧师访问她也好，还是医生想劝她让他们把尸体处理掉也好。正当他们要诉诸法律和武力时，她垮下来了，于是他们很快地埋葬了她的父亲。

当时我们还没有说她发疯。我们相信她这样做是控制不了自己。我们还记得她父亲赶走了所有的青年男子，我们也知道她现在已经一无所有，只好像人们常常所做的一样，死死拖住抢走了她一切的那个人。

三

她病了好长一个时期。再见到她时，她的头发已经剪短，看上去像个姑娘，和教堂里彩色玻璃窗上的天使像不无相似之处——有几分悲怆肃穆。

行政当局已订好合同，要铺设人行道，就在她父亲去世的那年夏天开始动工，建筑公司带着一批黑人、骡子和机器来了，工头是个北方佬，名叫荷默·伯隆，个子高大，皮肤黝黑，精明强干，声音洪亮，双眼比脸色浅淡。一群群孩子跟在他身后听他用不堪入耳的话责骂黑人，而黑人则随着铁镐的上下起落有节奏地哼着劳动号子。没有多少时候，全镇的人他都认识了。随便什么时候人们要是在广场上的什么地方听见呵呵大笑的声音，荷默·伯隆肯定是在人群的中心。过了不久，逢到礼拜天的下午我们就看到他和艾米丽小姐一齐驾着轻便马车出游了。那辆黄轮车配上从马房中挑出的栗色辕马，十分相称。

起初我们都高兴地看到艾米丽小姐多少有了一点寄托，因为妇女们都说："格里尔生家的人绝对不会真的看中一个北方佬，一个拿日工资的人。"不过也有别人，一些年纪大的人说就是悲伤也不会叫一个真正高贵的妇女忘记"贵人举止"，尽管口头上不把它叫做"贵人举止"。他们只是说："可怜的艾米丽，她的亲属应该来到她的身边。"她有亲属在亚拉巴马；但多年以前，她的父亲为了疯婆子韦亚特老太太的产权问题跟他们闹翻了，以后两家就没有来往。他们连丧礼也没派人参加。

老人们一说到"可怜的艾米丽"，就交头接耳开了。他们彼此说："你当真认为是那么回事吗？""当然是啰。还能是别的什么事？……"而这句话他们是用手捂住嘴轻轻地说的；轻快的马蹄得得驶去的时候，关上了遮挡星期日午后骄阳的百叶窗，还可听出绸缎的窸窣声："可怜的艾米丽。"

她把头抬得高高——甚至当我们深信她已经堕落了的时候也是如此，仿佛她比历来都更要求人们承认她作为格里尔生家族末代人物的尊严；仿佛她的尊严就需要同世俗的接触来重新肯定她那不受任何影响的性格。比如说，她那次买老鼠药、砒霜的情况。那是在人们已开始说"可怜的艾米丽"之后一年多，她的两个堂姐妹也正在那时来看望她。

"我要买点毒药。"她跟药剂师说。她当时已三十出头，依然是个削肩细腰的女人，只是比往常更加清瘦了，一双黑眼冷酷高傲，脸上的肉在两边的太阳穴和眼窝处绷得很紧，那副面部表情是你想象中的灯塔守望人所应有的。"我要买点毒药，"她说道。

“知道了，艾米丽小姐。要买哪一种？是毒老鼠之类的吗？那么我介——”

“我要你们店里最有效的毒药，种类我不管。”

药剂师一口说出好几种。“它们什么都毒得死，哪怕是大象。可是你要的是——”

“砒霜，”艾米丽小姐说。“砒霜灵不灵？”

“是……砒霜？知道了，小姐。可是你要的是……”

“我要的是砒霜。”

药剂师朝下望了她一眼。她回看他一眼，身子挺直，面孔像一面拉紧了的旗子。“噢噢，当然有，”药剂师说，“如果你要的是这种毒药。不过，法律规定你得说明作什么用途。”

艾米丽小姐只是瞪着他，头向后仰了仰，以便双眼好正视他的双眼，一直看到他把目光移开了，走进去拿砒霜包好。黑人送货员把那包药送出来给她；药剂师却没有再露面。她回家打开药包，盒子上骷髅骨标记下注明：“毒鼠用药。”

四

于是，第二天我们大家都说：“她要自杀了。”我们也都说这是再好没有的事。我们第一次看到她和荷默·伯隆在一块儿时，我们都说：“她要嫁给他了。”后来又说：“她还得说服他呢。”因为荷默自己说他喜欢和男人来往，大家知道他和年轻人在麋鹿俱乐部一道喝酒，他本人说过，他是无意于成家的人。以后每逢礼拜天下午他们乘着漂亮的轻便马车驰过：艾米丽小姐昂着头，荷默歪戴着帽子，嘴里叼着雪茄烟，戴着黄手套的手握着马缰和马鞭。我们在百叶窗背后都不禁要说一声：“可怜的艾米丽。”

后来有些妇女开始说，这是全镇的羞辱，也是青年的坏榜样。男子汉不想干涉，但妇女们终于迫使浸礼会牧师——艾米丽小姐一家人都是属于圣公会的——去拜访她。访问经过他从未透露，但他再也不愿去第二趟了。下个礼拜天他们又驾着马车出现在街上，于是第二天牧师夫人就写信告知艾米丽住在亚拉巴马的亲属家。

原来她家里还有近亲，于是我们坐待事态的发展。起先没有动静，随后我们得到确讯，他们即将结婚。我们还听说艾米丽小姐去过首饰店，订购了一套银质男人盥洗用具，每件上面刻着“荷·伯”。两天之后人家又告诉我们她买了全套男人服装，包括睡衣在内，因此我们说：“他们已经结婚了。”我们着实高兴。我们高兴的是两位堂姐妹比起艾米丽小姐来，更有格里尔生家族的风度。

因此当荷默·伯隆离开本城——街道铺路工程已经竣工好一阵子了——时，我们一点也不感到惊异。我们倒因为缺少一番送行告别的热闹，不无失望之感。不过我们都相信他此去是为了迎接艾米丽小姐作一番准备，或者是让她有个机会打发走两个堂姐妹。（这时已经形成了一个秘密小集团，我们都站在艾米丽小姐一边，帮她踢开这一对堂姐妹。）一点也不差，一星期后她们就走了。而且，正如我们一直所期待的那样，荷默·伯隆又回到镇上来了。一位邻居亲眼看见那个黑人在一天黄昏时分打开厨房门让他进去了。

这就是我们最后一次看到荷默·伯隆。至于艾米丽小姐呢，我们则有一段时间没有见到过她。黑人拿着购货篮进进出出，可是前门却总是关着。偶尔可以看到她的身影在窗口晃过，就像人们在撒石灰那天夜晚曾经见到过的那样，但却有整整六个月的时间，她没有出现在大街上。我们明白这也并非出乎意料；她父亲的性格三番五次地使她那作为女性的一生平添波折，而这种性格仿佛大恶毒，太狂暴，还不肯消失似的。

等到我们再见到艾米丽小姐时，她已经发胖了，头发也已灰白了。以后数年中，头发越变越灰，变得像胡椒盐似的铁灰色，颜色就不再变了。直到她七十四岁去世之日为止，还是保持着那旺盛的铁灰色，像是一个活跃的男子的头发。

打那时起，她的前门就一直关闭着，除了她四十左右的那段约有六七年的时间之外。在那段时期，她开授瓷器彩绘课。在楼下的一间房里，她临时布置了一个画室，沙多里斯上校的同时代人全都把女儿、孙女儿送到她那里学画，那样的按时按刻，那样的认真精神，简直同礼拜天把她们送到教堂去，还给她们二角五分钱的硬币准备放在捐献盆子里的情况一模一样。这时，她的捐税已经被豁免了。

后来，新的一代成了全镇的骨干和精神，学画的学生们也长大成人，渐次离开了，她们没有让她们自己的女孩子带着颜色盒、令人生厌的画笔和从妇女杂志上剪下来的画片到艾米丽小姐那里去学画。最后一个学生离开后，前门关上了，而且永远关上了。全镇实行免费邮递制度之后，只有艾米丽小姐一人拒绝在她门口钉上金属门牌号，附设一个邮件箱。她怎样也不理睬他们。

日复一日，月复一月，年复一年，我们眼看着那黑人的头发变白了，背也驼了，还照旧提着购货篮进进出出。每年十二月我们都寄给她一张纳税通知单，但一星期后又由邮局退还了，无人收信。不时我们在楼底下的一个窗口——她显然是把楼上封闭起来了——见到她的身影，像神龛中的一个偶像的雕塑躯干，我们说不上她是不是在看着我们。她就这样度过了一代又一代——高贵，宁静，无法逃避，无法接近，怪僻乖张。

她就这样与世长辞了。在一栋尘埃遍地、鬼影憧憧的屋子里得了病，侍候她的只有一个老态龙钟的黑人。我们甚至连她病了也不知道；也早已不想从黑人那里去打听什么消息。他跟谁也不说话，恐怕对她也是如此，他的嗓子似乎由于长久不用变得嘶哑了。

她死在楼下一间屋子里，笨重的胡桃木床上还挂着床帷，她那长满铁灰头发的头枕着的枕头由于用了多年而又不见阳光，已经黄得发霉了。

五

黑人在前门口迎接第一批妇女，把她们请进来，她们话音低沉，发出咝咝声响，以好奇的目光迅速扫视着一切。黑人随即不见了，他穿过屋子，走出后门，从此就不见踪影了。

两位堂姐妹也随即赶到，她们第二天就举行了丧礼，全镇的人都跑来看看覆盖着鲜花的艾米丽小姐的尸体。停尸架上方悬挂着她父亲的炭笔画像，一脸深刻沉思的表情，妇女们唧唧喳喳地谈论着死亡，而老年男子呢——有些人还穿上了刷得很干净的南方同盟军制服——则在走廊上、草坪上纷纷谈论着艾米丽小姐的一生，仿佛她是他们的同时代人，而且还相信和她跳过舞，甚至向她求过爱，他们把按数学级数向前推进的时间给搅乱了。这是老年人常有的情形。在他们看来，过去的岁月不是一条越来越窄的路，而是一片广袤的连冬天也对它无所影响的大草地，只是近十年来才像窄小的瓶口一样，把他们同过去隔断了。

我们已经知道，楼上那块地方有一个房间，四十年来从没有人见到过，要进去得把门撬开。他们等到艾米丽小姐安葬之后，才设法去开门。

门猛烈地打开，震得屋里灰尘弥漫。这间布置得像新房的屋子，仿佛到处都笼罩着墓室一般的淡淡的阴惨惨的氛围：败了色的玫瑰色窗帘，玫瑰色的灯罩，梳妆台，一排精细的水晶制品和白银作底的男人盥洗用具，但白银已毫无光泽，连刻制的姓名字母图案都已无法辨认了。杂物中有一条硬领和领带，仿佛刚从身上取下来似的，把它们拿起来时，在台面上堆积的尘埃中留下淡淡的月牙痕。椅子上放着一套衣服，折叠得好好的；椅子底下有两只寂寞无声的鞋和一双扔了不要的袜子。

那男人躺在床上。

我们在那里立了好久，俯视着那没有肉的脸上令人莫测的龇牙咧嘴的样子。那尸体躺在那里，显出一度是拥抱的姿势，但那比爱情更能持久、那战胜了爱情的熬煎的永恒的长眠已经使他驯服了。他所遗留下来的肉体已在破烂的睡衣下腐烂，跟他躺着的木床粘在一起，难分难解了。在他身上和他身旁的枕上，均匀地覆盖着一层长年累月积下来的灰尘。

后来我们才注意到旁边那只枕头上有人头压过的痕迹。我们当中有一个人从那上面拿起了什么东西，大家凑近一看——这时一股淡淡的干燥发臭的气味钻进了鼻孔——原来是一绺长长的铁灰色头发。

（杨岂深 译）

雪　国（节选）

川端康成

穿过县界长长的隧道，便是雪国。夜空下一片白茫茫。火车在信号所前停了下来。

一位姑娘从对面座位上站起身子，把岛村座位前的玻璃窗打开。一股冷空气卷袭进来。姑娘将身子探出窗外，仿佛向远方呼唤似地喊道：

“站长先生，站长先生！”

一个把围巾缠到鼻子上、帽耳耷拉在耳朵边的男子，手拎提灯，踏着缓步走了过来。

岛村心想：已经这么冷了吗？他向窗外望去，只见铁路人员当做临时宿舍的小板房，星星点点地散落在山脚下，给人一种冷寂的感觉。那边的白雪，早已被黑暗吞噬了。

“站长先生，是我。您好啊！”

“哟，这不是叶子姑娘吗！回家呀？又是大冷天了。”

“听说我弟弟到这里来工作，我要谢谢您的照顾。”

“在这种地方，早晚会寂寞得难受的。年纪轻轻，怪可怜的！”

“他还是个孩子，请站长先生常指点他，拜托您了。”

“行啊。他干得很带劲，往后会忙起来的。去年也下了大雪，常常闹雪崩，火车一抛锚，村里人就忙着给旅客送水送饭。”

“站长先生好像穿得很多，我弟弟来信说，他还没穿西服背心呢。”

“我都穿四件啦！小伙子们遇上大冷天就一个劲儿地喝酒，现在一个个都得了感冒，东歪西倒地躺在那儿啦。”

站长向宿舍那边晃了晃手上的提灯。

“我弟弟也喝酒了吗？”

“这倒没有。”

“站长先生这就回家了？”

“我受了伤，每天都去看医生。”

“啊，这可太糟糕了。”

和服上罩着外套的站长，在大冷天里，仿佛想赶快结束闲谈似地转过身来说：

“好吧，路上请多保重。”

“站长先生，我弟弟还没出来吗？”叶子用目光在雪地上搜索，“请您多多照顾我弟弟，拜托啦。”

她的话声优美而又近乎悲戚。那嘹亮的声音久久地在雪夜里回荡。

火车开动了，她还没把上身从窗口缩回来。一直等火车追上走在铁路边上的站长，她又喊道：“站长先生，请您告诉我弟弟，叫他下次休假时回家一趟！”

“行啊！”站长大声答应。

叶子关上车窗，用双手捂住冻红了的脸颊。

这是县界的山，山下备有三辆扫雪车，供下雪天使用。隧道南北，架设了电力控制的雪崩报警线。部署了五千名扫雪工和两千名消防队的青年队员。

这个叶子姑娘的弟弟，从今冬起就在这个将要被大雪覆盖的铁路信号所工作。岛村知道这一情况以后，对她越发感兴趣了。

但是，这里说的“姑娘”，只是岛村这么认为罢了。她身边那个男子究竟是她的什么人，岛村自然不晓得。两人的举动很像夫妻，男的显然有病。陪伴病人，无形中就容易忽略男女间的界限，侍候得越殷勤，看起来就越像夫妻。一个女人像慈母般地照拂比自己岁数大的男子，老远看去，免不了会被人看做是夫妻。

岛村是把她一个人单独来看的，凭她那种举止就推断她可能是个姑娘。也许是因为他用过分好奇的目光盯住这个姑娘，所以增添了自己不少的感伤。

已经是三个钟头以前的事了。岛村感到百无聊赖，发呆地凝望着不停活动的左手的食指。因为只有这个手指，才能使他清楚地感到就要去会见的那个女人。奇怪的是，越是急于把她清楚地回忆起来，印象就越模糊。在这扑朔迷离的记忆中，也只有这手指所留下的几许感触，把他带到远方的女人身边。他想着想着，不由得把手指送到鼻子边闻了闻。当他无意识地用这个手指在窗玻璃上划道时，不知怎的，上面竟清晰地映出一只女人的眼睛。他大吃一惊，几乎喊出声来。大概是他的心飞向了远方的缘故。他定神看时，什么也没有。映在玻璃窗上的，是对座那个女人的形象。外面昏暗下来，车厢里的灯亮了。这样，窗玻璃就成了一面镜子。然而，由于放了暖气，玻璃上蒙了一层水蒸气，在他用手指揩亮玻璃之前，那面镜子其实并不存在。

玻璃上只映出姑娘一只眼睛，她反而显得更加美了。岛村把脸贴近车窗，装出一副带着旅愁观赏黄昏景色的模样，用手掌揩了揩窗玻璃。

……

黄昏的景色在镜后移动着。也就是说，镜面映现的虚像与镜后的实物好像电影里的叠影一样在晃动。出场人物和背景没有任何联系，而且人物是一种透明的幻象，景物则是在夜霭中的朦胧暗流，两者消融在一起，描绘出一个超脱人世的象征的世界。特别是当山野里的灯火映照在姑娘的脸上时，那种无法形容的美，使岛村的心都几乎为之颤动。

在遥远的山巅上空，还淡淡地残留着晚霞的余晖。透过车窗玻璃看见的景物轮廓，退到远方，却没有消逝，但已经黯然失色了。尽管火车继续往前奔驰，在他看来，山野那平凡的姿态越是显得更加平凡了。由于什么东西都不十分惹他注目，他内心反而好像隐隐地存在着一股巨大的感情激流。这自然是由于镜中浮现出姑娘的脸的缘故。只有身影映在窗玻璃上的部分，遮住了窗外的暮景，然而，景色却在姑娘的轮廓周围不断地移动，使人觉得姑娘的脸也像是透明的。是不是真的透明呢？这是一种错觉。因为从姑娘面影后面不停地掠过的暮景，仿佛是从她脸的前面流过。定睛一看，却又扑朔迷离。

车厢里也不太明亮。窗玻璃上的映像不像真的镜子那样清晰了。反光没有了。这使岛村看入了神，他渐渐地忘却了镜子的存在，只觉得姑娘好像漂浮在流逝的暮景之中。

这当儿，姑娘的脸上闪现着灯光。镜中映像并未清晰到减弱窗外灯光的程度，灯光也没有把映像抹去。灯光就这样从她的脸上闪过，但并没有把她的脸照亮。这是一束从远方投来的寒光，模模糊糊地照亮了她眼睛的周围。她的眼睛同灯光重叠的那一瞬间，就像在夕阳的余晖里飞舞的妖艳而美丽的夜光虫。

（叶渭渠 译）

百年孤独（节选）

马尔克斯

奥雷连诺上校发动了三十二次武装起义，三十二次都遭到了失败。他跟十七个女人生了十七个儿子，这些儿子都在一个晚上接二连三被杀死了，其中最大的还不满三十五岁。他自己遭到过十四次暗杀、七十三次埋伏和一次枪决，但都幸免于难。他喝了一杯掺有士的宁的咖啡，剂量足以毒死一匹马，可他也活过来了。他拒绝了共和国总统授予他的荣誉勋章。他曾升为革命军总司令，在全国广大地区拥有生杀予夺之权，成了政府最畏惧的人物，但他从来没有让人给他拍过照。战争结束以后，他拒绝了政府给他的终身养老金，直到年老都在马孔多作坊里制作小金鱼为生。尽管他作战时经常身先士卒，但他唯一的伤却是他亲手造成的，那是结束二十年内战的尼兰德投降书签订之后的事。他用手枪朝自己的胸膛开了一枪，子弹穿过脊背，可是没有击中要害。这一切的结果不过是马孔多的一条街道拿他命了名。

然而，据他自己寿终之前不久承认，那天早晨，他率领二十一人的队伍离开马孔多，去投奔维克多里奥·麦丁纳将军的部队时，他是没有想到这些的。

…………

并非一切消息都是好的。奥雷连诺上校逃脱枪毙之后过了一年，霍·阿卡蒂奥和雷贝卡就迁进了阿卡蒂奥建成的房子。谁也不知道霍·阿卡蒂奥救了上校的命，新房子坐落在市镇广场最好的地方，在一棵杏树的浓荫下面；知更鸟在树上筑了三个巢；房子有一道正门和四扇窗子。夫妇俩把这儿搞成了一个好客之家。雷贝卡的老朋友，其中包括摩斯柯特家的四姊妹（她们至今还没结婚），又到这儿来一起绣花了，她们的聚会是几年前在秋海棠长廊上中断的。霍·阿卡蒂奥继续使用侵占的土地，保守党政府承认了他的土地所有权，每天傍晚都可看见他骑着马回来，后面是一群猎犬；他带着一支双筒枪，鞍上系着一串野兔。九月里的一天，快要临头的暴雨使他不得不比平常早一点回家。他在饭厅里跟雷贝卡打了个招呼，把狗拴在院里，将兔子拿进厨房去等着腌起来，就到卧室去换衣服。后来，据雷贝卡说，丈夫走进卧室的时候，她在浴室里洗澡，什么也不知道。这种说法是值得怀疑的，可是谁也想不出其他更近情理的原因，借以说明雷贝卡为什么要打死一个使她幸福的人。这大概是马孔多始终没有揭穿的唯一秘密。霍·阿卡蒂奥刚刚带上卧室的门，室内就响起了手枪声。门下溢出一股血，穿过客厅，流到街上，沿着凹凸不平的人行道前进，流下石阶，爬上街沿，顺着土耳其人街奔驰，往右一弯，然后朝左一拐，径直踅向布恩蒂亚的房子，在关着的房门下面挤了进去，绕过客厅，贴着墙壁（免得弄脏地毯），穿过起居室，在饭厅的食桌旁边画了条曲线，沿着秋海棠长廊蜿蜒行进，悄悄地溜过阿玛兰塔的椅子下面（她正在教奥雷连诺·霍塞学习算术），穿过库房，进了厨房（乌苏娜正在那儿准备打碎三十六只鸡蛋来做面包）。

“我的圣母！”乌苏娜一声惊叫。

于是，她朝着血液流来的方向往回走，想弄清楚血是从哪儿来的：她穿过库房，经过秋海棠长廊（奥雷连诺·霍塞正在那儿大声念：3＋3＝6，6＋3＝9），过了饭厅和客厅，沿着街道一直前进，然后往右拐，再向左拐，到了土耳其人街；她一直没有发觉，她是系着围裙、穿着拖鞋走过市镇的；然后，她到了市镇广场，走进她从来没有来过的房子，推开卧室的门，一股火药味呛得她喘不过气来；接着，她瞧见了趴在地板上的霍·阿卡蒂奥，身体压着他已脱掉的长筒皮靴；而且她还看见，已经停止流动的一股血，是从他的右耳开始的。在霍·阿卡蒂奥的尸体上，没有发现一点伤痕，无法确定他是被什么武器打死的。让尸体摆脱强烈的火药味，也没办到，虽然先用刷子和肥皂擦了三次，然后又用盐和醋擦，随后又用灰和柠檬汁擦，最后拿一桶碱水把它泡了六个小时。这样反复擦来擦去，皮肤上所刺的奇异花纹就明显地褪色了。他们采取极端的办法——给尸体加上胡椒、茴香和月桂树叶，放在微火上焖了整整一天，尸体已经开始腐烂，他们才不得不把它慌忙埋掉。死人是密封在特制棺材里的，棺材长二米三十厘米，宽一米十厘米，内部用铁皮加固，并且拿钢质螺钉拧紧。但是尽管如此，送葬队伍在街上行进的时候，还能闻到火药味。尼康诺神甫肝脏肿得像个鼓似的，在床上给死者作了祈祷。随后，他们又给坟围了几层砖，在所有的间隙里填满灰渣、锯屑和生石灰，但是许多年里坟墓依然发出火药味，直到香蕉公司的工程师们给坟堆浇上一层钢筋混凝土。棺材刚刚抬出，雷贝卡就闩上房门，与世隔绝了，她穿上了藐视整个世界的“甲胄”，这身“甲胄”是世上的任何诱惑力都穿不透的。她只有一次走上街头，那时她已经是个老妇，穿着一双旧的银色鞋子，戴着一顶小花帽。当时，一个流浪的犹太人经过马孔多，带来了那么酷烈的热浪，以致鸟儿都从窗上的铁丝网钻到屋里，掉到地上死了。雷贝卡活着的时候，人们最后一次看见她是在那天夜里，当时她用准确的射击打死了一个企图撬她房门的小偷。后来，除了她的女佣人和心腹朋友阿金尼达，谁也没有遇见过她。有个时候，有人说她曾写信给一个主教(她认为他是她的表兄)，可是没有听说她收到过回信。镇上的人都把她给忘了。

(高长荣 译)

Appendix Ⅱ.

Some Classifications and Basic Terms of Literature

Fiction

Literary works can be divided into two parts: fiction and non-fiction. Fiction refers to any narrative work that is wholly or in part the product of the imagination. Fiction can be classified according to their length or number of words. Classification by length includes short-short stories, short stories, novelette (or novelet), novella and book-length novel.

Novel and short story are the two genres that have dominated Western literary culture since the late eighteenth century.

Novel

The term "novel" is used in its broadest sense to designate any extended fictional narrative almost always in prose. In practice, however, its use is customarily restricted to narrative in which the representation of character occurs either in a static condition or in the process of development as the result of events or actions ... The term "novel" is an English counterpart of the Italian novella, a short compact, broadly realistic tale popular in the medieval period and best represented by those in the Decameron. In most European countries, the word "roman" is used rather than novel, thus linking the novel with the older romance, of which, in a sense, the novel is an extension. The conflict between the imaginative recreation of experience implied in roman and the realistic representation of the soiled world of common people implied in novel has been present in the form from its beginning, and it accounted for a distinction often made in the eighteenth and nineteenth centuries between the romance and the novel, in which the romance was the tale of the long ago, the far away, or the imaginatively improbable; whereas, the novel was bound by the facts of the actual world and the laws of probability.

The nineteenth century saw the flowering of the English novel as an instrument portraying middle-class society. Jane Austen produced novels of manners, and Scott created the historical novel and carried it to a high point in the first quarter of the century. The great Victorian novelists — Dickens, Thackeray and Trollope — created splendid fictional worlds loaded with an abundance of social types and arranged in intricate melodramatic plots. In Thomas Hardy and George Eliot the last half of the century found writers, who, in differing degrees, applied some of the tenets of Naturalism.

(Excerpted from *A Handbook to Literature*, 7th ed. by William Harmon and C. Hugh Holman, Prentice-Hall, 1996.)

Short Story

A short story is a work of fiction that is usually written in prose, often in narrative format. The short story format tends to be more pointed than that of fiction, such as novellas (in the 20th and 21st century sense) and novels. Short story definitions based upon length differ somewhat, even among professional writers, partly because of the fragmentation of the medium into genres. Since the short story format includes a wide range of genres and styles, the actual length is determined by the individual author's preference (or the story's actual needs in terms of creative trajectory or story arc) and the submission guidelines relevant to the story's actual market. Guidelines vary greatly among publishers.

Many short story writers define their work through a combination of creative, personal expression and artistic integrity. They attempt to resist categorization by genre as well as definition by numbers, finding such approaches limiting and counter-intuitive to artistic form and reasoning. As a result, definitions of the short story based upon length splinter even more when the writing process is taken into consideration.

(From *Wikipedia*)

Lyrical Poetry

Most poems are either narrative or lyrical ones. Narrative poems recount a story, and the two most familiar forms are the the epic and the ballad. Lyrical poetry attempts to communicate an author's emotional and intellectual responses to his or her own existence to the surrounding world. According to Samuel Taylor Coleridge, prose is "words in their best order", and poetry is "the best words in their best order".

The word "lyric" originated from the ancient Greek musical instrument "lyre", so musicality is one of the important factors of the lyrical poetry. Another important factor is human feeling, as William Wordsworth once wrote, "Poetry is the spontaneous overflow of powerful feelings: it takes its origin from emotion recollected in tranquility." And Robert Frost said, "Poetry is when an emotion has found its thought and the thought has found words."

Like narrative works, lyrical poems take various forms. Among them, the important ones are elegy, ode, aubade, occasional poem, meditation, pastoral and dramatic monologue.

Blank Verse

A poem written in unrhymed iambic pentameter is called blank verse. The iambic pentameter form often resembles the rhythms of speech. English blank verse was first written in the 16th century by Henry Howard in his translation of Virgil's *Aeneid*, and it developed by Marlowe and Shakespeare in their plays. In the 17th century, Milton extended the uses of blank verse to the epic in his *Paradise Lost*.

Free Verse

Free verse has no identifiable meter, although sometimes the lines may have a rhyme-scheme.

Philip Hobsbaum identified three major types of free verse:

1. Free iambic verse, which is an extension of the work of the Jacobean dramatists. Practitioners of this sort of free verse include T. S. Eliot, Hart Crane, and W. H. Auden.
2. Cadenced verse in the manner of Walt Whitman.
3. Free verse proper, where the discrepancies and variations of meter take centre stage.

Today, cadenced verse is based on rhythmical phrases that are more irregular than those of traditional poetic meter. When it is used, it tends to follow a looser pattern and a more open-ended syntactical structure. Free verse is poetry without the structuring devices of regular meter and rhyme schemes; other traditional elements of expression, such as diction and syntax, still play a prominent role in free verse.

Sonnet

Sonnet is a fourteen-line poem. The Italian Petrarchan has two stanzas: the first of eight lines is called octave and has the rhyme-scheme *a b b a a b b a*; the second of six lines is called sestet and has the rhyme *c d e c d e* or *c d c d c d*.

The Spenserian sonnet, developed by Edmund Spenser, has three quatrains and a heroic couplet, in iambic pentameter with rhymes *a b a b*, *b c b c*, *c d c d*, *e e*. The English sonnet, developed by William Shakespeare, has three quatrains and a heroic couplet, in iambic pentameter with rhymes *a b a b*, *c d c d*, *e f e f*, *g g*.

The Russian sonnet, developed by Pushkin in his verse-novel *Eugene Onegin*, has three quatrains and a heroic couplet in iambic pentameter, rhyming *a b a b*, *c c d d*, *e f f e*, *g g*.

Tragedy

According to Aristotle's definition, a tragedy is the imitation in dramatic form of an action that is serious and complete, with incidents arousing pity and fear wherewith it effects a catharsis of such emotions. The language used is pleasurable and throughout appropriate to the situation in which it is used. The chief characters are noble personages ("better than ourselves," says Aristotle) and the actions they perform are noble actions.

The tragic hero is a character of noble stature and greatness. If the hero's fall is to arouse in us the emotions of pity and fear, it must be a fall from a great height.

Though it arouses solemn emotion — "pity and fear", says Aristotle, "but compassion and awe might be better terms" — tragedy, when well performed, does not leave its audience in a state of depression. It produces a catharsis or an emotional release at the end, one shared as a common experience by the audience.

Comedy

Northrop Frye said that comedy lies between satire and romance. The essential difference between tragedy and comedy lies in the depiction of human nature. Tragedy shows greatness in human nature and human freedom whereas comedy shows human weakness and human limitation. The norms of comedy are primarily social; the protagonist is always in a group or emphasizes commonness.

The purpose of comedy is to make us laugh and at the same time, help illuminate human nature and human weaknesses. Conventionally, all the comedies have the happy ending.

Theme

A theme is the central idea or statement that unifies and controls a literature work. And it is an answer to the question, "What did you learn from this?" In some cases a literary work's theme is a prominent element and somewhat unmistakable. In some pieces of fiction, however, the theme is hard to define.

Too much focus on pinning down a story's theme can obscure the accompanying emotional context or the story's intentional ambiguity (especially for modern fictions). In fact, the function of some contemporary short stories is in part to make us confront the limitations of traditional processes of establishing meaning and coherence. In most cases, though, theme is still an important element of story construction (even in its absence), providing the basis for many valuable discussions.

Plot

Plot refers to the series of events that give a story its meaning and effect. In most stories, these events arise out of conflicts experienced by the protagonist. The conflicts may come from something external, or it may stem from inner evils, such as jealousy, loss of identity and overconfidence. As the character makes choices and tries to resolve the problem, the story's action is shaped and the plot is generated. In some stories, the author structures the entire plot chronologically. However, many other stories are told with flashbacks in which plot events from earlier times interrupt the story's "current" events.

All stories are unique, and in one sense there are as many plots as there are stories. In one general view of plot, however — and one that describes many works of fiction — the story begins with rising action as the character experiences conflict through a series of plot complications that entangle him or her more deeply in the problem. This conflict reaches a climax, after which the conflict is resolved, and the falling action leads quickly to the story's end.

Character

A character refers to a textual representation of a human being or another creature in a fiction or the dramatic personae of a play usually include a protagonist and an antagonist or antagonistic force. Most writers agree that character development is the key element in a story's creation, and in most pieces of fiction, identification with the characters is crucial to understanding the story. The story's protagonist is the central agent in generating its plot, and this individual can embody the story's theme. Characters can be either round or flat, depending on the level of development and the extent to which they change.

Authors achieve characterization with a variety of techniques, for instance, by using the narrative voice to describe the character, by showing the actions of the main character and of those reacting to the main character, by revealing the thoughts of the main character, or by showing the thoughts and dialogues of others in relation to the main character.

Style

Style refers to the language conventions used to construct a literary work. A writer can manipulate diction, sentence structure, phrasing, dialogue, and other aspects of language to create a style. Thus a story's style could be described as richly detailed, flowing, and barely controlled.

The communicative effect created by the author's style can be referred to as the story's voice. A story's voice may be serious, straightforward, comic or dramatically tense.

Point of View

Point of view refers to the source and scope of the narrative voice. In the first-person point of view, usually identifiable by the use of the pronoun "I", a character in the story does the narration. A first-person narrator may be a major character and often the protagonist. The author's choice of point of view has a significant effect on the story's voice and on the information given to the reader.

In the first-person narration, messages delivered to the reader are limited to the character's observation and thoughts, and any skewed perceptions of the narrator will be passed on to the reader.

The third-person point of view occurs when the narrator does not take part in the story. A character's thoughts, for example, are inferred only by what is expressed openly, in actions or in words. This point of view is also known as the third-person dramatic since it is generally the way drama is developed.

Setting

The setting refers to the historical moment in time and the geographic location where a story takes place in narrative works. Besides physical attributes, such as the climate, it can also include complex dimensions such as social contexts. Because particular places and times carry certain emotional connotations, the setting is also the one of the primary ways that a novelist establishes the mood of a story. Typically, short stories take place in limited locations and time frames, whereas novels may involve many different settings across widely varying landscapes. Even in short stories, however, readers should pay attention to subtle shifts in setting. The setting is often presented with narrative description, but it may also be shown with actions, dialogues, or characters' thoughts.

Techniques

The technique is the means a writer uses to present ideas in a literary work. The frequently-used techniques include image, symbol and allegory.

An image is a sensory impression used to create meanings. While visual imagery is typically prominent in story-making, it also includes imagery based on the other senses.

If an image in a story is used repeatedly and carries multiple layers of meaning, it may be significant enough to be called a symbol. Symbols are often objects, like a toy windmill or a rose, and they may be parts of a landscape, like a river. A symbol is often mentioned repeatedly and carries meanings essential to the story. Some symbols are universal, like water for cleansing, but others are culture-based. For example, a black cat is seen as good luck in some African societies, but in Western history, it has often been considered a symbol of evil omens. Novelists combine preexisting cultural associations and meanings drawn from the context of the story together to create symbols.

Allegory is a device in which symbols, characters, and events come to represent a different metaphysical, political, or social situation. In the West, allegories have often been used for instructive purposes around Christian themes.

Imagery

Literature communicates experience and experience comes to us largely through the five senses. Words that call upon our senses are referred to as images. Imagery may be defined as the representation through language of sense experience. The word "image" often suggests a mental picture, and visual imagery is the most frequently used kind of imagery in poetry. Imagery is often symbolic and metaphorical, in that it conveys meanings beyond the literal words.

Figures of Speech

Figures of speech refer to ways of adding extra dimensions to language. A writer often uses figures of speech to indicate he or she is using language in a figurative and not a literal way. In a broad sense, a figure of speech is any saying organised beyond the ordinary way. Some rhetoricians have classified as many as 250 figures of speech. Metaphor and simile are two figures of speech comparing things that are essentially unlike; in simile the comparison is expressed by the use of some word or phrase such as "like", "than", "similar to", "resembles" and "seems"; in metaphor the comparison is implied, that is, the figurative term is substituted for or identified with the literal term. Personification gives the attributes of a human being to an animal, an object, or a concept. Closely related to personification is apostrophe, which addresses someone absent or something non-human as if what or who being addressed were present and alive, could replying to what is being said. Synecdoche (the use of the part for the whole) and metonymy (the use of something closely related for the thing actually meant) are alike since both substitute some significant detail or aspect of an experience for the experience itself.

Rhythm

Like music, most oral poetry has its own timing of sounds and silences. This is rhythm in poetry. A poem must set its own rhythm. If it follows a rigid form, like a sonnet, the music will probably conform to other poems of the same form. The best way to find a poem's rhythm is to read it aloud. Listen to the rhythmic flow of sounds when the lines are spoken aloud. How do the words resonate with each other? How do the words flow when they are linked with one another? Do the words fit with each other? These are the questions you should consider while studying the rhythm of the poem.

Rhyme

Rhyme refers to correspondence of sound between words or the endings of words, especially when these are used at the ends of lines of poetry. A poem may or may not have a rhyme. In rhyming poetry, the words of the lines match with each other in some form. There are various kinds of phonetic similarity between words and different organization patterns of such similar-sounding words. Rhymes could be classified according to the degree and manners of phonetic similarity. Free verse, though, does not follow this system.

Meter

Meter is the basic structural make-up of the poem. Do the syllables match with each other? Every line in the poem must adhere to this structure. A poem is made up of blocks of lines, which convey a single strand of thought. Within those blocks, a structure of syllables which follow the rhythm has to be included. This is the meter or the metrical form of poetry.

The basic unit of meter is "foot", a specific sequence of syllable types, such as a combination of stressed and unstressed syllables.

Meters can be classified based either on number of syllables or on stress. The most common meters are as follows:

Iambic — two the short or unstressed syllable followed by the long or stressed syllable.

Trochaic — two syllables, with the long or stressed syllable followed by the short or unstressed syllable.

Anapestic — three syllables, with the first two short or unstressed and the last long or stressed.

Dactylic — three syllables, with the first one long or stressed and the other two short or unstressed.

Spondaic — two syllables, with two successive long or stressed syllables.

The most common meter in English is iambic pentameter, with a normative sequence of five iambic feet or five iambs per line. The most common in French is the *alexandrin*, with twelve syllables per line. In English, the alexandrine is called iambic hexameter.

Dramatic Dialogue

A dramatic dialogue is a conversation between dramatic characters, and it is one of the distinguishing features of drama. Dramatic dialogue is quite different from kinds of dialogue that make up so much of our ordinary lives, and it must include sufficient background information to fix the time, place, and circumstances of the action firmly in the mind of the audience.

Dialogue provides the substance of the play. A theatrical production without dialogue can not be a play. It can only be a ballet. The story of any play is taken forward by means of dialogue. The story is narrated to the audience through the dialogue written by the playwright. The success of a drama depends hugely on the content and the quality of the dialogues delivered by the actors of the play.